THE 1992

EUROPEAN

CHAMPIONSHIP

THE 1992
EUROPEAN
CHAMPIONSHIP

TONY LYNCH

THE OFFICIAL **ITV Sport** PUBLICATION

B☐XTREE

First published in 1992 by
BOXTREE LIMITED
36 Tavistock Street
London WC2E 7PB

13579108642

Text © Boxtree Limited 1992

Photographs © Action Images

Designed by Design 23

Printed and bound in Great Britain by
Butler & Tanner Ltd.,Frome, Sommerset

A CIP catalogue record for this book is available
from the British Library.

ISBN – 1 85283 733 0

Right: *Jan Wouters holds aloft the European
Championship trophy after Holland beat the USSR
2-0 in the final of 1988*

Contents

ALL TIMES ARE BST

ITV's Transmission Schedule

Saturday 6/6/92
13.10 Saint & Greavsie
15.15 England v Italy Schoolboys' international from Wembley - with European Championship reports from Sweden

Tuesday 9/6/92
23.40 - 00.30 Euro '92 Special. Presented from Sweden by Elton Welsby. A full preview.

Wednesday 10/6/92
19.00 The Opening Ceremony - live from Stockholm
19.15 Sweden v France - live from Stockholm

Thursday 11/6/92
22.40-23.3 Yugoslavia v England - highlights from Malmo

Friday 12/6/92
15.55 - 18.15 Holland v Scotland - live from Gothenburg

Saturday 13/6/92
13.10 Saint & Greavsie - expert views on the tournament so far

Sunday 14/6/92
15.45 France v England - live from Malmo

Monday 15/6/92
19.00 Holland v CIS - live from Gothenburg
Scotland v Germany - highlights from Norrkoping

Wednesday 17/6/92
22.40 Sweden v England - highlights from Stockholm
France v Yugoslavia - highlights from Malmo

Thursday 18/6/92
18.50 Scotland v CIS - live from Norrkoping

OR

Holland v Germany - live from Gothenburg

Saturday 20/6/92
13.10 Saint & Greavsie - more expert analysis and speculation on the final stages

Sunday 21/6/92
18.45 - 21.30 (22.00 if extra-time is played)
Live **semi-final** from Stockholm

OR

22.20 - 23.05 Highlights of Stockholm **semi-final**

Monday 22/6/92
19.00-21.30 (22.00 if extra-time is played)
Live **semi-final** from Gothenburg

OR

23.40 - 21.30 (22.15) Highlights of Gothenburg **semi-final**

Friday 26/6/92
19.00 - 21.30 (22.15 if extra-time is played)
THE FINAL - live from Gothenburg

Saturday 27/6/92
13.10 - 13.50 Saint & Greavsie - round-up of the championship

When the opening fixture – Sweden v France – kicks off in the Rasunda Stadium on 10 June, the ninth European Championship will be well and truly underway. Sixteen days and fourteen matches later we'll all know who are the new kings of European football.

Inbetween there will be plenty of action and it will all be captured by the cameras of ITV Sport whose transmission schedule appears opposite.

This book also contains a comprehensive history of the tournament, an in-depth look at the route to the finals taken by each of this year's qualifiers, profiles of each competing nation – and there's a results table on which the reader can chart the progress of the Championship.

Tony Lynch has asked me to speculate on the outcome of the tournament – a difficult thing to do since each of the eight competing nations has the potential to become European Champions. It all depends on which squads hit peak form at the time. And as Michel Platini, the French Manager, says elsewhere in this book, there are no easy games in the final stages of a European Championship.

Sweden have the obvious advantage of playing before their home crowd, a factor which can often lift a team . . . **Germany**, the current World Cup holders, are always difficult to beat and their squad is packed with talent . . .**Holland** will be anxious to regain the glory days of 1988 when they won this Championship, and they have the talent to do it . . . **The Commonwealth of Independent States** and **Yugoslavia** will both be formidable opponents for any side, despite the political and civil unrest in their respective homelands. I think Yugoslavia could prove to be the 'dark horse' of the tournament. . . **France**, the supposed favourites, have had a fabulous year and are obviously expecting to do well . . . **Scotland** have labelled themselves the underdogs and seem quite happy to do so. But don't be fooled into thinking they're going along just for the ride – anyone who writes off the Scots would be taking a big risk.

And **England?** Well, it would certainly be a fabulous way for me to bow out of the international arena if we were to win the Championship. . .

Foreword by Gary Lineker OBE

. . . But I won't tempt fate by predicting the winners. We'll just have to wait and see what happens. In the meantime, let's enjoy the football . . .

Jean- Pierre Papin,
*France's prolific
goalscorer.*

THE ROAD TO SWEDEN

On Monday 28 May 1990 the footballing fraternity was growing ever more excited at the prospect of the World Cup finals, due to begin in Italy less than two weeks later. The 24 qualifying nations were adding the finishing touches to their campaign plans. The English squad, already settled in an hotel in Cagliari, were due to take on the local league side next day. Scotland struck a somewhat nervy 2-1 victory in a friendly against Malta. The mighty Brazilians suffered a portentous 0-1 defeat to a 'scratch' team in Umbria. And the Swedish police announced that they would be sending a team of eight observers to Italia '90, as part of their security preparations for the 1992 European Championship.

The Svenska Fotbollförbundet (the Swedish FA) had originally applied to host the *1988* European Championship in partnership with Nordic neighbours Denmark, Finland and Norway. And when West Germany was eventually awarded that tournament the Swedish contingent immediately focused its attention on 1992's event. Subsequently, an initial dual application to stage the ninth Championship was made in conjunction with Denmark, with matches to be played in Stockholm, Gothenburg, Malmo and Copenhagen. But at that time Denmark was in the process of rebuilding her national stadium, The Idraetsparken, and since the completion date for the work was uncertain, the application finally came from Sweden alone - with Norrkoping replacing Copenhagen.

Several other applications were considered by UEFA, but the race was eventually run between Sweden and Spain. And, as Spain had already been granted the 1992 Olympic Games, the decision was finally made in favour of Sweden.

Lennart Johansson, president of both the Swedish FA and UEFA, was delighted by the decision. "We have to be there amongst the top sporting circles - that means football as well as other major international sports," he said. "European Championship football is of a very high standard and the attention created by this event will assuredly mean very positive long-term effects for soccer in Sweden. The

Qualifying Group 1

propaganda of the Championship cannot be over-estimated."

Now, as football's elite awaited the start of 1990's footballing festival in the Italian sunshine, the Albanian international squad was *en route* to Reykjavik to take part in the opening Group One qualifying match of the *1992* tournament. Their aircraft landed at Heathrow Airport for re-fuelling while its passengers sampled the delights of the duty free shop.

Unfortunately the entire 37-man squad - managers, coaches, officials, first team players and Under-21 players - was detained by the airport police on suspicion of shoplifting. However, after further investigation they were allowed to continue their journey without charges being made.

Thus, the Albanians arrived behind schedule in Reykjavik. Two days later they lost the match 2-0, in front of a crowd of 5,250, and could be forgiven for blaming their poor performance on the Heathrow experience. Iceland had two points in the bag and the ninth European Championship was officially underway.

The hugely successful Italia '90 was all wrapped up and the World Cup safely in the hands of West Germany by the time the next European Championship matches were played.

In Group One on 5 September Iceland were once again the home side. The visitors to

Reykjavik were France, under the generalship of Michel Platini and unbeaten in their previous nine outings. The match proved a routine assignment for the French side. Jean-Pierre Papin opened the scoring in the twelfth minute after Christian Perez had latched onto a poor goal-kick to supply the pass. Three chances fell to Iceland, the closest being a shot from Amor Gudjohnsen which rebounded off the post.

Papin was also involved in the build-up to the second French goal, glancing on a corner from Perez for Eric Cantona to head home – despite being down on his hands and knees – in the 73rd minute. Icelandic protests that Cantona had handled were dismissed by the Scottish referee and the goal stood.

Plucky Iceland rallied late in the game and were rewarded with a back-heeled goal from skipper Atli Edvaldsson six minutes from time.

Twenty-one days later Iceland visited Kosice and put up a creditable display against Czechoslovakia. The Czech's blushes were saved by the recently recalled striker Vaclav Danekwho scored the only goal of the game, with a diving header, shortly before half-time.

Iceland were also involved in the fourth Group One encounter, on 10 October. This time they travelled to Seville and, employing blanket defensive tactics, proved a huge frustration to Spain. Forty-four minutes of dour struggle passed before striker Emilio Butragueno, making his 55th international appearance, headed Spain ahead from a Juan Goicoechea cross. Carlos scored Spain's second after 64 minutes. Just two minutes later Iceland pulled one back when Siggi Jonsson (then on Arsenal's books) took advantage of a weak backpass by Manuel Sanchis.

Although Spain's two points were safe, warning bells were ringing and manager Luis Suarez was furious at his side's lacklustre display. "They should have approached the thing with flair, used the wings", he said. Instead, they had attempted to force a way through an almost impenetrable defence.

Platini's France played hosts to Czechoslovakia in Paris, on 13 October. Once again Jean-Pierre Papin effectively staked his claim to Europe's top striker spot, by scoring both French goals in a 2-1 victory. Tomas Skuhravy replied for Czechoslovakia.

Spanish woes were increased in Prague on 14 November with a 3-2 defeat by Czechoslovakia. To make matters worse Spain had built up a 2-1 lead at one stage in the proceedings. The opening goal came in the 17th minute when a cross from Lubomir Moravcik eluded the Spanish defence and found the trusty boot of Vaclav Danek who shot home.

A 30th minute penalty area scramble resulted in Spain's equaliser as Roberto's effort was deflected into the net by defender Kadlec. Ten minutes after half time Spain went ahead with a header from Carlos. Roberto almost made it 3-1 soon afterwards, but his fine header was thwarted by a magnificent Ludek Miklosko save. After this incident Czechoslovakia took control – they equalised when Danek eluded the offside trap to score his second of the game, his shot going in off 'keeper Zubizarreta's gloves after 69 minutes. The winner came eight minutes later when Moravcik slotted home, from a rebounding shot from full-back Kocian.

On 17 November Albania met France in Tirana. Both sides were affected by injury and France were without strikers Papin and Cantona. In the event defender Basile Boli headed the only goal of the game, in the 23rd minute. It was France's 13th consecutive victory, Albania's seventh successive defeat. French team boss Michel Platini was celebrating his second year in the hot seat.

Albania's eighth defeat in a row came in crushing style when they travelled to Seville to take on Spain, on 19 December. Albania went close early in the game, but that was practically the only chance they would have. By half time Spain were 4-0 ahead, with strikes from Amor,

Carlos, Butregueno and Hierro. The rout continued after the break. Butragueno hit three more, Carlos scored his second of the game and Baquero rounded things off at 9-0.

Butragueno's four goals took his international

Emilio Butragueno, *Spain's most prolific goal scorer.*

tally to 27, making him Spain's leading goalscorer of all time (a record previously held by Alfredo Di Stefano).

Spain were now lying second in the table behind France, but those nine goals had taken their total to 13, more than any other country in the tournament. The stage was well and truly set

for the France v Spain encounter due to be played on 20 February 1991.

That match, played in Paris in front of a 45,000 crowd, underlined the French supremacy in Group One, albeit after a shaky first-half performance in which Spain struck first - in the 11th minute, through Jose Baquero who successfully nipped behind the French defence to control and volley a right side cross. Four minutes later the balance was restored when the unmarked Franck Sauzee headed home Jean-Phillipe Durand's expertly taken free-kick.

It was a different story after the interval. The inevitable Jean-Pierre Papin shot France into the lead with a spectacular airborne scissor kick in the 58th minute. The scoreline was sealed at 3-1 after 77 minutes when Laurent Blanc's header fooled the stranded Zubizaretta. After the match Platini declared "I knew we had the guts to win".

Albania were the next visitors to Paris, on 30 March. As if the national team didn't already face an uphill task, the leading Albanian club Flamurtari Vlore refused to allow certain key players to travel on the grounds that they might not return to the country. To make matters worse three players *did* abandon the party in

Geneva and later claimed political asylum.

The match itself was a nightmare for Albania. A 30 yard free-kick, taken by Sauzee, hit the back of the net in the opening minute. Eighteen minutes passed before a repeat performance by Sauzee put France two up, this time from the edge of the penalty area after Lekbello had bundled Laurent Blanc to the ground.

The Czech side was somewhat depleted too, with three key players - Knoflicek, Danek and Skuhravy - out through injury. Nevertheless, Czechoslovakia had the upper hand throughout the match and won with two second half goals, from a Lubos Kubik free-kick after 47 minutes and Pavel Kuka's neatly worked strike which went in off a post twenty minutes later.

But the plucky Albanian side were allowed a moment of Euro glory on 26 May when they entertained Iceland in Tirana. Forward Eduard Abazi had recently signed for Yugoslavian side Hajduk Split, and thus became the first ever foreign-based player allowed into the Albanian line-up. His inclusion proved more than an interesting historical footnote as he scored the only goal of the game - after 56 minutes - to mark Albania's first victory in over six years (their previous victims were Belgium in 1984).

Lubos Kubic shot Czechoslovakia into the lead against Albania.

In the 34th minute the unfortunate Lekbello gave away a penalty which Jean-Pierre Papin converted. Papin made it four, from a Cocard cross, just before half time. Lekbello's nightmare was completed ten minutes from the final whistle when he put the ball into his own net during a goalmouth scramble.

By the time of Albania's next fixture, at home to Czechoslovakia on 1 May, several more of their top players were absent and actively seeking political asylum elsewhere in Europe.

Czechoslovakia's 1-0 victory over Iceland in Reykjavik on 5 June took them to within two points of France at the top of the Group One table. The goal came from midfielder Ivan Hasek after 15 minutes.

The next clash, therefore, Czechoslovakia v France on 4 September, promised to be a classic. It turned out to be a tough encounter dubbed 'The Battle of Bratislava' by the press. Czechoslovakia, without several key players due to illness, took the lead in the 21st minute when

Vaclav Nemecek capitalised on a poor clearance by Manuel Amoros. Nemecek's shot was deflected into the French net off defender Basile Boli.

It was the scoring power of Papin that saved the day for France. In the 53rd minute he met a long, hopeful cross from Perez and volleyed expertly home. With barely a minute left Papin swung the game in France's favour with a neatly taken close range goal. The 2-1 victory left Platini's side unbeaten in sixteen consecutive outings and needing but a single point from their two remaining games to ensure qualification for Sweden '92.

On 25 September Spain suffered a nightmare of monumental proportions when they travelled to a wet and windy Reykjavik for their second encounter with Iceland. New manager Vicente Miera had hoped to revitalise the Spanish Euro challenge, but his plans went completely awry as Iceland - also under a new manager, Asgeir Eliasson - put in a remarkable second half display which brought two goals in eight minutes. The first came from Thor Orlygsson who, on 71 minutes, hit home a Siggi Jonsson pass; the second in the 78th

from Eyjolfur Sverrisson.

It was a remarkable result not only in the 'giant killing' sense, but also because it meant Spain had failed to reach the finals of a major tournament for the first time in twelve years.

With only national pride left to play for, Spain faced up to France in Seville on 12 October. But Platini's men, seeking that solitary point, were

Vaclav Nemecek had the French worried in the 'Battle of Bratislava'.

magnificent. They were two up within the first quarter-hour, through Luis Fernandez - making a triumphant return to the midfield - and the inevitable Jean-Pierre Papin. Spain pulled one back, through Abelardo on 33 minutes, but were tactically outdone for the remainder of the game. The defeat represented Spain's

Group 1 Leading Scorers

9 - Papin *France.*
5 - Butragueno *Spain.*
4 - Carlos *Spain.*
3 - Sauzee *France,* **Cantona** *France,*
Danek *Czechoslovakia.*

first loss in the city of Seville in 68 years.

The two points earned by France made them the first squad to book a certain passage to Sweden.

Since only one team per group could qualify, the remaining fixtures in Group One were somewhat academic. In Olomouc on 16 October, Czechoslovakia beat Albania 2-1, with goals from Kula after 35 minutes and Lancz after 39. Zmijani replied for Albania on 62 minutes.

Spain restored a measure of pride in Seville on 13 November, with a 2-1 victory over Czechoslovakia. Goals from Abelardo and a Michel penalty, gave new team boss Vicente Miera his first taste of success. Nemecek had equalised for Czechoslovakia on the hour.

On 20 November France wrapped things up neatly with a 3-1 win against Iceland in Paris. Although the scoreline was 0-0 at half time, Iceland didn't really stand a chance and their 'keeper Kristinsson was the busiest player on the park. Amara Simba, standing in for the absent Papin, broke the deadlock in the 42nd minute and Eric Cantona added two more (on 60 and 68 minutes). Sverrisson replied for the opposition three minutes later.

We will never know the outcome of the one remaining Group One fixture, Albania v Spain, which was due to be played on 18 December. The match was cancelled.

Luis Fernandez helped book France's passage to Sweden

Group 1 Final Table	P	W	D	L	F	A	Pts
FRANCE	8	8	0	0	20	6	16
Czechoslovakia	8	5	0	3	12	9	10
Spain	7	3	0	4	17	12	6
Iceland	8	2	0	6	7	10	4
Albania	7	1	0	6	2	21	2

30/5/90 - Reykjavik
Ref: McKnight (N.Ire)
Attendance: 5,250

Iceland 2, Albania 0

Iceland: Kristinsson B, Thordarson, Edvaldsson, Bergsson, Jonsson Sa, Orlygsson T (Kristjan 46), Ormslev, Gretarsson, Gudjohnsen, Petursson, Tarfason, (Orlygsson O 67). Scorers: Gudjohnsen 42, Edvaldsson 88

Albania: Starkosha, Naga (Illadhi 75), Lekbello, Kove, Vata, Jera, Shehu (Arberi 46), Josa, Milo, Abazi, Demollari.

5/9/90, Reykjavik
Ref: Syme (Scotland)
Attendance: 8,388

Iceland 1, France 2

Iceland: Sigurdsson. Thrainsson, Edvaldsson, Bergsson, Jonsson Sa, Orlygsson (Margeirsson 63), Gretarsson, Thordarsson, Ormslev (Kristinsson 63), Gudjohnsen, Petursson. Scorer: Edvaldsson 84

France: Martini, Amoros, Boli, Sauzee, Casoni, Blanc (Durand 75), Pardo, Deschamps, Perez, Papin, Cantona (Fernandez 83). Scorers: Papin 12, Cantona 73

26/9/90 Kosice
Ref: Kolev (Bul)
Attendance: 30,184

Czechoslovakia 1, Iceland 0

Czechoslovakia: Stejskal, Kedlec, Kocian, Hipp, Bilek (Weiss 67), Hasek, Moravcik, Kubik, Danek, Skuhravy, Kula. Scorer: Danek 43

Iceland: Sigurdsson; Thrainsson, Bergsson, Edvaldsson, Jonsson Sa, Kristinsson R (Jonsson K 61), Gretarsson, Thordarsson, Jonsson Si, Gudjohnsen, Margeirsson (Ormslev 76)

10/10/90 Seville
Ref: Mintoff (Malta)
Attendance: 18,399

Spain 2, Iceland 1

Spain: Zubizaretta; Nando, Serna, Rafa Paz (Beguiristain 61), Sanchis, Fernando, Goicoechea, Michel, Butragueno, Martin Vasquez, Carlos (Valverde 71). Scorers: Butragueno 44, Carlos 64

Iceland: Sigurdsson; Thrainsson, Edvaldsson, Jonsson K (Gregory 80), Gretarsson, Jonsson Sa, Bergsson, Jonsson Si (Omslev 72), Gudjohnsen, Thordarsson, Margeirsson. Scorer: Jonsson Si 65

13/10/90 Paris
Ref: Courtney (Eng)
Attendance: 38,249

France 2, Czechoslovakia 1

France: Martini; Angloma (Fernandez 53) Durand, Boli, Casoni, Sauzee, Deschamps, Vahirua (Silvestre 83), Papin, Blanc, Cantona. Scorer: Papin 59, 80

Czechoslovakia: Stejskal, Kubik (Tittel 84), Kadlec, Hipp, Kocian, Kula, Bilek (Pecko 80), Knoflicek, Chovanec, Skuhravy, Moravik. Scorer: Skuhravy 87

14/11/90 Prague
Ref: Tritschler (Ger)
Attendance: 21,980

Czechoslovakia 3, Spain 2

Czechoslovakia: Miklosko; Kocian, Kadlec, Hipp, Hasek, Tittel, Moravcik, Kula, Bilek (Belak 80), Danek (Kuka 89), Skuhravy. Scorers: Danek 17, 69, Moravcik 77

Spain: Zubizaretta; Quique, Sanchis, Nando, Serna, Michel (Amor 85), Martin Vasquez, Roberto, Goicoechea, Butragueno, Carlos (Baquero 62). Scorers: Roberto 30, Carlos 55

17/11/90 Tirana
Ref: Galler (Switz)
Attendance: 12,972

Albania 0, France 1

Albania: Arapi; Leskaj (Ferko 46), Stafa, Ibro, Hodja, Lekbello, Zmijani, Demollari, Josa, Kushta, Majaci (Kacasi 56)

France: Martini; Boli B, Durand, Casoni, Blanc, Pardo, Deschamps, Sauzee, Tibeuf (Ginola 66), Ferreri, Vahirua Angloma 82). Scorer: Boli 23

19/12/90 Seville
Ref: Constantin (Belg)
Attendance: 12,972

Spain 9, Albania 0

Spain: Zubizaretta; Sanchis, Alcorta, Goicoechea (Baquero 75), Hierro, Amor, Manolo, Michel (Flores 62), Butragueno, Martin, Vazquez, Carlos. Scorers: Amor 9, Carlos 22, 63, Butragueno 30, 57, 66, 75, Hierro 37, Baquero 86.

Albania: Arapi, Ibro, Lekbello, Stafa, Demollari (Kola 38), Kushta, Millo, Dema (Mollari 39), Ferko, Zmijani, Tahiri.

20/2/91 Paris
Ref: Lanese (Italy)
Attendance: 45,000

France 3, Spain 1

France: Martini; Amoros, Boli, Casoni, Blanc, Pardo (Fernandez 50), Durand, Sauzee, Papin, Cantona, Vahirua (Deschamps 83). Scorers: Sauzee 15, Papin 58, Blanc 77

Spain: Zubizaretta; Quique, Nando, Juanito, Sanchis, Michel, Amor, Vizcaino (Soler 61), Goicoechea, Baquero, Butragueno (Manolo 75). Scorer: Baquero 11

30/3/91 Paris
Ref: Halle (Norway)
Attendance: 24,181

France 5, Albania 0

France: Martini; Amoros, Boli, Blanc, Durand, Frenandez, Sauzee (Deschamps 73), Cocard, Cantona, Papin, Vahirua (Baills 57). Scorers: Sauzee 1, 19, Papin 34 pen, 42, Lekbello (og) 79

Albania; Nallbani; Zmijani, Lekbello, Vata, Gjergi, Ocelli, Dume, Canaj, Demollari, Tahiri, Kepa.

1/5/91 Tirana
Ref: Longhi (Italy)
Attendance: 10,000

Albania 0, Czechoslovakia 2

Albania: Nallbani; Zmijani, Dema (Kola 73), Daja, Ocelli, Shpuza, Kushta, Memushi, Barbullushi (Dosti 63), Dume (Kola 70), Milori.

Czechoslovakia: Miklosko; Kula, Kadlec, Hasek (Hapal 19), Grussmann, Tittel, Nemec, Kubik, Kuka, Kukleta (Chylek 84), Moravcik. Scorers: Kubik 47, Kuka 67

26/5/91 Tirana
Ref: Varga (Hun)
Attendance: 8,000

Albania 1, Iceland 0

Albania: Nallbani; Memushi (Josa 17), Ocelli, Lekbello, Shpuza, Daja, Millo, Demollari (sent off 88), Milori, Kushta, Abazi. Scorer: Abazi 56

Iceland: Sigurdsson, Jonsson Sa, Bergsson, Gislason, Kristiansson, Kristinsson (Stefansson 62), Orlygsson, Thordarsson, Gretarsson, Sverrisson, Gregory (Marteinsson 75).

5/6/91 Reykjavik
Ref: Spillane (Rep of I)
Attendance: 5,102

Iceland 0, Czechoslovakia 1

Iceland: Sigurdsson; Jonsson, Bergsson, Edvaldsson, Gislason, Thordarsson, Gretarsson, Orlygsson, Kristinsson, Gudjohnsen, Sverrisson (Stefansson 70).

Czechoslovakia: Miklosko; Grussmann, Kocian, Tittel, Hasek, Hapal, Kubik, Kula, Nemec, Danek (Pecko 89), Skuhravy. Scorer: Hasek 15

4/9/91 Bratislava
Ref: Mikkelsen (Den)
Attendance: 51,000

Czechoslovakia 1, France 2

Czechoslovakia: Miklosko; Kocian, Tittel, Novotny, Knoflicek (Hapal 80), Kristofik (Frydek 22), Nemecek, Moravcik, Nemec, Pecko, Kuka. Scorer: Nemecek 21

France: Martini; Blanc, Amoros, Angloma (Durand 76), Boli, Casoni, Deschamps, Sauzee, Papin, Cocard (Perez 46), Vahiura. Scorer: Papin 53, 89

25/9/91 Reykjavik
Ref: Bakker (Holland)
Attendance: 3,900

Iceland 2, Spain 0

Iceland: Kristinsson; Valsson (Marteinsson 46), Ormslev, Bergsson, Jonsson Sa, Jonsson K, Gretarsson, Sverrisson, Thordarsson, Orlygsson, Bjarnasson (Magnusson 73). Scorers Orlygsson 71, Sverrisson 78.

Spain: Zubizaretta; Abelardo, Eusebio, Sanchis, Solozabal, Michel, Vizcaino, Martin Vazquez (Hierro 67), Goicoechea, Manolo, Butragueno.

12/10/91 Seville
Ref: Forstinger (Aust)
Attendance: 27,500

Spain 1, France 2

Spain: Zubizaretta; Cristobal, Solozabal (Eusebio 46), Abelardo, Sanchis, Vizcaino, Manolo, Bango, Butragueno, Martin Vazquez (Alvaro 73), Hierro. Scorer: Abelardo 33

France: Martini; Amoros, Blanc, Boli, Casoni, Deschamps, Angloma, Fernandez,(Durand 82), Perez (Garde 62), Cantona, Papin. Scorers: Fernandez 12, Papin 15

16/10/91 Olomouc
Ref: Lietskiewicz (Pol)
Attendance: 2,366

Czechoslovakia 2, Albania 1

Czechoslovakia: Miklosko; Jurasko, Tittel, Nemecek, Hapal, Moravcik, Lancz (Sedlacek 64), Frydek, Kula, Danek (Pecko 72), Kuka. Scorers: Kula 35, Lancz 39

Albania: Strakosha; Zmijani, Lekbello, Kacaj, Cipi, Josa, Milori (sent off 64), Kola (Daja 53), Gjondeda, Abazi, Barbullushi. Scorer: Zmijani 62

13/11/91 Seville
Ref: Rothlisberger (Sw)
Attendance: 20,500

Spain 2, Czechoslovakia 1

Spain: Zubizaretta; Abelardo, Soler, Solozabal, Sanchis, Hierro, Moya (Conte 59), Michel, Butragueno, Martin Vazquez (Nadal 46), Vizcaino. Scorers: Abelardo 10, Michel 79 (pen)

Czechoslovakia: Stejskal; Suchoparek, Glonek, Vik (Grussmann 65), Kristov, Nemecek, Nemec, Novotny, Pecko, Kula, Dubovsky (Latal 79). Scorer: Nemecek 59

20/11/91 Paris
Ref: Fredriksson (Sw)
Attendance: 35,000

France 3, Iceland 1

France: Martini; Angloma, Blanc, Casoni (Boli 46), Amoros, Deschamps, Fernandez, Perez, Cantona, Simba, Vahirua. Scorers: Simba 42, Cantona 60, 68

Iceland: Kristinsson; Valsson, Bergsson (Jonsson Sa 81), Jonsson K, Ormslev, Bjarnsson, Orlygsson, Jonsson K, Gudjohnsen, Torfasson (Sverrisson 56), Gretarsson. Scorer: Sverrisson 71

18/12/91 Tirana

Albania v Spain
Match cancelled

***Ally McCoist**. created Scotland's first goal of the Championship....*

Scotland's European Championship campaign kicked off on 12 September 1990, against Romania at Hampden Park, in front of a surprisingly small crowd of just 12,081. The Scottish team selected by Andy Roxburgh was described as 'makeshift' and 'experimental'. Nevertheless, the experiment paid off with a 2-1 victory.

Romania scored first after 13 minutes when Rodian Camataru slid in a cross from Lacatus. Scottish claims for offside were swept aside by referee Aziparte. Scotland's equaliser came in the 37th minute, when new cap John Robertson put the finishing touch to a neat move by McCoist and McAllister.

The Scots almost conceded a second half penalty for Brian Irvine's harsh challenge on full-back Petrescu. But the moment passed, and the winner eventually came in the 75th minute when Ally McCoist converted a John Robertson cross.

On the same day, Switzerland entertained Bulgaria in Geneva. After soaking up some early pressure the Swiss opened their account when Marc Hottiger hit a low drive to score his first international goal, in the 19th minute. Bulgaria went close twice early in the second half, but it was Thomas Bickel who settled the matter in Switzerland's favour after linking with Chapuisat in the 74th minute.

Bulgaria's team boss Ivan Vutsov was made to eat his words in Bucharest on 17 October. In a pre-match pronouncement he claimed that his side's chances of an away victory over Romania were "practically non-existent". But a remarkable, inspired performance by Bulgaria saw them thrash their more flamboyant neighbours 3-0.

By half time Bulgaria were one up through Nasko Sirakov. But it was second half substitute Niki Todorov who became man-of-the-match by scoring twice: first in the 46th minute with virtually his first kick of the game; and again in the 77th minute. The pass for Todorov's second was provided by Bulgaria's second substitute,

Emil Kostadinov. And the 3-0 scoreline represented Bulgaria's heaviest defeat of Romania in 65 years.

Also on 17 October Scotland staged their second home fixture of the campaign, against Switzerland. This time the crowd was a more

Qualifying Group 2

substantial 20,000-plus which saw a game dominated by penalty kicks. The first was taken by Ally McCoist after he had been fouled by Swiss 'keeper Walker. McCoist shot wide and the Swiss breathed again. When Andre Egli deliberately handled after half an hour John

... *for new cap* **John Robertson**..

Robertson stepped up and made no mistake with the spot kick.

In the 52nd minute the Swiss defence stopped short, expecting an offside decision. Finnish referee Palsi looked to his linesman but the flag stayed down. Gary McAllister took full advantage of the situation and netted his first goal for Scotland. Fourteen minutes later Alex McLeish bowled over Kubilay Turkyilmaz and the game saw its third penalty-kick. Adrian Knup converted the kick, and prompted a Swiss revival which saw them go close three times in the dying minutes. In the final minute Egli was given his marching orders after a deliberate foul on Gordon Durie.

Scotland next travelled to Sofia, to take on Bulgaria on 14 November. Within nine minutes the Scots were ahead when Tommy Boyd's shot was mishandled by 'keeper Mikhailov. Gordon Durie knocked it back into the fray and Ally McCoist hit home.

It was supersub Niki Todorov - the hero of the famous victory over Romania - who saved the day for Bulgaria. His 70th minute shot struck Stewart McKimmie and was deflected over Goram into the net.

November 14 was an historic day for football in San Marino. The Group Two qualifier against Switzerland in Serravalle was the first full international to be staged in the tiny principality. The San Marino team, made up of part-timers, were the obvious outsiders in the group. The minnows pitted against the big fish of Europe. But there the romance ended: A crowd of just 931 saw Switzerland go one up within eight minutes, through Alain Sutter. Further goals from Chapuisat, Knup and Chassot sealed the matter at 4-0.

San Marino fared even worse in their second game, in which 6,380 fans saw them thrashed 6-0 by Romania in Bucharest on 5 December. It was Romania's first victory in the tournament and manager Mircea Radulescu praised the confident performance, coming as it did in the wake of the disaster against Bulgaria.

The return San Marino v Romania fixture was played out on 27 March 1991 in Serravalle. Romania went ahead on 17 minutes with a Gheorghe Hagi penalty. Thirteen minutes later San Marino scored their first international goal - a penalty converted by Pasolini (it would also be the only goal San Marino would score in this tournament). On the stroke of half time Romania took command of the match with a goal from Florian Raducioiu. An unfortunate own goal by San Marino's Matteoni completed the scoreline at 3-1.

On the same day Scotland met Bulgaria for their second encounter, at Hampden Park. The match looked a certain 0-0 draw until substitute John Collins, with his first touch of the ball, shot the Scots ahead with just six minutes left to play. But the Hampden roar was subdued in the final minute when Emil Kostadinov equalised for the visitors. Despite the disappointment Scotland were sitting on top of the Group Two table and had yet to be beaten.

On 3 April Switzerland and Romania drew 0-0 in Neuchatel. It was a dour encounter with Switzerland's Christophe Ohrel fluffing the best chance late in the game.

May Day saw Bulgaria entertain Switzerland in Sofia. It was a remarkable match. With just three minute left to play Bulgaria were 2-1 ahead thanks to goals from Emil Kostadinov and Nasko Sirakov. Although Adrian Knup had pulled one back for the Swiss in the 58th minute, the last three minutes of the game were now ticking away and the crowd of 40,000 must have been certain of a homeward journey on which Bulgaria's victory would be the main topic of conversation.

But, in those closing minutes, Switzerland won the match. The equaliser came from Knup when 'keeper Mikhailov presented him with a weak clearance in the 88th minute.

The Bulgarians, on the pitch and in the stands, could hardly believe what had

Gordon Strachan finally opened the scoring against San Marino.

scored the second after 66 minutes.

Bulgaria were the next visitors to San Marino, on 22 May. The spectators, who barely qualified for the classification of 'a crowd', numbered 670. They saw a Lubislav Penev shot deflected to Zlatko Ivanov who headed home for Bulgaria after 12 minutes. In the 19th minute Nasko Sirakov hit the second from a free-kick on the edge of the box. Penev scored Bulgaria's third from the penalty spot on 59 minutes.

San Marino's next outing was to result in their heaviest defeat of the campaign - 7-0 against Switzerland in St Gallen on 5 June. The goals - from Knup (2), Hottiger, Sutter, Hermann, Ohrel and Turkyilmaz - made San Marinese 'keeper Benedittini the busiest man on the park, and took Switzerland to the top of the table ahead of Scotland. And that made the next fixture - Switzerland v Scotland - a vitally important one. Scotland simply had to do well if they were to stay in the race.

By half time in the match, played in Berne on 11 September, it looked to be all over for Scotland. Goals from Stephane Chapuisat and Heinz Hermann (making his 115th international appearance) had given Switzerland a comfortable lead.

Then two minutes after the restart

happened. And they had further reason for depression when, in injury time two minutes later, Kubilay Turkyilmaz scored a brilliant solo goal to seal the result at 3-2 in Switzerland's favour.

Also on 1 May Scotland were in Serravalle for their first encounter with San Marino. The Scots won 2-0, but took more than an hour to break the deadlock. The first goal came from the penalty spot and was scored by Gordon Strachan, who two days earlier had been voted the English football writers' Footballer of the Year for his inspirational leadership of Leeds United. Gordon Durie

2

Group | Leading Scorers

6 - **Knup** *Switzerland.*
4 - **McCoist** *Scotland,* **Sikarov** *Bulgaria.*
3 - **Todorov** *Bulgaria,* **Durie** *Scotland.*

Gordon Durie gave the Scots fresh hope when he pulled one back. Ally McCoist went close twice after that and was eventually rewarded with the equaliser with seven minutes left to play. It was his ninth international goal and a vital one for Scotland. With two games left to play the Scottish team were on 9 points; Switzerland were on 10, but had played one less game. Bulgaria (6 points from 6 games) and Romania (5 from 5) were lagging behind.

As far as Scotland were concerned there was everything to play for in the next fixture, against Romania on October 16 in Bucharest. But it turned out to be a dire Wednesday evening for the Scots. They did not look likely to score and spent most of the game in their own half, defending desperately. Then in the 75th minute, when it was beginning to look as if a point might be salvaged, Gordon Durie *punched* away a free-kick in the penalty area. Gheorghe Hagi scored from the spot to put the Scottish hopes back to square one.

Meanwhile Bulgaria were improving their fortunes by giving San Marino a 4-0 drubbing in Sofia. The goals came from a Stoichkov penalty, Yankov, Illiev, and an own goal by Valentini. San Marino's coach Giancarlo Gionginni was philosophical about his team's performances. "We're happy . . . we don't worry about results." he said.

On 13 November Switzerland ruined their chances of qualification by losing their last match to Romania in Bucharest. The Swiss were too intent on defence and paid the

Heinz Hermann scored in his 115th international.

penalty when Mateut scored the only goal of the game, in the 72nd minute.

On the same day Scotland, in their last fixture of the qualifying campaign, duly beat San Marino 4-0 at Hampden Park. Paul McStay opened the scoring with a header in the 10th minute. Richard Gough headed the second from a Gary McAllister corner on 32 minutes. Six minutes later Gordon Durie made it 3-0 and in the 63rd minute McStay set up Ally McCoist for Scotland's fourth.

The victory gave Scotland 11 points at the top of the table - but they now had to play an agonising waiting game. Romania, on 9 points could still progress on goal difference, providing they beat Bulgaria by two clear goals, or by 2-1, in the last match of the group.

That game, which would decide Scotland's fate, was played on 20 November in Sofia. The first half was full of incident with most of the attacking moves coming from Romania. Marius Lacatus had the ball in the net for Romania, but the goal was disallowed – and on 20 minutes Gheorghe Hagi missed a penalty. But the Romanians made the inevitable breakthrough after 30 minutes, when Adrian Popescu scored.

Eleven minutes of the second half had passed when Bulgaria's Stoichkov set up a chance for Sirakov. The chance was taken and the scores levelled at 1-1. And to the relief of Andy Roxburgh and his Scottish squad, that's the way it stayed.

Scotland had qualified for their first ever European Championship finals.

Group 2 Final Table	P	W	D	L	F	A	Pts
SCOTLAND	8	4	3	1	14	7	11
Switzerland	8	4	2	2	19	7	10
Romania	8	4	2	2	13	7	10
Bulgaria	8	3	3	2	15	8	9
San Marino	8	0	0	8	1	33	0

12/9/90 Glasgow
Ref: Aziparte (Spain)
Attendance: 12,081

Scotland 2, Romania 1

Scotland: Goram, McKimmie, Malpas, McAllister (Nevin 73), Irvine, McLeish, Robertson, McStay, McCoist, MacLeod, Connor (Boyd 59).   Scorers: Robertson 37, McCoist 75

Romania: Lung, Petrescu, Klein, Sandoi, Rotariu, Popescu, Lacatus, Mateut (Sabau 79), Camataru (Raducioiu 62), Hagi, Lupescu.   Scorer: Camataru 13

12/9/90 Geneva
Ref: Goethals (Bel)
Attendance: 12,500

Switzerland 2, Bulgaria 0

Switzerland: Walker, Geiger, Hottiger, Herr, Schepull, Hermann, Koller, Bickel, Sutter A (Piffaretti 87), Knup (Chapuisat 64), Turkyilmaz.   Scorers: Hottiger 19, Bickel 74

Bulgaria: Valov, Iliev, Zhelev, Vasev, (Bankov 59), Ivanov, Dachev, Yardanov, Yanchev, Kostadinov, Stoihkov, Balakov (Todorov 65).

17/10/90 Bucharest
Ref: Dos Santos (Por)
Attendance: 15,350

Romania 0, Bulgaria 3

Romania: Stelea, Petrescu, Klein (Sandoi 46), Andone, Rotariu, Popescu, Lacatus, Sabau, Raducioiu (Balint 46), Hagi, Lupescu.

Bulgaria: Mikhailov, Dochev, Ivanov, Vassev, Iliev, Yankov, Yanchev, Stoichkov, Balakov, Sirakov (Kostadinov 75), Yordanov (Todorov 46).   Scorers: Sirakov 35, Todorov 46, 77

17/10/90 Glasgow
Ref: Palsi (Fin)
Attendance: 20,740

Scotland 2, Switzerland 1

Scotland: Goram, McKimmie, Nicol, McCall, McPherson, McLeish, Robertson, McAllister (Collins 79), McCoist, MacLeod, Boyd (Durie 79).
Scorers: Robertson 34 pen, McAllister 52

Switzerland: Walker, Piffaretti (B Sutter 80), Schepull (Chassot 73), Herr, Egli (sent off 89), Bickel, Knup, Hermann, Turkyilmaz, A Sutter, Chapuisat.   Scorer: Knup 66 pen

---

14/11/90 Sofia
Ref: Kaupe (Aust)
Attendance: 40,000

Bulgaria 1, Scotland 1

Bulgaria: Mikhailov, Dochev, Mladenov, Yankov, Bankov, Yanchev (Todorov 52), Yordanov, Stoichkov, Penev, Sirakov, Balakov (Kostadinov 80).   Scorer: Todorov 70

Scotland: Goram, McKimmie, Malpas, McInally, McPherson, Gillespie, Durie (Nevin 67), McAllister, McCoist, McClair, Boyd.   Scorer: McCoist 9

14/11/90 Serravalle
Ref: Kapsos (Cyp)
Attendance: 931

San Marino 0, Switzerland 4

San Marino: Benedettini, Montironi, Guerra, Gobbi, Muccioli (Toccacelli 46), Bonini (Matteoni 46), Zanotti, Francini, Ceccoli, Pasolini, Macina.

Switzerland: Walker, Hottiger, Geiger, Herr, Sutter B, Bickel (Piffaretti 59), Chapuisat, Hermann, Sutter A, Turkilmaz (Chassot 46), Knup.   Scorers: Sutter A 8, Chapuisat 27, Knup 43,Chassot 85

5/12/90 Bucharest
Ref: Kirschen (Ger)
Attendance: 6,380

Romania 6, San Marino 0

Romania: Prunea, Petrescu, Iovan, Popescu, Rednic, Sabau, Mateut, Lupescu (Stanici 65), Dumitrescu (Bedea 46), Lacatus, Raducioiu.   Scorers: Sabau 2, Mateut 18, Raducioiu 41, Lupescu 57, Badea 78, Petrescu 85

San Marino: Benedettini, Montironi, Conti, Guerra, Zanotti L, Toccacelli, Matteoni, Ceccoli, Francini, Pasolini (Zanotti P 72), Macina (Bacchiochi 46).

27/3/91 Serravalle
Ref: Phillipi (Lux)
Attendance: 1,500

San Marino 1, Romania 3

San Marino: Benedettini, Canti, Guerra, Gobbi (Toccacelli 74), Muccioli, Matteoni, Francini, Pasolini (Mularoni 89), Ceccoli, Mazza M, Mazza P.   Scorer: Pasolini 30 pen

Romania: Prunea, Petrescu, Popescu (Timofte D 46), Lupescu, Klein, Sandoi, Mateut (Timofte I 65), Hagi, Lacatus, Raducioiu.   Scorers: Hagi 17 pen, Raducioiu 45, Matteoni 86 og

---

27/3/91 Glasgow
Ref: Fredrickson (Swe)
Attendance: 33,119

Scotland 1, Bulgaria 1

Scotland: Goram, McPherson, Malpas, McInally, Gough, McLeish, Strachan (Robertson 80), McClair, McCoist, McStay, Durie (Collins 80).   Scorer: Collins 84

Bulgaria: Mikhailov, Dochev, Ivanov, Kiryakov, Iliev, Yankov, Kostadinov, Yordanov, Penev, Sirakov (Alexandrov 86), Balakov (Tanev 86).   Scorer: Kostadinov 89

3/4/91 Neuchatel
Ref: Biquet (Fra)
Attendance: 15,700

Switzerland 0, Romania 0

Switzerland: Huber, Geiger, Hottiger, Ohrel, Herr, Koller, Bonvin (Bickel 33), Hermann, Aeby, Turkyilmaz (Sutter B 75), Knup.

Romania: Prunea, Petrescu, Klein, Sandoi, Lupescu, Popescu, Sabau, Hagi (Mateut 85), Lacatus, Raducioiu (Timofte I 89), Timofte D.

1/5/91 Sofia
Ref: Assenmacher (Ger)
Attendance: 40,000

Bulgaria 2, Switzerland 3

Bulgaria: Mikhailov, Dochev (Todorov 75), Kiriakov, Yankov, Iliev, Inanov, Yordanov, Penev, Sirakov (Tanev 65), Balakov, Kostadinov.   Scorers: Kostadinov 11, Sirakov 25

Switzerland: Huber, Egli, Herr, Hottiger, Ohrel, Bonvin, Hermann, Knup (Schepull 89), Koller (Chapuisat 46), Sutter B, Turkyilmaz   Scorers: Knup 58, 88, Turkyilmaz 90

1/5/91 Serravalle
Ref: Kaimi (Alb)
Attendance: 3,512

San Marino 0, Scotland 2

San Marino: Benedettini, Canti, Muccioli, Zanotti (Toccaceli 60), Gobbi, Guerra, Ceccoli, Mazza M, Mazza P, Francini, Pasolini (Matteoni 79)

Scotland: Goram, McKimmie, Nicol (Robertson 73), McCall, McPherson, Malpas, Gallacher, Strachan, McClair (Nevin 57), McAllister, Durie.   Scorers: Strachan 63 pen, Durie 66

22/5/91 Serravalle
Ref: Mintoff (Malta)
Attendance: 670

San Marino 0, Bulgaria 3

San Marino: Benedettini, Canti, Montironi, Muccoioli, Gobbi, Guerra, Ceccoli (Matteoni 82), Mazza M, Mazza P, Francini, Pasolini (Bacciocchi 64)

Bulgaria: Mikhailov, Dimitrov, Ivanov I, Kiriakov, Anghelov, Ivanov Z (Todorov 76), Kostadinov, Gheorghiev, Penev, Sirakov, Yotov (Metkov 56)   Scorers: Ivanov Z 12, Sirakov 19, Penev 59 pen

---

5/6/91 St. Gallen
Ref: Toroglu (Tur)
Attendance: 12,000

Switzerland 7, San Marino 0

Switzerland: Huber, Egli (Schepull 74), Herr, Hottiger (Ohrel 74), Hermann, Koller, Sutter A, Sutter B, Turkyilmaz, Chapuisat,Knup. Scorers: Knup 2, 86, Hottiger 12, Sutter B 28, Hermann 54, Ohrel 77, Turkyilmaz 89

San Marino: Benedettini, Muccoioli, Guerra, Gobbi, Canti, Matteoni (Valentini 46), Mazza, Francini, Zanotti, Pasolini, Bacciocchi (Malaroni 65)

11/9/91 Berne
Ref: Lanese (Italy)
Attendance: 48,000

Switzerland 2, Scotland 2

Switzerland: Huber, Hottiger, Ohrel, Herr, Sforza, Heldmann (Sutter B 64), Knup, Hermann, Turkyilmaz, Sutter A (Bikel 60), Chapuisat.   Scorers: Chapuisat 30, Hermann 39

Scotland: Goram, McKimmie (McClair 66), Boyd, McPherson, Malpas, Strachan, McCall, Nicol, Johnston (McAllister 40), Durie, McCoist.   Scorers: Durie 47, McCoist 83

16/10/91 Bucharest
Ref: Schmidhuber (Ger)
Attendance: 30,000

Romania 1, Scotland 0

Romania: Lung, Petrescu, Klein, Sandoi, Lupescu, Popescu, Lacatus, Timofte D (Timofte I 60), Raducioiu (Dumitrescu 75), Hagi, Munteanu.   Scorer: Hagi 75 pen

Scotland: Goram, McKimmie, Malpas, McCall, McPherson, Levein, Strachan, Galloway (Aitken 70), McClair, Durie, Boyd (Gallacher 59)

16/10/91 Sofia
Ref: Ulrich (Cze)
Attendance: 8,000

Bulgaria 4, San Marino 0

Bulgaria: Mikhailov; Kiriakov, Rakov, Vidov, Illiev, Yankov, Kostadinov, Stoichkov (Lechkov 69), Penev, Kolev (Yordanov 46), Balukov. Scorers: Valentini 20 og, Stoichkov 37 pen, Yankov 41, Illiev 85

San Marino: Benedettini; Toccachelli, Valentini, Matteooni, Gobbi, Guerra, Manzzaroli, De la Valle, Mazza P, Francini, Pasolini

---

13/11/91 Glasgow
Ref: Pedersen (Nor)
Attendance: 35,170

Scotland 4, San Marino 0

Scotland: Goram, McPherson (Johnston 45), Levein (Gallacher 60), Gough, McAllister, McCall, McStay, Malpas, McCoist, Robertson, Durie.   Scorers: McStay 10, Gough 32, Durie 38, McCoist 63

San Marino: Benedettini, Canti, Guerra, Gobbi, Muccioli, Zenotti, Mazza, Bonini, Franchini, Mozza, Pasolini (Manzaroli 67).

13/11/91 Bucharest
Ref: Blankenstein (Hol)
Attendance: 28,000

Romania 1, Switzerland 0

Romania: Lung, Popescu A, Popescu G, Sandoi, Klein (Munteanu 3), Lupescu, Timofte (Sabau 46), Hagi, Mateut, Lacatus, Raducioiu.   Scorer: Mateut 72

Switzerland: Huber, Hottiger, Sforza, Herr, Schepull, Ohrel, Sutter B (Bonvin 63), Hermann (Bickel 77), Sutter A, Turkyilmaz, Chapuisat.

20/11/91 Sofia
Ref: Mikkelsen (Den)
Attendance: 10,000

Bulgaria 1, Romania 1

Bulgaria: Mikhailov, Khubchev, Rakov, Kiriakov, Illiev (Mladenov 57), Yankov, Kostadinov (Yordanov 69), Stoichkov, Penev, Sirakov, Balakov.   Scorer: Sirakov 56

Romania: Lung, Popescu A, Munteanu, Sandoi (Timofte I 68), Lupescu, Popescu G, Lacatus (Dumitrescu 60), Sabau, Raducioiu, Hagi, Mateut.   Scorer: Popescu A 30

Andrei Kanchelskis, a
goal scoring Ukrainian
export to Britain.

Group Three promised a fascinating contest between Italy, fresh from staging a splendid World Cup in 1990 and finishing as the third placed team in the world; and the USSR, European Championship runners-up in 1988. Italy were favourites, however, as the USSR were embarking on a period of transition and rebuilding. Also included in the group were Hungary, Norway and potential also-rans Cyprus.

The group programme began on 12 September 1990, when the USSR played Norway in Moscow. The Soviets' new manager, Anatoli Bishovets, who had taken over from Valeri Lobanovsky, was a man with new ideas and a fresh squad. Only five members of the team which played against Norway - Oleg Kusnetsov, Oleg Protasov, Igor Dobrovolski, Igor Shalimov and Sergei Gorlukovich - had been in the World Cup squad. With goals from Andrei Kanchelskis and Oleg Kusnetsov - two players destined to play club soccer in Britain - the Soviets won comfortably.

10 October saw Norway play Hungary in Bergen. Despite being in command for most of the game, Norway conceded a point in a 0-0 draw. Goalkeeper Zsolt Petry was Hungary's hero, making at least three magnificent saves.

Italy got off to a poor start, finding themselves under almost constant pressure from a lively Hungarian side in Budapest on 17 October. The pressure paid off and Hungary scored in the 16th minute with a Laszlo Disztl near-post header following a corner. Italy salvaged a point when Roberto Baggio equalised from the penalty-spot after a foul on Di Napoli. But they were fortunate not to *concede* a penalty when the referee failed to acknowledge a foul by Ferri.

Cyprus entered the fray on 30 October when they faced Hungary in rain-soaked Budapest. The underdogs found themselves in immediate trouble by conceding a corner in the opening minute. The kick was taken by Istvan Kozma, the ball found the head of Emil Lorincz and then the back of the Cypriots' net.

Cyprus rallied and struck an equaliser 12 minutes later, through Xiurupas. But the glory didn't last, Hungary were ahead again on 20 minutes when George Christodolu deflected the ball past 'keeper Onisiforu and into his own goal.

Qualifying Group 3

A minute later the unfortunate Christodolu conceded a penalty by bringing down Kovacs. Josef Kiprich converted from the spot for 3-1.

Another penalty decision went against the Cypriots in the 69th minute, and once again Kiprich found the net. Angelo Tolakis pulled one

Christodolu *had a Budapest nightmare.*

back for Cyprus in the last minute. They had lost 4-2, yet the most disappointed man in the stadium was Hungarian team boss Kalman Meszoly who felt his side should have won by a far wider margin.

Italy's woes increased with the visit of the USSR to Rome on 3 November. The result, 0-0, underlined just how evenly-matched were the two teams. Even so, USSR almost won the game when Oleg Protasov attempted to capitalise on a Baresi error. But the Soviet striker missed an open goal.

The result did not please the Italian press, or the Italian fans, and there were calls for the sacking of team boss Azeglio Vicini.

Cyprus met Norway in Nicosia in the next match of the campaign, on 14 November. Predictably, the Norwegians won comfortably with goals from Sorloth, Bohinen and Brandhaug. Cyprus made no reply.

Italy were the next visitors to Nicosia, on 22 December, and this time they did not slip up. As expected, Italy took both points, with a 4-0 win. The goals came from Pietro Vierchowod, Aldo Serena (2) and Attilio Lombardo. And coach Vicini was given a reprieve of sorts.

A change of venue, from Nicosia to Limassol, did nothing to prevent Cyprus from suffering a third successive European Championship defeat, on 3 April 1991. The 2-0 scoreline was inflicted

Oleg Protasov missed an open goal in Rome.

by Hungary thanks to goals by Szlama and Kiprich.

For the first time in the competition, table toppers Hungary were to find themselves on the losing end in their next game, against the USSR in Budapest, on 17 April. The only goal of the game came after 30 minutes when Mikhailichenko finished off a move by Kanchelskis and Aleinikov. The second half was notable for the return to international action of Hungary's Lajos Detari, who almost celebrated his comeback from injury with a goal. But it wasn't to be.

Hungary were to suffer again when they met Italy in Salerno on 1 May. Prior to the game the press had been speculating again that Vicini was about to replaced in the hot seat by Arrigo Sacchi, but the 3-1 Italian victory saw his star rising once more.

On this occasion Vicini was able to field his strongest side and the selection paid off with two goals from Donadoni and a third from Vialli. It could have been four, but Vialli hit a penalty-kick against the crossbar. Gyorgy Bognar replied for Hungary from the penalty spot. On the same day Norway beat Cyprus 3-0 in Oslo.

Before embarking on their next European Championship encounter - against Cyprus - the USSR took part in the England Challenge Cup competition, in which they lost 3-1 to England

and drew 1-1 with Argentina. These disappointing results were clearly forgotten by the time the match with Cyprus was played, in a Moscow thunderstorm, on 29 May. The USSR won 4-0; a result which returned them to the top of the Group Three table.

Italy stumbled once more on their visit to Oslo on 5 June. Norway were a goal ahead within four minutes when Tore Dahlum headed home a Lars Bohinen corner-kick. Twenty minutes later Bohinen latched onto a poor back pass to slot home Norway's second. Italy struggled on but could not get back into the game, although they did score a consolation goal in the 79th minute through Schillaci. In the 89th minute Guiseppi Bergomi was brought on as a substitute for Riccardo Ferri - and before the ref's watch had ticked into its 90th minute Bergomi had been sent off for fouling both Sorloth and Lydersen in one flowing movement. In neither tackle had the Italian so much as touched the ball.

The result was an absolute disaster for Italy's European Championship prospects; and it effectivley ended Azeglio Vicini's reign as manager.

Lombardo sealed the Cypriots' fate in Nicosia.

Norway were now tucked in behind the USSR at the top of the table. Both had 7 points, although the USSR had a game in hand and a superior goal difference. The two sides met in Oslo on 28 August.

The Soviet side, selected by Anatoli Bishovets amid the growing political

Group **3**	Leading Scorers
5- **Kiprich** *Hungary*	
3- **Kanchelskis** *USSR*	
2-**Baggio** *Italy*, **Sorloth** *Norway*,	
Mikhailichenko *USSR*, **Dahlum** *Norway*	
Mostovoi *USSR*, **Serena** *Italy*, **Vialli** *Italy*	
Donadoni *Italy*	

turmoil within the country, contained six foreign-based players. The match was a close fought affair. Norway almost went ahead soon after half time, but Gunner Halle's shot rebounded off the post. The matter was settled in the 74th minute when Alexander Mostovoi scored from close range for the USSR. The Soviets now looked almost certain to qualify for Sweden.

The USSR next entertained Hungary, in Moscow on 25 September. Despite being on the defensive for most the opening quarter, Hungary opened the scoring in the 17th minute through Jozef Kiprich. On 41 minutes Igor Shalimov equalised for the USSR from the penalty spot. Shortly after half time Andrei Kanchelskis put the home side ahead after a long build-up involving four players. It looked as though the USSR had the match sewn up. They held onto their lead until the 86th minute, when Kiprich got his second after connecting with a long throw-in.

92,000 spectators turned out to see the crunch match between the USSR and Italy in Moscow on 12 October. Italy really needed to win if they were to consolidate their challenge on the Soviet position. In the event the 0-0 result favoured the Soviet side and left them needing just a single point in their one remaining fixture, against Cyprus.

For Azeglio Vicini it was the end of the road. He was dismissed as manager on 15 October. Despite Italy's relatively poor form of late, Vicini's record was exemplary. In 54 matches his national team had lost only seven times.

On 30 October Hungary and Norway drew 0-0 in Szombathely.

The two matches played on 13 November settled the outcome of the group. A new-look Italy, now under the managership of Arrigo Sacchi, only managed a 1-1 draw with Norway in Genoa, while the USSR were making absolutely sure of their finals place with an emphatic 3-0 victory over Cyprus. Oleg Protasov, Sergei Yuran and Andrei Kanchelskis scored the

*Soviet hero **Alexander Mostovoi**.*

Group **3**		P	W	D	L	F	A	Pts
Final Table								
USSR		8	5	3	0	13	2	13
Italy		8	3	4	1	12	5	10
Norway		8	3	3	2	9	5	9
Hungary		8	2	4	2	10	9	8
Cyprus		8	0	0	8	2	25	0

goals which booked their trip to Sweden in the summer.

The loose ends were neatly tied when Italy beat Cyprus 2-0 in Foggia on December 21, thereby ensuring themselves of the runners-up spot in Group Three and the outside chance of a place in the finals should the newly created Commonwealth of Independent States (formerly the USSR) be unable to compete for political reasons.

12/9/90 Moscow Ref: Forstinger (Aust) Attendance: 23,000	USSR 2, Norway 0	**USSR:** Uvarov, Chernishev, Gorlukovich, Kusnetsov, Tishenko (Kulkov 79), Shalimov, Mikhailichenko, Kanchelskis, Getso (Kolyvanov 70), Protasov, Dobrovolski Scorers: Kanchelskis 22, Kusnetsov 60	**Norway:** Thorstvedt, Lydersen, Pedersen T, Bratseth, Halle, Berg (Pedersen E 61), Ahlsen, Gulbrandsen, Jakobsen, Andersen, Fjortoft (Dalhum 66)
10/10/90 Bergen Ref: Spillane (Rep of I) Attendance: 6,300	Norway 0, Hungary 0	**Norway:** Thorstvedt, Halle, Pedersen T, Bratseth, Lydersen, Pedersen E, Ahlsen, Brandhaug, Jakobsen (Andersen 72), Sorloth, Fjortoft (Dalhum 78)	**Hungary:** Petry, Monos, Pinter, Szalma, Kovacs E, Limperger, Kiprich (Fodor 79), Kozma, Bognar, Lorincz, Kovacs K (Urbanyi 89)
17/10/90 Budapest Ref: Karlsson (Swe) Attendance: 24,600	Hungary 1, Italy 1	**Hungary:** Petry, Monos, Disztl, Garaba (Fodor 60), Szalma, Bognar, Limperger, Kiprich, Kozma (Urbanyi 87), Lorincz, Kovacs K Scorer: Disztl 16	**Italy:** Zenga, Bergomi, De Agostini, Baresi, Ferri, Marocchi, Donadoni, De Napoli, Schillaci (Serena 80), Giannini (Berti 87), Baggio Scorer: Baggio 54 pen
30/10/90 Budapest Ref: Kotherja (Alb) Attendance: 2,300	Hungary 4, Cyprus 2	**Hungary:** Petry, Disztl L, Monos, Garaba, Limperger, Szalma, Kozma (Discher 56), Bognar, Lorincz, Kiprich (Rugovics 75), Kovacs K. Scorers: Lorincz 1, Christodolou 20 og, Kiprich 21 pen, 69 pen	**Cyprus:** Onisiforou, Kalotheou, Miamiliotis, Christodolou, Socratous, Yiangudakis, Andreou (Tsolakis 59), Savva, Kastanas, Constantin (Orthanides 73), Xiurupas Scorers: Xiurupas 13, Tsolakis 89
3/11/90 Rome Ref: Van Langenhove (Bel) Attendance: 52,208	Italy 0, USSR 0	**Italy:** Zenga, Ferrara, Baresi, Ferri, Maldini, Di Napoli, Crippa, De Agostini, Mancini, Schillaci (Serena 70), Baggio	**USSR:** Uvarov, Chernishev, Kulkov, Tsveiba, Shalimov, Aleinikov, Mikhailichenko, Kanchelskis, Getso (Protasov 67), Mostovoi (Tatarchuck 85), Dobrovolski
14/11/90 Nicosia Ref: Petrovic (Yug) Attendance: 2,123	Cyprus 0, Norway 3	**Cyprus:** Charitou, Kalotheou (Kantilos 49), Miamiliotis, Kastanas, Socratous, Yiangudakis, Christodolou, Savva, Tsolakas (Constaninou 74), Nicolau, Xiurupas	**Norway:** Thorstvedt, Lydersen, Pedersen T, Bratseth, Lohen (Pedersen E 64), Halle, Brandhaug, Leonhardsen, Bohinen, Sorloth, Dahlum (Fjortroft 80) Scorers: Sorloth 40, Bohinen 47, Brandhaug 63
22/12/90 Nicosia Ref: Gregr (Cze) Attendance: 9,185	Cyprus 0, Italy 4	**Cyprus:** Onisiforu, Kalotheou, Miamiliotis, Christodolou, Socratous, Yiangudakis, Punna, Savva (Constaninou 56), Tsolakis, Nicolau, Papaavasiliu (Xiurupas 64)	**Italy:** Zenga, Bergomi, Ferrara, Eranio, Vierchowod, Crippa, Lombardo, Berti, Schillaci, Marocchi, Serena Scorers: Vierchowod 14, Serena 22, 51, Lombardo 42
3/4/91 Limassol Ref: Kapl (Aus) Attendance: 3,000	Cyprus 0, Hungary 2	**Cyprus:** Marangos, Constantinou G, Pittas (Kasianos 75), Ioannu, Constantinou C, Yiangudakis, Cristofi, Savva (Sotiriu 83), Savadis, Nicolau, Tsolakis	**Hungary:** Petry, Monos, Disztl L, Szalma, Nagy, Limperger, Kiprich, Bognar, Fischer (Maroszan 72), Lorincz, Kovacs K Scorers: Szalma 15, Kiprich 40
17/4/91 Budapest Ref: Schmidhiber (Ger) Attendance: 40,000	Hungary 0, USSR 1	**Hungary:** Petry, Disztl L, Garaba, Limperger, Monos, Kozma (Detari 63), Bognar (Vincze 71), Lorincz, Szalma, Kiprich, Kovacs K	**USSR:** Uvarov, Chernishev, Kulkov, Tsveiba, Galiamin, Shalimov, Aleinikov, Mikhailichenko, Kanchelskis, Yuran (Kusnetsov 86), Kolivanov Scorer: Mikhailichenko 30
1/5/91 Salerno Ref: Worral (Eng) Attendance: 45,000	Italy 3, Hungary 1	**Italy:** Zenga, Ferrara (Vierchowod 65), Ferri, Baresi, Maldini, Crippa, Di Napoli, Giannini, Donadoni (Eranio 37), Vialli, Mancini Scorers: Donadoni 4, 16 Vialli 56	**Hungary:** Petry, Monos, Disztl, Palackzy (Kozma 33), Limperger, Garaba, Kiprich (Gregor 46), Lorincz, Bognar, Detari, Kovacs K Scorer: Bognar 66 pen
1/5/91 Oslo Ref: Natri (Fin) Attendance: 7,833	Norway 3, Cyprus 0	**Norway:** Thorstvedt, Pedersen T, Bratseth (Ingebritsen 46), Lydersen, Halle (Pedersen E 75), Ahlsen, Brandhaug, Leonhardsen, Bjornbyre, Sorloth, Dahlum Scorers: Lydersen 49 pen, Dahlum 65, Serloth 89	**Cyprus:** Charitou, Nicolau (Sotiriu 89), Constantinou G, Ioannu, Costa, Kalotheu (Constaninou C 84), Savva, Yiangudakis, Pittas, Savvides, Xiurupas
29/5/91 Moscow Ref: Petrescu (Rom) Attendance: 20,000	USSR 4, Cyprus 0	**USSR:** Uvarov, Chernishev, Kulkov, Mostovoi (Kusnetsov 74), Galiamin, Shalimov, Mikhailichenko, Kanchelskis, Aleinikov, Kolivanov, Yuran (Korneyev 46) Scorers: Mostovoi 20, Mikhailichenko 51, Korneyev 83, Aleinikov 89	**Cyprus:** Charitou, Kalotheu, Pittas, Ioannu, Nicolau, Yiangudakis. Costa, Christofi, Savvidis, Christopulu (Constantinou G 88), Xiurupas (Savva 89)
5/6/91 Oslo Ref: Ven Der Ende (Hol) Attendance: 27,500	Norway 2, Italy 1	**Norway:** Thorstvedt, Pedersen T, Ahlsen, Bratseth, Lydersen, Dahlum (Pedersen E 46), Bohinen, Lokken, Ingebrightsen, Jakobsen, Sorloth Scorers: Dahlum 4, Bohinen 24	**Italy:** Zenga, Baresi, Ferrara, Ferri (Bergomi 89; sent-off 89), Maldini, Lombardo, Eranio, De Napoli (Schillaci 53), Crippa, Vialli, Mancini Scorer: Schillaci 79
28/9/91 Oslo Ref: King (Wal) Attendance: 25,472	Norway 0, USSR 1	**Norway:** Thorstvedt, Lydersen, Pedersen T, Bratseth, Nilsen R (Riisnaes 66), Lokken, Halle, Leonhardsen, Jakobsen (Skammelsrud 80), Sorloth, Fjortoft	**USSR:** Cherchesov, Chernishev, Kulkov, Tsveiba, Kusnetsov, Shulimov, Mikhailichenko, Kanchelskis (Kornyev 71), Aleinikov, Kolivanov, Yuran (Mostovoi 46) Scorer: Mostovoi 74
25/9/91 Moscow Ref: Petrovic (Yug) Attendance: 50,000	USSR 2, Hungary 2	**USSR:** Cherchesov, Chernisov, Kulkov, Tsveiba (Kusnetsov 28), Galiamin, Shalimov, Mikhailichenko, Kanchelskis, Aleinikov, Kolivanov, Mostovoi (Yuran 72) Scorers: Shalimov 41 pen, Kanchelskis 48	**Hungary:** Petry, Monos (Duros 46), Disztl L, Szalma, Linchei, Limperger, Kiprich, Lorincz, Kozma (Fischer 28), Detari, Kovacs K Scorer: Kiprich 17, 86
12/10/91 Moscow Ref: Galler (Switz) Attendance: 92,029	USSR 0, Italy 0	**USSR:** Cherchesov, Chernishev, Kulkov, Kusnetsov O (Tsveiba 46), Galiamin, Shalimov, Mikhailichenko, Kanchelskis, Aleinikov, Protasov (Kusnetsov D 69), Kolivanov	**Italy:** Zenga, Ferrara, Maldini, Crippa, Vierchowod, Baresi, Lentini (Lombardo 58), De Napoli, Vialli, Giannini (Mancini 69), Rizzitelli
30/10/91 Szombathely Ref: Biguet (Fra) Attendance: 10,000	Hungary 0, Norway 0	**Hungary:** Petry, Pinter, Urban, Lorincz, Nagy, Pisont (Eszenyi 83), Lipsei (Illes 71), Duro, Detari, Fischer, Kovacs	**Norway:** Grodas, Pedersen T, Bratseth, Ahlsen, Bjornebye, Lokken, Bohinen, Rekdal, Leonhardsen (Ingebrightsen 78), Jakobsen, Sorloth (Fjortoft 46)
13/11/91 Genoa Ref: Assenmacher (Ger) Attendance: 30,000	Italy 1, Norway 1	**Italy:** Pagliuca, Castacurta, Maldini, Berti (De Napoli 66), Ferri, Baresi, Baiano (Rizzitelli 55), Ancelotti, Vialli, Zola, Eranio Scorer: Rizzitelli 82	**Norway:** Thorstvedt, Loken, Ahlsen, Bratseth, Lydersen, Johnsen (Pedersen J 46), Rekdal, Ingebrightsen, Fjortoft, Sorloth, Jakobsen (Berg 77) Scorer: Jakobsen 60
13/11/91 Larnaca Ref: Waddell (Scot) Attendance: 4,000	Cyprus 0, USSR 3	**Cyprus:** Charitou, Costa, Pittas, Constantinou, Socratous, Larkou, Koliandris (Hadjiloukas 75), Savva, Savvides (Soteriou 89), Ioannu, Charalambous	**USSR:** Kharin, Chernishev, Kulkov, Tsveiba, Galiamin, Shalimov, Mikhailichenko, Kanchelskis, Kusnetsov, Protasov (Mostovoi 70), Kolivanov (Yuran 46) Scorers: Protasov 27, Yuran 79, Kanchelskis 82
21/12/91 Foggia Ref: Marko (Cze) Attendance: 25,000	Italy 2, Cyprus 0	**Italy:** Zenga, Baggio D, Costacurta, Baresi, Maldini, Albertini, Berti, Evani, Zola, Baggio R (Casiraghi 65), Vialli (Baiano 66) Scorers: Vialli 27, Baggio R 55	**Cyprus:** Christofi, Constantinou G, Pittas, Constantinou K, Nicolau, Michael (Andreu 62), Koliandris, Savva, Sotariu, Ioannu (Larku 80), Charalambous

Darko Pancev, *leading goal scorer in Group 4.*

The Group Four contest - between Austria, Denmark, the Faroe Islands, Northern Ireland and Yugoslavia - got off to a sensational start on 12 September 1990, when the Faroe Islands beat Austria 1-0.

Since the only suitable playing surfaces on the Faroes are of plastic and therefore banned by UEFA, the game was played on Swedish grass in Landskrona. Pre-match publicity had the Austrians predicting that they would win by a landslide. No one had reason to doubt the claim since the match would be the Faroe Islanders' first ever competitive international. Their team of part-timers comprised truck drivers, fish salesmen, students, carpenters and electricians, while Austria had appeared in the Italia '90 World Cup finals and boasted two world class strikers in Toni Polster and Gerhard Rodax, both of whom played their club football in the prestigious Spanish league.

The match was won in the 63rd minute when Torkil Nielsen unleashed a low, left foot drive which ended up in the back of the Austrian net; a strike which imbued Nielsen with a legendary status throughout the Islands. Another hero of the hour was 'keeper Jens Martin Knudsen. Wearing a woolly bobble hat, he performed magnificently to deny Polster, Rodax and all that the Austrians could throw at him. Knudsen's headwear became a hot fashion in the Faroes, with women knitting and selling 2,000 replicas of the hero's hat!

The result came as a shock - one of the biggest shocks in world football history - not only to the Austrians, but also to the Faroe Islanders. A national holiday was declared for the following day, and for weeks afterwards the players and their Icelandic coach Pall Gudlaugsson were feted by the press. In contrast, Gudlaugsson's Austrian contemporary Josef Hickersberger resigned immediately and honourably saying that, "Any manager whose team loses to the Faroes is a failure." Hickersberger was replaced by Alfred Riedl, his former assistant.

On the same day a victory of less sensational proportions was achieved by Yugoslavia over Billy Bingham's Northern Ireland, in Belfast. The Yugoslavian side, inspired by Dragan Stojkovic, dominated the proceedings. Following a break

Qualifying Group 4

along the left flank Stojkovic delivered the cross from which Pancev scored the opening goal in the 37th minute.

Northern Ireland had no answer to Yugoslavia's well-disciplined football, and 'keeper Paul Kee was called upon to pull off several superb saves. As the Irish desperately fought for the equaliser they were frequently caught out by the counter attack - and in the 89th minute Robert Prosinecki wrapped it all up with Yugoslavia's second goal.

The Faroe Islands came down from Cloud Nine with a crash when they played their second competitive international, against Denmark in Copenhagen on 10 October. Denmark won 4-1, but it could have been a lot more. The goals came from Michael Laudrup (2), Lars Elstrup and Flemming Povlsen. Allan Morkore replied for the Islanders. Even this defeat heartened coach Gudlaugsson. He said: "...to lose only 4-1 was a moral victory for us."

On 17 October Northern Ireland picked up their first point with a 1-1 draw against Denmark in Belfast. Jan Bartram opened the scoring for Denmark with an 11th minute penalty. Colin Clarke replied for Northern Ireland in the 57th minute.

Yugoslavia, playing their 500th international match, pressed their claim for superiority in Group Four with an emphatic 4-1 win over

Colin Clarke of Portsmouth and Northern Ireland.

Austria in Belgrade on 31 October. Still smarting from the Faroe Islands fiasco, Austria were on the defensive right from the start and 'keeper Konsel was kept busy - yet it was they who scored first when Andy Ogris hit home after a fine individual run on 15 minutes. Then the home side struck back with two goals in the space of eleven minutes, from Darko Pancev (32 mins) and Srecko Katanec (43 mins). Pancev headed Yugoslavia's third on 52 minutes, and four minutes from time he completed a hat-trick.

Another efficient Yugoslavian performance, away to Denmark on 14 November, further consolidated their position at the top of the table. Late in the second half the game seemed to be heading for a goalless draw. Then with 13 minutes left Mehmed Bazdarevic scored on the break for Yugoslavia. As Denmark pressed forward in a desperate search for the equaliser, they left themselves wide open at the back and a second, almost inevitable, Yugoslav goal came from Robert Jarni.

On the same day Northern Ireland took on Austria in Vienna. To say that football in Austria had drifted into the doldrums is something of an understatement. Morale within the national side and among supporters was at an all-time low. So concerned with the situation was the Osterreichischer Fussball-Bund, that they reduced the price of admission to the Prater Stadium for the Northern Ireland match. The

7,000 who took advantage of the offer witnessed little to raise their spirits. The result was a dreary goalless draw.

Billy Bingham next took his Northern Ireland squad to Belgrade where they faced an on-form Yugoslavia. Striker Darko Pancev was particularly on song - in the second half he notched his second hat-trick of the qualifying tournament. Before that Drasic Binic had opened the scoring in the 36th minute and Colin Hill had equalised moments before half time. But the match belonged to Pancev and the points to Yugoslavia.

In their next fixture, at home to Denmark in Belgrade on May Day, it was Yugoslavia's turn for a shock. The Danish side was considerably weakened by the absence of Michael and Brian Laudrup. The brothers had withdrawn from selection in protest against team boss Richard Moller-Nielsen.

Nevertheless Denmark were the dominant side right from the start. They scored in the 31st minute when Bent Christensen headed home a cross from Flemming Povlsen. Yugoslavia gradually got back into the game and equalised five minutes into the second half through Darko Pancev. The matter was sealed in Denmark's favour in the 62nd minute when Povlsen siezed on a defensive error by Robert Prosinecki. The ball found Christensen who netted his second of the game.

On the same day, the Faroe Islanders tasted another moment of glory when they drew 1-1 with Northern Ireland in Belfast. Portsmouth's Colin Clarke opened the scoring in the 44th minute, by which time the Irish should have been well ahead. But once again the bobble-hatted Jens Knudsen had been in top form between the posts and was the hero of the hour. Ten minutes into the second half Allan Morkore crossed the ball into the Irish penalty area, it was met by the head of Kari Reynheim and finished up in Paul Kee's goal. After the match the Faroe's coach Pall Gudlaugsson said: "...the margin between

Bent Christensen raised hopes for Denmark.

professionals and amateurs is closing all the time."

Perhaps so, but that point was the last the Faroe Islands would collect, and Reynheim's goal was the last they would score in the tournament. On 16 May a very professional Yugoslavia thrashed the Islanders 7-0 in Belgrade; and in Vienna six days later Austria avenged that humiliating opening match defeat - with a 3-0 win over the Faroes.

Denmark consolidated their challenge on Yugoslavia at the top of the group, with a 2-1 victory over Austria in Copenhagen on 5 June. Bent Christensen scored both for the Danes; Ernst Ogris replied for Austria. The result left Denmark in second place with 7 points from 5 games. Yugoslavia, however, were comfortably placed in top spot with 10 points from 6 games.

On 11 September the Faroe Islands played their second 'home' fixture, 900 miles from home, in Landskrona. This time the opponents were Northern Ireland; and this time there would be no repeat of the fairy tale result achieved against Austria a year earlier, nor of the draw against Northern Ireland in May. Colin Clarke saw to that by netting a hat-trick. Further goals from Kevin Wilson and Alan McDonald completed the demolition job.

But Northern Ireland's revival had come too late; those earlier dropped points meant they had very little chance of qualifying.

The Faroe Islanders had yet another rude awakening when they played Denmark in Landskrona two weeks later. The Danes were ahead after two minutes when Kim Christofte converted a penalty. Five minutes later the prolific Bent Chritensen made it 2-0. After such a demoralising start the Faroes hardly stood a chance - and it says a lot for their tenacity that the final scoreline stood at just 4-0. Franck Pingel and Kim Vilfort scored the Danes' remaining goals in the second half.

Denmark - still troubled with internal strife, several players now refused to play under team-boss Richard Moller-Nielsen - travelled to Vienna and inflicted further grief on the Austrians with a 3-0 victory on 9 October. The damage was done with goals from Flemming Povlsen, Bent Christensen and an unfortunate own-goal by Peter Artner. The result took Denmark to the top of the table.

Before the final whistle the home fans were booing their own team. After the match manager Alfred Riedl was sacked, having spent a little over a year in the hot seat. He was succeeded by Didi Constantini, as 'caretaker' manager.

By this time

Group 4 — **Leading Scorers**

10- **Pancev** *Yugoslavia*
6- **Christensen** *Denmark*
5-**Clarke** *Northern Ireland,*
4-**Povlsen** *Denmark*

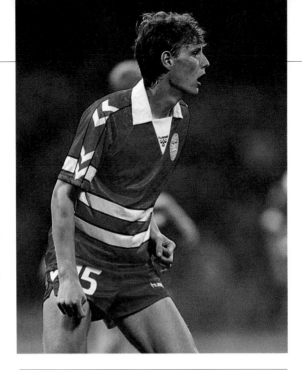

Flemming Povlsen of Denmark.

Yugoslavia was in the throes of a devastating civil war, and football was suffering the consequences along with every other aspect of life in that divided country. Indeed, for the away fixture against the Faroe Islands on 16 October team-boss Ivica Osim was forced to select his side chiefly from the two Belgrade-based clubs Red Star and Partizan: no Croatian-born players were available to him.

Robert Prosinecki, of Real Madrid, was to have been included in the team. However, reports that he was of both Serbian and Croatian descent placed him in a decidedly awkward situation and, reportedly, there was even a 'death threat' hanging over him. In the event an injury prevented Prosinecki from taking part in the match.

The result, a 2-0 victory for Yugoslavia, returned Ivica Osim's side to the top of the table and saw the Faroe Islands completing their first venture into European Championship football with a certain amount of pride, not to mention a special page in the history books.

Meanwhile, Northern Ireland were playing Austria in Belfast. Even under new management the Austrians were still a forlorn team. An Ian Dowie header from a Kingsley Black free-kick put Northern Ireland ahead in the 17th minute; and Black himself scored a second from a neatly placed pass by Robby Dennison on 40 minutes. Leo Lainer replied for Austria just before half time. Austria did stage something of a recovery in the second half and Lainer almost snatched an equaliser with five minutes to go.

The final outcome of Group Four was decided in the last two matches, both played on 13 November. Yugoslavia topped the table with 12 points and a goal difference of 18. Denmark lay second with 11 points and a goal difference of 10. This meant that a win for Yugoslavia against Austria would see them through. If that match was drawn then Denmark would need to beat Northern Ireland by a nine goal margin.

In the event, Yugoslavia had an easy passage through their match in Vienna, winning 2-0 against Didi Constantini's unsettled Austrian side. First-half goals from Vladen Lukic and Dejan Savicevic saw them safely through to Sweden.

Meanwhile, Denmark was putting on a terrific attacking display in Odense. They won 2-1, both goals scored by Flemming Povlsen. After the match team-boss Richard Moller-Nielsen - who had been at the centre of controversy and speculation for months - declared: "We're disappointed not to make it to the finals - after all we only dropped three points..." Unfortunately for him, Yugoslavia had dropped only two.

Yugoslavia also had the distinction of being the leading scorers, with 24 goals, in the qualifying competition and they boasted the leading individual goalscorer - Darko Pancev with ten goals.

Group 4 Final Table

	P	W	D	L	F	A	Pts
YUGOSLAVIA	8	7	0	1	24	4	14
Denmark	8	6	1	1	18	7	13
Northern Ireland	8	2	3	3	11	11	7
Austria	8	1	1	6	6	14	3
Faroe Islands	8	1	1	6	3	26	3

12/9/90 Landskrona, (Sweden) Ref: Nervik (Nor)	Faroe Islands 1, Austria 0	**Faroe Islands:** Knudsen, Jakobsen, Hansen T, Danielsen, Hansen J, Morkore A, Nielsen, Dam, Hansen A, Reynheim, Morkore K Scorer: Nielsen 63	**Austria:** Konsel, Russ, Pecl, Hartmann, Strieter, Peischl, Rodax, Linzmaier, Polster, Herzog (Pacult 63), Reisinger (Willfurth 63)
12/9/90 Belfast Ref: Uilenberg (Hol) Attendance: 9,008	Northern Ireland 0, Yugoslavia 2	**Northern Ireland:** Kee, Taggart, McDonald, Donaghy, Worthington, Wilson D, Rogan, Dennison (Clarke 66), Black, Wilson K, Dowie	**Yugoslavia:** Ivkovic, Vulic, Spasic, Jozic, Hadzibegic, Najdoski, Prosinecki, Savicevic, Pancev (Petrovic 87), Stojkovic, Binic Scorers: Pancev 37, Prosinecki 89
10/10/90 Copenhagen Ref: Haraldsson (Ice'd) Attendance: 38,563	Denmark 4, Faroe Islands 1	**Denmark:** Schmeichel, Sivebaek, Nielsen K, Olsen L, Heintze, Bartram, Vilfort, Elstrup (Rasmussen 73), Povlsen, Laudrup M, Laudrup B Scorers: Laudrup M 8, 49, Elstrup 39, Povlsen 89	**Faroe Islands:** Knudsen, Jakobsen, Hansen E, Danielsen, Hansen J, Morkore A (Jarnskor 88), Nielsen, Dam, Hansen A, Reynheim, Morkore K (Mohr) Scorer Morkore A 22
17/10/90 Belfast Ref: Phillipi (Lux) Attendance: 9,079	Northern Ireland 1, Denmark 1	**Northern Ireland:** Kee, Donaghy, Worthington, Taggart, McDonald, Rogan, Wilson D, O'Neill (McBride 72), Dowie, Clarke, Black Scorer: Clarke 57	**Denmark:** Schmeichel, Sivebaek, Nielsen K, Olsen L, Heintze, Bartram, Larsen, Vilfort, Povlsen, Laudrup M (Helt 70), Laudrup B, (Elstrup 70) Scorer: Bartram 11 pen
31/10/90 Belgrade Ref: Schmidhuber (Ger) Attendance: 11,422	Yugoslavia 4, Austria 1	**Yugoslavia:** Ivkovic, Vulic, Spasic, Katenec (Jarni 46), Hadzibegic, Jozic, Prosinecki, Susic (Boban 70), Pancev, Bazdarevic, Vujovic Scorers: Pancev 32, 52, 86, Katanec 43	**Austria:** Konsel, Aigner, Pecl, Strieter, Schottel, Reisinger, Ogris A, Artner, Polster, Herzog (Linzmaier 46), Hortnagl Scorer: Ogris 15
14/11/90 Copenhagen Ref: Midgley (Eng) Attendance: 40,000	Denmark 0, Yugoslavia 2	**Denmark:** Schmeichel, Olsen, Nielsen, Sivebaek, Heintze, Vilfort, Bartram, Molby (Elstrup 72), Laudrup M, Povlsen (Jensen 46), Laudrup B	**Yugoslavia:** Ivkovic, Vulic, Spasic, Katanec, Hadzibegic, Jozic, Jarni, Susic, Pancev (Boban 11), Bazdarevic, Vujovic (Najdoski 89) Scorers: Bazdarevic 77, Jarni 84
1· 11/90 Vienna Ret.: Biguet (Fra) Attendance: 7,062	Austria 0, Northern Ireland 0	**Austria:** Konsel, Schottel, Pecl, Poger, Artner, Willfurth, Peischl, Linzmaier, Hortnagl, Ogris, Polster (Pacult 70)	**Northern Ireland:** Kee, Donaghy, Taggart, McDonald, Worthington, Dennison, Wilson D, Rogan, Black (Morrow 82), Clarke (Dowie 65), Wilson K
27/3/91 Belgrade Ref: Namoglu (Tur) Attendance: 10,000	Yugoslavia 4, Northern Ireland 1	**Yugoslavia:** Ivkovic, Spasic, Vulic (Najdoski 85), Jozic, Jarni, Bazdarevic, Prosinecki, Boban, Pancev, Savicevic, Binic Scorers: Binic 36, Pancev 48, 61, 63	**Northern Ireland:** Kee, Donaghy, Hill, Taggart, Morrow, Rogan, Wilson K, Dennison (Quinn 70), Wilson D (Clarke 60), Black, Dowie Scorer: Hill 44
1/5/91 Belgrade Ref: Quiniou (Fra) Attendance: 26,000	Yugoslavia 1, Denmark 2	**Yugoslavia:** Ivkovic, Vulic, Jarni (Najdoski 84), Spasic, Hadzibegic, Jozic, Prosinecki, Savicevic, Pancev, Bazdarevic, Binic Scorer: Pancev 50	**Denmark:** Schmeichel, Sivebaek (Larsen 54), Nielsen K, Olsen L, Kristensen B, Bartram, Jensen (Goldbaek 82), Christofte, Povlsen, Vilfort, Christensen B Scorer: Christensen B 31, 62
1/5/91 Belfast Ref: Piraux (Fra) Attendance: 10,000	Northern Ireland 1, Faroe Islands 1	**Northern Ireland:** Kee, Donaghy, Worthington, Taggart, McDonald, Magilton, Wilson D (Dennison 83), Clarke, Dowie (Williams 83), Wilson K, Black Scorer: Clarke 44	**Faroe Islands:** Knudsen, Jakobsen T, Hansen, Danielsen, Muller, Morkore A, Nielsen, Dam, Hansen A, Reynheim, Morkore K Scorer: Reynheim 65
16/5/91 Belgrade Ref: Nikakis (Gre) Attendance: 6,745	Yugoslavia 7, Faroe Islands 0	**Yugoslavia:** Ivkovic (Lazic 80), Stanojkovic, Jarni (Suker 67), Vulic, Najdoski, Spasic, Prosinecki, Boban, Pancev, Savicevic, Mihajlovic Scorers: Najdoski 20, Prosinecki 24, Pancev 50, 74, Vulic 66, Boban 70, Suker 86	**Faroe Islands:** Knudsen, Jakobsen, Hansen T, Danielsen, Jarnskor, Morkore A, Nielsen, Dam, Hansen A, Reynheim, Morkore K (Muller 49)
22/5/91 Vienna Ref: Loizou (Cyp) Attendance: 13,000	Austria 3, Faroe Islands 0	**Austria:** Konsel (Wohlfarht 86), Baur, Russ, Pfeifenberger (Hortnagl 24), Hartmann, Stoger, Schottel, Herzog, Streiter, Wetl, Ogris A Scorers: Pfiefenberger 13, Streiter 48, Wetl 63	**Faroe Islands:** Knudsen, Jakobsen, Morkore A, Danielsen, Hansen T, Simonsen, Nielsen, Hansen A, Dam (Thomassen 71), Reynheim, Rasmussen (Mohr 85)
5/6/91 Copenhagen Ref: Listkiewicz (Pol) Attendance: 12,521	Denmark 2, Austria 1	**Denmark:** Schmeichel, Hansen, Nielsen K, Olsen, Bruun, Vilfort, Larsen, Nielsen BS, Nielsen C (Goldbaek 46), Povlsen (Rasmussen 78), Christensen Scorer: Christensen 2, 77	**Austria:** Konrad, Russ (Prosenik 72), Baur, Hartmann, Pfiefenberger, Streiter, Ogris E, Schottel (Hortnagl 66), Herzog, Stoger, Westerhaler Scorer: Ogris E 83
11/9/91 Landskrona (Sweden) Ref: Ruokonen (Fin) Attendance: 1,623	Faroe Islands 0, Northern Ireland 5	**Faroe Islands:** Knudsen, Jakobsen J (Morkore K 78), Hansen T, Danielsen, Thomassen (Muller 51), Morkore A (sent-off 67), Nielsen, Dam, Hansen A, Reynheim, Jonsson	**Northern Ireland:** Wright, Donaghy, Morrow, Taggart, McDonald, Magilton, Dennison, Wilson K (O'Neill 70), Dowie, Clarke, Black (McBride 70) Scorers: Wilson K 7, Clarke 13, 49, 70 pen, McDonald 15
25/9/91 Landskrona (Sweden) Ref: McCluskey (Scot) Attendance: 3,589	Faroe Islands 0, Denmark 4	**Faroe Islands:** Knudsen (Johannessen 46), Jakobsen, Hansen T, Danielsen, Morkore K, Dam, Jarnskor, Jonsson (Davidsen 83), Hansen A, Reyheim, Muller	**Denmark:** Schmeichel, Sivebaek, Nielsen K, Olsen L, Larsen H, Christofte (Molby Jo 60), Jensen J, Vilfort, Povlsen, Christensen, Elstrup (Pingel 68) Scorers: Christofte 2 pen, Christensen 7, Pingel 69, Vilfort 76
9/10/91 Vienna Ref: Van Den Wijngaert (Bel) Attendance: 10,000	Austria 0, Denmark 3	**Austria:** Konrad, Prosenik, Baur, Resch, Kogler, Schottel (Gschneidter 46), Ogris A, Artner, Herzog, Stoger, Pacult	**Denmark:** Schmeichel, Sivebaek, Nielsen K, Olsen L, Larsen H (Jensen B 81), Christofte (Molby Jo 59), Jensen J, Vilfort, Povlsen, Christensen, Elstrup Scorers: Artner 10 og, Povlsen 16, Christensen 37
16/10/91 Landskrona (Sweden) Ref: Habermann (Ger) Attendance: 2,345	Faroe Islands 0, Yugoslavia 2	**Faroe Islands:** Knudsen, Hansen T, Jakobsen, Danielsen, Morkore T, Dam, Hansen A, Reynheim, Jonsson, Morkore A (Davidsen 75) Moller	**Yugoslavia:** Omerovic, Brnovic B, Hadzibegic, Najdoski, Spasic, Yugovic, Jokanovic, Savicevic, Bazdarevic, Lukic (Stanic 70), Mihailovic (Mihatovic 65) Scorers: Yugovich 18, Savicevic 81
16/10/91 Belfast Ref: Sundell (Swe) Attendance: 8,000	Northern Ireland 2, Austria 1	**Northern Ireland:** Wright, Hill, Donaghy, Taggart, Worthington, Dennison, Magilton, Wilson K, Black, Dowie, Clarke Scorers: Dowie 17, Black 40	**Austria:** Knaller, Lainer, Rotter, Hartmann, Kogler, Zsak, Ogris A, Atrner, Keglevits, Stoger, Garger Scorer: Lainer 44
13/11/91 Odense Ref: Spirin (USSR) Attendance: 10,881	Denmark 2, Northern Ireland 1	**Denmark:** Schmeichel, Olsen, Neilsen K, Vilfort, Sivebaek, Christofte, Povlsen, Molby Jo, Larsen H, Piechnik, Elstrup (Pingel 53) Scorer: Povlsen 22, 36	**Northern Ireland:** Fettis, Hill, Donaghy, Taggart, Worthington, McBride, Hughes, Magilton, Wilson K, Black (Dennison 83), Clark (Dowie 67) Scorer: Taggart 71
13/11/91 Vienna Ref: D'Elia (Italy) Attendance: 8,000	Austria 0, Yugoslavia 2	**Austria:** Knaller, Zsak, Garger W, Kogler, Artner, Garger H, Stoger (Keglevits 53), Herzog, Lainer, Ogris A. Westerhaler (Baur 73)	**Yugoslavia:** Omerovic, Hadzibegic, Vujacic, Milanic, Novak (Brnovic 81), Jokanovic, Savicevic, Bazdarevic, Mihailovic, Lukic (Mijatovic 46), Pancev Scorers: Lukic 19, Savicevic 39

Ian Rush's first
international goal for 2
years came against
Belgium.

Group Five started life with five contenders: Belgium, East Germany, Luxembourg, Wales and West Germany. However, in the wake of the sweeping political changes which ultimately saw the reunification of Germany, *East* Germany withdrew from the competition and the contest was subsequently run on a four team basis.

The action kicked off on October 17 1990 when Terry Yorath's Wales entertained Belgium at the spiritual home of Welsh sporting endeavour, the Cardiff Arms Park.

Under Guy Thys Belgium had reached the Second Round of the 1990 World Cup only to be eliminated by England and David Platt's famous last-minute-of-extra-time goal. The Belgians were now expected to pose the most serious threat to Group Five favourites Germany. Ten members of Belgium's World Cup team which had faced England in Bologna now lined up against the Welsh including two of Europe's finest midfielders, Jan Cuelemans and the Italian-born Enzo Scifo.

But Yorath, the ex-Leeds , Coventry, Spurs and Bradford City favourite, had been nurturing a formidable squad of his own which boasted one of the world's best goalkeepers, Neville Southall and three of the top forwards in the Football League, Ian Rush, Dean Saunders and Mark Hughes. The rest of the side was based on solid and dependable stock, including Clayton Blackmore, Kevin Ratcliffe and team captain Peter Nicholas.

Belgium struck the first blow in the match when Scifo delivered a long ball into the Welsh defence in the 24th minute. It was met by Bruno Versavel who made no mistake in beating Southall. Ian Rush linked with Dean Sauders to level the scores on 29 minutes. The strike was a personal triumph for the Liverpool superstar as it marked his first international goal in over two years.

Late in the second half the match seemed destined for a draw, but then with eight minutes left to play Saunders shot the Welsh ahead. Not

to be outdone, Mark Hughes added a third in the 87th minute. Terry Yorath's side were off to a tremendous start.

Former West German international Berti Vogts had succeeded Franz Beckenbauer as team manager of the new Germany. He was now

Qualifying Group 5

embarking on his first major campaign and must have expected an easy win in the first fixture, away to Luxembourg on 31 October. Indeed, by half time Germany were leading 2-0 with goals from Jurgen Klinsmann and Uwe Bein, and when Rudi Voller added a third in the 49th minute the Germans appeared to be coasting to victory. Perhaps they were treating the game as something of a training excercise, perhaps an air of complacency set in - because when Luxembourg staged a remarkable fightback the German effort virtually disintegrated.

First Jean-Paul Girres (57 minutes) and then Roby Langers (66 minutes) scored for the home side, and twice after that Luxembourg almost snatched the equaliser. Only some sterling work by Bodo Illgner in the German goal denied them.

At full time the scoreline remained at 3-2 in Germany's favour, but they had ridden their luck and Berti Vogts knew it. Meanwhile, Luxembourg's team boss Paul Philip was singing his side's praises. "I've never seen them play so well," he said.

Unfortunately, the fixture had been marred by crowd trouble before, during and after the match.

The Welsh cause was boosted by a 1-0 away victory over Luxembourg on 14 November. Ian Rush scored on 16 minutes, following a Peter Nicholas free-kick. But, still bolstered by their

Dean Saunders linked with Rush to level the scores against Belgium.

Luxembourg could not stage another comeback, although they did manage four goal attempts in the second half.

Wales dropped their first point of the campaign in a hard-fought 1-1 draw with Belgium in Brussels on 27 March. Both goals came within an eleven minute spell early in the second half. Belgium struck first through Marc Degryse who had latched onto a weak back pass before lifting the ball over the rapidly advancing Neville Southall. The Welsh reply came after a Paul Bodin cross from the left wing was headed on by Ian Rush for Dean Saunders to volley home.

The point provided a pleasant present for team boss Yorath who was celebrating his 41st birthday, and the result meant Wales were very much in the qualification hunt. But they still had to face the mighty Germans - twice.

The spectre of hooliganism raised its ugly head prior to Germany's next fixture, against Belgium, in Hanover on May Day. Many shops and offices were damaged as some 500 troublemakers went on the rampage and fought a running battle with police: more than 250 arrests were made.

The German team included ex-East German

plucky performance in the previous match against Germany, Luxembourg had proved difficult to beat and once again were unlucky not to equalise. The Welsh side was depleted by the early sending off of Clayton Blackmore.

Luxembourg next travelled to neighbouring Belgium for the match on 27 February 1991, only to find the home side staging an attacking onslaught right from the start and going three goals to the good within 36 minutes. Erwin Vandenburgh, Jan Cuelemans and Enzo Scifo were the scorers for Belgium. Try as they might

players (Matthias Sammer and Thomas Doll) for the first time in the Championships. The only goal of the game came after three minutes when Lothar Matthaus's side foot

Above: Michel Preud'homme, *Belgium's goalkeeper*

shot was adjudged by referee Petrovic to have been taken over the line by Belgian 'keeper

Above: Neville Southhall denied the Germans a goal in Cardiff.

Michel Preud'homme. Although it had been a somewhat poor, uninspired German performance, the points were in the bag. Another good result, against Wales at the Arms Park on 5 June, would surely see Germany well on the way to Sweden.

But, if the World Champions considered that game to be a mere formality, they were in for a shock of monumental proportions. They arrived in Cardiff bolstered, as always, by their tremendous reputation and unbeaten in sixteen matches.

However, the Welsh squad was riding high and in a confident frame of mind - and the visitors appeared to be intent on defence and seeking the safety of a draw. When sweeper Thomas Berthold was sent off in the 61st minute, after walking all over Kevin Ratcliffe, Wales were able to exploit the situation. Eight minutes after the dismissal, Ian Rush confounded German expectations with the only goal of the game after outpacing Guido Buchwald to meet Paul Bodin's long pass. At the other end Neville Southall performed heroically to keep the German attack at bay.

It was arguably the most remarkable victory in Welsh international history. Although Germany had a game in hand, Wales were now 3 points ahead - but there was still the return match to come.

Meanwhile, Belgium and Luxembourg met in Luxembourg on 11 September. It was a familiar story for the home side who put in yet another plucky performance only to find themselves on the wrong end of a 2-0 scoreline. Belgium's goals came from Enzo Scifo and Marc Degryse.

Five weeks before the Germany/Wales clash the Germans played in an exemplary friendly against England at Wembley, and showed their true class while winning 1-0. Team captain Lothar Matthaus had been in particularly inspirational form and demonstrated just why he was the current European Footballer Of The Year. The vastly improved German team performance must have caused Terry Yorath one or two sleepless nights - and not without some justification, as things turned out.

Karlheinze Riedle headed the third past Southall in Nuremberg.

The re-match was played in Nurnberg on 16 October, with the German side at last looking like true World Champions. Quite simply, they outclassed Wales who were perhaps too intent on defending their slim advantage. The opening goal was scored by Andreas Moller on 34 minutes after a short left-sided corner and a neatly worked exchange with Matthaus. The second came five minutes later when Rudi Voller took advantage of a crazy backpass by Gavin Maguire, and headed the gifted ball beyond Southall's reach. Almost on the stroke of half time Karl-Heinz Riedle headed Germany's third from a Matthaus cross.

The situation grew gradually worse for Wales. Dean Saunders brought down Thomas Doll on tender age of 17 years 321 days became the youngest ever player to represent Wales. He replaced Eric Young with four minutes left to play.

Despite the defeat the Welsh were still in with a chance of qualification. They topped the Group with 7 points from 5 games. Germany, on 6 points from 4 games, had the obvious potential to overtake Wales.

To keep up the momemtum Wales needed to

*Manchester United's **Ryan Giggs** – the youngest ever Welsh international.*

59 minutes and was promptly sent off by French referee Quiniou. Ten minutes later Doll netted a fourth goal for Germany.

Wales had a small consolation when Paul Bodin scored from the penalty spot in the 85th minute. The match also saw the international debut of Manchester United's teenage sensation Ryan Giggs, who at the

win their last match, at home to Luxembourg, and in case the eventual outcome of the group was to be decided on goal difference, they needed to win by as big a margin as possible. Of course, before that could happen the fate of the Welsh would lie with the results of Germany's remaining fixtures, away to Belgium and at home to Luxembourg.

Group 5 Leading Scorers

3-Rush *Wales*, **Voller** *Germany*
2-Saunders *Wales*, **Degryse** *Belgium*, **Matthaus** *Germany*, **Riedle** *Germany*, **Scifo** *Belgium*, **Bodin** *Wales*

The Wales v Luxembourg match was played at the Arms Park on 13 November. The visitors almost went ahead in the opening minutes, but the Welsh blushes were saved by a well-timed Peter Nicholas tackle on the adventurous Malget. After that scare Wales made probing attacks but found the Luxembourg defence almost impenetrable. The deadlock was eventually broken by a Paul Bodin penalty in the 82nd minute.

The scoreline remained at 1-0. Wales had both points, but had hardly enhanced their goal difference as they'd hoped. On 20 November Germany beat Belgium 1-0 in Brussels, with a Rudi Voller goal. As with the previous fixture between the two nations, this match was tainted with sinister overtones. Some 300 Nazi-inspired hooligans were arrested after riots in the streets of the city.

Germany - now needing just a single point - finally sealed their qualification by beating Luxembourg 4-0 in Leverkusen on 17 December. The rout began in the 15th minute when Marcel Bossi brought down Karl-Heinz Riedle in the penalty area and Lothar Matthaus netted from the spot. Guido Buchwald made it 2-0 in the 44th minute and also provided the pass from which Riedle headed the third on 51 minutes. Thomas Hassler, substituting for Thomas Doll, struck a spectacular fourth in the 62nd minute. It was a fitting way for the reigning World Champions to tie up the loose ends.

Group 5 Final Table	P	W	D	L	F	A	Pts
GERMANY	6	5	0	1	13	4	10
Wales	6	4	1	1	8	6	9
Belgium	6	2	1	3	7	6	5
Luxembourg	6	0	0	6	2	14	0

Rudi Voller scored for Germany in Brussels.

17/10/90 Cardiff Ref: Rothlisberger (Switz) Attendance: 15,000	Wales 3, Belgium 1	**Wales:** Southal, Blackmore, Bodin, Aizlewood, Young, Ratcliffe, Horne, Nicholas, Rush, Hughes, Saunders Scorers: Rush 29, Saunders 82, Hughes 87	**Belgium:** Preud'homme, Gerets, Grun, De Wolf, Versavel, Emmers, Demol, Van der Elst, Nilis (Wilmots 73), Scifo, Ceulemans Scorer: Verseval 24
31/10/90 Luxembourg Ref: Nielsen (Den) Attendance: 9,512	Luxembourg 2, Germany 3	**Luxembourg:** Van Rijswijck, Malget, Bossi, Petry, Birsens, Groff, Hellers, Girres, Saibene (Jeitz 85), Weis, Langers Scorers: Girres 57, Langers 66	**Germany:** Illgner, Binz, Berthold, Kohler, Strunz, Hassler, Matthaus, Bein (Reinhardt 73), Brehme, Klinsmann, Voller Scorers: Klinsmann 14, Bein 30, Voller 49
14/11/90 Luxembourg Ref: Ulrich (Cze) Attendance: 6,800	Luxembourg 0, Wales 1	**Luxembourg:** Van Rijswijck, Malget, Bossi, Petry, Birsens, Saibene, Girres, Weis, Hellers, Morcutti (Krings 60), Langers	**Wales:** Southall, Blackmore (sent-off 11), Bodin, Aizlewood, Young, Ratcliffe, Horne, Nicholas, Rush (Speed 83), Hughes, Saunders (Allen M 88) Scorer: Rush 16
27/2/91 Brussels Ref: Loizu (Cyprus) Attendance: 24,505	Belgium 3, Luxembourg 0	**Belgium:** Preud'homme, Grun, Albert, Emmers, Versavel B, Dauwen, Scifo, Ceulemans, Degryse, Vandenbergh, Wilmots Scorers: Vandebergh 7, Cuelemans 17, Scifo 36	**Luxembourg:** Koch, Malget (Jeitz 46), Bossi, Birsens, Petry, Groff (Scuto 75), Hellers, Girres, Saibene, Weis, Krings
27/3/91 Brussels Ref: Aladren (Sp) Attendance: 25,500	Belgium 1, Wales 1	**Belgium:** Preud'homme, Gerets, Albert, Grun, Clysters, Versavel B, Van der Elst, Scifo, Degryse, Vandenbergh, Wilmots Scorer: Degryse 47	**Wales:** Southall, Phillips, Ratcliffe, Young, Aizlewood, Bodin, Horne, Nicholas, Hughes, Rush, Saunders Scorer: Saunders 58
1/5/91 Hanover Ref: Petrovic (Yug) Attendance: 56,000	Germany 1, Belgium 0	**Germany:** Illgner, Berthold, Reuter, Beiersdorfer, Brehme, Hassler, Sammer, Matthaus, Doll, Klinsmann (Helmer 77), Voller (Riedle 88) Scorer: Matthaus 3	**Belgium:** Preud'homme, Emers, Crasson, Grun, Albert, Van der Elst, Scifo, Vervoort, Versavel B, Degryse, Wilmots (Nilis 77)
5/6/91 Cardiff Ref: Karlsson (Swe) Attendance: 37,000	Wales 1, Germany 0	**Wales:** Southall, Phillips, Melville, Ratcliffe, Bodin, Aizlewood, Nicholas, Horne, Rush, Saunders, Hughes Scorer: Rush 69	**Germany:** Illgner, Reuter, Helmer, Berthold (sent-off 61), Kohler, Brehme, Buchwald, Sammer (Effenberg 76), Matthaus (Doll 46), Klinsmann, Voller
11/9/91 Luxembourg Ref: Harrel (Fra) Attendance: 7,440	Luxembourg 0, Belgium 2	**Luxembourg:** Van Rijswijck, Jeitz, Bossi, Petry, Wolf, Mirsens, Girres, Hellers, Groff, Langers (Thome 66), Morcutti (Krings 77)	**Belgium:** Preud'homme, Grun (Medved 75), Van der Elst, Demol (Dauwen 79), Borkelmans, Emmers, Staelens, Scifo, Vervoort, Degryse, Nilis Scorers: Scifo 23, Degryse 48
16/10/91 Nurnberg Ref: Quiniou (Fra) Attendance: 46,000	Germany 4, Wales 1	**Germany:** Illgner, Binz, Reuter, Kohler, Buchwald, Brehme, Matthaus, Moller, Doll (Effenberg 74), Voller, Riedle (Hassler 65) Scorers: Moller 34, Voller 39, Riedle 44, Doll 69	**Wales:** Southall, Ratcliffe, Bodin, Young (Giggs 86), Bowen, Hughes, Melville, Maguire (Speed 46), Horne, Rush, Saunders (sent-off 59) Scorer: Bodin 85 pen
13/11/91 Cardiff Ref: Puhl (Hun) Attendance: 20,000	Wales 1, Luxembourg 0	**Wales:** Southall, Phillips, Bowen (Bodin 72), Aizlewood, Young, Melville (Giggs 62), Horne, Nicholas, Rush, Hughes, Speed Scorer: Bodin 82 pen	**Luxembourg:** Van Rijswijck, Bossi, Birsens, Petry, Wolf, Girres (Jeitz 87), Hellers, Weis, Groff, Langers (Krings 69), Malget
20/11/91 Brussels Ref: Lanese (Italy) Attendance: 25,000	Belgium 0, Germany 1	**Belgium:** Preud'homme, Emmers, Grun, Demol (Medved 46), Albert, Borkelmans, Degryse, Scifo, Walem, Boffin, Wilmots (Nilis 67)	**Germany:** Illgner, Reuter, Buchwald, Binz, Kohler, Brehme, Doll, Matthaus, Moller (Effenberg 80), Voller, Riedle Scorer: Voller 15
17/12/91 Leverkusen Ref: Przemycki (Pol) Attendance: 23,000	Germany 4, Luxembourg 0	**Germany:** Illgner, Kohler, Binz, Buchwald, Reuter, Moller (Bein 70), Matthaus, Doll (Hassler 46), Brehme, Riedle, Voller Scorers: Matthaus 15 pen, Buchwald 44, Riedle 51, Hassler 62	**Luxembourg:** Van Rijswijck, Petry, Bossi, Birsens, Girres (Jeitz 83), Weis, Hellers, Groff (Holtz 78), Wolf, Malget, Langers

Marco Van Basten -
below par at Italia '90.

Group six comprised Finland, Greece, Malta, Portugal and reigning European Champions Holland. With their fine pedigree and their line-up of superstars, Holland were favourites to qualify - but the course of the group was not destined to be as clear-cut as that.

The action began in Helsinki on 9 September 1990 when Finland met Portugal. Against all expectations Finland were the dominant side and should have won easily, but Portugal - who were without star player Paulo Futre - clung on for a 0-0 draw.

However, the Portuguese side were to perform far better in their first home encounter, against Holland, in Lisbon on 17 October.

Since winning the 1988 European Championship under the management of Rinus Michels, the Dutch side had experienced a woefully inept attempt on the World Cup at Italia '90. With new team boss Leo Beenhakker at the helm, Holland only just squeezed into the Second Round where they were disposed of by their close rivals and eventual World Champions West Germany.

That match had seen the double sending off of West Germany's Rudi Voller and Holland's Frank Rijkaard. Somehow, the incident - sparked off by Rijkaard's dreadful foul on Voller and ending with the Dutchman spitting into the hair of the German - seemed to symbolise the malaise then raging within the Dutch camp.

In essence the internal wranglings had sprung from the players' general discontentment initially with Beenhakker's appointment over the more favoured Johan Cruyff and then with Beenhakker's tactical plans. The resulting atmosphere was having a devastating effect on the team's performances. The star players Ronald Koeman, Frank Rijkaard, Marco van Basten and Hans Van Breukelen all played below par, while Ruud Gullit was still suffering the effects of a knee injury sustained almost a year earlier. Three draws and a defeat were all they managed in Italy.

After Italia '90 Leo Beenhakker announced his resignation as national team boss. Michels, by then a director of the Koninklijke Nederlandsche Voetbalbond, offered the vacant position to Johan Cruyff. In turn, Cruyff demanded to know why he had not been given the job in the first

Qualifying Group 6

place. He then decided to stay with his club, Barcelona, but expressed a desire to manage Holland if they reached the final stages of the 1992 European Championship. Other candidates were then considered for the vacancy, but in the end the Voetbalbond decided to re-appoint Rinus Michels to the hot seat.

The news came as a great shock, especially to the star players in the Dutch squad, many of whom no longer saw eye-to-eye with their former boss. To make matters worse Frank Rijkaard, arguably the best of the bunch,

*The **Rijkaard/Voller** incident.*

decided that he'd had enough of the internal bickering and announced that he no longer wished to play for Holland.

It was in this grim atmosphere that the Dutch squad began its defence of the European Championship, in Oporto. Besides the absence of Rijkaard another stalwart of the side was also missing - central defender Ronald Koeman had been unceremoniously dropped by Rinus Michels for publicly criticising the defensive tactics advocated by the boss in a recent friendly against Italy.

The result was almost inevitable. An undisciplined Holland lost 1-0 to a lively Portuguese side. A moment's hesitancy by by new cap Frank De Boer was seized upon by Vitor Paniera who then crossed for Rui Aguas to score in the 54th minute. After the match Marco Van Basten had clashed with Veloso and found himself in grave danger of receiving a UEFA ban.

Greece and Malta entered the fray on 31 October, in Athens. As expected Greece won by a large margin - 4-0. The goals came from Tsiantakis and Karapialis in the first half; Saravakos and Borbokis in the second. Malta looked set to follow their usual 'also ran' route.

Meanwhile the problems were continuing for Rinus Michels. Prior to the home fixture with Greece, on 21 November in Rotterdam, Ruud Gullit withdrew from the squad - through injury and depression; Ronald Koeman and Berry Van Aerle were out through injury and Wim Kieft had walked out on the squad. In spite of all this the re-jigged Dutch side, with Marco Van Basten

wearing the skipper's armband, won the match 2-0 and looked a completely different proposition than they had against Portugal. The goals came from Dennis Bergkamp and Van Basten.

Malta enjoyed their one brief moment of glory in front of a 7,200 home crowd in the Ta'Qali National Stadium on 25 November. In the 73rd minute of the game against Finland Hubert Suda came on to replace Joe Zarb - and one minute later he scored the goal which put Malta 1-0 ahead. The game was heading for a famous Maltese victory when - with just three minutes left Erik Holmgren equalised for the visitors.

Frank Rijkaard retired from the international scene.

The rejuvenated Holland were the next visitors to Malta - on 19 December. This time the crowd swelled to 10,254, but they did not witness a single moment of Maltese glory. Holland's super-striker Marco Van Basten was back to his lethal best, scoring five goals (including a penalty) to complement those of his team-mates Dennis Bergkamp who scored twice, and Aron Winter. The 8-0 thrashing represented Malta's biggest ever home defeat and did Holland's goal difference a power of good. In fact, it was to be the biggest away win margin of the entire '90-92 qualifying competition.

The first Group Six game of 1991 took place in Athens. Portugal were the visitors: with an attack strengthened by the inclusion of Paulo Futre, making only his third international appearance since suffering a prolonged bout of muscle strain. He scored the second Portuguese goal, to give his side a 2-1 lead on 62 minutes.

But it wasn't enough. Greece pulled one back through Stelios Manolas six minutes later and Yotis Tsaluhidis headed Greece to victory with six minutes left.

Nevertheless, Portugal took over the leadership of the Group following their next match, a somewhat flattering 1-0 away win on 9 February over a Maltese side much changed since their heavy defeat by Holland. Futre was on target again, in the 26th minute, with a perfectly struck free-kick. But Portugal had to fight hard for their victory and had 'keeper Vitor Baia to thank for a number of excellent saves. Malta's Joe Galea was sent off in the 89th minute.

The return match took place eleven days later in Oporto and this time Portugal made no mistake. They won 5-0 to strenghten their lead. Once again Futre was the man-of-the-match and had a say in three of the goals.

Malta next visited Rotterdam, on 13 March, and gave a far better showing than they had done in the eight-goal drubbing three months earlier. Holland created many chances, but were able to manage just a single goal, from a Marco van Basten penalty in the 32nd minute.

Holland next chalked up a 2-0 home win over Finland on 17 April which took them to the top of the table. Marco van Basten and Ruud Gullit were the stars of the show. Gullit provided the cross from which van Basten scored the opening goal on 9 minutes. Then the dreadlocked superstar turned on his old magic for a solo strike in the 75th minute.

Finland entertained Malta in Helsinki on 16 May and duly recorded a 2-0 victory, with second half goals from Petri Jarvinen and Jari Litmainen.

Three weeks later the Finns were at home to a Dutch side which was depleted by injury - Van Breukelen, Gullit, Roy and Vanenburg were all absent. It was a hard game on a rough pitch and Holland did not break the deadlock until an hour had elapsed, when Frank De Boer scored his first international goal. But the Finns were far from finished and Erik Holmgren snatched the equaliser with 12 minutes left. Finland then threw everything into a last-ditch attempt at victory, but merely succeeded in bringing out the very best in 'keeper Joop Hiele (standing in for Van Breukelen). Wim Kieft, a late substitute for Pieter Huistra, unfortunately broke an arm.

Portugal, complete with new manager Carlos Queiroz, caught up with Holland at the top of the table after a 1-0 home victory over Finland on 11 September. Once again Paulo Futre proved Portugal's inspiration. The goal came on 22 minutes from Cesar Brito, and on the balance of play there should have been a lot more in Portugal's favour. Nevertheless, the points were in the bag; only Holland's superior goal difference separated the sides. The crunch match between the two countries was due to be played five weeks later.

Meanwhile, Finland and Greece played out a 1-1 draw in Helsinki on 9 October. Greece were the dominant side, but Finland unexpectedly took the lead through Kari Ukkonen in the 50th minute. Yotis Tsaluhudis saved the day for Greece with an equaliser after 73 minutes and he almost snatched victory with four minutes left, but his shot rebounded off the post.

Seven days later Portugal were in Rotterdam for the game against Holland. The Dutch side had been boosted by the return to the international scene of Frank Rijkaard. Indeed, he

Group 6 — **Leading Scorers**

8-**van Basten** *Holland*
4-**Bergkamp** *Holland*
3-**Borbokis** *Greece,* **Rui Aguas** *Portugal*

had already played in a friendly against Poland, some fifteen months after 'retiring' from the international scene. Since the disgraceful spitting episode in the 1990 World Cup, Rijkaard and Rudi Voller of Germany had shaken hands and put the incident behind them - and now it seemed that big Frank had also made his peace with Rinus Michels and the rest of the Dutch squad.

In the event, Holland won the match against Portugal by the only goal of the game - scored by Richard Witschge after 20 minutes. The result put the Dutch firmly in the driving seat although theoretically they could still slip up, to leave Portugal or Greece with the opportunity of a Swedish summer.

On 30 October Greece beat Finland 2-0 in Athens. Dimitri Saravakos opened the scoring with a brilliant solo strike on 50 minutes, and Stefanos Borbokis sealed the result with a headed goal two minutes later.

Greece next faced Portugal on 20 November at Benfica's magnificent Stadium of Light, in Lisbon. The only goal of the game was scored by Portugal's Joao Pinto. But the Greek hopes were still alive - if they could beat Holland and then Malta (by a wide margin) in their remaining matches,

Richard Witchge dashed Portugal's hopes.

they would leapfrog to the top of the table.

Portugal's fixture programme was now complete and their slim chances were reliant on Greece beating Holland by a (highly unlikely) 7 goal margin - and then dropping a point against Malta. Holland had only to draw against Greece to qualify. That match was played in Salonika on 4 December. Rinus Michels was again beset by a problem - this time at the last minute. Ruud Gullit was warming up for the match when he pulled a muscle and, much to Rinus' annoyance, was forced to withdraw from the encounter. Despite the hasty reshuffling and consequent unsettling of the Dutch line-up, the Greek side was unable to capitalise on the situation.

Holland's first goal came in the 38th minute when Jan Wouters put Dennis Bergkamp through to score. The result - and Holland's qualification for the finals - was sealed in the 87th minute when Danny Blind headed home from a Marco van Basten cross.

In the last match of the group Malta earned draw, at home to a somewhat experimental Greek side which had to fighthard for the equaliser.

Group 6 Final Table

	P	W	D	L	F	A	Pts
HOLLAND	8	6	1	1	17	2	13
Portugal	8	5	1	2	11	4	11
Greece	8	3	2	3	11	9	6
Finland	8	1	4	3	5	8	6
Malta	8	0	2	6	2	23	2

12/9/90 Helsinki
Ref: Marko (Cze)
Attendance: 10,242

Finland 0, Portugal 0

Finland: Huttunen, Europeus, Holmgrenn, Heikkinen, Petaja, Rinne, Hjelm, Litmanen, Paatelainen, Tarrikio (Paavola 67), Jervinen (Muuru 86)

Portugal: Silvino, Venancio, Veloso, Ferreira, Fonseca (Pacheco A 67), Andre, Pacheco J, Pinto, Rui Barros, Rui Aguas (Cadete 46), Paneira

---

17/10/90 Oporto
Ref: Kirschen (Ger)
Attendance: 17,198

Portugal 1, Holland 0

Portugal: Silvino, Joao Pinto, Oceano, Venancio, Veloso, Leal, Vitor Paneira, Semedo (Ferreira 89), Nelo (Costa Xavier 86), Rui Aguas, Cadete Scorer: Rui Aguas 54

Holland: Van Breukelen, Blind, Valckx, Van Tiggelen (Van't Schip 59), Rutjes, De Boer (Gillhaus 59), Vanenberg, Gullit, Witschge, Bergkamp, Van Basten

---

31/10/90 Athens
Ref: Gracunesciou (Rom)
Attendance: 7,768

Greece 4, Malta 0

Greece: Papadopulos T, Papadopulos G, Apostolakis, Manolas, Kalizakis, Tsaluhidis, Saravakos, Kofidis, Dimitriadis (Borbokis 35), Karapialis, Tsiantakis Scorers: Tsiantakis 37, Karapialis 43, Saravakos 59, Borbokis 88

Malta: Cini, Vella S, Carabott, Galea, Buttigieg, Laferla, Busuttil, Scerri, Suda (De Giorgio 41), Vella R, Zerafa

---

21/11/90 Rotterdam
Ref: Nemeth (Hun)
Attendance: 25,430

Holland 2, Greece 0

Holland: Van Breukelen, Blind, Rutjes, De Jong, Wouters, Vanenburg, Witschge, Van't Schip, Roy, Bergkamp (Winter 85), Van Basten Scorers: Bergkamp 7, Van Basten 19

Greece: Papadopulos T, Apostolakis, Papadopulos G, Manolas, Kalitzakis, Kofidis (Karageorgiou 56), Tsaluhidis, Karapialis, Saravakos, Borbokis, Tsiantakis

---

25/11/90 Ta'Qali
Ref: Deda (Tur)
Attendance: 7,200

Malta 1, Finland 1

Malta: Cluett, Carabott, Vella S, Galea, Scerri, Buttigieg, Busuttil, Vella R, Laferla, De Giorgio, Zarb (Suda 73) Scorer: Suda 74

Finland: Huttunen, Rinne (Petaja 46), Heikkinen, Europaeus, Holmgren, Myyry, Litmanen, Hjelm, Tauriainen, Tarkkio (Tegelberg 75), Paatelainen Scorer: Holmgren 87

19/12/90 Ta'Qali
Ref: Blattman (Switz)
Attendance: 10,254

Malta 0, Holland 8

Malta: Cluett, Camilleri E (Suda 46), Camilleri J, Galea, Laferla, Vella S, Carabott, De Giorgio, Scerri (Zerafa 70), Busuttil, Vella R

Holland: Van Breukelen, Blind, De Jong, Koeman E (Winter 46), De Boer, Wouters, Van't Schip, Gullit (Van Der Brom 71), Van Basten, Roy, Bergkamp Scorers: Van Basten 10, 20, 25, 68, 80 pen, Winter 51, Bergkamp 58, 70

23/1/91 Athens
Ref: Longhi (Ita)
Attendance: 20,000

Greece 3, Portugal 2

Greece: Serganis, Apostolakis, Popadopulos G, Manolas, Kalintsakis, Tsaluhidis, Kofides (Athanasiadis 69), Tursinides, Tsiantakis, Borbokis (Dinitriades 65), Sarvakos Scorers: Borbokis 7, Manolas 68, Tsaluhidis 84

Portugal: Vitor Baia, Joao Pinto, Veloso, Leal, Venancio, Vitor Paneira, Oceano, Rui Barros (Cadete 71), Futre, Rui Aguas, Sousa Scorers: Rui Aguas 18, Futre 62

9/2/91 Ta'Qali
Ref: Neuner (Ger)
Attendance: 5,000

Malta 0, Portugal 1

Malta: Cluett, Vella S, Azzopardi, Galea (sent-off 89), Laferla, Buttigieg, Busuttil, Vella R, Suda, De Giorgio, Zerafa

Portugal: Vitor Baia, Joao Pinto, Leal, Venancio, Veloso, Oceano, Vitor Paneira, Rui Barros (Cadete 67), Rui Aguas, Futre (Sousa 63), Semedo Scorer: Futre 26

20/2/91 Oporto
Ref: Spillane (N. Ire)
Attendance: 5,303

Portugal 5, Malta 0

Portugal: Vitor Baia, Joao Pinto (Cadete 46), Leal, Venancio (Madeira 67), Veloso, Oceano, Vitor Paneira, Sousa, Rui Aguas, Futre, Semedo Scorers: Rui Aguas 5, Leal 33, Vitor Paneira 40 pen, Scerri 48 og, Cadete 81

Malta: Cluett, Vella S, Azzopardi, Camilleri J (Scerri 38), Laferla, Buttigeig, Busuttil, Vella R, Suda (Carabott 51), De Giorgio, Zerafa

---

13/3/91 Rotterdam
Ref: Krchnak (Cze)
Attendance: 36,388

Holland 1, Malta 0

Holland: Van Breukelen, Blind, Vink, De Boer (Kieft 46), Van't Schip, Wouters, Witschge, Gullit, Bergkamp, Van Basten, Roy (Vanenburg 69) Scorer: Van Basten 32 pen

Malta: Cini, Laferla, Camilleri E, Vella S, Brincat (Suda 85), Camilleri J, Azzopardi (Saliba 89), Scerri, Vella R, De Giorgio, Zerafa

---

17/4/91 Rotterdam
Ref: Damgaard (Den)
Attendance: 25,000

Holland 2, Finland 0

Holland: Van Breukelen, Blind, Vink, De Jong, Gullit, Wouters, Berkamp (Kieft 72), Witschge, Van't Schip, Van Basten (Rutjes 76), Huistra Scorers: Van Basten 9, Gullit 75

Finland: Huttunen, Kanerva, Heikkinen, Europaeus, Holmgren, Ukkonen, Petaja, Litmanen (Tegelberg 46), Myyry, Tauriainen (Nyyssonen 83), Paatelainen

---

16/5/91 Helsinki
Ref: Pedersen (Nor)
Attendance: 5,150

Finland 2, Malta 0

Finland: Huttunen, Petaja, Holmgren, Heikkinen, Kanerva, Myyry, Litmanen, Ukkonen, Tarkkio (Taurianen 87), Paatelainen (Paavola 63), Jarvinen Scorers: Jarvinen 51, Litmanen 88

Malta: Cini, Buttigieg, Brincat, Vella S, Camilleri E (Zerafa 70), Laferla, Busuttil, Vella R, De Giorgio, Scerri, Suda

---

5/6/91 Helsinki
Ref: McGinlay (Sco)
Attendance: 21,207

Finland 1, Holland 1

Finland: Huttunen, Petaja, Heikkinen, Ukkonen (Hjelm 81), Holmgren, Paavola, Myyry, Litmanen, Jaervinen, Tarkkio, Paatelainen (Tegelberg 66) Scorer: Holmgren 78

Holland: Hiele, Rutjes, Blind, Wouters, De Boer, Koeman R, Winter, Witschge, Van't Schip, Van Basten, Huistra (Kieft 75) Scorer: De Boer 60

11/9/91 Oporto
Ref: Martine (Switz)
Attendance: 30,000

Portugal 1, Finland 0

Portugal: Vitor Baia, Joao Pinto, Samuel, Couto, Leal, Veloso, Brito (Cadete 80), Rui Barros, Rui Aguas (Oceano 56), Futre, Guimaraes Scorer: Brito 22

Finland: Huttunen, Tauriainen (Vurela 59), Holmgren, Heikkinen, Petaja, Paavola, Myyry, Ukkonen (Litmanen 72), Jarvinen, Tarkkio, Paatelainen

---

9/10/91 Helsinki
Ref: Kusainov (USSR)
Attendance: 5,225

Finland 1, Greece 1

Finland: Huttunen, Heikkinen, Holmgren, Petaja, Myyry, Jarvinen (Paatalainen 63), Tarkkio (Tegelberg 82), Ukkonen, Hjelm, Litmanen, Vuorela Scorer: Ukkonen 50

Greece: Sarganis, Apostolakis (Athanasiadis 60), Karageorgiu, Mistsibonas, Kaliitzakis, Tsaluhidis, Saravakos, Papaioannu, Borbokis (Tursinidis 70), Karapialis, Tsiantakis Scorer: Tsaluhidis 73

16/10/91 Rotterdam
Ref: Courtney (Eng)
Attendance: 50,000

Holland 1, Portugal 0

Holland: Van Breukelen, Blind, Koeman R, Van Tiggelen, Koeman E, Wouters, Rijkaard (Winter 70), Witschge (Van't Schip 87), Gullit, Van Basten, Bergkamp Scorer: Witschge 20

Portugal: Vitor Baia, Joao Pinto, Samuel, Couto, Leal, Veloso, Brito (Cadete 80), Rui Barros, Rui Aguas (Oceano 56), Futre, Guimaraes

---

30/10/91 Athens
Ref: Kapl (Aust)
Attendance: 17,000

Greece 2, Finland 0

Greece: Sarganis, Apostolakis, Karageorgiou, Mitsibonas, Tsaluhidis, Kalitzakis, Saravakos, Papaioannu, Athanasiadis (Borbokis 46), Karapialis (Tursunides 73), Tsiantakis Scorers: Saravakos 50, Borbokis 52

Finland: Huttunen, Holmgren, Heikkinen, Petaja, Vuorela (Paatelainen 54), Huhtamaki (Tegelberg 83), Litmanen, Ukkonen, Jarvinen, Tarkkio, Hjelm

---

20/11/91 Lisbon
Ref: Constantin (Belg)
Attendance: 20,000

Portugal 1, Greece 0

Portugal: Vitor Baia, Pinto I, Bento, Couto, Leal, Peixe, Paneira (Oceano 46), Barros, Pinto II, Semedo (Figo 15), Aguas Scorer: Pinto II 17

Greece: Sarganis, Apostolakis, Karageorgiou, Mitsibonas, Tsaluhidis, Kalitzakis, Saravakos, Papaioannu (Athanasiadis 64), Borbokis (Dimitriadis 69), Karapiakis, Tsiantakis

---

4/12/91 Salonika
Ref: Karlsson (Swe)
Attendance: 30,000

Greece 0, Holland 2

Greece: Sarganis, Papaioannu (Karageorgiu 46), Lagondis, Kalintzakis, Mitsibonas, Tsaluhidis, Saravarkos, Papadopulos, Tsiantakis, Nioplias, Karapialis (Tursunidis 61)

Holland: Van Breukelen, Blind, Van Tiggelen, Koeman R, Koeman E, Wouters, Rijkaard (Winter 61), Witschge, Bergkamp, Van Basten, Kieft (Bosz 83) Scorers: Bergkamp 38, Blind 87

22/12/91 Ta'Qali
Ref: Girard (Fran)
Attendance: 8,000

Malta 1, Greece 1

Malta: Cluett, Brincat, Galea, Vella S, Saliba, Laferla, Busuttil, Vella R (Camilleri 68), Scerri (Sultana 33), Gregory, De Giorgio Scorer: Sultana 42

Greece: Plitsis, Papaioannu, Kapuranis, Mitsibonas, Kalitzakis, Tsaluhidis, Thonis (Giotsas 56), Marangos (Marinakis 44), Dimitriadis, Nobilias, Tsiantakis Scorer: Marinakis 67

John Aldridge, *Ireland's hat-trick hero against Turkey.*

According to most soccer pundits in England, Group Seven had an all too familiar ring about it. England were joined by perennial opponents Poland, the Republic of Ireland and Turkey.

Poland and England were footballing adversaries from way back. Indeed the deciding match of the 1974 World Cup Group Five qualifying tournament - played at Wembley on 17 October 1973 - marked one of the low points in English international history. England had to win in order to qualify for the following year's finals in West Germany. Sir Alf Ramsey's side dominated the game and went close to scoring on numerous occasions. Yet it was Poland who struck first when Norman Hunter lost the ball to winger Lato who, then raced down the left wing and crossed for Domarski to score. England fought back to equalise through an Allan Clarke penalty - and would surely have won the match but for the incredible, if eccentric, goalkeeping of Jan Tomaszewski. It was a display which effectively took Poland to West Germany where they eventually finished in third place.

The two sides met

Jan Tomaszewski eccentric goalkeeping in 1973.

again in Monterrey in the opening round of the 1986 World Cup. England won 3-0 with a Gary Lineker hat-trick. And in two Italia '90 World Cup qualifiers of 1989, England again came out on top after a 0-0 draw in Katowice and a 3-0 win at Wembley.

Qualifying Group 7

The Republic of Ireland had played ten matches against England since 1946; half had been friendly games, the remainder in the World Cup and the European Championships. The most recent of these encounters had been a 1-1 draw in Cagliari during the 1990 World Cup finals, a tournament which confirmed the Republic's emergence as a true international footballing force - thanks largely to the inspired leadership of Jack Charlton.

Turkey and England have only *ever* met in serious international competition: there have been no 'friendly' matches between the two sides. In two qualifying games for the 1986 World Cup Turkey had conceded no less than 13 goals to England. And in the qualifiers for the 1988 European Championship a 0-0 draw in Izmir was followed by England's 8-0 trouncing of the visitors, at Wembley.

And so, in a distinct atmosphere of deja vu, the 1990-92 European Championship Group Seven action began on 17 October 1990, when England played Poland at Wembley, and the Republic of Ireland entertained Turkey in Dublin.

The Polish squad arrived in London still reeling from a surprise 3-2 home defeat in a friendly against the USA. The American side - continually gaining international experience prior to staging the '94 World Cup - had led 3-0 at half time and it took a supreme Polish effort to

Gary Lineker recieves treatment for a head injury, later requiring eight stitches.

get back into the game. England team boss Graham Taylor had attended the game, witnessing the worst and the best of Polish football.

England had recently beaten Hungary 1-0 in a Wembley friendly, a match which marked Taylor's debut as manager, and saw Gary Lineker wearing the captain's armband for the first time and scoring the solitary goal.

The England v Poland encounter marked precisely the 17th anniversary of the game which had seen England booted out of the '74 World Cup. But this time the result went England's way. The first goal came after a Gary Lineker header was punched away by midfielder Nawrocki. Lineker scored from the consequent penalty.

Early in the second half captain Lineker sustained a gash on his head, which later

required no less than eight stitches. He was substituted by Chris Waddle on 56 minutes while Steve Bull was replaced by Peter Beardsley. Ultimately it was Beardsley who secured the match with a fine swerving drive which beat 'keeper Jozef Wandzik in the last minute.

John Aldridge was Ireland's hero, with a hat-trick in a 5-0 thrashing of Turkey at Dublin's Lansdowne Road stadium. The match also saw Kevin Moran come out of international 'retirement' to help out Jack Charlton's injury hit squad. Moran came on as a 75th minute substitute for Andy Townsend. The remaining goals were scored by Niall Quinn and David O'Leary.

England next met the Republic at Lansdowne Road, in decidedly windswept conditions on 14 November. The flamboyant talents of Paul Gascoigne were sidelined by Graham Taylor, to be replaced by the more down-to-earth style of Gordon Cowans. Also drafted into the team were Tony Adams and Steve McMahon. It was a line-up expected to "do a job", as Taylor explained.

The job they did was to produce a rather dour 1-1 draw. David Platt eventually opened the scoring in the 67th minute after meeting a low cross from Lee Dixon and slotting it home at the far post. Twelve minutes later Tony Cascarino equalised for the Republic, heading home a Steve Staunton cross after climbing above Adams and McMahon.

On the same day Turkey entertained Poland in Istanbul, only to lose 1-0. The goal which secured Poland's first victory came on 36 minutes from Celtic's Darius

Tony Cascarino *saved the day for Ireland at home to England.*

'Jacki' Dziekanowski who had followed up on a speculative shot by Roman Kosecki.

On 27 March 1991 England met the Republic of Ireland in the rematch at Wembley. Despite going ahead on 7 minutes through Lee Dixon - whose shot was deflected into the goal off Steve Staunton - England struggled throughout the match and had to resort to some desperate defending. The Irish side, most of them steeped in the traditions and tactics of the Football League, knew precisely how to frustrate and harass the English. The equaliser came in the 27th minute when Niall Quinn connected with a right-side cross from Paul McGrath. That feeling of deja vu persisted: this was the third successive 1-1 draw between the two sides.

Poland caught up with England and the Republic of Ireland thanks to a 3-0 victory over Turkey in Warsaw on 17 April. But the Poles left it very late and didn't open their account until the 75th minute when Ryszard Tarasiewicz struck

Roman Kosecki *snapped up a third goal for Poland against Turkey.*

with a brilliantly taken free-kick from 25 yards. The remaining goals came from a clever back-heel by Jan Urban on 82 minutes, and an opportunist strike by Roman Kosecki who

latched onto a disastrous back pass six minutes later. The result belied the skill of the Turkish side who until those last fifteen minutes had kept pace with Poland.

May Day at last saw a breaking of the deadlock. The Republic of Ireland and Poland played out a 0-0 draw in Dublin, which left both on five points. Meanwhile, England beat Turkey 1-0 in Izmir, to go ahead with six points.

The match in Dublin was a listless affair which the Irish should have won. They went close several times and John Aldridge had a goal disallowed and a penalty appeal turned down by the Dutch referee.

England carried memories of those huge recent victories over Turkey. But this time the Turkish side were no push-over. Although Dennis Wise slid home the only goal of the game on 32 minutes, Turkey defended well. And, inspired by Dilman Ridvan, they made many forays into attack and almost scored three times in the last minutes of the game. Afterwards Graham Taylor showed his relief and claimed: "This is a damned good result...we are in a hard group". His job now was to keep up the momentum in the run-in to qualification.

On 16 October, the Republic of Ireland let slip the chance to redress the balance in Poznan. Twice they led Poland, twice Poland staged a comeback to pull back the deficit. The game ended at 3-3.

On the same day, at Wembley, England once again struggled to beat Turkey. This time the line-up included the recalled Bryan Robson, as well as Chris Waddle, Gary Mabbutt and new

Tugay's shot zipped past the upright.

After the game the disenchanted English fans booed their team off the pitch. Manager Taylor was apologetic. "I can understand the crowd's reaction...people aren't fools. They don't like what they see." Nevertheless, the two points gained meant that England needed no more than a draw in their last game against Poland, to ensure qualification.

The match was played in Poznan on 13

Dennis Wise scored England's only goal against Turkey in Izmir.

cap David Batty. Arsenal's Alan Smith headed the only goal of the game in the 21st minute, following a Stuart Pearce cross. And it took a magnificent second half save by Chris Woods to prevent a Turkish equaliser from a Fayyaz header. A minute later a Turkish counter-attack almost resulted in a goal, but

November. Graham Taylor experimented yet again by throwing two new caps, Andy Gray and Andy Sinton, in at the deep end. Both were substituted in the course of the game and by the time Sinton left the field to be replaced by Tony Daley with twenty minutes left to play, the situation was

Group	7	Leading Scorers

3-Aldridge *Republic of Ireland,*
Cascarino *Republic of Ireland,*
2-Byrne *Republic of Ireland,*
Lineker *England,*
Quinn *Republic of Ireland,* **Urban** *Poland*

looking desperate for England.

Poland had taken the lead in the 32nd minute when a free-kick taken by Roman Szewczyk was deflected into the net by Gary Mabbutt. Since then each successive English attack had been thwarted either by the sturdy Polish defence or through missed opportunity.

left on the clock, bury it he did. David Rocastle took a corner-kick, Gary Mabbutt headed the ball towards the far post. Lineker saw it coming, "It was a bit high but I just smashed it," he said later while describing the

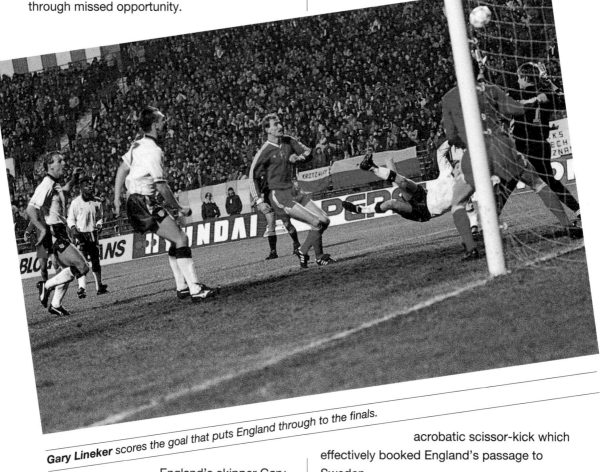

Gary Lineker scores the goal that puts England through to the finals.

England's skipper Gary Lineker had been virtually marked out of the game, he had hardly had a touch of the ball all night. He later explained: "As I saw the chances falling to the others, I prayed for one for myself. 'Give it to me,' I thought, 'I'll bury it'."

And when the chance came, with just thirteen minutes

acrobatic scissor-kick which effectively booked England's passage to Sweden.

Simultaneously, the Republic of Ireland were beating Turkey 3-1 in Istanbul, with two goals from Johnny Byrne and one from Tony Cascarino. But the Irish luck had run out, and Jack Charlton's side was left to rue the missed opportunities of earlier games.

Ireland were out. England were in.

Group 7 Final Table	P	W	D	L	F	A	Pts
ENGLAND	6	3	3	0	7	3	9
Republic of Ireland	6	2	4	0	13	6	8
Poland	6	2	3	1	8	6	7
Turkey	6	0	0	6	1	14	0

17/10/90 Wembley Ref: Lanese (Ita) Attendance: 77,040	England 2, Poland 0	**England:** Woods, Parker, Wright, Walker, Dixon, Platt, Gascoigne, Pearce, Bull (Beardsley 56), Lineker (Waddle 56), Barnes Scorers: Lineker 39 pen, Beardsley 89	**Poland:** Wandzik, Czachowski, Kaczmarek, Wdowczyk, Warzycha R, Tarasiewicz, Szewczyk, Furtok (Warzycha K 75), Nawrocki, Kosecki (Kubicki 85), Ziober
7/10/90 Dublin Ref: Fredriksson (Swe) Attendance: 46,000	Republic of Ireland 5, Turkey 0	**Republic of Ireland:** Bonner, Irwin, Staunton, McCarthy, O'Leary, Hughton, Townsend (Moran 75), Houghton, Quinn (Cascarino 69), Aldridge, Sheridan Scorers: Aldridge 15, 57, 72, O'Leary 41, Quinn 66	**Turkey:** Engin, Riza, Turgay, Kemal, Gokhan, Erkan (Metin 46), Bulent, Oguz, Mehmet, Hami, Sercan (Tanju 46)
14/11/90 Dublin Ref: D'Elia (Italy) Attendance: 45,000	Republic of Ireland 1, England 1	**Republic of Ireland:** Bonner, Morris, McCarthy, O'Leary, Staunton, Whelan (McLoughlin 72), McGrath, Houghton, Townsend, Quinn (Cascarino 60), Aldridge Scorer: Cascarino 79	**England:** Woods, Dixon, Adams, Walker, Wright, Pearce, Platt, Cowans, McMahon, Beardsley, Lineker Scorer: Platt 67
14/11/90 Istanbul Ref: Spirin (USSR) Attendance: 4,868	Turkey 0, Poland 1	**Turkey:** Engin, Riza, Ulgen (Sercan 67), Bulent, Gokhan, Yusuf, Muhammet (Mehmet 67), Unal, Oguz, Tanju, Hami	**Poland:** Wandzik, Kubicki, Warzycha R, Wdowczyk, Kaczmerek, Nawrocki, Tarasiewicz, Prusik, Warzycha K, Dziekanowski (Ziober 73), Kosecki Scorer: Dziekanowski 36
27/3/91 Wembley Ref: Rothlisberger (Swz) Attendance: 77,753	England 1, Republic of Ireland 1	**England:** Seaman, Dixon, Adams (Sharpe 46),Walker, Wright M, Pearce, Barnes, Robson, Platt, Beardsley, Lineker (Wright I 75) Scorer: Dixon 7	**Republic of Ireland:** Bonner, Irwin, O'Leary, Moran, Staunton, Townsend, McGrath, Houghton, Sheedy, Quinn, Aldridge (Cascarino 70) Scorer: Quinn 27
17/4/91 Warsaw Ref: Salomir (Rom) Attendance: 1,000	Poland 3, Turkey 0	**Poland:** Wandzik, Kubicki, Kaczmarek (Czachowski 62), Wdowczyk, Jakolcewicz, Warzycha K, Warzycha R, Tarasiewicz, Urban, Kosecki, Ziober (Soczynski 70) Scorers: Tarasiewicz 75, Urban 82, Kosecki 88	**Turkey:** Engin, Riza, Tayfun, Gokhan, Kemal, Bulent, Feyyaz, (Faruk 80), Muhammet, Mehmet, Tanju, Abdullah (Osman 70)
1/5/91 Izmir Ref: Wiesel (Ger) Attendance: 20,000	Turkey 0, England 1	**Turkey:** Hayrettin, Riza, Ogun, Gokhan, Recep, Muhammet, Unal, Ridvan, Mehmet, Tanju, Ali (Feyyaz 72)	**England:** Seaman, Dixon, Pearce, Wise, Walker, Pallister, Platt, Thomas G (Hodge 46), Smith A, Lineker, Barnes Scorer: Wise 32
1/5/91 Dublin Ref: Blankenstein (Hol) Attendance: 48,000	Republic of Ireland 0, Poland 0	**Republic of Ireland:** Bonner, Irwin, Staunton, O'Leary, Moran, Townsend, McGrath, Houghton, Quinn (Slaven 70), Aldridge (Cascarino 70), Sheedy	**Poland:** Wandzik, Kubnicki, Jakolcewicz, Wdowczyk, Soczynski, Warzycha R, Tarasiewicz, Czachowski, Furtok (Kosecki 89), Urban (Warzycha K 88), Szewczyk
16/10/91 Poznan Ref: Goethals (Bel) Attendance: 17,000	Poland 3, Republic of Ireland 3	**Poland:** Wandzik, Kubicki (Lesiak 32), Czachowski, Soczynski, Wdowczyk, Nawrocki (Skrzypczak 81), Tarasiewicz, Ziober, Urban, Kosecki, Furtok Scorers: Czachowski 54, Furtok 76, Urban 87	**Republic of Ireland:** Bonner, Morris, Staunton (Phelan 56), Irwin, McGrath, Moran, O'Leary, Sheedy, Keane, Townsend, Cascarino Scorers: McGrath 10, Townsend 62, Cascarino 68
16/10/91 Wembley Ref: Navarette (Sp) Attendance: 50,896	England 1, Turkey 0	**England:** Woods, Dixon, Pearce, Batty, Walker, Mabbutt, Robson, Platt, Smith A, Lineker, Waddle Scorer: Smith A 21	**Turkey:** Hayrettin, Recep, Ogun, Gokhan, Tugay, Turhan, Feyyaz (Hami 76), Riza, Unal, Oguz, Orhan
13/11/91 Istanbul Ref: Petrovic (Yug) Attendance: 42,000	Turkey 1, Republic of Ireland 3	**Turkey:** Hayrettin, Recep (Bulent 69), Turhan, Gokhan, Tugay, Ogun, Feyyaz (Ridvan 46), Riza, Hami, Oguz, Orhan Scorer: Riza 12 pen	**Republic of Ireland:** Bonner, Hughton, O'Leary, McCarthy, Phelan, Byrne, McGrath, Staunton, Sheedy, Cascarino, Aldridge Scorers: Byrne 7, 88 Cascarino 55
13/11/91 Poznan Ref: Forstinger (Aus) Attendance: 15,000	Poland 1, England 1	**Poland:** Bako, Warzycha R, Szewczyk (Fedoruk 77) Waldoch, Soczynski, Czachowski, Kosecki, Skrzypczak (Kowalczyk 79), Ziober, Furtok, Urban Scorer: Szewczyk 32	**England:** Woods, Dixon, Pearce, Gray (Smith 46), Walker, Mabbutt, Platt, Thomas, Rocaslte, Lineker, Sinton (Daley 70) Scorer: Lineker 77

The draw for the final stages of the ninth European Championship took place on Friday 17 January 1992, in Gothenburg's new Conference Centre. As host nation, Sweden was automatically placed in Group One, to ensure that each of their opening round matches would

The Draw for the Finals

be played at the Rasunda Stadium in Solna. Holland, as current European Champions, were installed at the head of the Group Two list. The six remaining places in the schedule were drawn by Nils Liedholm, a Swedish soccer legend and captain of the 1958 World Cup final team. Eventually the tournament schedule was completed as follows:

Group 1 Teams

Team 1: SWEDEN
Team 2: FRANCE
Team 3: YUGOSLAVIA
Team 4: ENGLAND

Group 2 Teams

Team 5: HOLLAND
Team 6: SCOTLAND
Team 7: COMMONWEALTH
OF INDEPENDENT STATES
Team 8: GERMANY

Above: Tommy Svensson meets Michel Platini at the draw ceremony.

The draw ceremony was a rather elaborate affair conducted in a kind of low key razzmatazz, with Swedish schoolgirls placing the team names in the appropriate slots on the giant fixtures board as they were drawn. The proceedings were conducted by Gerhard Aigner general secretary of UEFA - and the draw itself was made by Swedish soccer legend Nils Liedholm.

Group 1 — Score Chart

10 June - Stockholm
SWEDEN ☐ v ☐ **FRANCE**

11 June - Malmo
YUGOSLAVIA ☐ v ☐ **ENGLAND**

14 June - Stockholm
SWEDEN ☐ v ☐ **YUGOSLAVIA**

14 June - Malmo
FRANCE ☐ v ☐ **ENGLAND**

17 June - Stockholm
SWEDEN ☐ v ☐ **ENGLAND**

17 June - Malmo
FRANCE ☐ v ☐ **YUGOSLAVIA**

Group Winner: _____

Runner-up: _____

Group 2 — Score Chart

12 June - Gothenburg
HOLLAND ☐ v ☐ **SCOTLAND**

12 June - Norrkoping
CIS ☐ v ☐ **GERMANY**

15 June - Gothenburg
HOLLAND ☐ v ☐ **CIS**

15 June - Norrkoping
SCOTLAND ☐ v ☐ **GERMANY**

18 June - Gothenburg
HOLLAND ☐ v ☐ **GERMANY**

18 June - Norrkoping
SCOTLAND ☐ v ☐ **CIS**

Group Winner: _____

Runner-up: _____

SEMI FINALS

21 June - Stockholm
Group 1 Winner _____ ☐ v ☐ _____ Group 2 Runner-up

22 June - Gothenburg
Group 2 Winner _____ ☐ v ☐ _____ Group 1 Runner-up

THE FINAL *26 June - Gothenburg*

_____ ☐ v ☐ _____

THE CHAMPIONS

_____

If two or more teams have equal points after the group programme is completed, then the team with the greatest goal difference will qualify for the semi-final. If the goal difference is equal, the team having scored most goals will qualify. If this is not conclusive, the qualified team will be determined by the result of the match previously played between the teams concerned. Failing this, the qualified team shall be determined by a drawing of lots.

If a semi-final match or the final ends in a draw after ninety minutes, extra-time will be played. If the scoreline remains level after extra time, the winners will be decided via a penalty shoot-out.

Above: *The Rasunda Stadium, Solna, is the northernmost venue in the 1992 European Championship finals. Sweden will play all their Group One games here. Workers in the 'Dallas-like' office block which overlooks the staduim, must enjoy one of the best free views in Europe.*

Left: *The Malmo Stadium complex also incorporates an ice rink, a bowling alley, several training pitches and Sweden's only sporting museum.*

Sweden does not boast a single stadium the size of a San Siro, a Wembley, or a Nou Camp. As far as the Swedish FA is concerned, it's more a case of 'small is beautiful'. The Ullevi Stadium in Gothenburg, where three Group Two matches, the second semi-final and the Final of the 1992 Championship will be played, is Sweden's largest sporting venue, with a current capacity of 35,000. Construction of The Nya (New) Ullevi Stadium commenced in May 1957 and was completed twelve months later, over budget but on schedule, and in time for the 1958 World Cup finals. The first football match played at the stadium saw a Gothenburg XI take on Sweden's national team, on 29 May 1958.

In the '58 World Cup the Ullevi staged six matches, and is notable as the venue for the World Cup debut of a certain Pele who took to the field for Brazil against the USSR in a Group Four match.

The ground's record attendance for a soccer match, set in pre-safety restriction times, is 52,914 for a league game between IFK Gothenburg and Orgryte IS in June 1959. The Ullevi is home to both these clubs as well as GAIS - all three are currently in the Swedish Premier Division and the stadium therefore enjoys no less than twelve local derbies per season. In its time the Ullevi has also staged the 1983 and 1990 European Cup-Winners' Cup Finals (won by Aberdeen and Sampdoria, respectively), and the home legs of the 1982 and 1987 UEFA Cup Finals (both won by IFK Gothenburg), championship boxing, ice hockey, rock concerts and athletics; and its cinder track is home to the Karparna speedway team.

The Nya Ullevi,

with its architecturally pleasing 'shell-like' roof, is sister to the Malmo Stadium in the south of the country. Both were built at the same time and are of similar design. Malmo, the home ground of Malmo FF, was also used for the '58 World Cup; its first match of that competition, between Argentina and West Germany on 8 June 1958,

Championship Venues

set the stadium's attendance record at 31,156. The current capacity is restricted to 26,000.

The Malmo Stadium will host three Group One matches in the 1992 tournament, including England's encounters with Yugoslavia and France.

UEFA have decreed that, for the first time in a major international tournament, 'player recognition' is to be improved. Each squad member's designated 1-20 number will not only appear on the back of his shirt as per current regulations, but also in the middle of the shirt-front. In addition, his surname will be emblazoned across his shoulders. This greater clarification will aid commentators, reporters and fans alike - and brings UEFA's specifications into line with FIFA's plans for the 1994 World Cup finals in the United States.

The Rasunda Stadium stands in Stockholm's northern suburb of Solna, and occupies the site of a former lake bed. The present structure is the home ground of the AIK and Djurgardens IF Premier Division clubs. It also houses the headquarters of the Svenska Fotbollforbundet, is the venue for the annual Swedish Cup Final, and was the setting for the 1958 World Cup Fnal between Sweden

Above: *The tiny Idrottspark in Norrkoping will stage two of Scotland's Group Two matches, plus the CIS v Germany clash*

and Brazil.

The Rasunda's record attendance is 52,943, for the Sweden v West Germany World Cup qualifier of September 1965 (Sweden lost). The stadium's present all-seater capacity is 27,000. Each of Sweden's Group One games will be played here, as well as the first semi-final.

The smallest of the Championship venues is the Idrottspark in the delightful town of Norrkoping, often called 'the Paris of the North'. With a woefully small capacity of 17,000 the stadium hardly seems an adequate stage for the CIS v Germany clash on June 12, nor indeed the Scotland v Germany and Scotland v CIS fixtures which follow.

The Idrottspark was completed in 1903, and is home to Premier Division club IFK Norrkoping. The ground's record attendance was set at 32,234 in June 1956 for a League Championship decider between IFK Norrkoping and Malmo FF (IFK won and collected their sixth title). The stadium was also used in the 1958 World Cup finals.

A great deal of reconstruction work was necessary to bring The Idrottspark up to UEFA's specifications for the 1992 tournament. This included the construction of new terracing on 'the mountain', formerly little more than a grass slope with barriers, behind the northern goal. The main stand was also completely refurbished, with its ageing wooden benches being replaced by more comfortable seating.

The Ullevi Stadium in Gothenburg, venue for the Final.

Tomas Brolin was arguably the only outstanding Swedish player during the 1990 World Cup finals, in which he scored a memorable goal against Brazil. And, despite Sweden's early return home, the blond-haired striker became the target for a number of clubs. For a while speculation was rife that he was about to come to England, but eventually he settled for Parma of Italy where he's been dubbed 'The Little Viking'.

Jonas Thern, another of Sweden's top-class exports, plays his club football for Benfica with whom he reached the 1990 European Cup Final. Was a star turn in Benfica's disposal of Arsenal in this season's European Cup. Thern is Sweden's captain.

THE SQUADS

When the draw for the finals was made in Gothenburg, Swedish manager Tommy Svensson seemed absolutely delighted, especially with the opening fixture of his campaign: "What a dream match on the first day - against France," he said. "The French play wonderful football and for us it will be very stimulating to meet perhaps the best team in Europe right at the start."

Despite his show of enthusiastic optimism, Tommy Svensson is beset with problems. While things have gone reasonably smoothly for Sweden in the administrative build-up to the Championship, it has been an entirely different matter on the field.

As host nation with automatic entry into the final stages, the national side has obviously been denied the competitive edge that comes with the rigours of qualification. Instead they have played a number of build-up matches, against teams of varying quality. Unfortunately for Svensson, none of the recent results have shown the Swedish squad as potential European Champions.

An early blow came before Svensson assumed control, when Sweden were over-run 3-1 by world champions West Germany at the Rasunda Stadium in October 1990. The defence was in some disarray, and after the match captain Glenn Hysen announced his retirement from the international scene.

In Svensson's first match in charge, against Greece in Athens on 17th April 1991, the side recovered from an early own goal to take a 2-1 lead through Magnus Erlingmark and Hakan Mild. It looked for all the world like being a good

Sweden

The Manager

Born 4.3.45, **Tommy Svensson** took charge of the Swedish national team in July 1990, after the disastrous World Cup finals campaign in Italy. Between 1967-73 Svensson was a winger, who played for Osters IF and Standard Liege, and was capped on 40 occasions. He appeared in the 1970 World Cup in Mexico. Before taking over from Olle Nording as Sweden's coach, Svensson had been coaching the Norweigan club Tromso. His father was the former Chairman of Osters IF

debut for the new boss, but then Stefanos Borbokis spoilt the party with an 83rd minute equaliser. The result stood at 2-2.

On May Day 1991 a hat-trick against Austria by Kennet Andersson was supplemented by two goals from Martin Dahlin and another by Stefan Rehn. Austria had no reply and the display underlined Svensson's commitment to attacking football.

Unfortunately, the defence proved a little suspect in the next friendly encounter, against visitors Colombia on 5 June. Tomas Brolin opened the scoring for Sweden on 32 minutes, but then Colombia clawed their way to a 2-1 lead with less than 20 minutes left to play. Kennet Andersson saved the day with a 73rd minute equaliser.

Tommy Svensson experienced his first defeat in the Scania 100 tournament, a four-nation competition played in the four European Championship venues. Sweden began well in their opening match against the USSR, going ahead after just four minutes when the ever-sharp Brolin hit home a Jonas Thern cross. The Soviets eventually replied through Sergei Yuran on 69 minutes. The match went into extra time, during which Oleg Kusnetsov put the USSR ahead, Brolin equalised - then Igor Kornyev snatched the winner for the Soviets with just three minutes left. Sweden had performed well, particularly in the first half, and could be forgiven for thinking themselves unlucky.

Two days later, in Norrkoping, they played an understrength Denmark in the third-place play-off and won by a convincing 4-0 scoreline. (Scania 100 was won by Italy, who beat the USSR after a penalty shoot-out in the final.)

An encouraging 2-1 win against neighbouring Norway on 8 August, this despite the sending off of Peter Larsson, was followed by a devastating 2-1 defeat by Poland in Gdansk, two weeks later. The Swedish defence once again showed its vulnerability, while the attack created few chances at the other end. Afterwards Svensson declared it Sweden's worst performance so far.

Yugoslavia, under-strength because of the repercussions of the civil unrest at home, provided Sweden's next friendly opposition on 4 September in Solna. And, although Sweden won 4-3 in a hugely entertaining match, Yugoslavia were the dominant side throughout and might have scored six goals against that suspect defence.

Squad Contenders

	Club	Date of Birth	Caps	Goals
Goalkeepers				
Thomas Ravelli	IFK Goteburg	13.8.59	85	0
Lars Eriksson	Norrkoping	21.9.65	8	0
Defenders				
Peter Larsson	AIK Stockholm	8.3.61	47	4
Jan Eriksson	Norrkoping	24.8.67	15	1
Magnus Erlingmark	Orebro	8.7.68	16	1
Mats Gren	Grasshoppers Zurich	20.12.63	21	0
Stefan Schwarz	Benfica	18.4.69	11	2
Roger Llung	UNFC Zurich	8.1.66	28	2
Roland Nilsson	Sheffield Wednesday	27.11.63	43	1
Mikael Nilsson	IFK Goteburg	28.9.68	7	0
Midfielders				
Stefan Rehn	IFK Goteburg	22.9.66	21	5
Jonas Thern	Benfica	20.3.67	30	5
Joakim Nilsson	Sporting Gijon	31.3.66	25	1
Klas Ingesson	Mechelen	20.8.68	19	6
Hakan Mild	IFK Goteburg	14.6.71	8	1
Forwards				
Anders Limpar	Arsenal	24.9.65	29	4
Thomas Brolin	Parma	29.11.69	14	9
Martin Dahlin	Borussia Monchengladbach	16.4.68	7	6
Kennet Andersson	Mechelen	6.10.67	12	6
Mats Magnusson	Benfica	10.7.63	30	9
Stefan Pettersson	Ajax	22.3.63	24	1

Record against European Championship Finalists up until April 1992

SWEDEN	P	W	L	D	F	A
v. England	13	3	6	4	14	23
v. France	10	4	5	1	10	16
v. Germany	30	13	11	6	51	53
v. Holland	18	7	8	3	40	33
v. Yugoslavia	11	4	5	2	21	19
v. Scotland	7	2	4	1	8	11
v. Soviet Union (CIS)	20	6	7	7	27	41

A visit to Switzerland on 10 October did nothing to lift Swedish morale. They lost 3-1 and Svensson complained that lack of concentration throughout his team was largely to blame.

Sweden's 1992 preparations for the summer continued with a tour of Australia - albeit without the squad's foreign based players. Nevertheless, what should have been little more than a polishing up operation, became an absolute nightmare for Tommy Svensson.

In Sydney on 25 January, the Australians held the Swedes to a 0-0 draw and Svensson conceded that his side had been fortunate not to lose. Four days later they did lose, 1-0 in Adelaide. And on 2 February, in Melbourne, Sweden concluded a miserable tour with another 1-0 defeat.

In the remaining build up period to the Championship Svensson's squad will have had further try-outs against Tunisia, Poland and Hungary. But on the evidence so far, it seems highly unlikely that Sweden's name will be engraved on the Henri Delaunay Cup - not, at least, in 1992.

Thomas Ravelli is Sweden's longest-serving goalkeeper and is noted for his aggressive style. His outstanding form was a decisive factor in IFK Gothenburg's title win of 1990.

Stefan Rehn had a brief, unsuccessful, spell in English football with Everton before returning to Sweden to join IFK Gothenburg. He became the prime mover in IFK's 1990 Championship-winning season and the Allvenskan's Player of the Year.

Fact File

Governing Body:
Svenska Fotbollforbundet (SFF)

Year of Formation: **1904**

National Stadium:
Rasunda, Solna

National team colours:
Yellow shirts, blue shorts, yellow stockings with blue trim

Change colours:
Blue shirts, white shorts, yellow stockings

International Record

World Cup, final stages
1930 - did not enter
1934 - 2nd Round
1938 - 4th place
1950 - 3rd place
1954 - did not qualify
1958 - hosts & runners-up
1962 - dnq
1966 - dnq
1970 - 1st round
1974 - 2nd round
1978 - 1st round
1982 - dnq
1986 - dnq
1990 - 1st round

European Championship
1960 - did not enter
1964 - quarter-finalists
1968 - 1st round
1972 - 1st round
1976 - 1st round
1980 - 1st round
1984 - 1st round
1988 - 1st round

European Championship record 1962-1991
Played 46; won 19, drawn 11, lost 16; Goals 63 for - 56 against.

*Defender/sweeper **Vasily Kulkov** was drafted into the USSR squad after their poor showing at Italia '90. He led Spartak Moscow to the European Cup semi-finals in 1991 and was very impressive against England in the Challenge Cup match at Wembley. Made a big money move to Benfica of Portugal last summer.*

As with most other aspects of life in the former Soviet Union, football has been overshadowed by the momentous political changes that have taken place there during the past two years. As the former states of the USSR regained their independent status, under the umbrella of the newly created Commonwealth of Independent States, it appeared that the 'national' team which had won through to the European Championship finals was also likely to fragment.

The situation left FIFA and UEFA with a diplomatic dilemma which simply had to be resolved. Joao Havelange and Lennart Johansson, the respective Presidents of the two bodies, trod cautiously through the political maze before decreeing, on 13 January 1992, that: 'The Association of Football Federations of the Commonwealth of Independent States, formed in Moscow on the territory of the former USSR will be considered as a successor to the USSR Football Federation until further notice. The newly formed Association will take part [in the European Championship finals] under this name.'

Ever mindful of the spirit of fair play, they also declared that 'Every player in the area of the former USSR Football Federation will be entitled to play for this selection.' All of which means that CIS team manager Anatoli Bishovets, has at least the prospect of fielding his strongest possible squad in Sweden.

At the draw in Gothenburg, the Commonwealth was represented by assistant manager Vladimir Salkov who was philosophical about his side's chances of success in Sweden. "We have problems in our country, everyone knows that. However, I still believe that we will come to the finals with the same strong team

Commonwealth of Independent States

The Manager

Appointed in August 1990 to replace Valeri Lobanovsky, **Anatoli Bishovets** was a former player under Lobanovsky for both Dinamo Kiev and the Soviet Union. Born 23.4.46, Bishovets was an oustanding winger in the fine Dinamo Kiev side of the 1960s and 1970s winning 66 caps betwen 1966-72. Injury brought about his early retirement from the playing side and he went onto the Kiev coaching staff. He moved to the national role after taking the Olympic team to the 1988 gold medal at Seoul, and had between 1988-90 been coaching Dinamo Moscow.

that carried us to victory in our qualifying group. All of those who have been called up have agreed to play. So, despite the somewhat chaotic situation, I'm an optimist."

It is to be hoped that Salkov is right. His players certainly deserve the opportunity to see the job through to its end. It is virtually certain that this will be the last time the squad will play together, with Estonia, Latvia, Lithuania and possibly the Ukraine and Georgia playing independently in the future.

Alexei Mikhailichenko, arrived at Ibrox Park in July 1991 for a Rangers' club record of £2 million.

Squad Contenders

The following statistics combine appearances and goals for the old Soviet Union and the new CIS.

	Club	Date of Birth	Caps	Goals
Goalkeepers				
Stanislav Cherchasov	Spartak Moscow	2.9.63	10	0
Alexsandr Uvarov	Maccabi Tel Aviv	13.1.60	11	0
Dimitri Kharin	CSKA Moscow	16.8.68	10	0
Defenders				
Vasili Kulkov	Benfica	11.2.66	21	0
Andreij Cherniskov	Dinamo Moscow	7.1.68	21	0
Dimitri Geliamin	Espanol	8.11.63	13 (1)	0
Ahrik Tsveiba	Dynamo Kiev	10.9.66	21	2
Oleg Kuznetsov	Glasgow Rangers	22.3.63	59	1
Sergey Gorlukovich	Borussia Dortmund	19.11.61	21	1
Sergey Aleinikov	Lecce	7.11.61	74	6
Kkhaber Tskahadadze	Sundsvall	7.9.68	4	0
Midfielders				
Igor Schalimov	Foggia	2.2.69	21	1
Alexey Mikhailitchenko	Glasgow Rangers	30.3.63	36	9
Andreij Kanchelskis	Manchester Utd	23.1.69	18	3
Dimitri Kuznetsov	Espanol	28.8.65	15	2
Alexandr Mostovoi	Benfica	22.8.68	14	2
Andreij Mokh	Espanol	20.10.65	2	0
Forwards				
Oleg Protassov	Olympiakos Pireus	4.11.64	68	29
Igor Dobrovolsky	Servette Geneva	27.8.67	25	7
Igor Kolivanov	Foggia	6.3.68	20	2
Sergey Yuran	Benfica	11.6.69	12	4
Igor Kornijev	Espanol	4.9.67	5	3
Sergey Kiriakov	Dynamo Moscow	1.1.70	6	3

Andrei Kanchelskis has proved one of Alex Ferguson's shrewdest buys for Manchester United. His sudden bursts of speed have been a feature of the Old Trafford title challenge in 1991-92.

Record against European Championship Finalists up until April 1992

CIS (SovietUnion)	P	W	L	D	F	A
v. England	11	3	5	3	13	19
v. France	12	4	2	6	17	12
v. Germany	13	0	10	3	11	38
v. Holland	6	2	3	1	4	8
v. Yugoslavia	17	11	2	4	33	17
v. Scotland	4	3	0	1	6	2
v. Sweden	20	7	6	7	41	27

Fact File

Governing Body:
Association of Footbal Federations of The Commonwealth of Independent States

Year of formation: **1992**

National Stadium
(as Soviet Union): Lenin, Moscow

National Colours:
Red shirts, white shorts, red stockings

Change Colours: **All white**

International record
(as Soviet Union):
World Cup, final stages
1930 not eligible
1934 ne **1938** ne
1950 did not enter
1954 dne
1958 quarter-finalists
1962 quarter-finalists
1966 4th place
1970 quarter-finalists
1974 did not qualify
1978 dnq
1982 2nd round
1986 2nd round
1990 1st round

European Championships
1960 Champions
1964 runners-up
1968 4th place
1972 runners-up
1976 quarter-finalists
1980 1st round
1984 1st round
1988 runners-up.
European Championship record (1958-1991):
Played 71; won 41, drawn 18, lost 12; Goals 120 for - 53 against

Among the quickest defenders on the international scene, **Des Walker** is virtually irreplaceable either for England or Nottingham Forest. Immaculate timing is a Walker speciality.

Stuart Pearce is one of the hardest defenders in world football and the most probable successor to Gary Lineker in the captain's armband for England. A free-kick specialist with a penchant for attack.

At the draw for the final stages of the 1992 European Championship, both England's Graham Taylor and Scotland's Andy Roxburgh had hoped that their sides would avoid one another in the first round. Their wishes were granted, with England having arguably the easier draw of the two.

This point was immediately taken up by the press, but Graham Taylor was under no such illusions. "We're playing the host country - and that in itself could produce problems which might not arise elsewhere," he said. "Yugoslavia have arguably the most technically gifted individual players. If they can get their act together they will prove worthwhile and strong opponents for anyone.

"France are undefeated in nineteen games - they've won sixteen and drawn three. If anyone wants to describe this as an easy group, they don't know what football is about - certainly not at this level."

A month later Taylor's England brought France's unbeaten run to an abrupt end with a fine, morale-boosting, 2-0 victory at Wembley. England's preparations then continued with an experimental side drawing 2-2 with Czechoslovakia in Prague, followed by further rehearsals

against the Commonwealth of Independent States, Hungary, Brazil and Finland.

Since taking over as England's manager, Graham Taylor has not been afraid to try many combinations, by now though, he *must* know his best team...

The Manager

Born 14.9.44 in Worksop, Nottinghamshire.
Graham Taylor joined Grimsby as a junior and played 189 league games at full back between 1963 and 1967. He then moved on to Lincoln City, making 152 league appearances between 1967-72.
He entered management with Lincoln City, and took the club to the Fourth Division Championship in 1976, before leaving to join Elton John at Watford in 1977. Watford were promoted to Division 2 in 1978, and to Division 1 in 1979. The club finished runners-up in the first Division in 1982, and reached the 1984 FA Cup Final,where they lost 2-0 to Everton. Taylor moved on to Aston Villa in May 1985, and took the club to the runners-up spot in Division 1 in 1990. He was appointed England manager to succeed Bobby Robson after the 1990 World Cup.

Squad Contenders

	Club	Date of Birth	Caps	Goals
Goalkeepers				
Chris Woods	Sheffield Wed	14.11.59	28	0
David Seaman	Arsenal	19.9.63	8	0
Stephen Pears	Middlesbrough	22.1.62	0	0
Nigel Martin	Crystal Palace	11.8.66	0	0
Defenders				
Rob Jones	Liverpool	5.11.71	1	0
Stuart Pearce	Nott'm Forest	24.4.62	45	2
Mark Wright	Liverpool	1.8.63	41	1
Martin Keown	Everton	24.7.66	2	1
Gary Pallister	Man United	30.6.65	5	0
Des Walker	Nott'm Forest	26.11.65	39	0
Lee Dixon	Arsenal	17.3.64	12	1
Tony Dorigo	Leeds Utd	31.12.65	8	0
Paul Parker	ManUtd	4.4.64	17	0
Midfielders				
David Platt	Bari	10.6.66	26	7
Paul Gascoigne	Tottenham	25.7.67	20	2
Geoff Thomas	Crystal Palace	5.8.64	9	0
Paul Stewart	Tottenham	7.10.64	2	0
Carlton Palmer	Sheffield Wed	5.12.65	0	0
David Rocastle	Arsenal	3.5.67	13	0
David Batty	Leeds Utd	2.12.68	7	0
Neil Webb	Man United	30.7.63	17	0
Forwards				
Gary Lineker	Tottenham	30.11.60	73	47
John Barnes	Liverpool	7.11.63	66	10
Alan Shearer	Southampton	13.8.70	1	1
Mark Hateley	Rangers	7.11.61	32	9
Paul Merson	Arsenal	20.3.68	2	1
Ian Wright	Arsenal	3.11.63	4	0

Record against European Championship Finalists up until April 1992

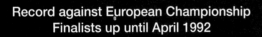

ENGLAND	P	W	L	D	F	A
v. France	21	15	4	2	62	27
v. Germany	19	9	6	4	36	25
v. Holland	10	4	2	4	16	10
v. Yugoslavia	14	5	4	5	23	20
v. Scotland	107	43	40	24	188	168
v. Sweden	13	6	3	4	23	14
v. Soviet Union (CIS)	11	5	3	3	19	13

Mark Wright played the 'libero' role to perfection in Bobby Robson's World Cup scheme in 1990. He now occupies a central defensive role under Graham Taylor's leadership.

Left: Striker on the rebound. **Mark Hateley** must have believed that his international career was over. He hadn't pulled on the famous white shirt for almost four years, but then a marvellous season with Rangers brought about his recall by Graham Taylor for the friendly against Czechoslovakia in March 1992.

Above: England's 'keeper **Chris Woods** has proved himself a worthy successor to Peter Shilton - and a model of professional patience. He had been waiting and watching from the wings for seven seasons, as Shilts' total of caps climbed inexorably to a record 125. Nowadays close competition for the 'keeper's jersey, from David Seaman, Tony Coton, Stephen Pears and Nigel Martyn, keeps Chris on his toes.

Fact File

Governing Body:
The Football Association

Year of formation: **1863**

National stadium:
Wembley

National Colours:
White shirts, navy shorts, white stockings

Change Colours:
Red shirts, white shorts, red stockings

International record:
World Cup, final stages
1930 not eligible
1934 ne
1938 ne
1950 1st round
1954 quarter-finalists
1958 1st round
1962 quarter-finalists
1966 hosts & Champions
1970 quarter-finalists
1974 did not qualify
1978 dnq
1982 2nd round
1986 quarter-finalists
1990 4th place.

European Championships
1960 dne
1964 1st round
1968 3rd place
1972 quarter-finalists
1976 1st phase
1980 quarter finalists
1984 1st phase
1988 quarter-finalists.

European Championship Record (1962-1991):
Played 60; won 36, drawn 14, lost 10; Goals 126 for - 44 against

Right: Basile Boli is a key man in the French defence. He's also a menacing figure at set-piece free-kicks in and around the opposition penalty-area.

Above: The so-called enfant terrible of French football, Eric 'the 'orrible' Cantona has a tendency to hit the headlines just as often off the field as he does on it. In 1987 he was fined for striking his own goalkeeper. In 1988 he was banned from the national team for insulting coach Henri Michel. In 1991 he was suspended for using a referee as target practice and then losing his temper during the resulting disciplinary hearing. In 1992 he walked out on Nimes before crossing the English Channel initially expecting to join Sheffield Wednesday on loan but eventually landing at Leeds United where he became an integral part of the League Championship campaign.

The French team, unbeaten in the qualifiers, was first past the post for the 1992 European Championship finals. Their form which made them the most consistent national side in Europe in 1991 give the French joint-favourite status, with Germany, to win the title.

The inspiration behind this remarkableFrench revival is team boss Michel Platini who motivated his squad by warning them that, having failed to qualify for the '88 European Championship *and* the '90 World Cup finals, they now stood a good chance of becoming the 'forgotten generation' of French football. The message was received and understood.

But Michel Platini knows that his team side still has it all to do in Sweden. "In a European Championship you have to be ready for tough matches, however the draw comes out. There aren't any easy games, as there often are in a World Cup. And we French are proud that we

have the chance to start the finals by playing Sweden."

If the outcome of that particular match follows form, with France as the eventual winners. Platini's team must then overcome the more formidable obstacles of England and Yugoslavia if the manager is to write yet another special chapter in the history books.

The Manager

One of the world's finest midfielders, Michel Platini became the first player to be elected European Footballer of the Year three times in succession - in 1983, 1984 and 1985. He was the architect behind the French team which won the 1984 European Championship and were World Cup semi finalists in 1982 and 1986, playing in a fine midfield with Tigana and Giresse.

Michel Platini was born 21.6.55 at Joeuf, in Lorraine. His father was technical director at AS Nancy, which became his first senior club from 1972-1979. After the French Cup win with Nancy in 1979, he moved to St Etienne from 1979-82, winning a league title in 1981. Platini was then signed by Juventus for whom he played between 1982-87 winning league titles in 1984 and 1986, the European Cup in 1985, and the Italian Cup in 1983.

Platini scored 348 goals in 648 senior games before his retirement in 1987, including a French record 41 goals in 72 internationals. With no training experience, he was asked to take over the national team in November.

Squad Contenders

	Club	Date of Birth	Caps	Goals
Goalkeepers				
Bruno Martini	Auxerre	25.1.62	20	0
Gilles Rousset	Lyon	22.8.63	2	0
Defenders				
Manuel Amoros	Marseille	1.2.62	78	1
Basile Boli	Marseille	2.1.67	33	1
Bernard Casoni	Marseille	4.9.61	22	0
Emmanuel Petit	Monaco	22.9.70	2	0
Laurent Blanc	Napoli	19.11.65	20	4
Jocelyn Angloma	Marseille	7.8.65	8	0
Franck Silvestre	Sochaux	5.4.67	10	0
Midfielders				
Didier Deschamps	Marseille	15.10.68	18	3
Jean-Philippe Durand	Marseille	11.11.60	17	0
Luis Fernandez	Cannes	2.11.59	55	6
Franck Sauzee	Marseille	28.10.65	23	6
Remi Garde	Lyon	3.4.66	4	0
Forwards				
Jean-Pierre Papin	Marseille	5.11.63	34	19
Eric Cantona	Leeds Utd	24.5.66	22	12
Christian Perez	Paris Saint Germain	13.5.63	17	2
Pascal Vahirua	Auxerre	9.3.66	11	0
Christophe Cocard	Auxerre	23.11.67	3	0
Stephane Paille	Caen	25.6.65	8	1

Record against European Championship Finalists up until April 1992

FRANCE	P	W	L	D	F	A
v. England	21	4	15	2	27	62
v. Germany	19	7	8	4	33	39
v. Holland	15	6	8	1	28	42
v. Yugoslavia	25	8	10	7	28	39
v. Scotland	10	4	6	0	11	12
v. Sweden	10	5	4	1	16	10
v. Soviet Union (CIS)	12	2	4	6	12	17

Jean-Pierre Papin was voted the 1991 European Footballer of the Year in the wake of his consistent performances for Marseille and France. He has been the leading scorer in the French League for the past four seasons, and could be described as a good, old fashioned centre-forward with an aggressive, opportunist style. Papin is bound to move on to one of the Italian or Spanish giants sooner or later. Not bad for a lad who was a self-confessed late-developer in the game.

*Laurant Blanc -
sweeper supreme and
expert penalty-taker for
France.*

*Consistently good
between the posts for
France, **Bruno Martini**
is a key member of
Platini's squad.*

Fact File

Governing Body:
**Federation Francaise De
Football**

Year of formation: **1919**

National Stadium:
Parc des Princes

National Colours:
**Blue shirts, white shorts,
red stockings**

Change colours:
**White shirts, blue shorts,
red stockings**

International record:
**World Cup, final stages
1930** 1st round
1934 1st round
1938 hosts & quarter-
finalists
1950 dnq
1954 1st round
1958 3rd place
1962 dnq
1966 1st round
1970 dnq **1974** dnq
1978 1st round
1982 1st round
1986 semi-finalists
1990 dnq.

**European Championships
1960** semi-finalists
1964 2nd round
1968 quarter-finalists
1972 1st round
1976 1st phase
1980 1st round
1984 Champions
1988 1st round.

**EuropeanChampionship
record (1958-1991):
Played 59; won 31,
drawn 13, lost 15;
Goals 116 for - 73
against**

*German skipper **Lothar Matthaus** has an impeccable footballing pedigree. He was voted World Player of the Year in 1991, by the team coaches of 56 national squads.*

Having survived the Welsh scare in the qualifying contest, the Germans are confident of success in Sweden. "I'm very conscious of the fact that we'll be coming to the Championship as favourites, as we are World Champions," said team manager Berti Vogts. "That doesn't disturb us at all. I don't have much to say about the draw. If we're going to be the Champions again then we have to beat everybody sooner or later."

Such a clinical attitude has served (West) Germany well in recent years. They have become three times winners and three times runners-up in the World Cup; twice winners and once runners-up in the European Championship - all by the simple expedient of 'beating everybody sooner or later' and, of course, having the depth of playing talent with which to do it.

The reuniting of the old East and West German football authorities has made available

Germany

even more talent (Doll, Matthias, Thom et al) for Berti Vogts to consider. Reunification has also had the healthy effect of making competition for first team places even tougher - especially in the midfield where Vogts is almost spoilt for choice. This summer the German success machine could prove even more difficult to stop than usual.

The Manager

Hans-Hubert 'Berti' Vogts took over from Franz Beckenbauer after the 1990 World Cup triumph - Vogts had come through the coaching system and had previously been in charge of the U-21 squad. As a player, he had a fine career with 96 caps for West Germany, and a World Cup winners medal in 1974. First capped in 1967, he ended his international career after the 1978 World Cup. Vogts was a one-club man, joining Borussia Menchengladbach in 1965 when they were in the second division. His club was quickly promoted to the Bundesliga, where he collected five league medals, two UEFA Cup medals, and was elected the West German Footballer of the Year in both 1971 and 1979. He played 419 games in the Bundesliga.

From 1979-90, Vogts was employed by the West German FA, and was in charge of all representative sides below the national team, until his appointment as manager of West Germany - and now Germany - in August 1990.

Above: Rudi Voller's striking power has long been a vital facor in Germany's soccer success.

Below: England's footballers have good reason to fear the talents of German goalkeeper **Bodo Illgner**. It was his superb form in the 1990 World Cup semi-final penalty shoot-out which effectively removed England from the tournament.

Squad Contenders

	Club	Date of Birth	Caps	Goals
Goalkeepers				
Bodo Illgner	Cologne	7.4.67	33	0
Andreas Kopke	Nurnberg	12.3.62	1	0
Defenders				
Dietmar Beirsdorfer	Hamburg SV	16.11.63	1	0
Manfred Binz	Eintracht Frankfurt	22.9.65	8	0
Andreas Brehme	Inter Milan	9.11.60	67	8
Guido Buchwald	VFB Stuttgart	24.1.61	48	1
Thomas Helmer	Borussia Dortmund	21.4.65	6	0
Stefan Reuter	Juventus	16.10.66	31	2
Michael Schulz	Borussia Dortmund	3.9.61	1	0
Midfielders				
Uwe Bein	Eintracht Frankfurt	26.9.60	14	3
Thomas Doll	Lazio	9.4.66	8 (29)	1
Thomas Haessler	AS Roma	30.5.66	26	2
Lothar Matthaus	Inter Milan	21.3.61	93	18
Matthias Sammer	VFB Stuttgart	5.9.67	4 (23)	0
Markus Schupp	Wattenscheid	7.1.66	0	0
Forwards				
Ulf Kirsten	Bayer Leverkusen	4.12.65	0(49)	0
Jurgen Klinsmann	Inter Milan	30.7.64	34	9
Stefan Kuntz	Kaiserslautern	30.10.62	0	0
Karl Heinz Riedle	Lazio	16.9.65	19	6
Andreas Thom	Bayer Leverkusen	7.9.65	1(51)	1
Rudi Voller	AS Roma	13.4.60	80	42

Note: Numbers in brackets indicate the caps won when playing for the old East Germany.

Record against European Championship Finalists up until April 1992

GERMANY	P	W	L	D	F	A
v. England	19	6	9	4	25	36
v. France	19	8	7	4	39	33
v. Holland	30	12	7	11	64	51
v. Yugoslavia	24	14	7	3	44	29
v. Scotland	10	3	3	4	15	17
v. Sweden	30	11	13	6	53	51
v. Soviet Union (CIS)	13	10	0	3	38	11

Fact File

Governing Body:
Deutsche Fussball-Bund

Year of formation: **1900**

National stadia:
**Olympic Berlin
Olympic Munich**

National Colours:
White shirts with black/red trim, black shorts, white stockings

Change Colours:
Green shirts, white shorts, white stockings

International Record:

World Cup, final stages
1930 did not enter
1934 3rd place
1938 1st round
1950 not eligible
1954 Champions
1958 4th place
1962 quarter-finalists
1966 runners-up
1970 3rd place
1974 Champions
1978 2nd round
1982 runners-up
1986 runners-up
1990 Champions.

European Championships
1960 dne **1964** dne
1968 1st round
1972 Champions
1976 runners-up
1980 Champions
1984 quarter-finalists
1988 semi-finalists.
European Championship record (1967-1991):
Played 60; won 39, drawn 15, lost 6; Goals 109 for - 33 against.

*Former East German international **Thomas Doll** was bought by Lazio of Italy when Paul Gascoigne's proposed transfer was put on hold.*

Ruud Gullit *hit the heights with Holland in the 1988 European Championship campaign, when he was captain. Since then, a recurring knee injury, requiring four separate operations, has hampered his progress somewhat. But Ruud, he of the unmistakable 'dreadlocks' and once described by Paul Gascoigne as a 'hairy yetti', is determined to play on beyond this year's European Championship and into the qualifiers for the '94 World Cup.*

Team manager Rinus Michels must be relieved that the internal problems which have dogged the Dutch squad in recent years appear to have been put on hold. The highly publicised rift between Michels and Ruud Gullit has been bridged; Frank Rijkaard is happy to be back in the fold - and it seems that the squad is once more behind their manager and determined to wipe out the memory of their poor showing in the 1990 World Cup by retaining the Championship of Europe which they won, for the first time, four years ago.

Michels, whose key players perform in the Italian and Spanish leagues confessed after the draw in Gothenburg, that he would be keeping a close eye on developments in those countries prior to the European finals. "During the spring I'm going to be a great fan of AC Milan. If they can secure the league championship early, then maybe the team bosses will allow three of my key players Rijkaard, Gullit and van Basten to rest in the last matches - in which case I'd have them a lot earlier than 24 May when the final

Holland

Italian league games are played. I also have players at Barcelona where the league season ends even later - but in their case the manager's name is Johan Cruyff, and I hope he has a certain understanding for my situation."

Cruyff will indeed have an abiding interest in Holland's fortunes - he is due to take over the managership of the squad if they reach the World Cup finals in 1994.

The Manager

Born 9.2.28, Rinus Michels is the oldest trainer of all Europe's 34 International teams, and was recalled after the disappointing spell of Dutch leadership under Thijs Librechts and then Leo Beenhakker. Michels is the man who took Holland to the 1988 European Championship, then appeared to have set the seal on a glittering career - however, he was recalled in July 1990 after a poor World Cup showing by the Dutch. Michels spent his playing career at Ajax, as a centre forward, in the 1940s and 1950s and won five caps. After a brief managerial spell at JOS, he joined Ajax in 1965 and shaped the great team under Johann Cruyff that won the European Cup from 1971-73. He then left for Barcelona, with Cruyff and Neeskens, but returned to take Holland to the 1974 World Cup final with his creed of total football. In 1975, he went back to Ajax, then went to Los Angeles Aztecs and Cologne. Michels returned again as Dutch trainer, but 'retired' in 1985 after a heart attack. Answering the call again, he took charge of the Dutch side through the qualifying stages and on to the European Championship triumphs of 1988. This campaign, he has said, will be his last.

Squad Contenders

	Club	Date of Birth	Caps	Goals
Goalkeepers				
Hans Van Breukelen	PSV Eindhoven	4.10.56	66	0
Stanley Menzo	Ajax	15.10.63	3	0
Defenders				
Berry van Aerle	PSV Eindhoven	8.12.62	27	0
Ronald Koeman	Barcelona	21.3.63	54	10
Erwin Koeman	PSV Eindhoven	20.9.61	28	2
Adrie van Tiggelen	PSV Eindhoven	10.6.57	49	0
Danny Blind	Ajax	1.8.61	17	1
Henk Fraser	Feyenoord	7.7.66	5	0
Midfielders				
Frank Rijkaard	AC Milan	30.9.62	50	3
Jan Wouters	Bayern Munich	17.7.60	45	4
Richard Witschge	Barcelona	20.9.69	19	1
Aron Winter	Ajax	1.3.67	19	1
Johnny van't Schip	Ajax	30.12.63	33	2
Rob Witschge	Feyenoord	22.8.66	4	0
Peter Bosz	Feyenoord	21.11.63	2	0
Forwards				
Ruud Gullit	AC Milan	1.9.62	55	15
Marco van Basten	AC Milan	31.10.64	48	23
Wim Kieft	PSV Eindhoven	12.11.62	37	11
Dennis Bergkamp	Ajax	10.5.69	10	5
Peter van Vossen	Beveren Waas	21.4.68	1	0

Record against European Championship Finalists up until April 1992

HOLLAND	P	W	L	D	F	A
v. England	10	2	4	4	10	16
v. France	15	8	1	6	42	28
v. Germany	30	7	12	11	51	64
v. Yugoslavia	7	3	3	1	9	10
v. Scotland	9	2	5	2	10	13
v. Sweden	18	8	7	3	33	40
v. Soviet Union (CIS)	6	3	2	1	8	4

The superb form of **Frank Rijkaard** was a vital factor in Holland's 1988 European Championship-winning campaign. In 1990 he made what appeared to be his last international appearance, following the incident with West Germany's Rudi Voller in the World Cup. But Frank has been welcomed back into the Dutch fold in his favourite central midfield role.

Fact File

Above, left: *Goalkeeper **Hans Van Breukelen** is the most experienced member of the current Dutch squad with over 65 caps to his name. At the ripe old age of thirty-five he has announced that he will be retiring from the international scene after the European Championship and intends to serve for just one more season with PSV Eindhoven before turning to sports journalism.*

Above, right: *Richard **Witschge's** goal against Portugal, his first in international, secured Holland's place in the finals. His elder brother, Rob, is also a Dutch international.*

*The goal-scoring sensation of the 1988 European Championship, **Marco van Basten** is still regarded as the most lethal striker in Europe.*

Governing Body:
Koninklijke Nederlandsche Voetbalbond

Year of formation: **1889**

National Stadium:
Feyenoord, Rotterdam

National Colours:
Orange shirts, white shorts, orange stockings

Change Colours:
All white

International record:
World Cup, final stages
1930 did not enter
1934 1st round
1938 1stround
1950 dne **1954** dne
1958 did not qualify;
1962 dnq **1966** dnq
1970 dnq
1974 runners-up
1978 runners-up
1982 dnq **1986** dnq
1990 2nd round.

European Championships:
1960 dne
1964 2nd round
1968 1st round
1972 1st round
1976 3rd place
1980 2nd round
1984 1st round
1988 Champions.

European Championship record (1962-1991):
Played 66; won 42, drawn 10, lost 14; Goals 146 for - 58 against.

*The versatile **Brian McClair** has enjoyed a marvellous 1991-92 season for Manchester United and has been at the heart of the Old Trafford title challenge. During his international career he's been called upon to perform more of a variety of roles, in all areas of the midfield and as a striker.*

Scotland arrive in Sweden, and at their first ever European Championship finals, via a somewhat tortuous route - having had to await the outcome of a match played hundreds of miles away in Sofia (Bulgaria 1, Romania 1; if Romania had won by two goals or more, they would have qualified with a superior goal difference over the Scots). Now they have been drawn in arguably the toughest group in the opening stage of the finals, along with Holland, Germany and the Commonwealth of Independent States.

Nevertheless, manager Andy Roxburgh remains optimistic about Scotland's chances of success: "I'm quite delighted to be in with the Big Guns," he said after the draw. "Obviously we're going to be playing against the World Champions and the current European Champions, and in a way that adds to the challenge. After all, we felt it was a success to get to our first finals. We knew we were going to be in with the top teams - so they might as well give us the best."

In terms of 1991 form, however, Scotland have the lowest success rate of any of the eight contenders. In that year they played six matches and won only two of them - both against the tiny principality of San Marino in the European Championship qualifiers.

Scotland will certainly need to perform far better in Sweden than they did against Finland at Hampden Park in March of this year. Apart from a superb goal involving some stunning approach work by debutant David Bowman and spectacular finishing by Paul McStay, Scotland

Scotland

The Manager
Born 5.8.43, Andy Roxburgh has been in charge of the national team since taking over from Alex Ferguson in July 1986. Roxburgh set a Scottish record in becoming the first to take the side to the European finals. Roxburgh is the 'quiet man' in terms of achievement - as a player he was with Queen's Park, Partick Thistle, Falkirk and the now defunct East Stirlingshire Clydebank. Instead of club management, he moved to the Scottish FA coaching staff in 1975, guiding the Scots to the European Youth Championship in 1982. He succeeded Alex Ferguson, who was himself a temporary choice following the death of Jock Stein.

Squad Contenders

	Club	Date of Birth	Caps	Goals
Goalkeepers				
Andy Goram	Glasgow Rangers	13.4.64	19	0
Henry Smith	Hearts	10.3.56	2	0
Defenders				
Stewart McKimmie	Aberdeen	27.10.62	14	1
Tom Boyd	Celtic	24.11.65	7	0
Davie McPherson	Hearts	28.1.64	17	0
Richard Gough	Glasgow Rangers	5.4.62	54	5
Maurice Malpas	Dundee Utd	3.8.62	47	0
David Robertson	Glasgow Rangers	17.10.68	1	0
Steve Nicol	Liverpool	11.12.61	27	0
Midfielders				
Gordon Strachan	Leeds Utd	9.2.57	50	5
Paul McStay	Celtic	22.10.64	54	8
Stuart McCall	Glasgow Rangers	10.6.64	14	1
John Collins	Celtic	31.1.68	8	2
Gary McAllister	Leeds Utd	25.12.64	12	1
David Bowman	Dundee Utd	10.3.64	1	0
Forwards				
Ally McCoist	Glasgow Rangers	24.9.62	35 1	1
Gordon Durie	Tottenham	6.12.65	17	4
John Robertson	Hearts	2.10.64	7	2
Maurice Johnston	Everton	13.4.63	38	14
Kevin Gallacher	Coventry	23.11.66	8	0
Brian McClair	Man Utd	8.12.63	20	0
Robert Fleck	Norwich City	11.8.65	4	0

Record against European Championship Finalists up until April 1992

SCOTLAND	P	W	L	D	F	A
v. England	107	40	43	24	168	188
v. France	10	6	4	0	12	11
v. Germany	10	3	3	4	17	15
v. Holland	9	5	2	2	13	10
v. Yugoslavia	8	2	1	5	16	11
v. Sweden	7	4	2	1	11	8
v. Soviet Union (CIS)	4	0	3	1	2	6

looked decidedly lethargic - and not the stuff of potential European Champions.

The subsequent tour of the USA and Canada and the match against Norway, hardly seemed an appropriate approach to the Championship. But as Andy Roxburgh says: "When it really matters, we'll be ready. We'll be totally committed for the European Championship."

*Ex-Coventry City boss Terry Butcher rates **Kevin Gallacher** as one of the best attackers in Britain and estimates that his value has at least trebled since Coventry signed him from Dundee United for £900,000 in 1989.*

Fact File

Above: *A £2.2 million transfer from Chelsea to Spurs in 1991, gave a confidence-building boost to* **Gordon Durie's** *career and he was subsequently recalled to the Scottish squad in the European Championship qualifiers against Switzerland, San Marino and Bulgaria.*

Right: **Paul McStay** *is listed among Europe's finest midfielders. He's invariably involved in the build-up to many promising Scottish moves. And he has an eye for goal, a fact confirmed by his superb strike against Finland at Hampden Park in March '92. McStay's contract with Celtic soon expires - which means there will undoubtedly be a queue of top clubs anxious to snap him up.*

Governing Body:
Scottish Football Association

Year of formation: **1873**

National stadium:
Hampden Park, Glasgow

National Colours:
Dark blue shirts, white shorts, red stockings

Change Colours:
White, yellow and blue hooped shirts, dark blue shorts, dark blue stockings with yellow trim

International record:
World Cup, final stages
1930 not eligible
1934 ne **1938** ne
1950 withdrew after qualification
1954 1st round
1958 1st round
1962 did not qualify
1966 dnq **1970** dnq
1974 1st round
1978 1st round
1982 1st round
1986 1st round
1990 1st round.

European Championships
1960 dne **1964** dne
1968 1st round
1972 1st round
1976 1st round
1980 1st round
1984 1st round
1988 1st round.

European Championship record (1966-1991):
Played 48; won 19, drawn 14, lost 15
Goals 66 for - 56 against.

Almost by tradition Yugoslavia is described as 'the best team never to have won the World Cup', or indeed the European Championship. The country also has a reputation for producing world class players who inevitably find fame and fortune abroad - the current estimate is that

Yugoslavia

against the squad. "We're not Germans," says team manager Osim. "We have a Balkan temperament and that's why we can be erratic at times."

On a far more serious note, Yugoslavia's realistic chances of success in Sweden have been deeply affected by the civil strife which has torn the country apart. As with the troubled Commonwealth of Independent States, FIFA and UEFA took serious note of the situation in Yugoslavia. But since the Yugoslav Football Assosciation was still in operation at the time of the draw in Gothenburg it was decided that 'for the time being [there is] no call for reviewing

some 120 Yugoslav footballers make their living elsewhere in Europe.

England's team manager Graham Taylor, along with many other experts, considers Ivica Osim's squad to be the most technically gifted in the entire European Championship: "In Pancev, Prosinecki and Savicevic they have three outstanding players," he said.

When on song Yugoslavia play a flowing, attacking game, a fact borne out by their 24 goals in the qualifying tournament - the highest tally of the 1992 championship. There is, however, a slight question of dubious temperament and indiscipline marked

Record against European Championship Finalists up until April 1992						
YUGOSLAVIA	P	W	L	D	F	A
v. England	14	4	5	5	20	23
v. France	25	10	8	7	39	23
v. Germany	24	7	14	3	29	44
v. Holland	7	3	3	1	10	9
v. Scotland	8	1	2	5	11	16
v. Sweden	11	5	4	2	19	21
v. Soviet Union (CIS)	17	2	11	4	17	33

their participation in the European Championship final rounds. Every player in the territory represented by Yugoslavia will, similarly, be entitled to play'.

If the unthinkable should happen and Yugoslavia finds it impossible to participate in the finals their place will be taken by Qualifying Group Four runners-up Denmark.

Reputedly Dragan Stojkovic's first transfer, to Red Star Belgrade, involved five new players and a complete set of floodlight pylons for his old club FK Radnicki Nis. This oustanding midfield talent - a corner-kick and free-kick specialist - went on to play in France and Italy.

Fact File

The Manager

Ivica Osim was appointed manager of the Yugoslav national team in October 1986, and, after a fine show in the 1990 World Cup under difficult circumstances, he was asked to continue. Osim currently doubles as trainer of Partizan Belgrade. Born 6.5.41, he was a tall, cultured midfielder from the FC Zeljeznicar club of Sarajevo, but also played in France for Strasbourg and Sedan. He scored 8 goals in 16 games for Yugoslavia from 1964-69, and had an outstanding 1968 European Championship until injury forced him out of the game. He returned from France to coach Zeljeznicar before taking over the national team.

Squad Contenders

	Club	Date of Birth	Caps	Goals
Goalkeepers				
Fahrudin Omerovic	Partizan	26.8.61	7	0
Defenders				
Darko Milanic	Partizan	18.12.67	4	0
Vujadin Stanojkovic	Partizan	10.9.63	21	1
Faruk Hadzibegic	Sochaux	7.10.56	59	6
Ilja Najdoski	Red Star	26.3.64	10	1
Dzoni Novak	Partizan	2.9.69	3	0
Budimir Vujacic	Partizan	4.1.64	7	0
Branko Brnovic	Partizan	8.8.67	5	0
Midfielders				
Mehmed Bazdarevic	Sochaux	28.9.60	54	4
Vladimir Jugovic	Red Star	30.8.69	3	1
Sinisa Mihailovic	Red Star	20.2.69	4	0
Pedrag Mijatovic	Partizan	19.1.69	8	0
Slavisa Jokanovic	Partizan	16.8.68	5	0
Forwards				
Darko Pancev	Red Star	7.9.65	26	17
Dejan Savicevic	Red Star	15.9.66	26	10
Dragan Stojkovic	Verona	3.5.65	40	9
Vladim Lukic	Red Star	16.2.70	3	2
Mario Stanic	Zeljeznicar	10.4.72	2	0

Governing Body:
Yugoslav Football Association

Year of formation: **1919**

National Stadium:**?-**

National Colours:
Blue shirts, white shorts, red stockings

Change Colours:
All white

International record:
World Cup, final stages
1930 semi-finalists
1934 did not qualify
1938 quarter-finalists
1950 1st round
1954 quarter-finalists
1958 quarter-finalists
1962 4th place
1966 dnq **1970** dnq
1974 2nd round
1978 dnq
1982 1st round
1986 dnq
1990 quarter-finalists.

European Championships
1960 runners-up
1964 2nd round
1968 runners-up
1972 quarter-finalists
1976 4th place
1980 1st round
1984 quarter-finalists
1988 1st round.

European Championship record (1959-1991):
Played 66; won 37, drawn 11, lost 18; Goals 128 for - 80 against.

Henri Delaunay, *founder of the European Chaampionship*

THE HISTORY OF THE EUROPEAN CHAMPIONSHIP

On 21 May 1904 Henri Delaunay, a young printer with an abiding interest in association football, attended a meeting in Paris together with Dutchman CAW Hirschman and fellow Frenchmen Robert Guerin and Jules Rimet. Also present were other representatves from Belgium, Denmark, Spain and Switzerland.

Inspired by the ever-increasing popularity of football throughout the world, these men thrashed out the foundations of the Federation International de Football Association (FIFA) and proclaimed their intention to organise a 'world championship'. They even went to the prudent lengths of inserting a clause into the Federation's constitution, which boldly stated that FIFA had the sole right to organise and administer such a tournament.

But a further 26 years would pass before the first World Cup competition was staged. In the intervening period Jules Rimet and Henri Delaunay had worked tirelessly towards this ultimate goal. Their efforts were impeded, of course, by the 1914-18 war, fought largely on French soil, and it wasn't until the early 1920s that the idea began to look anything like a reality.

After a great deal of painstaking organisation, the inaugural World Cup finals were eventually staged in the summer of 1930, in Uruguay - chosen as the host nation in the wake of gold medal soccer success at the Olympic Games of 1924 and 1928. By then Uruguay had also won the South American Championship six times (also known as the Copa America, this tournament was established in 1916).

Only thirteen nations entered the new World Cup and, much to the disappointment of the South American contingent, just four of the competing teams - Belgium, France, Romania and Yugoslavia - were from Europe. This, despite the Uruguayan government's pledge to underwrite the not inconsiderable travelling expenses of their European brothers.

The competition coincided with the centenary of Uruguay's independence - and to mark both occasions a brand new sporting venue, the

Centenary Stadium, was built in Montevideo in just eight months. It was there on 30 July 1930, in front of 90,000 frenzied

Left, Jules Rimet
Right, The Jules Rimet Trophy

supporters, that Uruguay played Argentina in the first ever World Cup final.

The event was not without incident. National fervour was at its height and cries of 'victory or death' were heard amid the celebratory fireworks. The Centenary Stadium was ringed by armed soldiers, the crowd was searched for weapons and the referee agreed to proceed with the game only after his life had been insured. The match itself resulted in a 4-2 victory for Uruguay and a national holiday was declared for the following day. The champions' trophy handed to team captain Nasazzi was a small statuette designed in France by Abel Lafluer and called The Golden Cup. In 1946 it would be re-named as The Jules Rimet Trophy in recognition of Rimet's unstinting efforts towards the creation of the competition and of his presidency of FIFA (an office he held between 1921 and 1954).

That first World Cup was the beginning of an

The Henry Delaunay Cup.

international footballing festival which, excluding wartime, has continued at four-yearly intervals ever since; it is a tournament which has given us some of the best of times and some of the worst of times on a football pitch. And it was the model and inspiration for the European Championship.

The idea for a European tournament was first mooted by Henri Delaunay in 1927, by which time he had become Secretary to the Federation Francaise de Football (FFF). The suggestion was greeted without enthusiasm among his fellow FIFA executives, who were understandably more concerned that the first *World* Cup should be launchedsmoothly . And so the idea lay dormant.

Meanwhile, a number of small international tournaments saw the light of day. The Nordic Cup, contested by Denmark, Finland, Norway and Sweden, was begun in 1924. 1927 saw the first Central European Championship, later known as the Dr Gero Cup; and of course the British Isles had, since 1883, held its own Home International Championship.

Delaunay's vision of a broader continental contest was given new life with the creation of the Union European de Football Associations (UEFA), of which he became the first General Secretary. UEFA was formed on 15 June 1954, in Basel, Switzerland, under the auspices of FIFA. In essence a bonding of the leading national football associations throughout the continent, UEFA effectively became the controlling body and organiser of the European game at both club and international levels.

Within two years of UEFA's foundation, the first European Cup competition was staged. Sixteen of the leading continental clubs were invited to participate. Real Madrid began their early domination of the tournament by beating French club Stade de Riems 4-3 in the Final in Paris, on 13 June 1956. Since then each season's league champions throughout Europe have gained automatic entry to the competition.

Sadly, Henri Delaunay died in 1955, before his dream became a reality. When the concept of an international championship within Europe was finally accepted by UEFA and FIFA, the tournament was christened The European Nations' Cup and would be contested in the years between World Cup competitions. The first qualifying tournament was set to begin in 1958, after the Swedish World Cup. The first finals were to be staged two years later and, as a mark of respect to the memory of Henri Delaunay, they were sheduled to be played in France. And his name lives on with every passing championship: the trophy which now symbolises the pinnacle of European footballing endeavour is called The Henri Delaunay Cup.

To begin with, the European Nations Cup competition was greeted with a distinct lack of enthusiasm among the football playing nations of Europe. UEFA had set the minimum number of entries required at 16 (with an entry fee of £25). In the event only 17 nations applied. Among the most notable absentees were 1954 World Champions West Germany,1958 World Cup hosts Sweden and the four home nations of Great Britain.

The Republic of Ireland did enter but, in order to even up the number of entrants, were selected to play in a two-leg preliminary round against Czechoslovakia. The first ever match in the European Nations' Cup, therefore, kicked-off in Dublin, on Saturday 5 April 1958.

The first goal of the tournament was scored for the Republic by Shamrock Rovers' winger Liam Tuohy. A penalty by West Ham's Noel Cantwell sealed the matter at 2-0. But it was to be a different story on 10 May in Bratislava. Czechoslovakia won 4-0 and, with a 4-2 aggregate, joined the fifteen other entrants in the first round proper.

The draw for the first European Nations' Cup, made during the World Cup finals in Sweden, was largely ignored by press and public alike. Nevertheless, the course of the competition was set. The first rounds and the quarter final would proceed on a two-leg, knock-out basis. The semi final, the third place match and the final itself would all be contested in France.

As the autumn of 1958 drew in, and with memories of the brilliant Brazilians - the new World Champions - still fresh in the minds of football aficionados everywhere, the European competition continued on its way.

And, as if in defiance of the initial apathy shown towards the tournament, 100,572 spectators turned out for the first USSR v Hungary tie in the Central Stadium, Moscow, on 28 September 1958.

Both sides had experienced a disappointing World Cup in Sweden. Hungary, who had been hailed as the 'Magical Magyars' in the early '50s, had not progressed beyond the first round. The Soviet Union had reached the quarter-finals only to be bundled out by the host nation and eventual finalists, Sweden. Consequently, both sides were now in something of a transitional

1958-1960
Final Hosts: France
Champions: USSR

period and were experimenting with fresh team selections and tactical changes.

The Soviets were obviously conducting the more successful experiment since, to the delight of that huge home crowd, they won the match by an emphatic 3-1 margin. In the second leg, played in Budapest on 27 September 1959, the USSR duly finished the job by despatching Hungary with a 1-0 victory.

France had finished in third place in the World Cup, behind Brazil and Sweden. Their centre-forward Just Fontaine had notched up 13 goals during the finals, a record which still stands today (and given these defence-minded times, seems likely to remain forever). They opened their first European Nations' campaign at the Parc des Princes Stadium in Paris on 1 October 1958, against Greece. The result was a resounding 7-1 victory for the impressive French team who attacked for most of the game, with captain Kopa giving a particularly fine performance. He scored one goal, as did Vincent. Fontaine hit two and Cisowski netted a hat-trick. Yfantis replied for Greece. The scoreline would represent the biggest margin in the entire tournament.

The Greek side were greatly improved for the return match in Athens two months later. They held the French to a 1-1 draw, both goals coming in the second half (Papaemmanuel for Greece, Bruey for France).

European Nations'
Cup Final
10 July 1960
Parc des Princes, Paris
Attendance: 17,966

**USSR 2,
YUGOSLAVIA 1**
(after extra time)

USSR: Yashin; Tchekeli,
Kroutikov, Voinov,
Maslenkin, Netto,
Metreveli, Ivanov,
Ponedelnik, Bubukin,
Meshki.
Scorers: Metreveli 50,
Ponedelnik 113

Yugoslavia: Vidinic,
Durkovic, Jusufi, Zanetic,
Miladinovic, Perusic,
Sekularac, Jerkovic,
Galic, Matus, Kostic.
Scorer: Galic 40

Yugoslavia beat neighbouring Bulgaria 2-0 on 31 May 1959, with goals from Galic and Tasic. And a 1-1 draw in Sofia five months later put the Yugoslavs through to the quarter finals.

Czechoslovakia, having won the right to be in the opening round, progressed to the quarter finals after an emphatic 5-1 defeat of Denmark in the second leg. Danish hopes had been high after a 2-2 draw in the first leg.

In the remaining first round ties Spain beat Poland on a 7-2 aggregate; Romania beat Turkey on a 3-2 aggregate; Austria beat Norway 6-2 (agg) and Portgual depatched East Germany with an aggregate of 5-2.

The easiest passage through the quarter final stage went to the USSR. They had been drawn against Spain, but the Spanish authorities, then under the control of General Franco, refused the squad permission to travel to Russia - a reaction against Soviet involvement in the Spanish Civil War of 1938-39. Consequently, the USSR were given a 'walk over' into the semi finals.

France won both legs of their tie against Austria, to finish with a resounding 9-4 aggregate score. Czechoslovakia also won both legs against Romania, scoring five goals without reply.

The remaining semi final berth went to Yugoslavia who had a far more difficult passage than any of the other surviving sides. They lost the first leg 2-1 away to Portugal and were not expected to progress further in the tournament. But a spirited attacking display in the home leg in Belgrade saw a Yugoslavian revival which brought about a 5-1 victory to carry them through.

Both semi finals took place on 6 July 1960. At the Parc des Princes in Paris, France were leading Yugoslavia 4-2 by the 62nd minute and looked set for the final. But a combination of yet another Yugoslavian revival, and an astonishing loss of confidence by French goalkeeper Georges Lama saw Yugoslavia score three goals in four minutes to take the match 5-4.

Meanwhile, in Marseille, the great Soviet 'keeper Lev Yashin was involved in one of the matches of his life, against Czechoslovakia. Time after time in the early stages Yashin halted the Czech attack and it was only his skill that kept the USSR in the match at that stage. Later the Soviet side took control and won 3-0 with goals from Ivanov (2) and Ponedelnik.

France suffered further disappointment in the third place play-off match in Marseille on 9 July: they lost 2-0 to Czechoslovakia after a dispirited display in front of a crowd of just 9,438.

The first European Nations' Cup final was staged at the Parc des Princes Stadium on 10 July 1960. A mere 17,966 spectators were treated to a fine game (refereed by Englishman, Arthur Ellis). Yugoslavia were pre-match favourites thanks to their spirited displays in earlier stages of the tournament. Indeed, they attacked right from the start and once again Lev Yashin in the Soviet goalmouth was called upon to perform near miracles. The pressure paid off in the 40th minute when Galic's shot was deflected into the net by Netto.

Then came a Soviet revival. After the interval the Soviet Union looked a different side, within five minutes of the restart they equalised through winger Slava Metreveli. The scoreline remained at 1-1 after 90 minutes, and the match went into extra time. The Soviet players proved the fitter at this stage of the game and their stamina was the deciding factor. After 113 gruelling minutes Meshki's cross was hit home by Victor Ponedelnik. It was the winning goal.

Twenty-nine nations entered the second European Nations' Cup competition. England, Wales and Northern Ireland were among the entrants. Scotland, West Germany, Cyprus and Finland were the notable absentees. Once again the competition would proceed along knock-out lines until the semi final and final stages. When the four semi-finalists were known a venue for the final stages would be chosen from amongst them.

The draw was made after the completion of the 1962 World Cup finals, held in Chile and won by Brazil. Consequently, the beginnings of the second European tournament attracted a lot more attention than its predecessor had done

In order to have 16 nations competing in the second round, Austria, Luxembourg and the USSR were given byes directly to the second stage. Upon being drawn to play Albania, Greece immediately withdrew from the competition as the two countries had been in a state of uneasy truce for many years. In view of the Greek decision UEFA awarded the tie to Albania.

England, managed by Sir Walter Winterbottom, began their first Nations Cup campaign at Hillsborough, against France in the 'glamour' tie of the first round, on 3 October 1962. The game turned into something of a nightmare for the home side who were outclassed and out-manoeuvred by a French 4-2-4 system modelled on the Brazilian original. Nevertheless, the game ended all-square at 1-1. Gujon scored first for France in the 8th minute. Ron Flowers equalised with a penalty early in the second half.

The game was Sir Walter Winterbottom's last in a distinguished managerial career which had begun in 1946. The Football

Association had originally wanted Jimmy Adamson, the ex-Burnley captain and assistant to Winterbottom, to take over the running of the national team. But Adamson refused the post and it was offered in turn to Alf Ramsey, the ex-Spurs and England defender who had recently

1962-1964
Final Hosts: Spain
Champions: Spain

managed Ipswich Town to the Second Division title and the League Championship in successive seasons (1960-61 & 1961-62). Ramsey accepted the job on condition that the archaic 'selection committee' system would be abolished and that he would have the exclusive right to select the team. The FA agreed. Ramsey took up the challenge and prophesied that he would one day lead England to the Championship of the World.

Meanwhile, England had it all to do in the European Nations' tournament. Ramsey's first official match in charge was the away leg against France in Paris, on 27 February 1963. His policy was to gamble on attack with a five-man forward line of proven goal-getters: John Connelly of Burnley, Bobby Tambling of Chelsea, Bobby Smith and Jimmy Greaves of Spurs and Bobby Charlton of Manchester United. That forward line did produce two goals - from Smith and Tambling. Unfortunately the French produced five of their own to take the tie with a 6-3

Ron Flowers, England's left-half.

Danny Blanchflower, *Northern Ireland.*

aggregate.

Wales also went out at the first stage, losing 3-1 to Hungary in Budapest, on 7 November 1962 and drawing 1-1 in the return match in Cardiff four months later.

Northern Ireland fared better than either of their British counterparts, recording two splendid and unexpected 2-0 victories over Poland in Katowice and Belfast, to progress to the second round. Cultured captain Danny Blanchflower, who had worn the green No.4 shirt more or less consecutively since his first appearance for Northern Ireland in October 1949, made his bow out of the international arena after the second leg. The Republic of Ireland also reached the second round, eliminating Iceland on a 5-3 aggregate.

Perhaps the biggest casualty of all in the opening round was 1962 World Cup runners-up Czechoslovakia, who had been among the hot favourites to lift the Nations' Cup. Instead they were dumped unceremoniously out of the tournament by East Germany. The German side won their home tie 2-1, on 21 November 1962, a close match settled by a Liebrecht penalty. In the second leg in Prague on 31 March '63, the

Germans battened down the hatches and defended their narrow lead. That match finished all-square at 1-1 and Czechoslovakia were out of the running.

In the second round Northern Ireland met Spain and achieved yet another marvellous result in the away leg in Bilbao on 30 May 1963. The 1-1 draw made the Irish side favourites to win the tie in the home leg in Belfast on 30 October. In the event Spain won the game, by a single goal.

The most remarkable performance of the second round was that of Luxembourg. Not only did they choose to play both legs of their tie against Holland in Amsterdam and Rotterdam respectively, they also drew the first game 1-1, and won the second 2-1. The Grand Duchy's heroes of the second game were striker Dimmer who scored both goals, and goalkeeper Nico Schmitt who finished the game with a dislocated shoulder. The result was one of the biggest upsets in European footballing history.

The plum tie of the second round was between the USSR and Italy. The first leg, played in rainy Moscow on 13 October 1963, attracted 102,000 spectators who witnessed a battle royal with Italy reduced to nine men in the first half. Striker Sormani was taken off with a head wound after just twelve minutes. Ponedelnik scored for the USSR in the 22nd minute when he latched onto a rebounding ball from the packed Italian penalty area. Then Pascutti was sent off after head-butting Dubinski. Sormani returned before the interval, but by then the Soviets had taken control of the game and Chislenko added a second as half time approached. The scoreline remained at 2-0.

The great Soviet goalkeeper Lev Yashin was recalled to the line-up for the rematch in Rome on 10 November, and coach Konstantin Beskov also strengthened his midfield in preparation for the defence of his slender lead. The USSR went ahead early in the game through Gusarov, and then threw everything into defence. Italy were given a penalty in the 57th minute. Mazzola

European Nations'
Cup Final
21 June 1964
Bernabau Stadium,
Madrid
Attendance: 120,000

SPAIN 2, USSR 1

Spain: Iribar; Rivilla, Calleja, Fuste, Olivella, Zoco, Amancio, Pereda, Marcellino, Suarez, Laperta.
Scorers: Pereda 6, Marcellino 84

USSR: Yashin; Chustikov, Mudrik, Voronin, Shesternjev, Anitchkin, Chislenko, Ivanov, Ponedelnik, Kornaev, Khusainov.
Scorer: Khusainov 8

struck it; Yashin saved it. Italy did equalise in the final minute, through Rivera, but by then the tie was lost.

Luxembourg almost pulled off another miracle in the quarter finals, taking Denmark to a third match after two splendid draws. Denmark won the decider - played in neutral Amsterdam - by a single goal from Ole Madsen who had scored all the previous Danish goals in the tie.

Spain played the Republic of Ireland, winning the home leg 5-1 and the away leg 2-0, and enjoying a far easier passage than they'd had against Northern Ireland in the previous round.

The USSR met Sweden, the form team of the moment, who were enjoying a long unbeaten run during which they had eliminated previous Nations' Cup finalists Yugoslavia from the current series. The first leg, played in Stockholm on 13 May 1964, ended in a 1-1 draw. Ivanov netted for the USSR and Kurre Hamrin equalised in the 87th minute.

Before the start of the return match, in Moscow on 27 May, Lev Yashin was presented with the European Footballer of the Year trophy. And, as if to underline his right to the title, he went on to put in yet another superb goalkeeping display, as Sweden attacked relentlessly from the start.

Yet it was the USSR who went ahead, through Ponedelnik shortly before half time. He added another in the 60th minute. Hamrin replied for Sweden and for a while it seemed that a Swedish revival was imminent. But when Voronin hit Russia's third the Swedish run was definitely at an end, as was their survival in the Nations' Cup.

In the fourth quarter final pairing Hungary despatched France with a 5-2 aggregate.

UEFA selected Spain as the host nation for the final stages, the games to be played in Barcelona and Madrid in late June 1964.

The USSR played Denmark in the Barcelona-based semi final on 17 June. Goals from Voronin, Ponedelnik and Ivanov sealed the Soviet's entry into their second final of the competition.

On the same day in Madrid, Spain played Hungary. Home advantage told and the host nation won 2-1 after extra time, with goals from Pereda and Amancio. Bene scored for Hungary.

The Third Place match was played in Barcelona on 20 June. Hungary, fielding six reserves, took the lead through Bene on 11 minutes. Denmark, shadowed by memories of a 6-0 thrashing by the Hungarians in their previous meeting, played well to stay in the game and were rewarded with an equaliser by Berthelsen in the 81st minute. The match went into extra time, during which Hungarian defender Novak scored twice, from the penalty spot and from a free-kick, to make the final score 3-1.

The final, between Spain and the USSR, was played in Madrid, on 21 June. 120,000 people turned out to see the spectacle, among them General Franco whose government had four years earlier refused the Spanish squad permission to travel to the USSR: an attitude which had since been relaxed.

The match proved a dour encounter. Spain took the lead on 6 minutes when Luis Suarez intercepted a pass out of the Soviet defence. He passed to Pereda, who was unmarked and had the simple task of slotting the ball home. Within two minutes the USSR had drawn level with a soft goal by Khusainov, his shot completely mishandled by 'keeper Iribar. The winning goal came in the 84th minute with a spectacular diving header from Marcellino which connected with a long cross by Pereda.

Spain were the new holders of the European Nations' Cup and former champions USSR had suffered their first defeat in the competition.

The third series saw the European Nations' Cup undergo a change of name to The European Championship. There was also a change in the structure of the qualifying tournament to accommodate the entry of 31 countries. The previous 1st and 2nd round two-leg, knock-out

1966-1968
Final Hosts: Italy
Champions: Italy

system was replaced by eight qualifying groups, each of which would be contested on a league basis. Seeding was also introduced for the first time, with one seeded nation per group.

The winners of each group would progress to the quarter finals which would be played on the two-leg, knock-out system. The host nation for the final stages would be chosen from the four semi final qualifiers.

Among the favourites for the title were England, the 1966 World Cup winners: Alf Ramsey's prophecy had become a reality and he had been knighted for his efforts. Now his squad were the seeded nation in Group 8 which also included Northern Ireland, Scotland (taking part for the first time) and Wales. This group also doubled as the Home International Championships for 1966-67 and 1967-68.

England duly won the group, but not without a scare or two along the way - chiefly from the 'Auld Enemy' Scotland. England had not been beaten in 19 matches (a run which included the World Cup success) when the two sides met at Wembley on 15 April 1967. It was also the first England v Scotland encounter since the summer

Denis Law.

of '66, and the match was dubbed 'Scotland's World Cup Final'. Thousands of tartan-clad supporters crossed the border and made their way south to Wembley.

Scotland's new team boss, Bobby Brown, was experimenting with his line-up which included Celtic's Ronnie Simpson in goal, winning his first full international cap at the age of 36.

The Scottish contingent were treated to a great game. Their side were on top form, inspired by the magical skills of Jim Baxter and the inventive wing-play of Bobby Lennox and Willie Wallace. They proved a real handful for the English defence which was decidely weakened when big Jack Charlton hobbled off with a broken toe.

Eventually, Denis Law opened the scoring - and so superior were the Scots that it looked as if the floodgates might open. In the circumstances England defended well, thanks to the class of Bobby Moore and his able lieutenants Alan Ball and Nobby Stiles. The final scoreline read 3-2 to Scotland, their remaining goals coming from Jim McCalliog and Bobby Lennox. England replied with strikes by Geoff Hurst and Jack Charlton who returned to the fray late in the game.

After that stirring victory Scotland looked to be in the driving seat and were favourites for the trip to Italy. They needed further victories over Wales and Northern Ireland to ensure that a single point in the last tie against England at Hampden Park would see them through.

But things went disastrously wrong for the Scots when they travelled to Belfast to take on Northern Ireland on 21 October 1967. A certain George Best was in top form for the Irish and he inspired the home side to a 1-0 win, the goal coming from Coventry City's Dave Clements.

On the same day England got their act together again with a 3-0 win against Wales in Cardiff - goals courtesy of Alan Ball, Bobby Charlton and Martin Peters. England eventually progressed to the quarter final stage, a single point ahead of Scotland.

George Best.

Reigning European Champions Spain also went through, after a close run race with Czecho-slovakia in Group One. The tie in Prague got off to an unfortunate start when the brass band played the old Republican Spanish national anthem instead of its replacement. The Czechs then proceeded to beat the Spanish by a single goal which can only be ascribed to goalkeeper error. Iribar completely mistimed his dive at Horvath's hopeful shot, and the ball flew over his back and into the net.

The return fixture in Madrid saw a much improved Spanish side record a 2-1 victory with goals from Pirri and Garate. Kuna hit a late reply for Czechoslovakia.

This was Spain's last game in the qualifying tournament. They were sitting on top of the group with 8 points, but their fate was still in the hands of others. Czechoslovakia were on 6 points, but with two games in hand: away to Turkey and at home to The Republic of Ireland.

Czechoslovakia were obviously confident of going through, but managed only a single point with a 0-0 draw against Turkey. And then an understrength Republic of Ireland side provided the shock of the group by notching up a famous

2-1 victory, with goals from Ray Treacy and Turlogh O'Connor. They even provided the Czech's goal too, when John Dempsey scored an unfortunate own goal.

Portugal were the firm favourites in Group Two, having enjoyed an unbeaten run at home since May 1964, and boasting one of the world's greatest players in Eusebio. But they were in for a surprise with the visit of Sweden to Lisbon for the first of their encounters. Eusebio scored first in the 20th minute and things seemed to be going to plan for Portugal. Twenty minutes later, a thirty yard shot from Inge Danielsson screamed into the back of the Portuguese net, and with just three minutes left Danielsson further stunned the home crowd by hitting the winner.

But neither of these sides were to progress to the quarter finals, that honour went to Bulgaria who won the group four points ahead of Portugal. The USSR won Group Three by the same margin, their only upset coming with a 1-0 defeat by Austria.

West Germany were making their first appearance in the championship and looked to have an easy passage to the next stage. After all, they had been World Cup runners-up to England in '66 and they were now drawn in the smallest group, Group Four, along with Albania and Yugoslavia. Predictably they won their first European

*Portugese hero **Eusebio**.*

Championship encounter against Albania by a 6-0 margin - but then lost 1-0 to Yugoslavia in Belgrade. In turn, Yugoslavia beat Albania 2-0, putting themselves firmly on top of the table.

Martin Peters put England ahead against Spain in Madrid.

qualifying stage, finishing second in Group Five, three points behind winners Hungary. In the deciding game Hungary were quite brilliant in disposing of the Germans with a 3-1 victory and a performance that smacked of the 'Magical Magyars' of the mid-50s. Janos Farkas was the outstanding player and scored all three of Hungary's goals.

Italy won the Group Six contest with the widest points margin (5) in the entire competition. In fact, they dropped only a single point, in a 2-2 draw with Switzerland.

Group Seven was a close-run thing with Poland, Belgium and

The return West Germany v Yugoslavia fixture, the Germans' opportunity to restore their challenge, was played in pouring rain at the Volksparkstadion in Hamburg. The opportunity was seized and West Germany won 3-1.

Yugoslavia duly won their next game with Albania, by a 4-0 margin - leaving West Germany needing to beat the Albanians in Tirana to be sure of qualification. But, as the Germans piled on the pressure, Albania defended magnificently and to the delight of the 21,000 crowd the scoreline remained at 0-0. West Germany were out, and the Yugoslavians could hardly believe their good fortune.

East Germany were also eliminated at the

France all level-pegging on seven points with only the France v Luxembourg fixture left to complete. France had a superior goal difference and needed only a draw to be sure. In the event France won by a comfortable 3-1 margin with a hat-trick from Loubet. Klein scored for the Grand Duchy, Luxembourg's only successful strike of the campaign.

The quarter finals saw England drawn against Spain - the World Champions v the European Champions. A Bobby Charlton goal gave England a 1-0 victory at Wembley.

England's defence, intent on securing that slender lead, were magnificent in the return match in Madrid a month later and goals by

European Championship Final
8 June 1968
Olympic Stadium, Rome
Attendance: 88,000

ITALY 1, YUGOSLAVIA 1
(after extra time)

Italy: Zoff; Burgnich, Facchetti, Ferrini, Guarneri, Castano, Domenghini, Juliano, Anastasi, Lodetti, Prati
Scorer: Domenghini 81

Yugoslavia: Pantelic; Fazlagic, Damjanovic, Pavlovic, Paunovic, Holcer, Petkovic, Acimovic, Musemic, Trivic, Dzajic.
Scorer: Dzajic 40

Replay
10 June 1968
Olympic Stadium, Rome
Attendance: 70,000

ITALY 2, YUGOSLAVIA 0

Italy: Zoff; Burgnich, Facchetti, Rosato, Guarneri, Salvadore, Domenghini, Mazzola, Anastasi, De Sisti, Riva
Scorers: Riva 13, Anastasi 30

Yugoslavia: Pantelic; Fazlagic, Damjanovic, Pavlovic, Paunovic, Holcer, Hosic, Acimovic, Musemic, Trivic, Dzajic.

Geoff Hurst *clinched third place for England in Rome.*

Martin Peters and Norman Hunter gave England a 2-1 victory. Amancio replied for Spain.

France were halted by Yugoslavia who recorded a 6-2 aggregate victory. Italy went close to elimination with a 3-2 defeat by Bulgaria in Sofia, and a spirited performance was required in Naples to secure a 2-0 escape act.

The USSR were also beaten in their away leg, 2-0 by Hungary, but they too came back to grab a semi final placing with a 3-0 victory in the return match in Moscow.

UEFA decided that Italy would host the final stages between 5-8 June. The semi finals saw Italy take on the USSR in Naples, and England v Yugoslavia in Florence. The first game was a defensive stalemate which went into extra time and still stood at 0-0. Incredibly, the tie was settled in Italy's favour on the lucky toss of a coin.

England, still reeling from a tough 'friendly' encounter with West Germany just a few days earlier (West Germany had won 1-0), met a far fresher Yugoslavia in Florence. It was a tough game for the English side, made even tougher when Alan Mullery earned the unwanted distinction of being the first English player ever to be sent off in an international match, following a robust challenge on Trivic and an Oscar-worthy display of histrionics by the Yugoslav player. The scales were tipped by the incident and Yugoslavia won the match when Dragan Dzajic scored in the last minute.

England had the consolation of winning the Third place match at Rome's Olympic Stadium, on 8 June. A goal each from Bobby Charlton and Geoff Hurst saw the beating of the USSR (2-0) in a particularly good game.

Later that day the final, between Italy and Yugoslavia, was staged at the same venue. Italy were somewhat weakened by injury and Yugoslavia proved the dominant team, going ahead through Dzajic after 40 minutes. In the 81st minute Italy were given a free-kick which was quickly taken by Domenghini and ended up in the Yugoslavian net. The referee, Dienst, who had been busily pushing back the Yugoslav wall when the kick was taken, awarded the goal despite the protests of the defending side. The goal stood and the game went into extra time, after which the scoreline remained at 1-1.

The replay took place in Rome two days later, by which time Italy had completely reorganised their forces. Yugoslavia, fielding virtually the same side, looked a different, dispirited outfit. Italy took command of things and won the match 2-0 with goals from Riva and Anastasi.

For the second time the host nation had won the championship.

Thirty-two nations entered the 1970-72 series which was run on the same basis as its predecessor, it was also the first European Championship in which substitutes were permitted.

By then England had lost their grip on the

1970-1972
Final Hosts: Belgium
Champions: West Germany

World Cup after an epic quarter final encounter with West Germany in Mexico in the summer of 1970; and the Jules Rimet trophy was now in the permanent possession of Brazil, in recognition of their third success in the tournament.

Sir Alf Ramsey's leadership of the English sqaud was drawing to its close. Although his team won the European Championship Group Three campaign unbeaten, they had made rather heavy weather of the two matches against Switzerland. Indeed,

Martin Chivers opened the scoring in Athens.

England's winning 3-2 scoreline in the away leg, in Basle, was completed only by courtesy an own goal from Weibel.

The return leg at Wembley should have been a cut-and-dried affair in favour of the home side, but the Swiss scored first through Odermatt, and only a Mike Summerbee equaliser saved England's blushes. Nevertheless, qualification was secured in the final match of the group with a 2-0 victory over Greece, in Athens on 1 December 1971. Martin Chivers and Geoff Hurst scored the goals that took England to the quarter

finals.

Wales were drawn in Group One along with Czechoslovakia, Finland and Romania. Czechoslovakia were favourites to win this qualifying campaign, but their team selection had been thrown into disarray following the banning of several World Cup stars, who had alledgedly indulged in certain commercial activities which had been frowned upon by the authorities. The hastily gathered new squad was quite unprepared for the opening home leg against Finland, in Prague. The supporters stayed away in droves and a mere 5,000 spectators watched a disappointing 1-1 draw.

After their next match, a 3-2 away victory over Wales, the Czechoslovakian authorities relented and the banned players were reinstated. Yet that poor start against Finland was the root cause of the Czechs' failure to reach the quarter finals. In the end that honour fell to Romania who went through on goal difference.

Hungary won Group Three, ahead of Bulgaria, France and Norway, in perhaps the toughest, most evenly-matched contest of all.

Northern Ireland were in Group Four with Cyprus, the USSR and Spain. The Soviets made all the running and ended the qualifying campaign unbeaten at the top of the table.

Scotland finished third in Group Five, winning all three home legs against Denmark, Portugal and Belgium - but losing all the corresponding away fixtures. The fate of the group was settled in the last game, in Lisbon, between Portugal and Belgium. Portugal needed to win by a three goal margin; Belgium would go through with just a draw. The Portuguese attacked constantly, but it was the visitors who scored first, through

Lambert after 61 minutes. A late penalty for Portugal was converted by Peres, but the 1-1 scoreline saw Belgium progress to the quarter finals

Italy went through from Group Six, which also included the Republic of Ireland, Sweden and Austria. The Irish began with a respectable 1-1 draw with Sweden in Dublin, but then proceeded to lose all their remaining fixtures to finish bottom of the table.

Yugoslavia qualified from Group Seven. Beginning with a 1-1 draw away to Holland, they then strung three consecutive victories together: 2-0 at home to Holland; 2-1 away to East Germany; and 2-0 away to Luxembourg. This seven point cushion proved extremely useful in the latter stages of the programme. The deciding factor in the group was Holland's excellent 3-2 victory over East Germany, a match notable for a fine performance from Holland's Johan Cruyff. He dominated the game and created all three of the Dutch goals, further adding to his fast-growing reputation as one of the world's finest players. The result left Yugoslavia needing to gain just two points from two remaining fixtures, a task they managed - but only just- with 0-0 draws against both East Germany and Luxembourg (a result which provided the Grand Duchy's only point in the tournament).

West Germany were widely expected to win Group Eight with ease. Albania, Poland and Turkey were their opponents, of whom Poland posed the only serious threat. However, Germany's opening encounter at home to Turkey provided one of the shocks of the tournament.

Johan Cruyff, one of the world's finest.

Turkey scored first through Kamarun who capitalised on a defensive error by Weber in the 16th minute. Gerd Muller equalised with a penalty in the 37th minute. But after that, try as they might, Germany could not take command and at the end of 90 minutes the scoreline remained at 1-1.

Albania provided West Germany's next opposition, in Tirana, and memories of that shock 0-0 draw between the two countries in the previous European Championship must have caused a few nervous moments in the German camp. In the event they won 1-0 with a goal from Muller. After that, West Germany began to look its old, efficient self and qualification was clinched with a 3-1 away win against Poland and a 0-0 draw in the return match.

England met West Germany in the quarter finals. The first leg was played at Wembley on 29 April 1972. Like Czechoslovakia earlier in the campaign, West German football was now in the midst of internal turmoil, following accusations of bribery within the Bundesliga. The resulting inquiry meant several key players were unavailable for national team selection by manager Helmut Schoen. However, they did have Franz Beckenbauer and Gunter Netzer in midfield - and between them they commanded the match.

In the first half Hoeness opened the scoring for West Germany. Francis Lee equalised early in the second, then a Netzer penalty put the Germans back in front. The matter was finally sealed at 3-1 by a goal from Gerd Muller.

The return fixture, in Berlin on 13 May, turned out to be a rather dour affair with Germany

European
Championship Final
18 June 1972
Heysel Stadium,
Brussels
Attendance: 43,437

**WEST GERMANY 3
USSR 0**

West Germany: Maier;
Hottges,
Schwarzenbeck,
Beckenbauer, Brietner,
Hoeness, Wimmer,
Netzer, Heynckes,
Muller, Kremers
Scorers: Muller (2),
Wimmer

USSR: Rudakov;
Dzodzuashvili,
Khurtsilava, Kaplichny,
Istomin, Troshkin,
Kolotov, Baidachni,
Konkov (Dolmatov),
Banishevski
(Kozinkievits),
Onishenko

*Triumphant West German captain, **Franz Bechenbauer.***

revival.

The USSR beat Yugoslavia with a 3-0 aggregate and the semi final line-up was completed when Hungary beat Romania, although they took three matches before breaking the deadlock.

Belgium was chosen to host the final stages. They met West Germany in the semi final in Antwerp, on 14 June 1972, in front of 60,000 spectators. But the great Gerd Muller yet again demonstrated his goal-getting genius, with an astonishing header which completely bamboozled 'keeper Piot in the 20th minute. Muller scored again late in the second half and Polleunis replied for Belgium. But West Germany were through to their first European Championship final.

defending throughout - once more under the generalship of Franz Beckenbauer - to achieve a 0-0 draw. England were out. And amid ever increasing criticisms of a negative style of play, Sir Alf Ramsey's days in charge were now definitely numbered.

Belgium's stolid defensive tactics were rewarded with a 0-0 draw in the away leg of their quarter final against Italy. The return was played at the Park Astrid, home of Anderlecht, which was packed to the rafters with 38,000 spectators. It was a tough game with Belgium determined to cling on to their advantage. They went ahead on 23 minutes through Van Moer who was to be stretchered off with a broken leg twenty mintues later, following a vicious tackle by Bertini. The incident served to increase Belgium's resolve and with 19 minutes left to play they went two up with a Van Himst goal. Riva replied from the penalty spot, but by then it was too late for an Italian

They were joined by the USSR who beat Hungary 1-0 with a goal from Konkov. In contrast to the Belgium/West Germany match this encounter, in Brussels, was attended by just 3,500 spectators.

Belgium beat Hungary 2-1 in the Third Place match, played in Liege on 17 June. Lambert and Van Himst scored for Belgium; Ku replied for Hungary with a penalty.

The final, between the USSR and West Germany, took place in Brussels on the 18th. The incredible combination of Beckenbauer, Netzer and Muller proved too much for the Soviets. Muller scored twice and Wimmer once for a 3-0 scoreline.

The West German side were now unquestionably masters of European football, and two years later they became masters of the world, beating Holland 2-1 in the 1974 World Cup final in Munich.

The 1976 finals in Yugoslavia, the first international competition to be held in an Eastern Bloc country, were to prove the finest and most exciting to date. But first came the long and winding road of qualification.

England were drawn in Group One, together with Cyprus, Czechoslovakia and Portugal. Things had come to a head for Sir Alf Ramsey after England failed to qualify for the 1974 World Cup finals - no thanks to that well remembered 1-1 draw against Poland at Wembley in 1973. He presided over just two more internationals after that and was then replaced by 'caretaker' boss Joe Mercer.

Ramsey's record remains the most impressive of any England manager. Between February 1963 and October 1973 he was in charge of 113 games of which England won 68, drew 28 and lost just 17. Under his leadership England had become World Champions in '66; European Championship semi finalists in 1968, quarter finalists in 1972; and they had won nine Home International Championships (including three shared titles).

Joe Mercer took over for seven matches before Don Revie took the reins on a permanent basis. Like Ramsey before him Revie had enjoyed a successful playing career followed by an equally successful period in club management. He had built Leeds United into one of the country's top clubs and had led them out

1974-1976
Final Hosts: Yugoslavia
Champions: Czechoslovakia

of the Second Division to twice win the League Championship, in 1969 and 1974, the FA Cup in 1972, the Football League Cup in 1968 and the European Fairs Cup in 1968 and 1971. But Revie was not destined to find much glory in the England hot seat. He remained as manager for just 29 matches in which he constantly experimented with the team selection and never really achieved a balanced line-up.

However, his first match in charge ended on an optimistic note, with a 3-0 victory over Czechoslovakia at Wembley in the opening match of Group One, on 30 October 1974. The goals came from Colin Bell (2) and Mick Channon.

England's next European qualifier was also played at Wembley, on 20 November, against Portugal. But this time things did not go so well for the home team. The Portuguese won the midfield battle and defended exceptionally well to achieve a 0-0 draw.

Following a heartening 2-0 friendly win for England over West Germany (England's 100th Wembley international), Cyprus were the next Championship visitors to Wembley. They were beaten 5-0, with Newcastle United's Malcolm 'SuperMac' Macdonald scoring all five.

Colin Bell – *2 goals against Czechs.*

Malcolm Macdonald

Czechoslovakia, having recovered from that opening defeat, next began to chase England with two high scoring victories in succession - 4-0 against Cyprus and 5-0 against Portugal. England collected two more points in Cyprus with a 1-0 win from a Kevin Keegan goal. Czechoslovakia further strengthened their cause by beating England 2-1 in Bratislava on 30 October 1975. Then they joined England at the top of the table following a 1-1 draw against Portugal.

If England were now to qualify they needed to win their last encounter, against Portugal, by three goals or more. It didn't happen. A 1-1 draw left England on eight points, leaving the Czechs with the relatively easy job of beating Cyprus. They did so with a 3-0 scoreline, to progress to the quarter finals.

Scotland and Northern Ireland also failed to qualify. Northern Ireland finished a creditable second, with six points, behind Yugoslavia in Group Three. Scotland finished third in Group Four, with seven points, behind qualifiers Spain and second placed Romania.

The British success story of the 1974-76 series belongs to Wales, managed by Mike Smith. They were drawn in Group Two with Austria, Hungary and Luxembourg. After losing their first encounter, away to Austria in Vienna on 4 September 1974, the Welsh recorded a

*Welsh wizard **John Toshack**.*

magnificent 2-0 home win over Hungary with goals from John Toshack and Arfon Griffiths. A 5-0 home drubbing of Luxembourg and a splendid 2-1 away victory over Hungary (goals by Toshack and Mahoney) were followed by a 3-1 away win against Luxembourg which put Wales on top of the group with 8 points, but only one game left - against Austria.

Austria posed the most serious threat with 5 points and three games left to play. When they met Hungary in Budapest it was the 120th meeting between the two sides and Austria had not won the away fixture in fifteen seasons. Thankfully for the watching Welsh, the match brought yet another defeat, 2-1. But Austria then beat Luxembourg by a comfortable 6-2 margin, which put them on 7 points, one behind Wales. All hinged on the last fixture in the group – Wales v Austria, in Wrexham on 19 November 1975.

Wales needed only a draw to go through, but they did better than that. Local hero Arfon Griffiths became a national hero when he scored the only goal of the game to ensure Wales of a quarter final berth.

Holland won a close run race in Group Five, ahead of Poland on goal difference, with Italy and Finland bringing up the rear. The USSR progressed from Group Six, leaving the Republic of Ireland, Switzerland and Turkey in their wake. The Irish side had enjoyed one glorious moment of triumph, when they beat the USSR 3-0 in Dublin with a hat-trick from QPR's Don Givens.

In Group Seven two unexpected draws by Iceland 1-1 away to East Germany and 0-0 at home to France proved the fly-in-the-ointment for both those countries. The dropped points effectively allowed Belgium to top the group and progress to the next stage.

Reigning European Champions and 1974 World Champions West Germany were drawn in Group Eight, with Bulgaria, Greece and Malta. But as in the 1970-72 series things began badly for the group favourites.

Greece performed magnificently in the home leg in Athens, to twice take the lead. West Germany equalised both goals and the scoreline remained at 2-2. Then came a narrow 1-0 win away to Malta and another draw, 1-1 this time, at home to Bulgaria.

The next match, the home leg against Greece, on 11 October '75 in Dusseldorf, was also something of a nightmare for West Germany. The Greek side, despite a shock 2-0 defeat by Malta, were still in with a slim chance of qualification providing they took both points against the Germans. Once again Greece played brilliantly and completely dominated the first half. Then West Germany were fortunate to go ahead through Heynckes early in the second period. Delikaris equalised for Greece in the 88th minute and the match ended at 1-1. West Germany had ridden their luck, and they knew it. A return to form saw them safely through the remaining two games - a 1-0 win over Bulgaria and an 8-0 thrashing of Malta. The reigning champions were through.

The Welsh dream faded in the quarter finals against Yugoslavia. Employing

Ondrus *scored for both sides in Zagreb.*

cautious defensive tactics in Zagreb, Wales went down 2-0 with Vuktovic and Popivoda scoring for the Yugoslavs. In the return game at Ninian Park, Cardiff, things began badly for Wales and were to get even worse. Katalinski opened the scoring for the visitors with a penalty; Ian Evans equalised for Wales. Then to the frustration of the crowd, the East German referee Rudi Glockner disallowed a Welsh goal because of dangerous play. Beer cans flew, a pitch invasion followed and play was suspended. After the restart another Welsh goal was disallowed and a Terry Yorath penalty attempt was saved by 'keeper Maric. From the moment he blew the final whistle, referee Glockner required a police escort from the pitch.

West Germany drew 1-1 with Spain in Madrid, but went through to the semi finals with an emphatic 2-0 home victory in the second leg. Holland despatched Belgium with a 7-1 aggregate and Czechoslovakia, who had eliminated England at the group stage, now put out the USSR - thanks to a fine 2-0 home victory. The return was a far more difficult affair which ended at 2-2.

Yugoslavia was selected to host the final stages and were drawn to play West Germany in Belgrade. With Czechoslovakia drawn against Holland in Zagreb, the stage looked set for a repeat of the '74 World Cup final between Holland and West Germany.

But, during a driving rainstorm, Holland's team of superstars were outplayed by the Czechs who had tightened up their defence and hardly allowed the Dutch class to show at all. Ondrus scored first for Czecho-slovakia with a mighty header, but soon afterwards he was guilty of deflecting the ball into his own goal to

European
Championship Final
20 June 1976
Belgrade
Attendance: 45,000

**CZECHOSLOVAKIA
2, WEST GERMANY 2**
(after extra time)
**Czechoslovakia won
5-3 on penalties**

Czechoslovakia: Viktor;
Dobias (Vesely F),
Pivarnik, Ondrus,
Capkovic, Gogh, Moder,
Panenka, Svehlic
(Jurkemik), Masny,
Nehoda.
Scorers: Svehlic, Nehoda

West Germany: Maier;
Vogts, Beckenbauer,
Schwarzenbeck, Dietz,
Bonhof, Wimmer (Flohe),
Muller D, Beer (Bongartz),
Hoeness, Holzenbein.
Scorers: Muller,
Holzenbein

even up the score. Then came three sendings-off by Welsh referee Clive Thomas. First went Pollak for Czechoslovakia for a foul on Neeskens; next went Neeskens for a grim tackle on Nehoda; then Van Hanegem received his marching orders for dissent. The game went into extra time during which Nehoda restored Czechoslovakia's lead, and Moder put the result beyond doubt at 3-1 in the final minute.

Next day, 17 June 1976, 75,000 spectators watched Yugoslavia take on West Germany in Belgrade. The home side were magnificent in the first half. They ran the world champions' defence ragged and scored the opening goal, through Popivoda from a long, high cross by Oblak. They struck again when Dzajic capitalised on 'keeper Maier's weak clearance of a Zungul cross. Time and again the Yugoslavian attack ripped through the West German defence, but no more goals were forthcoming in the first half.

The second half told another story altogether. Yugolsavia seemed content to sit on their two goal advantage. Consequently, West Germany were able to attack with more conviction. Heinz Flohe came on as a substitute and scored West Germany's first, long-awaited, goal. And a second substitute, Dieter Muller, was to prove even more effective. He headed the equaliser which ultimately took the game into extra time. Muller also scored the two goals which completed a remarkable rescue act and took West Germany to their second European Championship final.

In the Third Place match, played on 19 June in Zagreb, Holland beat Yugoslavia 3-2 after extra

Rene Van der Kerkhoff.

time. Holland were without Cruyff and Neeskens, but nevertheless showed their true class. Their goals came from Geels (2) and Van der Kerkhoff. Katalinski and Dzajic scored for the hosts.

The final, between Czechoslovakia and West Germany, played in Belgrade on 20 June before a crowd of 45,000, was a classic. At first Czechoslovakia looked the stronger side and scored first when goalkeeper Maier failed to clear a shot from Svehlic. Nehoda pushed the ball back to Svehlic who hit it home. Then Franz Beckenbauer - making his 100th international appearance - made a poor job of clearing a Masny free-kick and Dobias was on hand to hit it home via the crowded penalty area. Before half time Dieter Muller pulled one back for Germany, heading home a cross from Bonhof.

Fighting hard to cling on to their lead, Czechoslovakia grew decidedly weary, and eventually the relentless German pressure paid off with the equalising goal from Holzenbein who headed in a Bonhof corner. For the fourth time in the finals, the game went into extra time, after which the score still remained at 2-2.

For the first time a European Championship final was to be decided by a penalty shoot-out. The stalemate was broken when Uli Hoeness shot over the bar for a German miss. Then Panenka chipped the ball over Maier and into the net for Czechoslovakia's victory.

The sixth series saw a vast change in the structure of the tournament. The final stage would now be decided via a two group system split among the eight qualifying nations. The winners of each group would contest the final, the runners-up would play-off for third place. For the first time the host nation was chosen in advance and would receive automatic entry to the finals, as happened in the World Cup. The first country so honoured was to be Italy. The remaining 31 entrants were divided into seven qualifying groups - three of five teams, four of four teams.

England were drawn in Group One together with Bulgaria, Denmark and, together for the first time in an international competition, Northern Ireland and the Republic of Ireland. The first leg between the Irish sides took place in Dublin on 20 September 1978. It ended in stalemate at 0-0.

Meanwhile, England were playing Denmark in Copenhagen. The English squad was now under the managership of Ron Greenwood, the former Chelsea, Bradford Park Avenue, Brentford and Fulham defender who had gone on to enjoy a successful coaching and managerial career, most notably with West Ham United (where he had nurtured the talents of 1966 World Cup heroes Bobby Moore, Martin Peters and Geoff Hurst). His predecessor Don Revie had left under a cloud of controversy and was now working in the United Arab Emirates.

Greenwood's early days in charge produced arguably the best English squad since the glory days of '66. It harnessed the talents of Kevin Keegan, by then with SV Hamburg, Ray Wilkins, Trevor Brooking, Steve Coppell and Trevor Francis.

Trevor Francis.

The match in Copenhagen was a real ding-dong battle. England were two ahead after 23 minutes, both goals coming from Keegan. Denmark levelled the score within the space of two minutes. In the second half England took control once more with goals from Everton's Bob

Latchford and Liverpool's Phil Neal. Denmark struck again in the last minute and the final score was 4-3 to England.

England went on to win Group One unbeaten with only one point dropped, making sure of qualification with a 5-1 drubbing of Northern Ireland in Belfast on 17 October 1979. Northern Ireland finished second in the table, the Republic of Ireland third.

Belgium went through from Group Two, which also included Scotland, Austria, Norway and Portugal. The Scottish campaign, under Jock Stein's management, fell apart towards the end but it did finish with a flourish - a 4-1 home victory over Portugal.

Wales were drawn in Group Seven together with Malta, Turkey and West Germany, the obvious favourites for qualification. However, while Wales began with confident victories over Malta (7-0) and Turkey (1-0), the German side were experiencing some unexpected jitters. In fact they only just held on for a goalless draw against Malta in Ta'Qali, and were fortunate that two Maltese goals had been disallowed. Then came another 0-0 draw away to Turkey.

The tide turned for West Germany when they played Wales in Wrexham on 2 May 1979. They recorded an efficient 2-0 victory with goals from Zimmermann and Fischer. The return fixture in Koln, on 17 November, was an even more emphatic victory for West Germany, 5-1. From then on the Germans took control of the group and eventually qualified. Wales finished third behind Turkey.

1978 World Cup runners-up Holland topped Group Four ahead of Poland, East Germany, Switzerland and Iceland. Reigning European Champions Czechoslovakia qualified from Group Five, leaving France, Sweden and Luxembourg to fight another day.

The most remarkable performance of the qualifying competition came from Greece who, despite starting badly with defeats by Finland (away) and the USSR (away), hit top form in the return against the Finns to win 8-1. Next came a 0-0 draw in Hungary and a 1-0 home victory over the USSR which virtually assured Greece of qualification.

Another Group Six surprise saw former European Championship experts USSR finishing at the foot of the table.

The eight qualifiers

Ray Wilkins

travelled to Italy for the two-group quarter final competition which kicked-off on 11 June 1980. The two group winners would progress to the final, while the two second placed teams would play-off for third place.

The first match in Group One saw West Germany beat Czechoslovakia 1-0 in Rome. Then Holland were fortunate to beat Greece in Naples: the match was won only after the Greek 'keeper Konstantinou had tripped Nanninga to give away a penalty, duly converted by Kist.

A hat-trick by Klaus Allofs gave West

Germany a 3-1 lead over Holland, with just 23 minutes left to play of their clash in Naples. The Dutch staged a remarkable revival and pulled one back through Willi Van Der Kerkhof in the 86th minute. Germany only just managed to hold on to the lead, but they had four precious points in the bag.

The Greek dream ended in tragedy with a 3-1 defeat by Czechoslovakia, which effectively ended Greek hopes of any further glory in the competition. Czechoslovakia then drew 1-1 with Holland, thereby ensuring that West Germany could not be caught. In the last match of the group West Germany drew 0-0 with Greece.

In Group Two England played Belgium in Turin. The result - a 1-1 draw - was somewhat overshadowed by the behaviour of a certain section of the English support: the beginnings of a poor reputation which was to grow in the coming years, eventually culminating in the 1985 UEFA ban on English clubs from European competition.

In the first half the Belgians employed the offside trap to near perfection, much to the frustration of the English attack. But then Ray Wilkins scored an inspired goal generally considered to be one of the finest in English international history. He first intercepted a clearance out of the Belgian defence, then lobbed the ball over the advancing pack and slipped through them to receive his own pass before beating 'keeper Pfaff by shooting just under the bar.

European Championship Final
22 June 1980
Olympic Stadium, Rome
Attendance: 47,864

WEST GERMANY 2, BELGIUM 1

West Germany: Schumacher; Briegel (Cullmann 55), Forster K, Dietz, Schuster, Rummenigge, Hrubesch, Muller, Aloffs, Stielike, Kaltz.
Scorer: Hrubesch 10, 89

Belgium: Pfaff; Gerets, Millecamps, Meeuws, Renquin, Cools, Van der Eycken, Van Moer, Mommens, Van der Elst, Ceulemans.
Scorer: Van der Eycken 71 pen

Belgium replied within minutes, through Cuelemans from a Van Moer corner. It was then that the worst of the crowd trouble erupted, involving elements of the English and Italian contingents. The police, using tear gas, stepped in to quell the outbreak. Unfortunately the gas also affected the players and play was held up for six minutes. Late in the game Tony Woodcock found the net, but his strike was ruled offside and the result stood at 1-1.

Meanwhile, Italy met Spain in Milan. The match was played in an unusual atmosphere - generated by the hostile reception of the home side by the fans in the wake of a bribery scandal within the Italian League. No doubt this contributed to the poor performance of the Italians: the match ended goalless.

Spain then lost 2-1 to Belgium, while England were playing Italy in Turin. Although England were the better team they lost by the only goal of the game scored by Tardelli in the 83rd minute. The result meant that England, stuck on one point, stood no chance of progressing, although they did increase their points tally by winning 2-1 against Spain in their last match of the tournament.

The fight for top spot was between Belgium and Italy. Both were on three points, both had the same goal difference. But Belgium had scored two more goals than Italy and were therefore in the driving seat, requiring only a draw. Italy had to win to go through.

The game, played in Rome, developed into a rough-house with fouls coming thick and fast from both sides. Belgium defended well as the Italians seemed uninspired in attack. The game ended 0-0 and Belgium went through to the final.

Czechoslovakia eventually won the Third Place match against Italy, but the outcome was settled with a penalty-shoot-out after the score had remained at 1-1 after extra time.

The final between Belgium and West Germany was played on 22 June 1980, at the Olympic Stadium in Rome. The Germans were dominant from the start, going close in the 4th minute with only a finger-tip save from Belgian 'keeper Pfaff denying Muller. In the tenth minute the youngster Bernd Schuster played a delicate one-two with Allofs and then floated the ball into the path of Hrubesch who controlled it with his chest before shooting past Pfaff for the opening goal.

*The winning goal came from **Hrubesch**.*

The second half saw an injury to German midfielder Hans-Peter Briegel who had been the star player in the match. He was replaced by Cullmann, but the substitution seemed to upset West Germany's equilibrium and Belgium began to get back into the game. In the 71st minute Van Der Eycken equalised from the penalty spot after Van Der Elst had been brought down by Stielike. Then with just a minute remaining, and the match seemingly destined for extra time, Hrubesch scored the winner from a Rummenigge corner. West Germany had won their second European Championship.

France was chosen as the finals venue for the 1982-84 series and UEFA made two more changes to the structure of the tournament. A proper semi final stage was introduced, to be contested by the top two teams in each of the final groups. The somewhat redundant Third

1982-1984
Final Hosts: France
Champions: France

Place match was abolished. Once again 32 nations entered the contest.

England were in Group Three with Denmark, Greece, Hungary and Luxembourg. Ron Greenwood had resigned as manager following the 1982 World Cup finals in Spain - in which England had failed to progress beyond the second stage. He had been succeeded by Bobby Robson, a former England international who had enjoyed a reasonably successful club career with Fulham and West Bromwich Albion, followed by a sensational spell in club management with Ipswich Town, Alf Ramsey's earlier seat of power.

Robson led the Suffolk club through its second great period, in which they won the FA Cup in 1978 and the UEFA Cup in 1981 and were England's second most consistent club, after Liverpool. He also instigated a youth policy at Ipswich through which many talented young players were developed. Robson later became manager of the England 'B' squad, from which position he became the natural successor to Ron Greenwood.

But Robson's England, which admittedly was going through a period of transition, was to be overshadowed in the 1982-84 European Championship, by Denmark.

Danish football had gradually emerged as a potent force since the introduction of semi-professionalism in their domestic game in 1978.

A year earlier their star player Allan Simonsen had been voted European Player Of The Year for his performances with Bayern Munich.

The first Denmark v England game was played in Copenhagen on 22 September 1982. Although Trevor Francis opened the scoring after 7 minutes, England looked the less confident side. Allan Hansen equalised for Denmark with a penalty in the 69th minute. But England seemed to be riding their luck when Francis hit a second with ten minutes left. A goalmouth scramble led to Denmark's second equaliser, scored by Jesper Olsen, in the last seconds.

By the time the two sides met for the second leg, at Wembley a year later, England was on top of the table with 8 points, Denmark second with 7. Both knew that this was the crunch match. Denmark was the dominant side and put the emphasis on attack - they won thanks to an Allan Simonsen penalty in the 39th minute, after Phil Neal had handled the ball. From then on Denmark never looked back and won the group one point ahead of England.

Scotland won their opening Group One encounter, 2-0 against East Germany at Hampden Park, but failed after that to record any further wins in the qualifiers. They finished fourth behind Belgium, Switzerland and East Germany. Belgium won the group a clear three points ahead of the pack. Wales fared rather better, finishing second in Group Four, a single point behind qualifiers Yugoslavia.

Northern Ireland began badly in Group Six, losing 2-0 away to Austria. But in their next match, in rainy Belfast on 17 November 1982, they beat West Germany 1-0 thanks to an Ian Stewart goal in the 18th minute. By the end of the campaign the Irish side failed to qualify only on goal difference behind the Germans.

Portugal qualified for the finals for the first time, winning the Group Two campaign and despatching the USSR, Poland and Finland. Romania topped the Group Five table ahead of Sweden, Czechoslovakia, Italy and Cyprus.

The final qualifying berth was claimed by Spain, who won Group Seven, although they did leave it to the last minute. In the final match of the group Spain needed to beat Malta at home by eleven clear goals in order to qualify ahead of Holland. Despite Malta's poor showing in the

masterful dominance of the finals. In France's next encounter, against Belgium in Nantes, he struck a hat-trick in a 5-0 victory. The other goals were scored by Giresse and Fernandez. Three days later Platini scored his second hat-trick of the championship in the 3-2 win over Yugoslavia

Trevor Francis scores against Denmark.

competition so far, this was a seemingly impossible task. Yet Spain achieved precisely that target with a 12-1 scoreline, the last goal scored with four minutes to go.

The finals were held in France between 12-27 June 1984. France entered the tournament in the opening match, in Group One, against Denmark at the Parc des Princes, in Paris. It was a good game with attacking flair coming from both sides. It was also an extremely physical encounter, in which Allan Simonsen suffered a badly broken leg shortly before half-time following a poorly timed tackle by Leroux. Later the French full-back Amoros was sent off for head-butting Jesper Olsen.

French captain and European Footballer Of The Year, Michel Platini, eventually resolved the deadlock by firing home the winner in the 77th minute.

This was only the beginning of Platini's

in St. Etienne. The six points took France through to the semi finals. Denmark, second in the group with 4 points, also progressed to the semis.

Spain were on the rebound from their poor showing in the 1982 World Cup, which they had hosted. The Spanish squad had a lot to prove and did it in some style by topping Group Two on goal difference ahead of their neighbours Portugal. Unexpectedly, West Germany were left out of the running, along with Romania.

The France v Portugal semi final, played in Lyon on 23 June, was a classic and ranks among the best in European Championship history. Platini was once again the dominant figure and France seemed to have the edge in the opening period. They went ahead after 24 minutes through Domergue and still held the lead at half time with the Portugese beginning to tire.

But in the second half Portugal revived and began to take over the proceedings. In the 73rd

European
Championship Final
27 June 1984
Parc des Princes, Paris
Attandance: 47,368

FRANCE 2, SPAIN 0

France: Bats; Battiston (Amoros), Le Roux, Bossis, Domergue, Giresse, Platini, Tigana, Fernandez, Lacombe (Genghini), Bellone.
Scorers: Platini 56, Bellone 90

Spain: Arconada; Uriquiaga, Salva (Roberto), Gallego, Camacho, Francisco, Julio Alberto (Sarabia), Senor, Victor, Carrasco, Santillana

minute their efforts were rewarded when Jordao headed home a Chalana cross for the equaliser. Platini went close on several occasions before the whistle blew for time, but still the score remained at 1-1.

The match moved into extra time and still Portugal pressed for the winner. Then, in the 97th minute, Jordao again met a Chalana cross. This time he volleyed the ball past Bats to give Portugal the lead. But France were not yet beaten.

With just six minutes to go Domergue scored his second to bring the scores level again. Then in the last minute, the inevitable Platini, who had scored in every round so far, met a cross from Tigana and hit home the winner. France were in the final for the first time.

The second semi final, on the following day, saw Denmark play Spain in Lyon. The Danes struck first through Soren Lerby in the 6th minute, and they continued to rule the roost throughout the first half. But the pressure began to tell and in the second half Denmark began to look decidedly weary. To make matters more difficult for Denmark, Spain brought on the speed merchant Sarabia who began to

cause all sorts of problems for the opposition.

In the 66th minute Maceda equalised for Spain. The scoreline remained at 1-1 and the match went into extra time. No more goals were forthcoming in the added thirty minutes, but Denmark found themselves reduced to ten men when Berggren was sent off by referee George Courtney for a seemingly mild tackle on Camacho. The game was eventually settled by a penalty shoot-out which Spain won 5-4.

The France v Spain final at the Parc des Princes on 27 June turned out to be another classic. Giresse went close for France in the opening minute. Both sides mounted promising attacks. The 47,368 crowd were splendidly entertained and the teams went in at the interval with no score.

The deadlock was broken eleven minutes into the second half when Platini curled a free-kick around the Spanish wall. Goalkeeper Arconada appeared to have it covered. He got his hands to the ball, but then allowed it to slip from his grasp to roll under his body and into the net.

Michel Platini scored in every round of the contest.

Le Roux was dismissed by the referee with six minutes to play and Spain attempted to take advantage by pushing up for the equaliser. It was while the Spanish were on one of these sorties that Tigana gave a massive clearance from defence. The ball reached Bellone, unmarked in the Spanish half. He cooly advanced on Arconada and chipped the ball over him and into the goal. The hosts were the champions.

The eighth European Championship culminated in West Germany between 10-25 June 1988, and the tournament followed the pattern established in 1986.

England, with Bobby Robson still at the helm, had enjoyed a reasonably sound 1986 World Cup in Mexico, reaching the quarter finals before going out to Maradona's Argentina (ably assisted by the 'hand of God'). Gary Lineker in particular had returned from Mexico a world star by becoming the leading scorer in the tournament, with six goals. Back home the domestic game was still suffering the trauma of the ban imposed by UEFA on English clubs in continental competition, following the Heysel Stadium riots of 1985.

In the European Championship England were drawn in Group Four together with Northern Ireland, Turkey and Yugoslavia. The first match, against Northern Ireland, was played at Wembley on 15 October 1986. Appropriately it was Gary Lineker, by then a Barcelona player, who opened the scoring after 33 minutes. Further strikes by Chris Waddle (78 minutes) and a second by Lineker (80 minutes) gave England a confident start in the tournament. Indeed, from then on Robson's side dropped only a single point - an away draw with Turkey - to win the group comfortably, ahead of Yugoslavia.

Wales were drawn in Group Six with Denmark, Czechoslovakia and Finland. But despite fine home victories over Finland (4-0) and group favourites Denmark (1-0), Wales finished in third place. Denmark went through as expected.

Under the new management of Andy Roxburgh, Scotland were still seeking their first qualification in the European Championship. They began the '86-88 Group Seven campaign with a 0-0 draw against Bulgaria, at Hampden Park on 10 September 1986. Also in the group

1986-1988
Final Hosts: West Germany
Champions: Holland

were Belgium, Luxembourg and the Republic of Ireland.

The Republic of Ireland had a long tradition of producing quality players, but had never achieved very much of note on the international scene. Then along came Jack Charlton, a World Cup winner with England back in '66, to take over the management of the Republic's squad. Taking full advantage of the new qualification/selection rules, he selected a number of players of tenuous Irish descent born in England and Scotland and bearing accents from broadest

Liam Brady kept Ireland's hopes alive.

cockney to gruffest Glaswegian. Charlton pulled the squad together, instilled a more positive attitude within it and perfected a direct, long-ball game which was to unsettle many a more 'sophisticated' team.

Like Scotland, the Republic also began with a draw, 2-2 against Belgium, thanks to a late penalty by Liam Brady. And there was yet another stalemate, at 0-0, when Scotland travelled to Dublin on 15 October.

But it was a different story when the rematch took place at Hampden Park in February '87. Mark Lawrenson opened the scoring in the 8th minute, following a John Aldridge free-kick. The Irish side then fell back on defence, soaked up the frenetic Scottish pressure and successfully protected their lead till the end.

Midway through the Group Seven programme Belgium looked the most likely qualifiers, they led the group with 7 points after a 0-0 draw with Ireland in Dublin. But the Republic went on to win all three of their remaining games while Belgium, Bulgaria and Scotland effectively cancelled each other out.

The Boys in Green were through to the finals and, whatever the outcome in Germany, the consensus of opinion in the Emerald Isle was that Big Jack Charlton had performed wonders for Irish football.

Spain progressed from Group One, ahead of Romania, Austria and Albania. Italy atoned for their poor showing in the 1982-84 championship, by qualifying from Group Two leaving Sweden, Portugal, Switzerland and Malta in their wake. The USSR won Group Three, eliminating the reigning European Champions France as well as East Germany, Iceland and Norway.

Holland's team of orange-shirted superstars, captained by the 1987 European Footballer Of The Year Ruud Gullit, won Group Five with relative ease. They were undefeated, had conceded just a single goal, and finished 5 points ahead of nearest rivals Greece. Poland, Hungary and Cyprus brought up the rear. Managed once again by Rinus Michels - the man who had led the Dutch side to the very brink of World Cup success fourteen years earlier - Holland were favourites for the title. West Germany permitting.

The host nation opened the finals tournament against Italy in Dusseldorf's Rheinstadion on 10 June 1988. Italy attacked immediately and Giannini almost scored what would have been a sensational opening goal, but 'keeper Immel saved the moment. Italy continued to press for

most of the first half, with West Germany making but a few attempts on goal. Yet the Italians could not make the breakthrough and at half time the scoreline still stood at 0-0.

The deadlock was broken in the 51st minute

Roberto Donadoni snapped up his chance.

when, following a misunderstanding between Matthaus and Herget, Donadoni gratefully intercepted the ball and passed to Mancini who hit it home. The Germans replied in the 55th minute after 'keeper Zenga had been penalised. Littbarski's free-kick set up Brehme for a shot which was deflected into the Italian goal. Result 1-1.

In Hanover on the following day, Spain beat Denmark 3-2 in the second Group One match, with goals from Michel, Butragueno and Gordillo.

Denmark replied through Laudrup and Pouslen. West Germany and Italy went on to claim semi final berths by beating Spain and Denmark. Germany topped the group on goal difference.

England had a dreadful time of it in Group

and went on to re-think his strategy and prepare his squad for the Italia '90 World Cup campaign in which he took England to fourth place.

Despite his side's fine victory over England, Jack Charlton also suffered the disappointment of losing out in the quarter finals.

The USSR topped the group by virtue of a 1-0 victory over Holland: both went through to the semi finals - and both survived. Holland beat West Germany 2-1 in Hamburg on 21 June. It was the first Dutch victory over their neighbours in 32 years. The first half was full of incident, but saw no goals. Nine minutes after the restart Lothar Matthaus opened the scoring for the home side with a penalty after Frank Rijkaard was adjudged to have brought down Jurgen Klinsmann. Holland's reply also came from the penalty spot. Ronald Koeman

Marco van Basten *brought defeat for Germany in the dying seconds.*

Two. Fielding what was considered one of their strongest sqauds in years, the English team had flown to Germany full of high hopes and expecting at least a semi final place. Instead, they lost 1-0 to Jack Charlton's Irish team, 3-1 to a devastating Dutch side and 3-1 to the USSR.

This disaster met with howls of derision from the English Press together with vehement calls for Bobby Robson's resignation or sacking. To his eternal credit Robson weathered the storm - although at times he looked an exhausted man -

converted after Marco Van Basten had gone flying over a defender's leg on the edge of the box. The tie was decided when Jan Wouters laid on a marvellous through-ball for Van Basten to hit home with barely a minute left to play.

The following day in Stuttgart the USSR met Italy in the second semi final. This was a tough, physical encounter with the Soviets dishing out most of the crunching tackles. Kusnetsov was booked for one such incident early on - thereby ruling himself out of a potential final place, because of a previous yellow card offence in an earlier game.

A quarter of an hour into the second half Litovchenko finished off a break-away attack, instigated by Kusnetsov, with the first goal of the game. Three minutes later Protasov wrapped things up when he met a splendid pass from Zavarov who had made a great run along the left wing. The USSR had reached their fourth European Championship final.

The final was played in front of 72,308 spectators in Munich's Olympic Stadium, on 25 June. It was a terrific match, full of red-blooded end-to-end play. Holland went close in the 6th minute when Ronald Koeman's forceful free-kick flew over the crossbar. The USSR went closer still, but Litovchenko's shot was safely gathered by Van Breukelen in the Dutch goalmouth.

With Kusnetsov absent, the USSR's defence was considerably weakened and the Dutch pressure eventually told after 33 minutes when Gullit headed home from a move which had begun as a corner kick.

Holland had some defiant defending to do early in the second half, as the USSR tried to find the equaliser. Then in the 54th minute, Van Basten finished off a superb move involving Van Tiggelen and Muhren, to give Holland a 2-0 lead. There was still more drama left in the match when, on the hour, Van Breukelen gifted the USSR with a completely unnecessary penalty. Astonishingly, he then proceeded to save Belanov's spot-kick. From then on it was Holland all the way. They held on to the lead for the sweetest moment in Dutch footballing history.

Hans Van Breukelen

European Championship Final
25 June 1988
Olympic Stadium, Munich
Attendance: 72,308

**HOLLAND 2
USSR 0**

Holland: Van Breukelen; Van Arle, Van Tiggelen, Wouters, Koeman R, Rijkaard, Vanenburg, Gullit, Van Basten, Muhren, Koeman E.
Scorers: Gullit 33, Van Basten 54

USSR: Dassayev; Khidiatulin, Aleinikov, Mikhailichenko, Litovchenko, Demianenko, Belanov, Gotsmanov (Baltacha), Protasov (Pasulko), Zavarov, Rats.

Ruud Gullit celebrates Holland's 1988 Euro victory.

A TV control room (above) and a TV camera 0n location (Right) working to ensure that all the action is beamed into your living rooms.

BRINGING IT ALL BACK HOME

Such is the power of modern television, that every goal of the 1992 European Championship will be seen and commented upon and analysed somewhere in the world. Every pass, shot, header, save, penalty, free-kick, corner-kick, tantrum and throw-in will be viewed by millions of armchair soccer fans. There will be slow-motion replays, reverse angle shots, cut-away views of the benches, the crowd, the banners and, of course, we will see the climax of the tournament when the victorious captain lifts the Henri Delaunay Cup.

The average viewer now takes it for granted that these crisp, immediate, urgent, dramatic pictures should spill from his or her TV screen. Yet bringing these images into our homes requires a logistical operation of such vast proportions, that it would have good old John Logie Baird goggling in disbelief and delight (and no doubt flicking channels to see how Scotland are doing).

The basic coverage of the 1992 European Championship will be provided by the Swedish network SVT, whose images will be beamed around the world via satellite. ITV Sport will plug into this source, but will also have supplementary unilateral cameras specifically and exclusively for its own use.

ITV Sport's Senior Producer John D. Taylor explains: "There won't be a 'blind spot' anywhere on the pitch," says John. "The director, Ted Ayling, should be able to see *everything*."

Ted Ayling will be situated in the ITV Outside Broadcast van close to the stadium. The van contains a bank of screens and it is from these that Ted will give his instructions and make his choice of the pictures that viewers will see.

Meanwhile, via his headphones, the commentator - either Brian Moore or Alan Parry - can hear all the director's instructions. If Ted Ayling tells his camera team to find a close-up of, say, Gary McAllister, then Brian or Alan will

ITV's On-Screen Team In Sweden

be primed to expect that image - and as soon as McAllister appears on the monitor, their commentary will flow naturally and seamlessly towards him.

"Director and commentator are very much a team," says John. "And being a commentator is an extremely difficult job. He has to know a great deal about the technicalities of football, and he must be saturated with information about the personalities involved." The amount of a commentator's 'homework' is quite staggering. For example, during the preparation for the coverage of a normal League game on ITV's *The Match*, Brian Moore will visit each team in training during the week. He will talk to the managers and the leading players about possible tactics and any injury worries. He will also make copious notes about the potential squad members of each club so that he will be fully versed and armed with a 'fact file' to which he can refer during the the game. He has to be right first time, there are no second chances.

Sitting alongside the commentator at each match will be a summariser - either a current player or an ex-player. And a panel of experts will analyse the game under the chairmanship of presenter Elton Welsby. ITV's commentators in Sweden will be ably assisted by Ron Atkinson, Jack Charlton and Denis Law - as well as that well-known double-act Ian St. John and Jimmy

Greaves.

"Knowing the game from the inside as they do there are certain insights that only a player could have. We encourage them to inject their view into the commentary as often as possible," says John D. Taylor.

ITV's transmission schedule for the first phase of the tournament was mutually agreed with the BBC. "Consequently there are no head-to-head clashes until the final itself. On the days when we don't transmit a 'live' match, we'll be showing highlights - and it will be vice versa at the BBC. In terms of viewer satisfaction, I believe it's important that we don't clash."

In addition to the match coverage ITV Sport will also have camera crews and reporters with the English and Scottish squads throughout their stay in Sweden. In England's case the reporter will be Jim Rosenthal, while Scotland will be accompanied by Gary Newbon. "We have a small studio in the hotels where the squads are based from where we produce either pre-recorded reports, or live interviews," says John.

"The entire package is put together so that every ITV viewer gets the best seat in the house."

Elton Welsby The relaxed Elton Welsby will be ITV's presenter in Sweden, intoducing the matches and conducting the half time analyses.
Born in St. Helens in 1951, Elton was educated in Liverpool. His debut commentary came about quite unexpectedly in 1979, when the regular Granada commentator Gerald Sinstadt was taken ill. The match was a prestigious one, Manchester United v Arsenal, and young Elton must have made a good job of it because the following week he was sent to Goodison Park for another First Division commentary. Elton Welsby has established himself as one of ITV's leading sports personalities. He has presented **The Match** as well as coverage of rugby league darts championships and the 1988 Olympics from Seoul.

Thanks to his many years of work on television, **Brian Moore** 'the Voice of Soccer' is now as well-known as any player in the game.
After spending two years in the RAF, Brian turned to sports journalism with **World Sports**, **Exchange Telegraph** and **The Times**. Later he spent six years as a football correspondent with the BBC. In 1968 Brian joined London Weekend Television to work on The Big Match and On The Ball. Since then he has become ITV Sport's leading soccer commentator covering all levels of the game including relegation battles, cup-ties, Home International Championships, European Championships, five World Cups and more than 20 FA Cup finals.

Alan Parry Alan hails from Liverpool, and joined a local newspaper at the tender age of 16, eventually becoming the sports editor. His journalistic career later continued with an evening 'paper in Wigan.
In 1970 he joined BBC Radio Merseyside as sports editor. Two years later he moved to the BBC's national sports unit in London In 1981 Alan joined the BBC's Match of the Day commentary team. Three years later he moved to ITV Sport.

Jim Rosenthal will be with the England squad for the duration of their European Championship campaign. He was born in Oxford in 1948 and worked on two local newspapers in the city before moving on to BBC Radio in Birmingham, for whom he covered the 1976 Montreal Olympics. He later became presenter of the prestigious **Sport on Two** programme from where he joined ITV Sport in 1980.

Gary Newbon, who will accompany the Scottish squad throughout the European Championship, is a vastly experienced sports journalist. He worked with news agencies and the Sunday Mirror before joining Westward Television in 1968. In 1971 he joined ATV's sports coverage team and has reported on many of ITV's major sporting productions including the last two World Cups and the 1972 and 1980 Olympic Games. He has also appeared on **World of Sport**, **Star Focus**, **Midweek Sports Special** and **The Match**.

As a player, **Ron Atkinson** helped Oxford United's rise from the Fourth to the Second Division. As a manager he has enjoyed success with West Brom, Manchester United, Atletico Madrid and Sheffield Wednesday. He currently manages Aston Villa, the club where his career began.

Ian St John was a tenacious and fearless striker for Motherwell and Liverpool and he won 21 caps for Scotland. In 1979 he became the resident presenter of **World Of Sport's** regular **On The Ball** feature - and a year later formed TV's most popular sporting double act with **Jimmy Greaves**. Their Saturday lunchtime show **Saint And Greavsie** is now required viewing for football fans all over the country.

EVERYTHING OLD IS NEW AGAIN...

WITH A G.F. TWIST

By **Therese Anne Edwards**

The Inventive Cook:

For… The Busy Mother, The Home Entertainer, or those who just love to cook and have found it necessary to cook for the Gluten Intolerant.

Over a lifetime of cooking for a family or cooking commercially, my passion for cooking remains constant.

No matter what your lifestyle, whether you are cooking for 1 or 2, a small or large family, for a dinner party, or unexpected guests, the main ingredient, the trick if you will, is a well thought-out Pantry.

By having a well-stocked pantry, cooking becomes far less stressful, and far more pleasurable, it can even become "Fun", and believe it or not save you a lot of time, effort and money.

It also means that shopping becomes easier and quicker.

All you have to do is restock that which you have used previously instead of trying to think ahead and usually forgetting a prime ingredient.

Do not pale when you see "the list" you will find that you already have most of these ingredients in your cupboard.

It will not be very costly at all to fill the gaps, just buy a few extra items each time you shop to add to your store.

So carry-on cooking and enjoy!

Everything Old
Is New Again...
With a G.F. Twist

Therese Anne Edwards

Therese Anne Edwards

To order additional copies of this book, contact:
Xlibris
1-800-455-039
www.xlibris.com.au
Orders@Xlibris.com.au

ISBN: Softcover   978-1-7960-0509-7
        EBook   978-1-7960-0510-3

Print information available on the last page

Rev. date: 09/27/2019

Your Tool --- The Pantry

The Cupboard

Apricots dried
Asparagus tinned
Beans: baked in tomato sauce, Tex Mex beans, 3 or 5 mixed, kidney beans tinned
Beetroot tinned
Baking powder
Bi-carb soda
Champignons tinned
Cherries tinned
Chick peas tinned
Cooking chocolate
Coconut: desiccated, shredded
Couscous
Dried fruit
Flour*: plain, Self-raising, Gluten free, Corn flour, Buckwheat flour (is great for the GF)
Honey

Lentils
Milk: long life, carnation reduced cream, condensed and evaporated
Oils (olive, vegetable, spray, or your own favourites)
Pastas and Noodles* (GF options)
Pasta sauce/Passata
Potatoes
Rice: white, brown
Sugar: white, brown
Spices and herbs, dried: Any good selection not forgetting mixed herbs, nutmeg, cinnamon, paprika, Chinese 5 spice, Cloves, and your favourite mixture
Soup mixes*: French onion, spring vegetable, Dutch curry... all excellent for flavour boosters

Stock*: beef, chicken, a good gravy mix (not really necessary but very handy)
Tomato: paste, tinned tomatoes whole or diced
Sauces: Worstershire/black, soy sauce (fountain brand or black pearl I find are the best), sweet chilli sauce, fish sauce, hoi sin sauce, teriyaki sauce
Vinegar .malt, white wine, balsamic, apple cider, red wine, rice wine
Yeast

The Freezer

Chicken: whole, thighs, breasts, wings, mince
Crepes*: store bought
Ice cream
Meat: beef, lamb, veal, pork, bacon
Pureed fruit such as raspberries, strawberries, mango frozen when in season
Pastry*: shortcrust, puff, homemade or store bought
Pizza bases*

Seafood: fish fillets, green prawns, calamari, or your favourite variety
Stocks, homemade is the best

Terry's Tip: It is also good to keep a variety of nuts in the freezer, pine nuts, hazelnuts, pecans, walnuts, almonds, macadamia's, they stay fresher longer.

The Refrigerator

Cheese: cheddar, gruyere, parmesan and your own favourites

Cream: cooking, sour cream, crème fresh

Curry pastes: red; green, chilli, harissa

Deli meats: ham, Strasberg, salami, the list is endless

Eggs

Fresh vegetables are always great to have on hand: carrots, onions, celery, zucchini, cabbage, cauliflower, spring onions, fresh ginger, capsicum, parsley, chives, lettuce; all of your favourites!

Homemade mayonnaise will keep in a jar for 3 weeks

Jams: Apricot, strawberry, red current. They have an added effect on desserts, slices and slow cooked meat dishes. You can make your own!

Olives: black green, multi coloured, pitted, whole, paste. Never underestimate the power of the olive

Sugar syrup: ratio 1 cup sugar, 1 cup water - great for poaching fruit, a quick dessert in a few minutes

Terry's Tip: Add your own favourites to this list especially the products necessary for GF cooking.

Autobiography

I come from a family of cooks and chef's so it seems natural to me to be fascinated by the art of cooking and to share that interest with those who also have a love of cooking, particularly those who still cook the old recipes handed down from their parents, aunts and uncles and also grandparents.

I personally, as a sole trader or as a partner have owned a number of businesses over the years, most of which were in the food industry, so it is a natural progression to write a book of recipes. Since I have recently found myself to be gluten intolerant, I have found it most rewarding to have been able to convert the greater majority of our recipes into gluten free meals.

Many will recognize their families own recipe even if I have not stipulated who gave it to me.

I would like to thank everyone for their patience, help and contribution in getting this book published especially my family Ian, Andrew, Nicole, Danielle, Meagan and Kristen and their partners and children for their patience and help.

My Editors … Nicole for love of cooking and her many hours of work and fortitude with me and my computer "skills" (or rather lack there-of!), Meagan for her infinite knowledge of cooking, food and desserts, and Kristen for taking on the final edits and getting my book to the publishers.

SO WELCOME TO:
EVERYTHING OLD IS NEW AGAIN… WITH A G.F. TWIST

Contents

Entrée /
Finger Food /
Bread

Corn, Chickpea And Zuccini Fritters *GF

This recipe has evolved over the years; it was handed down from my mother, who had been taught it by her German Jewish grandmother, Hanna Levy. There are now 3 variations of this recipe which I've provided below!

Preparation time: 20 minutes
Cooking time: 10 to 45 minutes
Servings, 3 variations

Ingredients

400 gram can chickpeas, drained & rinsed
½ cup reduced-fat milk
2 eggs
3/4 cup self-raising flour*
½ teaspoon baking powder
1 large zucchini
310 gram can corn kernels, drained
2 tablespoons fresh mint leaves, chopped
1 onion or 4 shallots, thinly sliced
Salt & pepper
Olive oil cooking spray
Salad leaves and tomato chutney to serve

Method

In a food processor, blend the chickpeas until roughly chopped
Grate the zucchini and squeeze out the excess liquid
Whisk milk, eggs, flour and baking powder in a bowl until smooth
Into the mixture, stir in the chickpeas, zucchini, corn, mint, onion, salt and pepper
Spray a frying pan with oil on medium to high heat

Variation 1 — Main Meal, makes 4 fritters

Add a quarter of the mixture to the pan and spread lightly and evenly with a spatula
Cook for 2 or 3 minutes on each side or until golden or cooked through.
Repeat to make 3 more fritters spraying the pan each time

Variation 2 — Finger Food, makes approximate 18 pieces

Drop teaspoonsful of the mixture into hot oil for 1 or 2 minutes, turn if required
Drain on kitchen towel

Variation 3 — Finger Food, makes 16 squares

Preheat oven to 180°C
To the batter mixture add an additional 3 beaten eggs
Pour into a square baking dish lined with baking paper
Sprinkle with ½ cup of grated cheese and bake for 30 to 45 minutes until cheese is golden brown
Leave to cool and cut into squares to serve

Coconut Crusted Fish Fillets *GF

This is a yummy finger food, entrée or even an easy dinner time recipe.

Preparation time: 15 minutes
Cooking time: 10 minutes
Serves

Ingredients

500g small fillets of fish - whiting, small flathead, or any small fillets skinned
and boned
1 cup plain flour or gluten free flour*
½ teaspoon salt
½ teaspoon pepper
200 g shredded coconut
2 eggs
½ cup milk
Oil for frying
Lime or lemon wedges as garnish
Green leaf salad

Method

Place the flour, salt and pepper on a plate, mix together

Place the shredded coconut on a separate plate

Whisk eggs in a bowl

Dust fillets in the seasoned flour until well coated

Dip into egg mixture, drain of excess egg

Then coat with the shredded coconut, press with your fingers to ensure it sticks to the fish

Line a baking tray with baking paper, place fillets on tray and refrigerate for 30 mins.

Heat oil in a non- stick frying pan and at a medium heat, cook the fillets for a few minutes either side until cooked through and golden

Drain on paper towel

Serve with your pre-prepared salad so that the fish can be eaten as soon as it's cooked

Terry's Tips: If you only have large fish fillets cut them into 3cm batons or fingers to maximise the crunchie coconut flavour. As an entrée, the deconstructed Guacamole on the next page would be an ideal choice to accompany this crunchy fish. For finger food and entrée think about serving it with a sweet chilli sauce or lemon mayonnaise.

Deconstructed Guacamole *GF

Very simple and tasty dip, salad or BBQ accompaniment – this is a large amount so you could halve the ingredients if you wish to make a smaller batch.

Preparation time: 20 minutes
Servings vary

Ingredients

1 telegraph cucumber, diced
4 large tomatoes, diced
1 red onion, diced very finely
3 large avocados, diced
2 mangos diced
1 cup roughly chopped coriander, leaves and stems
½ red chilli, chopped

Dressing Ingredients

60ml lime juice
60ml virgin olive oil
4 cloves garlic diced
1 teaspoon salt
1 pinch white sugar
1 pinch pepper
½ tabasco sauce

Method

Prepare and mix salad ingredients gently in a large bowl
Add all dressing ingredients to a bowl and whisk
Pour over salad, toss and serve

Mushroom Cups *GF

Pam an old caravaning friend passed on this tasty recipe.

Preparation time: 10 minutes
Cooking time: 8 minutes
Serving of 12 pieces

Ingredients

12 small mushrooms stems removed
Rocket & cashew dip or any other dip of your choice (tomato relish is also really tasty)
2 rashes of chopped bacon (or you could use pastrami)
Small handful chopped cashew nuts
Grated cheese to sprinkle on top (you could also use Philadelphia cream cheese or feta if you prefer)
Butter

Method

Mix the dip, bacon and nuts together in a mixing bowl
Place the mushrooms with the cup side up on a baking tray and place a
spoonful of the mixture in each
Top with the cheese and a dollop of butter
Bake at 180°C for 5 to 8 minutes

Terry's Tips: This receipt can be served as an entrée, or use larger mushrooms
and garnish with a small salad for lunch or light dinner. You can also serve
it as hors d'oeuvre with pre dinner drinks!

Thai Style Chicken Patties *GF

This is an easy 5 o'clock drinks recipe that we often have at Ellis Beach. I think I just made it up over the years. Adding or subtracting a bit of this and a bit of that, depending on what's in the caravan fridge!

Preparation time: 20 minutes
Cooking time: 15 minutes
Makes 10-12 patties

Ingredients

500 g chicken mince
2 tablespoons Sweet chilli sauce
2 tablespoons fresh coriander
1 clove garlic crushed
1 tablespoon finely grated lemon rind
1 cup of fresh breadcrumbs or gluten free breadcrumbs*
2 tablespoons peanut oil

Garnish Ingredients

1/3 cup sour cream
1 tablespoon sweet chilli sauce
2 teaspoons coriander
Lemon zest (optional)
Fresh coriander to garnish (optional)

Method

Combine the mince, sweet chilli sauce, coriander, garlic, rind and peanut oil in a bowl, mix well

With wet hands shape the mixture into small balls then flatten into patties

Roll the patties in the breadcrumbs and set aside

Heat oil in large pan and cook the patties in batches

Drain on absorbent paper

For the garnish, combine the sour cream, sweet chilli sauce, and coriander and lemon zest in a small bowl, mix well and serve with the patties

Vietnamese Rice Paper Rolls *GF

My daughter Kristen made these rice paper rolls for the first time about 15 years ago and she got us all involved in the rolling process. We had a lot of fun working out how to soften the rice paper rolls and seeing who could do it without tearing it. It's a really tasty and fun dish to make with family and friends.

Preparation time: 30 minutes
Cooking time: 10 minutes
Makes 12-15 rolls

Ingredients

2 tablespoons peanut oil
1 chicken breast cut into thin strips
1 tablespoon sesame oil
1 tablespoon mirin
1 stick lemon grass
2 teaspoons fish sauce
2 teaspoons ketjap manis
1 tablespoon fresh ginger
2 teaspoons chopped garlic
Juice of 1 lime

Assembling Ingredients

Half a packet of vermicelli rice noodles
1 packet rice paper sheets
½ bunch fresh mint
1 red onion, thinly sliced
1 carrot, match sticks
1 cucumber, match sticks
½ cup crushed cashews
½ punnet bean sprouts
1 red chilli, chopped

Method

Place all ingredients from first section into a wok or frypan and cook lightly, place in a bowl to cool
Prepare the vermicelli rice noodles and allow to cool
In separate bowls place the mint, sliced red onion, carrot and cucumber sticks, crushed cashews, bean sprouts and chopped chilli so you are ready to assemble the rolls
Prepare a warm bowl of water; dunk the rice paper roll into the water and leave to soften (30 seconds to a 1 minute)
In the centre of each sheet place a small amount of the chicken mixture, few mint leaves, couple of slices of onion, a couple of carrot sticks and cucumber sticks, a few crushed cashews, a few sprouts and a small amount of chilli
You will need to do one roll at a time and completed quite quickly to avoid the rice paper drying out
Place the roll on a place and cover with a damp tea towel or cloth as you go
Serve with a dipping sauce, either sweet chilli sauce, peanut sauce or make your own

San Choy Bow *GF

Preparation time: 15 minutes
Cooking time: 10 minutes
Makes 12 servings

Ingredients

2 tablespoons peanut oil
500 grams minced pork
100 grams of rice noodles* or vermicelli noodles*
Half a bunch English spinach, chopped
3 garlic clove, crushed
4 spring onions, chopped
2 tablespoons light soy sauce
1 tablespoon rice vinegar
1 teaspoon sambal oelek
1 tablespoon sesame oil

Serving ingredients

1 iceberg lettuce
1 lime
Half a bunch of coriander

Method

Soak the lettuce in a bowl of cold iced water for 10 minutes (this allows the leaves to separate easily)

Heat the peanut oil in a pan and lightly brown the pork mince

Boil a pot of water to soften the noodles, once softened chop into 1-2cm pieces

Add the chopped noodles and other ingredients to the pork and stir fry for 5 minute

Serve the mixture in the lettuce leaves with a sprinkle of coriander and a squeeze of lemon juice

Collie's Salt & Pepper Squid *GF

Who doesn't love a bit of fried squid! This recipe came from my daughter Nicole who owned a café with me before going on to run a club bistro and catering service. I'm sure she's cooked up millions of plates of these over the years!

Preparation time: 15 minutes
Cooking time: 20 minutes
Serves 4

Ingredients

3 medium squid tubes
½ cup self-raising flour*
½ cup corn flour
1 teaspoon chilli powder (add a little more if you like it really hot)
1 heaped teaspoon ground white pepper
2 heaped teaspoons salt
1 cup canola oil, for shallow frying

Garnish Ingredients

½ bunch coriander
1 medium red chilli
1 lemon

Method

Add all of the dry ingredients to a bag and shake to mix well
Wash and pat dry the squid tubes then slice into half cm rings
Heat oil on high
Place the squid rings into the bag a few at a time, then drop them into the oil and cook for 90 seconds
Drain on paper towel
Serve with lemon wedges and mayonnaise

Terry's Tips: Be sure not to overcook the squid otherwise it goes tough and chewy! You can also serve with a garnish of coriander and finely chopped chilli sprinkled over the top of the top of the calamari.

Lemon Grass And Coriander Chicken Skewers Or Chicken Balls *GF

This is another one of Kristen's recipes, and it can be made 2 ways. Both variations are great for entertaining.

Preparation time: 20 minutes
Cooking time: 30 minutes

Ingredients

500g minced chicken
1 ½ cups fresh white breadcrumbs*
2 garlic cloves, crushed
1 lemongrass stalk, white part only finely chopped (lemon zest will do)
2 teaspoons lime zest
½ cup coriander
1 tablespoon fish sauce
2 teaspoons brown sugar
Sweet chilli sauce

Method 1 – Makes 12 skewers

Mix the mince, breadcrumbs, garlic, lemongrass, lime zest, coriander, fish sauce and brown sugar in a large bowl

Divide into 12 portions and then shape each portion around a skewer

Refrigerate for 30 minutes

Heat you grill or BBQ to medium heat

Spray the skewers with oil and cook for 6-8 minutes, turning often until cooked through

Serve with sweet chilli sauce and herb salad

Method 2 – Makes 40 balls

Mix the mince, breadcrumbs, garlic, lemongrass, lime zest, coriander, fish sauce and brown sugar in a large bowl

Divide mixture into approximately 40 bite sized balls

Shallow fry the meatballs in oil, drain and cool slightly

To serve, wrap each ball in a mint leaf, skewered with a toothpick

Filo Parcels *GF

Quick and easy, this is a traditional Greek dish. This recipe was given to me by several of my Greek friends and neighbours so I just had to include it.

Preparation time: 15 minutes
Cooking time: 20 minutes
Makes 12 pieces

Ingredients

1 can chick peas
½ bunch Spinach
1 stalk lemongrass
1 tablespoon coriander
1 chilli
1 lemon zest
Salt and pepper
200 grams feta cheese
12 sheets filo pastry*
Melted butter
2 tablespoons vegetable oil
Greek yoghurt
Honey

Method

Drain and wash the chickpeas

Chop the chickpeas, spinach, lemongrass, coriander and chilli finely, place in a bowl and crumble the feta cheese, mix well

On a chopping board, lay out 1 sheet of pastry and brush with melted butter, fold in half and then half again

Put a spoonful of the chickpea and spinach mixture into the centre of the pasty and lift up edges to form a parcel, squeeze the top to encase the filling

Heat the oil in a pan

Place the parcels into the hot oil on the stove top for 2 to 3 minutes to crisp the bottom of each parcel

Then place the whole pan into a hot oven until golden all over

Serve with a drizzle of honey and yoghurt or serve the honey and yoghurt on the side with a tasty cucumber and tomato salad

Terry's Tip: To make this dish gluten free you can make your own gluten free filo pastry! I have tried to re-create this using gluten free wraps but it is not as good.

Peach & Passionfruit Bread *GF

This is a sweet bread, similar to banana bread. It melts in the mouth when served with butter and is also great cut into thick slices, toasted and spread with butter!

Preparation time: 10 minutes
Cooking time: 30 to 40 minutes
Makes 1 loaf

Ingredients

2 cups self-raising flour* or Buckwheat flour*
½ cup brown sugar
2 eggs
¼ cup light olive oil
½ cup skim milk
410 can peaches in passionfruit flavoured sauce

Method

Heat oven to 180°C

Line a loaf tin with baking paper

In a bowl, add the flour, brown sugar and mix together

In a separate bowl, beat the two eggs then add the olive oil, skim milk and peaches in passionfruit

Add the mixture into the dry ingredients and stir lightly until combined

Pour into loaf tin and bake for 30-40 minutes or until well risen, firm to touch and golden brown

Cool on a rack before cutting

Beer Bread

Margaret Lawdon gave me this recipe. It's a lot of fun to make, just like the lady who gave it to me. A wonderful quick bread that has the texture and taste of a farmhouse loaf with gorgeous, yeasty smells and can be made in a jiffy without all that planning for hours, bowls of dough rising in the hot-water cupboard, kneading and fiddling about. You don't even have to take off your rings to make this one. Unfortunately this recipe cannot be made gluten free but it was too good to not include.

Preparation time: 10 minutes
Cooking time: 35 minutes to 1 hour
Makes 1 large loaf 20 x 10 cm or 2 smaller loaves

Ingredients

3 cups of plain flour
3 teaspoons baking powder
1 teaspoon of salt
1 can of beer
1 handful of grated cheese

Method

Preheat the oven to 200°c

Quickly mix the flour, baking powder, salt and beer

Pour mixture into a greased or non-stick loaf tin and top with the grated cheese

A large tin (20x10cm) will take 1 hr to cook, 2 x smaller tins (8x15cm) will take 35-40 minutes

Terry's Tips: Do not use low alcohol beer as the recipe will not work!

Savoury Pies, Tarts & Quiches

Ham & Cheese Quiche *GF

This s a very, very easy quiche recipe handed down by my mother Granny Smith.

Preparation time: 15 minutes
Cooking time: 45-50 minutes
Serves 4 to 6

Ingredients

1 sheet frozen pre-rolled short crust pastry, thawed*
2 large eggs beaten
150ml cream or milk (or half/half)
100gm smoked leg ham, finely chopped
½ red capsicum, seeded and finely chopped
1 white or Spanish onion, finely chopped
125gm packet cheese spread with chives, diced
Salt & pepper
Green leaf salad

Method

Preheat oven to 200°C

Place the pastry sheet into a deep 20cm lose-bottomed fluted flan tin or a quiche dish

Press from the centre to edge, and then carefully press into each flute

Trim edge and prick the base with a fork

Line the greaseproof paper and a layer of dried beans or baking beads and bake "blind" for 10 minutes

Meanwhile, beat the eggs and cream/milk and combine the ham, capsicum, onion and cheese spread in a bowl

Remove the pastry case from the oven and remove the paper and beans/beads

Return pastry case to the oven for a further 5 minutes or until golden

Pour the filling into the pastry case and bake for a further 30-35 minutes or until the filling is puffed, golden and set

Allow the quiche to cool slightly, then transfer to a serving plate and garnish with parsley

Serve warm with a green leaf salad

Terry's Tip: You can use any vegetables or protein you like or have in the fridge; this is just how I remember my mum making it!

English Spinach & Cheese Pie *GF

Preparation time: 20 minutes
Cooking time: 1 hour 30 minutes
Serves 4 (main meal) to 20 (finger food)

Ingredients

2 tablespoons olive oil
1 brown onion, finely chopped
2 bunches English spinach
2 tablespoons dill, finely chopped
200gm feta, crumbled
½ cup tasty cheddar cheese
½ teaspoon ground nutmeg
4 eggs lightly beaten
60 grams melted butter
10 sheets filo pasty

Method

Preheat oven to 180°C
Lightly brush a 26cmx16cmx 3cm deep pan with melted butter
Fry onion for 3 minutes
Add roughly shredded spinach and cook for 2 minutes, remove from the heat and cool

In a mixing bowl, add dill, feta, cheddar cheese, nutmeg, eggs and the cooked spinach and onion, season with salt and pepper

Place a sheet of filo on a flat board brush with melted butter and top with another sheet of filo, repeat 4 times

Line the pan with the pastry, spoon over the prepared spinach mixture

Prepare remaining filo as before, layering with melted butter and lay over the filling

Trim the edges and brush the top with remaining butter

Lightly cut filo into either bite size squares (finger food) or into four-six squares for a main meal.

Bake for 40-45 minutes or until golden and cooked through.

Serve with your favourite salad

Terry's Tips: For a gluten free option, omit the filo and add 2 tablespoons of corn flour to the mixture and pour into a heavily greased casserole dish. Cook for 20 minutes or until golden brown. This makes a magic pie!

Tomato Tart *GF

This recipe has been passed on to me from Paul Benstead's Aunty, Carmel and Connie's Mum and my own mum Granny Smith; it's another magic tart to add to the list!

Preparation time: 20 minutes
Cooking time: 35 minutes
Serves 4 to 6

Ingredients

Shortcrust pastry (see Dessert recipes)*
2 onions, chopped
2 teaspoons garlic, chopped
8 large tomatoes, peeled and coarsely chopped
1 tablespoon tomato passata sauce
100 grams almonds, crushed
½ teaspoon sugar
½ cup basil leaves, roughly chopped
1 cup mozzarella cheese, grated
2 tablespoons parmesan cheese, grated
Salt and pepper

Method

Preheat oven to 180°C
Place pastry in flan dish, blind bake for 15 minutes
Sauté onion and garlic till translucent, add tomatoes and cook until the moisture evaporates then leave to cool
Stir in the passata, almonds, sugar and mozzarella cheese
Pour mixture into the pastry shell
Baste lightly with oil
Sprinkle with parmesan cheese
Bake for approximately 15-20 minutes, until golden brown
Serve with a rocket salad

Terry's Tip: You can use a store bought gluten free pastry base or make your own gluten free alternative.

Smoked Leg Ham Quiche *GF

This is just a little bit different to the normal quiche. I thought it deserved a mention particularly since its gluten free and some people feel they don't always have many options.

Preparation time: 20 minutes
Cooking time: 45-50 minutes
Serves 4 to 6

Ingredients

Puff Pastry Sheets* (1 or 2 depending on size)
100 grams smoked leg ham, finely chopped
½ red capsicum, seeded and finely chopped
1 white or Spanish onion finely chopped
2 large eggs beaten
150ml cream or milk (or half & half)
125 gram packet cheese spread with chives, diced
¼ cup parsley, chopped
Salt and pepper to season

Method

Preheat oven to 200°C

Place the pastry sheet(s) into a deep 20cm lose-bottomed fluted flan tin or quiche dish

Press from centre to edge then carefully press into each flute, trim the edges and prick the base

Cover the pastry with greaseproof or baking paper and blind bake with a layer of dried beans, rice or baking beads for 10 minutes

Meanwhile, combine the ham, capsicum, onion, eggs, cream, milk and cheese spread in a bowl

Remove the pastry case from the oven, remove the paper and beans and return to the oven for a further 5 minutes or until golden

Pour the filling mixture into the pastry case and bake for a further 30-35 minutes or until the filling is puffed, golden and set

Allow the quiche to cool slightly, then transfer to a serving plate and garnish with parsley

Serve warm with a green or mixed salad of your choice

Impossible Pie *GF

This generations old recipe was given to me by my friend Anne Wilkinson. Many European friends have shared similar recipes with me also but they call it Frittata, every culture seems to have one. This pie is a quick and easy entrée or main meal or it can be cut into smaller squares for 5 o'clock drinks!

Ingredients

4 eggs
3/4 cup plain flour or gluten free flour*
1/3 cup melted butter
2 cups milk
Salt and pepper
1 large onion sliced
1 tin asparagus spears or fresh cooked asparagus
5 rashes bacon
Grated cheese

Method

Pre heat oven to 200°C

Combine the eggs, flour, butter, milk in a mixing bowl, season with salt and pepper and beat well

Fry the sliced onion in butter or olive oil

Place the egg mixture in a 20 cm square pan and top with bacon, asparagus, fried onion and cheese

Bake for 35 minutes or until set

Cool for 5 minutes and cut into squares then serve hot.

Terry's Tips: You can use any combination of topping you fancy, roasted pumpkin, capsicum, mushroom and feta is another great combination.

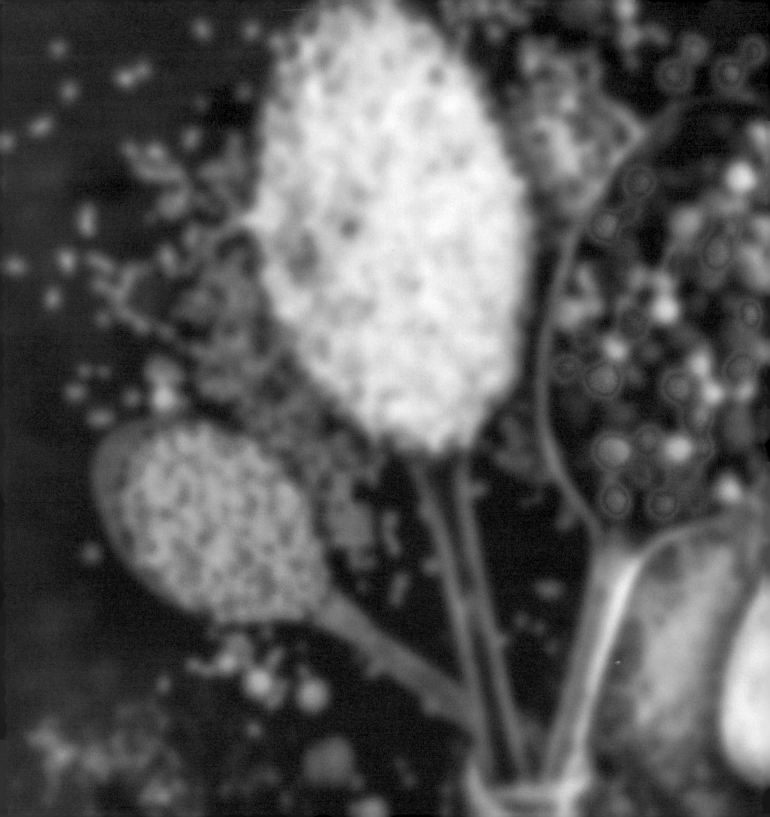

Chicken & Duck

Vegetable & Chicken Noodle Stir-Fry *GF

This recipe came from Kristen, my youngest daughter who has given me several of her recipes and like her siblings is a very good cook.

Preparation time: 20 minutes
Cooking time: 15 minutes
Serves 4

Ingredients

2 tablespoons peanut oil
2 full chicken breasts cut into strips
1 red onion, chopped
1 teaspoon ginger, finely diced
4 garlic cloves, finely chopped
400 grams baby corn, blanched (or 1 tin, strained of liquid)
200 grams French green beans, blanched and finely sliced
1 red capsicum, cut into 2cm strips on the diagonal
3 baby bok choy, shredded
1 tablespoon oyster sauce
1 tablespoons sweet chilli sauce
1 tablespoon black bean sauce
1 tablespoon soy sauce
2 teaspoons rice wine vinegar
4 sprigs of fresh coriander, chopped

Method

Heat the peanut oil in wok then add the chicken breast and stir fry till cooked, remove from wok

Add the red onion, ginger, garlic, baby corn, beans and capsicum, stir fry for 2 minutes and then return the chicken to the wok

Combine the oyster sauce, sweet chilli sauce, black bean sauce, soy sauce and rice wine vinegar and add to the wok and stir fry for 5 minutes

To serve sprinkled with chopped coriander

Terry's tip: Accompany the stir fry with your choice of rice or noodles*. If adding noodles, prepare and add to the wok and toss through to coat with the sauce before serving.

Chicken Pesto Pasta *GF

This is such an easy and tasty pasta recipe that my daughter Nicole often makes for the kids. It's a quick easy meal if you use a store bought pesto or if you've got the time and ingredients, then take the time to make a fresh pesto for added flavour. Nicole's recommendation is to use fettuccini pasta but really any pasta from the pantry will do!

Preparation time: 10 minutes
Cooking time: 20-30 minutes
Serve 4-6

Ingredients

1kg chicken breast or chicken thigh fillet
1 packet of pasta*
1 large onion, finely chopped
3-4 garlic cloves, finely chopped
3 rashes bacon, diced
4-5 medium sized mushrooms, sliced
100 grams basil pesto ((you can add more or less depending on your own taste)
350-500ml thickened or fresh cream
1 chicken stock cube
2 tablespoons olive oil
Salt & pepper to season

Method

In a saucepan boil water and cook pasta to your liking

Dice the chicken into approximately 2cm pieces

Heat the oil in a frying and add the chicken cooking for approximately 4 minutes, then add the onion, garlic and bacon cooking for another 4 minutes until onion has softened

Add the mushrooms and cook for a further couple of minutes

Add the chicken stock cube and mix to combine

Once chicken is cooked through, turn heat to low and add the basil pesto, stir in the cream and mix well

Simmer for 5-10 minutes

Once the pasta is cooked, add it to the pan and stir through the cream sauce

Add salt and pepper to taste

Terry's Tip: If cooking for adults, you can add a splash of white wine with the stock cube to give it a bit more zing! You can also include additional vegetables such as zucchini, capsicum or peas if you want to bulk this out to feed more guests.

Tarragon Chicken *GF

Preparation time: 15 minutes
Cooking time: 30 minutes
Serve 4

Ingredients

4 chicken breasts
2 tablespoons fresh tarragon, chopped
2 tablespoons fresh parsley, chopped
2 tablespoons seeded mustard
2 tablespoons pine nuts
2 cloves garlic
100grams butter sliced into 4
1 tablespoon oil
¼ cup white wine or apple juice
⅔cup water
2 chicken stock cubes*
½ cup cream
1 tablespoon fresh tarragon, chopped

Method

Preheat oven to 180°C

Flatten fillets

Mix together the herbs, garlic, mustard, pine nuts, salt and pepper

Spread a layer of the mixture and 1 slice of butter on each fillet, then roll up, fix each piece with a toothpick or two

Heat the oil and brown the rolled chicken on each side in the pan

Place chicken in baking tray and add the wine, water and stock cubes

Bake in the oven for approximately half an hour, chicken should be golden on all sides

Remove chicken from baking dish and set aside

Add the cream and extra tarragon to the pan juices, cook over low heat until warm

To serve, pour the cream sauce over the plated chicken

Granny's Lemon Chicken *GF

My Favourite Birthday special for the Edwards family, in fact I couldn't even count how many celebrations this dish has accompanied. A definite family favourite for all ages!

Preparation time: 20 minutes
Cooking time: 1 hour 10 minutes
Serves 8 to 10

Ingredients

1.5-2 kg chicken, cut into 6 to 8 pieces
2 cups self-raising flour*
3 teaspoons paprika
3 teaspoons Chinese 5 spice
3 teaspoons salt
3 teaspoons course ground pepper
2 tablespoons olive or vegetable oil

Lemon Mixture Ingredients

Juice of 2-3 lemons
5 garlic cloves, chopped
½ cup of soy sauce*
2 cups of water

Method

Heat Oven to 200°C

Place all the ingredients of the lemon mixture into a container/jug, preferably with a lid and refrigerate

Pour oil into a large baking tray and heat in the oven for a few minutes

In a large freezer bag place the flour, paprika, Chinese five spice, salt and pepper and shake well

Put about 4 pieces of chicken in to the bag at a time and shake well to coat

Remove the baking tray from the oven and carefully place the chicken into the hot oil, it's alright for the chicken to be squashed but ensure that it is in a single layer, use a second tray if there is too much chicken for one tray

If there is any of the flour mixture left over, sprinkle it evenly over the chicken

Bake for 15 minutes then turn them over and bake for a further 20 minutes

You are looking for the chicken to be brown and crispy; you may need to move the pieces around during the baking process if they are squashed together - do not overcook

Turn the oven down to 175°C

Take the chicken out of oven and pour the lemon mixture evenly over the chicken

Return to oven and bake for a further 30 minutes

Terry's Tips: We usually serve the chicken with baked potatoes, pumpkin and minted peas but you can serve it with any vegetable combination you like. It also goes well with fried rice and a salad (see the Vegetables & Side Dishes section for my famous fried rice recipe!).

Greek Lemon Chicken With Potatoes *GF

This is a one pan dish and looks stunning and smells amazing as it comes out of the oven and is placed on to the table. Quite a number of my Greek friends have given me variations of this recipe. In particular both of my next door neighbours!

Preparation time: 15 minutes
Cooking time: 55 minutes
Serves 4

Ingredients

8 chicken thigh cutlets skin on
1-2 tablespoons olive or vegetable oil
300 grams Chat potatoes, cut into quarters
1 medium red onion, cut into wedges
1 medium capsicum, cut into strips
4 garlic cloves, unpeeled
½ cup chicken stock*
2 medium lemons
250 grams cherry truss tomatoes
½ cup pitted Kalamata olives
2 tablespoons fresh flat parsley leaves, chopped
1 tablespoon fresh basil leaves, chopped
100 grams feta cheese

Method

Pre heat oven to 200°C

Brown the chicken on all sides in the oil

Place chicken in a large baking dish or casserole pan

Arrange potatoes, onions, garlic and capsicum around the chicken

Pour over the stock and add the juice and zest of one lemon, season with salt and pepper

Roast for 30 minutes at 200°C, then reduce oven to 160°C and roast for a further 15 minutes

Add tomatoes and olives and cook for a further 10 to 15 minutes or until the chicken thighs are cooked through and the tomatoes are just starting to collapse

Combine the parsley, basil and grated lemon zest and sprinkle over chicken mixture

Crumbled feta cheese over the top just before serving

Serve with lemon wedges

Terry's Tip: Replace chat potatoes with sweet potato slices for a low carb dish option.

Peperonata *GF

Two fine old Italian recipes with basic ingredients but full of flavour. I have found that most cultures have a version of the same.

Preparation time: 15 minutes
Cooking time: 30 minutes
Serves 4

Ingredients

2 chicken breasts
3 tablespoons of olive oil
4 onions, sliced lengthways
4 tomatoes, sliced lengthways
1 chilli, finely diced
1 jar tomato passata
4 garlic cloves, finely chopped
2 tablespoons tomato paste
1 cup water
6 cherry tomatoes, halved
1 cup of olives
1 tablespoon baby capers
1 tablespoon lemon juice
½ cup basil leaves
Salt and pepper to taste

Method

Heat 2 tablespoons of the oil in a fry pan, add the onions and fry for 5 minutes, add the garlic, chilli, tomatoes, passata, tomato paste and water and cook for a further 5 minutes

Place the sauce in a heat proof dish

Pre heat oven to 180°C

Slice the chicken breasts lengthways to make 4 fillets

Heat 1 tablespoon of the oil in a fry pan and lightly brown the fillets on both sides

Place on top of the Peperonata with the cherry tomatoes, olives, capers and lemon juice, season with salt and pepper and bake for 25 minutes

Garnish with roughly chopped basil leaves

Terry's Tip: You can substitute the chicken with steak, fish or even lamb if you prefer.

Peperonata With Bacon & Chilli *GF

Preparation time: 15 minutes
Cooking time: 20 minutes
Serves 4

Ingredients

1 can of chopped tomatoes
1 teaspoon of chilli flakes
2 onions
1 cup water
2 rashes bacon, chopped
½ cup of basil, shredded
½ cup pine nuts, toasted
1 cup of cheese (parmesan, crumbled feta or cheddar)

Method

Blend the can of chopped tomatoes, chilli, onions and water
Fry the bacon in oil until crisp then add the blended ingredients
Bring to boil then simmer for 10 minutes
Boil 300g macaroni until aldente
Drain the pasta and add the sauce to the pasta with basil and pine nuts
Top with your favourite cheese

Chicken And Pumpkin Pasta Bake *GF

This is a delicious one dish pasta bake that can be prepared ahead of time and heated later, or is as an easy to prepare dish for a group gathering. Robyn Black a long-time friend, and a very good cook, gave this recipe to me.

Preparation time: 15 minutes
Cooking time: 30 minutes
Serves 4 (as a main meal), up to 20 (as a side dish)

Ingredients

1 kg butternut pumpkin
3 cups pasta* (wholemeal, gluten free or any variation)
300ml light thickened cream
1 tablespoon wholegrain mustard
2 cups barbeque chicken, cooked and shredded
Salt and pepper to taste
150g ricotta (you can use reduced fat ricotta if preferred)

Method

Pre heat oven to 180°C

Peel and cut the pumpkin into 1.5cm pieces, spray or coat with cooking oil and bake for 20 minutes

Cook the pasta, strain and add to an 8 cup casserole dish

Mix the cream, wholegrain mustard, chicken and baked pumpkin together and then stir through the pasta and season with salt and pepper

Add dollops of ricotta to the top of the mixture

Place in oven to brown the ricotta for 5-10 minutes

Terry's Tips: Robyn usually serves any green boiled vegetables such as baby spinach, beans, zucchini or broccoli with this dish. If she's cooking for a crowd she would usually add some additional cooked vegetables to the pasta before topping with the ricotta.

Herby Crispy Lemon Chicken Thighs *GF

Another popular chicken recipe passed on by a number of friends. These thighs are also good served cold for a picnic basket or school lunches.

Preparation time: 10 minutes
Cooking time: 40 minutes
Serves 4

Ingredients

8 chicken thighs with skin on and bone in
1 heaped tablespoon chopped thyme
1 heaped tablespoon chopped rosemary
1 heaped tablespoon marjoram
1 heaped tablespoon oregano leaves
6 garlic clove, crushed
1 lemon, zest and juice
60ml olive oil
1 teaspoon each salt and pepper

Method

Pre heat oven to 180°C
In a large bowl mix the thyme, rosemary, marjoram, oregano, garlic and
lemon zest and juice
Coat the chicken in the olive oil then place in the bowl with the herbs and
coat well
Put the chicken skin side up on a wire rack placed on an oven tray
Roast for 30 to 40 minutes, until crispy and cooked through

Terry's Tip: Accompany this chicken dish with quinoa, tabouli, couscous,
fried rice or a bulky salad.

Easy Chicken Bake *GF

Another simple tasty succulent stove to table dish with layers of flavour.
Good for left over BBQ or any cooked chicken, easy and quick to prepare.

Preparation time: 15 minutes
Cooking time: 20 minutes
Serves 4

Ingredients

2 cups of cooked chicken
1 large onion, chopped
1 cup of celery, chopped
1 cup capsicum, chopped
1 cup frozen mixed vegetables
2 cups of cheese sauce or rue (see Preserves, Pickles, Sauces & Dressings)
4 chicken stock cubes, melted in ½ cup water
1 cup cheddar cheese
1 can asparagus spears (optional)

Method

Head a fry pan, in 1 tablespoon of oil, fry off the onion, celery, capsicum and 1 cup of frozen mixed vegetables
In a casserole dish, layer the cooked chicken and vegetables
Make your cheese sauce, add chicken stock and stir
Pour over the chicken and vegetables and top with tasty cheese
Bake for 15 minutes or until cheese browns

Terry's Tip: I like to add a can of asparagus spears, laid on top of the cheese sauce.

Roast Chicken With Bacon And Lentils *GF

This is a very old recipe at least 3 generations, but still a goody. A very simple dish, which is now a little different from the old version and very tasty

Preparation time: 15 minutes
Cooking time: 1 hour
Serves 4 to 6

Ingredients

1 baking bag
1 whole chicken,
½ teaspoon of salt
½ teaspoon pepper
1 chicken stock cube or 1 teaspoon of stock powder*
6 bacon rashers
½ cup lentil
½ cup water
½ cup olive oil
1 cup water
1 Packet French onion soup mix*

Method

Rub the chicken with a mixture of salt, pepper and a crushed chicken stock cube

In a fry pan, cook the bacon till crispy

Roughly chop the bacon and mix with the lentils, water and a pinch of salt

Stuff chicken with mixture

Place chicken in a baking bag with olive oil, water and French onion soup mix

Place into baking dish and bake in the baking bag for 1 hour

Remove the chicken from the bag and reserve the liquid to serve as your gravy

Terry's Tip: You can add a bit of oil and roast some potatoes and pumpkin in the baking dish outside the bag so they'll be ready at the same time as the chicken. You can find gluten free French onion soup mix; both Continental and Maggi have a version.

Five Spice Mango Chicken *GF

I first had this dish in a Parramatta riverside restaurant many years ago, and after many attempts at making it, I came up with this version.

Preparation time: 15 minutes
Cooking time: 15 hour
Serves 8

Ingredient

750gm chicken fillets
2 large mangoes peeled
6 tablespoons mango chutney
200ml Greek yoghurt
1 tablespoon Chinese five spice powder
Juice of 1 lemon
A few drops of tabasco sauce
8 mild peppadew peppers, sliced (bought from the supermarket in a jar)
4 sprigs Parsley, chopped

Method

In a hot pan, fry the chicken fillets till golden on both sides and cooked through

Set aside to cool

For the mango sauce, cut the flesh of 1 mango roughly into pieces and put in food processor, add the mango chutney, Greek yoghurt, Chinese five spice, lemon juice and tabasco, whiz until smooth and blended

Season with salt and pepper

Once cooled, cut the chicken into neat pieces and mix with the mango sauce in a bowl

Cut the flesh of the remaining mango into 1cm pieces and add to the chicken mixture

Spoon into a large salad bowl lined with salad leaves and decorate peppadew pepper slices and sprinkle with parsley

Terry's Tips: This dish is best served cold and is also succulent with a small amount of chopped avocado added. It can also be served in individual portions which look lovely.

Chicken And Orange Infused Noodles *GF

Another quick and easy recipe that can be produced in about 15 minutes, and it's a nice change from the ordinary. Rice noodles, rice or Hokkien noodles are all good for this change of flavour chicken dish.

Preparation time: 15 minutes
Cooking time: 10 minutes
Serves 6 to 8

Ingredients

3 cups of boiling water
1 orange, rind and juice
4 chicken breasts
Noodles of your choice
1 handful of snow peas
Fresh pink ginger, 2cm slice grated
4 Shallots, sliced
1 teaspoon sesame oil
1 tablespoon rice wine vinegar

Method

Pour 3 cups of boiling water into a jug, add orange rind and juice and leave for 3-4 minutes

Place the chicken breasts in a heavy based pan over medium heat and pour over orange mixture, cook for 7-8 minutes

Remove pan from heat and leave chicken in liquid until slightly cooled enough to handle

Reserve the liquid

Shred the chicken

Prepare the noodles according to packet directions

Place shredded chicken, snow peas, sliced pink ginger and sliced green shallots in a bowl and combine

Toss cooked noodles in 1 teaspoon sesame oil and 1 tablespoon of rice wine vinegar

Serve chicken mixture with noodles

Sprinkle with sesame seeds, spoon over warm reserved liquid

Terry's Tips: If you don't have fresh pink ginger which does have a more delicate flavour grated, fresh ordinary ginger will do.

Stir Fried Chicken Fillets With Cashews *GF

Preparation time: 25 minutes (plus 30 minutes refrigeration)
Cooking time: 15 minutes
Serves 4 to 6

Ingredients

1kg chicken thigh fillets, cut into 3cm squares
1 cucumber
¼ cup vegetable oil
1 cup of roasted cashews
6 garlic cloves
2 tablespoons of Chinese sherry or dry sherry
2 teaspoons of sea salt
4 spring onions

Marinade Ingredients

2 tablespoons dry sherry
2 tablespoons cornflour*
1 tablespoon cold water
1 teaspoon salt

Method

Combine all marinade ingredients together in a bowl and add the chicken
Cover and refrigerate for at least 30 minutes
Cut the cucumber in half lengthways, scoop out the seeds using a spoon, then finely slice on the diagonal and set aside
Heat 2 tablespoons of oil in a hot wok, add half the marinated chicken and fry for 1 minute
Add the remaining chicken and stir fry for I minute, set aside
Add remaining oil to the wok and stir fry the nuts and garlic for 30 seconds, stirring constantly
Return chicken to wok, pour in sherry and fry another 30 seconds
Add salt, fry for another 30 seconds or until chicken is just cooked through and lightly browned
Lastly add cucumber and stir fry for 10 seconds
Arrange chicken on platter and garnish with chopped spring onion
Serve immediately

Terry's Tip: Accompany this stir fry with a medley of Asian greens either steamed or fried and steamed rice.

Crispy Duck With Bloodplum Sauce *GF

This dish is easy enough to make but it is slightly time consuming. I have not had a lot to do with duck, only cooking it only occasionally, however the duck we had at the Koi restaurant in Hunters Hill were my daughter Meagan worked for a time was so delicious that I just had to search for a good recipe. This one, although not exactly the same, I feel meets the bill.

Preparation time: 45 minutes (plus overnight refrigeration)
Cooking time: 2 hours
Serves 4

Ingredients

1½ kg whole duck
½ tablespoon Sichuan pepper
1 tablespoon sea salt
¼ cup cornflour
Vegetable oil for deep frying

Blood Plum Sauce Ingredients

2 cups water
1 cup white sugar
4 ripe blood plums, halved
½ cup fish sauce

6 star anise
2 cinnamon quills
1/3 cup lime juice

Method

Wash and clean the duck then pat dry and rub all over with the Sichuan pepper and salt

Cover the duck and refrigerate overnight

In a steam basket cook the duck for 1½ hours, do not overcook

Gently place duck on a tray breast side up, allow it to cool slightly then refrigerate

For the sauce combine water, sugar and plums in a small saucepan and bring to boil

Turn to low and simmer for about 5 minutes or until reduced by half

Add fish sauce and spices and simmer for a further 2 minutes

Stir in lime juice and remove from heat

Keep the sauce warm while you fry the duck

Cut the duck in half lengthways and carefully remove the carcass from the meat, leaving thighs, legs and wings intact

Lightly toss each side in the flour to coat, shake off excess

Heat oil in a wok and when quite hot, deep fry each half for about 3 minutes or until crisp and golden

Remove duck from oil, drain on a paper towel and leave to rest for 5 minutes

Finally slice the duck and arrange on a platter

To serve, pour over the hot plum sauce

Beef, Veal & Lamb

Beef Stroganoff *GF

Jan Hilliard and Judy Hogan, two of my oldest friends passed on this recipe so it's only fitting that they feature first in the Beef, Veal and Lamb section! Jan's and Judy's husbands Peter and Kevin both butchers served my family's meat for a good number of years!

Preparation time: 20 minutes
Cooking time: 1 hour 30 minutes
Serves 6 to 8

Ingredients

1kg rump steak
2 tablespoons vegetable or olive oil
250 grams bacon, chopped
250gm mushrooms, sliced
3 onions, diced
4 garlic cloves, crushed
2 tablespoons plain flour or corn flour*
500 grams tomato paste
2 teaspoons caraway seeds
1 packet of continental stroganoff mix*
1 packet bouquet garnet
1 cup red wine
6 beef stock cubes with 1 litre water
Salt and pepper to season
500 grams sour cream

Method

In a large heavy saucepan lightly fry the beef in hot oil, small portions at a time, until lightly coloured
Remove beef from the pan and set to the side
Add bacon, mushrooms, garlic and onion to the saucepan and fry until brown
Add the flour, tomato paste, caraway seeds, stroganoff mix, bouquet garnet, wine, stock and beef to the pot and mix together
Bring to the boil, then put lid on top and simmer for 1 to 1.5 hours
Add the sour cream just before serving

Terry's Tips: Stroganoff can be served with mashed potato and green vegetables, or over pasta with a sprinkle of poppy seeds or with boiled rice and tomato wedges.

Massaman Beef Curry *GF

This Thai dish is another one from my daughter Kristen who enjoys cooking Asian food. It takes a while to cook but once it's on the stove and you can smell the aromas you'll be glad you did.

Preparation time: 20 minutes
Cooking time: 2 hour 20 minutes
Serves 4

Ingredients

500 grams beef, diced (blade or chuck Steak)
1 tablespoon peanut oil
2 tablespoons Massaman curry paste*
2 medium onions, halved and sliced
2 carrots, batons
4 kaffir lime leaves
4 medium potatoes, diced
1 teaspoon tamarind paste (optional)
2 cups water
1 can coconut milk
Pinch of salt and pepper
1 lime, juice
20 grams roasted peanuts
2 teaspoons fish sauce
2 teaspoons white sugar
4 sprigs fresh coriander, chopped

Method

In a heavy based saucepan, brown the beef in the peanut oil
Add Massaman curry paste and onions and cook until onions are soft
Add sliced carrot, lime leaves, potato, tamarind, water, coconut milk and season with salt and pepper
Cook for 2 hours on medium to low heat with a lid on, or until meat is tender
Add lime juice, roasted peanuts, fish sauce and sugar
Cook for another 5 minutes
Serve with steamed basmati or jasmine rice and Asian greens, sprinkle curry with fresh coriander leaves

Meat Loaf, Meat Balls Or Rissoles *GF

A combination of several recipes from friends but all tried and true. This is quite a large amount and will make 2 loaves or 24 rissoles or 50 meatballs, we're used to cooking for a crowd! Cut the recipe in half if more convenient.

Preparation time: 30 minutes to 1 hour
Cooking time: 1 hour 30 minutes (for Meatloaf) or 30 minutes to 1 hour (for Rissoles and Meatballs)
Serves, 3 variations below

Ingredients

1kg sausage mince*
1kg hamburger mince*
1kg pork mince*
2 onions, finely diced
2 capsicums, diced
3 carrots, peeled and grated
4 garlic cloves, crushed
¼ cup soy sauce
½ cup tomato sauce
2-3 teaspoons mixed herbs
2 cups of boiled rice or 3 cups bread crumbs*
Salt and pepper to season
2 onions thickly sliced (for Meatloaf only)
2 tomatoes sliced thickly (for Meatloaf only)
2 eggs (for Rissoles and Meatballs only)
Vegetable oil for shallow fry (for Rissoles only)

Method for Meatloaf, makes 2

Preheat oven to 180°C

Mix the sausage mince, hamburger mince, pork mind, diced onions, capsicums, carrots, garlic, soy sauce, tomato sauce, mixed herbs and rice or breadcrumbs together in a bowl, generously season with salt and pepper

Line the bottom of each meat loaf tin with baking paper

Then spread a layer of sliced onion and a layer of sliced tomatoes to cover the base

Press meat mixture firmly on top of the layered onion and tomato

Bake for 1½ hours

When the loaf is cooked, up turn it onto a serving platter for a decorative effect

Terry's Tips: The raw mixture freezes well so you can make a batch for 2 and freeze. The cold slices of meatloaf are great for lunches.

Method for Rissoles and Meatballs, makes 20-30 rissoles or 40-50 meatballs (depending on size of each)

To the mixture add 2 eggs

For the Rissoles, form the mixture into balls, roll in flour*, flatten and shallow fry in small batches

For the Meatballs, roll into balls, roll in breadcrumbs* and shallow fry in small batches or place on baking trays and cook for 30 minutes

Terry's Tips: You can halve or quarter this recipe for smaller quantities. You can omit the breadcrumbs and bake in the oven or shallow fry if you want to use to make meatballs and spaghetti.

Beef Stew (By Any Other Name) *GF

Preparation time: 20 minutes
Cooking time: 3 hours 20 minutes
Serves 10

Ingredients

2 tablespoons oil
2kg topside beef or fresh silverside cut into 2cm cubes
1 cup of plain flour*
4 onions, diced
4 carrots, diced
4 medium potatoes, diced
4 garlic cloves, finely chopped
1 capsicum, chopped
4 sticks celery, chopped
2 teaspoons paprika
1 cup passata
Salt and pepper to season
Water

Method

In a large heavy base saucepan heat the oil

Coat the beef in flour then cook/brown in small batches (otherwise the meat will stew)

When all the meat is cooked, add it back to the saucepan and add the onions

Cook for a further 3 to 4 minutes, then add carrots, potatoes, garlic, capsicum, celery, paprika and passata, and season with salt and pepper

Cover with water and cook slowly for 3 hours, stirring occasionally so the meat doesn't stick to the pot

Add extra water if necessary

Serve with mashed potato or boiled rice

Terrys Tips: You can also add 1 tablespoon soy sauce, 2 tablespoons tomato paste or 3 tablespoons Worcestershire sauce for extra flavour. The addition of dumplings with this recipe is great too. Any scone recipe will do for dumplings. If adding dumplings, make sure the lid is firmly on the pot, they'll need 20 minutes to cook.

Hungarian Goulash (With A Dash Of Aussie) *GF

Goulash Ingredients

Add these to the basic mixture above:
1 red capsicums, chopped
½ cup soy sauce or tamari*
1 dessert spoon of vegemite
4 tomatoes, chopped

Serve with boiled rice and garnish with tomato wedges and parsley

Terry's Tip: These recipes are both pressure cooker and slow cooker friendly.

Beef Olives *GF

This family recipe has evolved over many years and is a family favourite –
just watch out for the toothpicks!

Preparation time: 40 minutes
Cooking time: 1 hour 30 minutes
Serves 6 to 8

Ingredients

1kg silverside or rump, thinly sliced
1 jar tomato passata
1 tin diced or crushed tomatoes
2 cups of water
8 olives cut in half

Seasoning Ingredients

2 cups breadcrumbs*
3 teaspoons mixed herbs
1 egg, lightly beaten
1 onion
3 garlic cloves
½ bunch parsley
4 rashers bacon
Salt and pepper to season

Method

Preheat oven to 180°C

Place all of the seasoning ingredients in a blender and mix until combined

Bash out the meat and place a heaped spoonful of the seasoning mix in the centre, roll up and secure with a toothpick, repeat for each slice of beef

Coat each beef roll in flour and place them in a greased baking dish, do not pack the rolls too tightly together

Add the olives and water to the passata and tomatoes, pour over the beef rolls

Cook on 180°C for about 1-1.5 hours, adding water if the meat looks as if it is drying out (there should be sauce left in the pan serve over the top of the beef rolls)

Serve with boiled chat potatoes and green beans

Beef And Ginger With Rice *GF

A nice little tasty stir fry, easy and quick to make.

Preparation time: 10 minutes
Cooking time: 15 minutes
Serve 4

Ingredients

500 grams rump steak thinly sliced
Plain flour or corn flour*
4 garlic cloves garlic, crushed
2cm piece of fresh ginger, grated
½ cup soy sauce
½ cup mirin or sherry
1 tablespoons peanut oil
6 shallots, thinly sliced
2 celery sticks, thinly sliced
Half a bunch of coriander, chopped
300 grams rice

Method

Cook the rice

Coat the beef in flour, heat oil in a large frypan or wok and cook in batches until brown all over and remove from pan

Combine ginger and celery in a bowl with half of the soy sauce and half of the mirin and add to wok, stirring for 5 minutes, add the beef and the rest of the soy and mirin

Serve mixture over rice in individual bowls, sprinkle with fresh shallots and coriander on top of each bowl

Veal With Mushrooms And Mustard Cream Sauce *GF

Another simple steak recipe with an easy, succulent sauce.

Preparation time: 15 minutes
Cooking time: 15 minutes
Serves 4 to 6

Ingredients

1 tablespoon of oil
8 veal steaks
10 grams butter
2 garlic cloves, crushed
150 grams button mushrooms, thickly sliced
1/3 cup dry white wine
1 tablespoon wholegrain mustard
½ cup cream
¼ cup chicken stock
1 teaspoon fresh thyme leaves
Salt and pepper to season

Method

Heat oil in a large frypan

Cook the steak in batches with the melted butter, crushed garlic, and salt and pepper until browned on both sides or cooked as desired

Put on a plate and cover

In the same pan, fry the mushrooms lightly then add the wine, chicken stock, mustard, cream and thyme leaves

Stir over medium heat until slightly thickened

Pour over the steak

Served with any salad of your choice

Terry's Tips: Rump steak can be used in the place of veal if sliced thinly and pounded slightly with a mallet. Personally I prefer the flavour of rump to that of veal. You can use powered mustard mixed with vinegar in the place of the wholegrain mustard if you're on a no sugar regime. This recipe is a nice low calorie meal option.

Steak Diane *GF

Everyone has their own version of this traditional recipe, and this is mine.

Preparation time: 10 minute
Cooking time: 10 minutes
Serves 4

Ingredients

4 steaks, thinly sliced
3 garlic cloves, crushed
100 grams butter
½ cup Worcestershire sauce (black sauce)*
½ cup of chopped parsley
½ cup cream

Method

Melt the butter and the fry steak in a frypan on medium to high heat garlic on one side until lightly coloured, turn and add Worcestershire sauce and parsley, cook for one minute more then remove steak to serving dish
Add cream to pan, cook till warm
Pour sauce over steak
Serve with mashed potatoes or chips, and green vegetables

Tarragon Steak *GF

Preparation time: 10 minutes
Cooking time: 10 minutes
Serves 4

Ingredients

1 tablespoon melted butter
4 rump steaks thinly sliced & pounded to make even thinner
2 cloves garlic
150 grams button mushrooms, sliced thickly
2 cups dry white wine
1 tablespoon wholegrain mustard
½ cup cream
¼ cup beef stock or 2 beef cube melted in ½ cup water
1 teaspoon of fresh tarragon leaves

Method

In pan brown steaks and cook for about 3 minutes either side. Place on serving dish cover to keep warm
Add garlic and mushrooms to pan stirring till just soft
Add wine and mustard and cook for 2 minutes
Add cream and stock

Bring to boil then reduce heat and simmer for approximately 5 minutes, or until sauce thickens slightly, then stir in tarragon and cook for another minute

Terry's Tips: Serve with your favourite pasta, I suggest Bow or with mashed potatoes and steamed mixed vegetables. This is also a handy recipe for left over BBQ meat.

Warm Beef And Chilli Salad *GF

Preparation time: 15 minutes
Cooking time: 15 minutes
Serves 4

Ingredients

2 tablespoons peanut oil
750 grams beef fillets, thinly sliced
2 small red chillies, deseeded and chopped very finely
2 tablespoons light soy sauce
1 teaspoon fish sauce
1 tablespoon sweet chilli sauce
2 tablespoons lime juice
250 grams cherry tomatoes, halved
3 cups finely shredded Chinese cabbage (wombok)
¾ cup mint leaves, lightly packed
1 medium cucumber, deseeded and thinly sliced
1 cup bean sprouts

Method

Heat half of the oil in wok

Stir fry beef in batches until brown all over

Heat remaining oil in wok, stir fry onion, chilli and garlic until onion softens

Return beef to the wok with combined sauces, lime juice, tomatoes and cabbage

Stir fry until cabbage wilts

Place mixture in a serving bowl and stir in mint, cucumber and sprouts

Serve immediately with rice or additional salad or vegetables

Veal With Lemon And Capers *GF

A lovely lady called Marcelles who was the nurse at my doctor's surgery passed on this recipe. Unfortunately I have lost contact with her over the years. It's a very simple, but very tasty dish.

Preparation time: 10 minutes
Cooking time: 15 minutes
Serves 4

Ingredients

8 small pieces of veal schnitzel
Plain flour*
50 grams butter
2 garlic cloves, crushed
½ cup white wine
½ cup chicken stock
2 tablespoons capers
1 tablespoon lemon juice
1 tablespoon parsley, chopped

Method

Coat each piece of veal with flour
Heat 40 grams butter in pan
Cook veal in batches until light brown on both sides
Remove from pan, cover with foil and put aside
Heat remaining butter in same pan with garlic and cook for a minute or so
Add wine and stock and simmer until thickened
Return veal to pan, top with capers, lemon juice and parsley, spooning sauce over veal until warmed through
Serve with buttered chat potatoes, green beans and a crisp salad

Baked Glazed Corned Beef * GF

A friend and neighbour, Celia Delaney passed on this recipe from her electricity commission days.

Preparation time: 40 minutes
Cooking time: 4 hours
Serves 8

Ingredients

2 kg corned beef
1 level teaspoon mixed spice
1 large stalk of celery, chopped
1 onion, chopped
1 carrot, chopped
6-10 cloves

Paste Ingredients

1/3 cup brown sugar
1 tablespoon of prepared mustard
½ cup orange juice

Method

Place meat in a large pot and cover with cold water and add spice and vegetables

Bring to the boil, cover with a lid and simmer for 3 hours

Remove pot from heat and leave beef to cool in the broth

Pre-heat oven to 150°C

Once cool, place the meat in a baking dish, score the fat layer with a knife and then stud with the cloves

Pour the paste over meat and bake for 1 hour, basting frequently with the pan juices

After 30 minutes, pat a little more sugar on the meat

Serve with Parsley sauce (see Preserves, Pickles, Sauces and Dressings), mashed potato and steamed vegetables

Terry's Tip: This basting technique gives a delicious glaze to the meat. It makes a great presentation as hot or cold meat for a buffet luncheon or dinner.

Asian Lamb With Red Salad *GF

Preparation time: 40 minutes
Cooking time: 4 hours
Serves 8

Ingredients

4 Lamb back straps
1 tablespoon oil (or 2 tablespoons butter)
1 tablespoon red currant jelly
1 tablespoon fish sauce
1 tablespoon soy sauce

Salad Ingredients

Red salad leaves
Red onion
Beetroot sticks

Salad Dressing Ingredients

½ cup Vinegar
½ cup Mint leaves, finely sliced
½ teaspoon sugar

Method

Heat oil or butter in a frypan, add the red currant jelly, fish sauce and soy sauce and fry the meat, cook for a few minutes

Remove the lamb from the pan and thinly slice, return to the pan and coat with the sauce

To serve, prepare the salad and dressing, mix together and then add the lamb

Pork & Ham

Pork & Coriander Dumplings *GF

My daughter Kristen lived in Hong Kong but even before she did, she loved to cook Asian inspired dishes. Kristen and her husband Neil have been cooking these dumplings for years and it became a tradition to cook them with their friends when celebrating Chinese New Year.

Preparation time: 20 minutes
Cooking time: 20 minutes
Makes 30 servings

Ingredients

300g pork mince
3 green onions (scallions), chopped
½ teaspoon finely grated ginger
1 tablespoon kecap manis
1 tablespoon sweet chilli sauce
¼ cup chopped coriander leaves
1 eggwhite
30 wonton wrappers*
Vegetable oil, for pan-frying

Dipping Sauce Ingredients

2 tablespoons lime juice
1 tablespoon brown sugar
1 teaspoon fish sauce
1 large red chilli, seeds removed and finely chopped

Method

Combine all dipping sauce ingredients in a bowl and stir until the sugar dissolves, set aside

Place the pork, green onion, ginger, kecap manis, sweet chilli sauce, coriander and eggwhite in a bowl and mix until combined

Place one teaspoon of the pork mixture into the centre of each wrapper

Brush the edges with water and fold to enclose, pinching the edges to seal

Prepare a large saucepan of boiling water and cook the dumplings in batches for 2–3 minutes or until cooked through

Drain on absorbent paper to remove excess water

Heat the oil in a large non-stick frying pan over high heat and cook the dumplings for 1 minute each side or until golden

Serve immediately with the dipping sauce

Pork San Choy Bow *GF

Preparation time: 10 minutes
Cooking time: 10 minutes
Serves 2 to 4

Ingredients

8 Iceberg lettuce leaves, trimmed
2 teaspoons canola oil
2 garlic cloves crushed
6 scallions, finely sliced
500g lean pork mince
1 tablespoon oyster sauce
1 tablespoon cold water
1 tablespoon soy sauce* or tamari
1 tablespoon sherry or Mirren (optional but nice)
½ cup each celery and capsicum finely diced
½ x 227 gram can water chestnuts, drained and finely chopped
100 grams green beans very finely sliced on the diagonal
Mung beans or bean sprouts

Method

Place the iceberg lettuce leaves in a bowl of iced water for 10mins
Heat oil in pan to low and fry garlic and scallions for 1 minute
Increase heat to medium-high and add mince stir until browned
Combine oyster sauce, soy sauce, sherry and cold water and add to pan
Add the rest of the ingredients and stir fry for 2 minutes or until beans
are tender
Remove the leaves from the cold water and pat them dry
To serve, place mixture in a bowl with the leaves on the side

Terry's Tip: Baby cos leaves make an easier to handle method of eating,
although the iceberg lettuce is more traditional.

Almond Pork Chops *GF

Ingredients

4 pork chops
1 tablespoon oil
1 packet continental spring vegetable soup*
½ cup capsicum, diced
½ cup onion, diced
½ cup celery, diced
2 tablespoon soy sauce
1 cup water
16 whole almonds without skin
Salt & pepper to taste

Method

Fry the pork chops until brown on both sides, ensure not to overcook
Remove from the pan and set aside
Pour off most of the oil/fat from the pan, and then add the packet of spring onion soup
Stir with a spoon to get up all the crunchy bits from the bottom of the pan

Add capsicum, onion and celery to the pan and fry lightly
Add water, soy sauce and almonds, stir to combine
Just before serving, add the pork chops back to the pan and heat through

Terry's Tips: I find Fountain Brand to be the best soy sauce to use, followed by Black Pearl Dark. Fried rice makes a good accompaniment for this dish or an Asian herb salad, or I also serve it with mashed potatoes and vegetables.

Pan Fried Pork With Proscuitto, Sage & Capers *GF

My good friend Kay Brooks gave me this recipe. It's a great quick, easy and delicious pork dish. Kay says "the sauce is sooooo good you may want to lick the plate!"

Preparation time: 5-10 minutes
Cooking time: 5-10 minutes
Serves 4

Ingredients

4 thin pork cutlets or escalopes
4 slices prosciutto
1/3 cup olive oil
12 fresh sage leaves
2 tablespoons drained baby capers
1 tablespoon butter
1 lemon

Method

Preheat oven to 150°C

Sprinkle pork with black pepper

Wrap a slice of prosciutto around the centre of each piece

Heat a large pan on high and drizzle 1 tablespoon of oil into pan and add 2 pork pieces

Cook 2 minutes on each side or until golden brown and just cooked through

Transfer pork to a rimmed baking tray and place in oven to keep warm

Repeat with remaining pork pieces

Once you've removed the pork, do not wipe out the pan

Immediately add 1 tablespoon oil and sage and cook for 1 minute

Remove pan from the heat and add capers and butter

Grate lemon zest over capers

Swirl the pan to melt butter and combine flavours

Cut the lemon in half and squeeze strained juice into caper mixture

Stir in any juices that have accumulated around the pork whilst resting in the oven

Place pork on serving plates and spoon sauce evening over the pork

Terry's Tips: Kay usually serves this with wilted baby spinach, bok choy or couscous.

Creole Pulled Pork *GF

A great week end meal for the family.

Ingredients

1 shoulder of pork
1 onion roughly chopped
3 garlic cloves
½ teaspoon mixed spice
½ teaspoon cinnamon
1 bouquet garni
Salt and pepper
1 bottle of coca cola (750ml)

Method

Place all ingredients into a heavy pot and cover with a bottle of coca cola
Bring to the boil and simmer for 1 ½ hours
Skim the top once or twice during the cooking
Allow the pork to sit in the juices until cooled
When cool enough to handle lift the pork and separate (Pull) the meat from the bones and any fat and gristle
Thicken the pan juices with a little corn flour to make delicious gravy
Serve on crusty bread rolls* with the gravy and a little Chilli sauce

Terry's Tips: Accompany with any salad or sides you prefer, I like a beetroot salad myself! I've also tried this on a gluten free wrap which works really well.

Seafood

Salmon/Tuna Patties *GF

I've been making these patties since I owned a fish and chip shop when I was in my early 20's in Petersham in Sydney. They were a shop favourite. Children seem to love these, and they've been a family favourite through the generations.

Preparation time: 30 minutes
Cooking time: 30 minutes
Makes 20 patties

Patty Ingredients

4 medium potatoes peeled, chopped
2 cloves of garlic, chopped
2 large onions, chopped
1 medium to large bunch of parsley or coriander, chopped
1 x 425 gram can tuna or salmon
1 teaspoon salt
1 teaspoon pepper

Batter Ingredients

2 cups of plain flour or buckwheat flour*
2 cups of cold water
1½ teaspoons salt
1 teaspoon pepper

Method

Boil the potatoes, once cooked mash and mix in all other ingredients
Allow to cool slightly
Create balls out of the mixture, squeeze out any air then roll balls in flour and flatten
Place all ingredients for the batter mixture into a large bowl and whisk well
Add more flour or water to achieve the consistency of thick cream
Dip the patties into the batter ensuring the whole patty is completely covered
Fry the patties in batches in very hot oil for 2-3 minutes each side or until golden brown
Drain off excess oil on paper towel

Terry's Tip: I have found that tuna is stronger and cheaper that salmon and that Greenseas Tuna is the best. You can make the mixture into small balls for finger food or larger for a main meal.

Prawns And Spinach *GF

This is a very quick and easy prawn dish that is really tasty and looks appealing. It's just something I made up out of the caravan fridge but has now become a firm favourite with fellow campers.

Preparation time: 5 minutes
Cooking time: 10 minutes
Serves 4 to 6

Ingredients

50 grams butter (a bit more if you are not on a low-fat diet)
250 grams peeled green prawns
1 onion thinly sliced
150 ml cream
2 tablespoons vermouth (Cinzano)
2 teaspoons horse radish
2 teaspoons mustard
Salt and pepper

1 packet fresh baby spinach leaves
1 French stick thinly sliced*

Method

In a pan melt the butter, add onion and prawns and sauté until the prawns just change colour

Add the cream, vermouth, horse radish and mustard, season with salt and pepper

Arrange spinach on a platter

When all of the ingredients are heated through, place on spinach to serve

Serve with toasted baguette slices*

Smoked Salmon Salad With Herb Dressing *GF

Preparation time: 5 minutes
Cooking time: 10 minutes
Serves 2

Ingredients

¼ cup dill sprigs
1/3 cup parsley or watercress
3 shallots roughly chopped
1 cup natural yoghurt
Zest of 1 lemon
220 grams smoked salmon, sliced
½ red onion, finely sliced
3 eggs (optional)
2 sprigs of coriander, chopped
Baby cos lettuce or iceberg shredded

Method

Place herbs, shallots, yoghurt and lemon zest in to the bowl of a food processor and puree
Arrange lettuce, red onion and salmon on a platter, drizzle generously with herb sauce, sprinkle with coriander
Serve with bagels or rye bread*

Terry's Tip: Served cold as an entrée or light lunch.

Crab With Ginger *GF

Preparation time: 5 minutes
Cooking time: 10 minutes
Serves 2

Ingredients

1 crab (separate from shell) or use tinned crab
2 teaspoons sesame oil
1 tablespoon ginger, shredded
½ teaspoon small red chilli, diced
2 garlic cloves, finely chopped
1 onion, diced
½ cup capsicum, small sticks
1 teaspoon sugar
2 teaspoons oyster sauce
2 teaspoons wine vinegar
1 tablespoon white wine
1 bunch coriander
4 scallions

Method

Stir fry the crab, ginger, chilli, onion, garlic and capsicum in the sesame oil in a hot wok for 30 seconds

Add the oyster sauce, wine vinegar and white wine and stir fry till the crab is coated and opaque

Chop the scallions on the diagonal and add to pan whilst hot

Garnish with generous amount of coriander leaves

Use the shell to decorate

Crab Omlette *GF

Preparation time: 5 minutes
Cooking time: 5 minutes
Serves 1 to 2

Ingredients

60 grams blue swimmer crab, cooked (flesh only)
3 egg yolks, beaten
3 egg whites, beaten until fluffy
30 grams cream
Salt
Pepper
2 teaspoons sorrel, chopped
½ lemon

Method

Gently mix yolks, whites and cream together
Melt 1 tablespoon butter, add the egg mixture to the pan and cook until
golden on one side
Add the crab meat to one half, and then fold the omelette in half
Slide on to a serving plate and garnish with sorrel and lemon wedge

Salmon And Prawn Skewers *GF

So simple for the BBQ!

Preparation time: 15 minutes
Cooking time: 10 to 12 minutes
Serves 2 to 4

Ingredients

650gms skinless salmon fillets
16 green prawns, shelled with tails intact
8 bamboo skewers
2 tablespoons coriander
1 Birdseye chilli

Garlic Butter Ingredients

Butter
90gms butter
2 garlic cloves, crushed
1 Lime, zest

Method

Slice salmon into cubed pieces approximately 2cm

Thread the salmon and prawns alternately onto the skewers beginning with and ending with a piece of salmon

To make the garlic butter, melt the butter in a pan, stirring until butter is melted then add the garlic and lime zest

Brush half of the garlic butter over the skewers

Heat a chargrill pan or BBQ grill on medium heat

Cook skewers, turning every 3 to 4 minutes and basting with the garlic butter

To serve, scatter with chopped coriander and finely chopped chilli

Vegetables & Side Dishes

Potato Bake *GF

Just so easy, I think everyone already has one of these recipes up their sleeve but I thought I would add it anyway as it's a great accompaniment to any meal.

Preparation time: 20 minutes
Cooking time: 1 hour 30 minutes
Serves 10

Ingredients

4-5 medium size potatoes
1½ cup tasty cheese, grated
½ cup breadcrumbs*
250ml cream
250ml milk
Salt and pepper to season

Method

Preheat oven to 180°C
Thinly slice the potatoes
In a baking dish, layer the potato placing a sprinkling of cheese between in layer
Mix the cream and milk, salt and pepper together in a bowl and pour over the potatoes
Mix half a cup of cheese and the breadcrumbs then sprinkle on top.

Season with salt and pepper, and bake for 1½ hours

Variations:

#1 Add fried chopped bacon, salami or chorizo for a meaty crunch
#2 Add corn, peas, beans, lightly cooked onion, broccoli or any other vegetable
#3 Replace the potatoes for sweet potatoes for a low carb dish, they won't need to be baked for as long

Terry's Tips: Never throw out your stale bread, bake it in the oven until crisp then place in a blender for fresh bread crumbs.

Asparagus Mornay Bake With Eggs *GF

Preparation time: 10 minutes
Cooking time: 15 minutes
Serves 8

Ingredients

1 tin of asparagus spears or a bunch of fresh asparagus
750 ml cheese sauce (see Preserves, Pickles, Sauces and Dressings)
3-4 eggs
½ cup tasty cheese
½ cup bread crumbs*

Method

Preheat oven to 180°C
In a pot, boil the eggs and allow to cool
Arrange asparagus in a buttered dish
Once you've made your cheese sauce, pour it over the asparagus
Slice the eggs into quarters and arrange on top of the sauce
Sprinkle grated cheese and breadcrumbs* over the top
Bake for 15 minutes until bread crumbs and cheese are brown

Tomato, Onion, Cheese & Breadcrumb Bake *GF

This one has become almost a must at any of our BBQ's as it's so easy and so very tasty, definitely one of my favourites.

Preparation time: 15 minutes
Cooking time: 30 to 40 minutes
Serves 10

Ingredients

3-4 tomatoes, sliced
2 onions, sliced
1½ cup grated cheese
½ cup breadcrumbs*
30 grams butter, diced
Salt and pepper to season

Method

Preheat oven to 180°C

In a medium casserole dish place thin layers of the sliced tomato, sliced onion, grated cheese and breadcrumbs, making sure to salt the tomato on each layer

Do 3 layers finishing with the breadcrumbs

Dollop the butter in the breadcrumbs and then finish on top of the dish

Bake for 30 to 40 minutes, until tomato and onion is soft and the breadcrumbs are golden brown

Mixed Baked Vegetables

I have had many variations of this dish from my Italian friends over the years, this is one that I have come up with that incorporates the many versions! This is a dish that can be served at BBQ's or a side dish for a family dinner.

Preparation time: 20 minutes
Cooking time: 1 hour 15 minutes
Serves 10

Ingredients

2 medium zucchini cut into 3cm rounds
2 carrots cut in 3cm rounds
3 potatoes medium dice
1 sweet potato medium dice
½ yellow capsicum cut in strips
½ red capsicum cut in strips
3 small onions, halved
1 cup red wine
1 jar tomato passata
Plenty of salt and pepper
1 cup of feta cheese, crumbled
1 cup fresh mixed herbs such as marjoram, parsley, chives, mint, sage or thyme

Method

In a casserole dish layer the vegetables
Mix the passata, wine and 3/4's of the mixed herbs, then gently spread over the vegetables
Sprinkle crumbled feta cheese on top and bake covered for 1 hour
Uncover and bake for a further 15 minutes
To serve, sprinkle with the rest of the fresh herbs

Terry's Tip: If you prefer not to use wine, then it's easily replace with a cup of water. If you don't have any fresh herbs in the fridge or garden, you can replace with a few teaspoons of dry mixed herbs of similar varieties.

Quinoa Tabouleh *GF

Preparation time: 20 minutes
Cooking time: 25 minutes
Serves 10

Ingredients

300 grams quinoa (combination red, black and white)
3 cups water
Pinch of salt
3 large tomatoes, finely diced
½ large red onion, finely diced
½ cup Lebanese cucumber, finely diced
½ cup mint leaves
1 cup parsley

Dressing Ingredients

3 garlic cloves, finely chopped
½ cup lemon juice
½ cup olive oil
Pinch sugar
Salt and pepper

Method

Wash the quinoa then add to a pot of water and salt
Bring to the boil, leave to boil for 10 minutes over high heat
Simmer for 10 minutes
Cover with the lid and simmer for another 5 minutes
To make the dressing whisk all the ingredients together in a jug
Place cooled quinoa in a bowl and fluff it up with a fork
Add the tomatoes, red onion, cucumber, mint parsley and the dressing
and toss

Fried Cabbage *GF

This is an especially easy and tasty side dish, very handy to accompany a roast dinner, BBQ's or any occasion.

Preparation time: 15 minutes
Cooking time: 10 minutes
Serves 6

Ingredients

¼ head of cabbage or wombok
3 rashes of bacon
4 cloves garlic, grated
¼ cup of butter (butter makes it better)

Method

Melt the butter in a shallow fry pan
Fry the bacon and garlic in the butter until the bacon is cooked
Add the cabbage, season with salt and pepper
Simmer gently turning occasionally so that the cabbage doesn't catch at the bottom of the pan, till the cabbage is cooked

Terry's Tip: If using wombok, make sure to keep an eye on it as it cooks very quickly.

Terry's Special Fried Rice *GF

Whenever I take this to any function I'm always asked for the recipe, so friends... here it is!

Preparation time: 20 minutes
Cooking time: 30 minutes
Serves 10-20 as a side dish

Ingredients

2 cups rice
½ cup of oil or butter (or half and half)
4-5 cups of water
½ teaspoon salt
1/3 cup soy sauce (good quality)
4 chicken stock cubes
3 eggs
4 rashes of bacon
1 capsicum
4 celery sticks
1 onion
Small tin of prawns

Method

To a heavy fry pan or electric frying pan add the uncooked rice and oil or butter and toast gently until the rice is brown stirring occasionally

Combine the water, salt, soy sauce and chicken stock cubes and add to the rice

Cook until the water is absorbed – do not stir the rice – it should take about 15 to 20 minutes

Whilst rice is cooking, beat 3 eggs and fry in a separate pan, remove to cool and then chop into small pieces

Fry then chop the bacon, chop the capsicum, celery and onion

Once the liquid has been absorbed, add the egg, bacon, capsicum, celery and onion to the pan with the rice

To serve, heat the rice on low for 5 minutes and gently stir to mix ingredients through the rice

Desserts

Sweet Shortbread Pastry

This is a very old recipe which I believe can never be beaten. I have several versions from friends who have raided their mother's recipe books over the years; Nanna Edwards, Margaret from Ellis Beach, Grandmother Hickey, Anne Wilkinson, the Hinchcliffe sisters and more ...

Preparation time: 30 minutes
Makes enough for 1 pie

Ingredients

1 ½ cups self-raising flour
1 ½ cups plain flour
½ cup sugar
½ teaspoon salt
125 grams butter
1 tablespoon lard - optional but best or additional 25 grams butter
1½ caps vanilla
150 grams cream
½ cup milk
1 egg yolk

Method

Sift together dry ingredients, rub in butter and lard

In a separate bowl, mix together milk, cream, vanilla and egg yolk

Make a hole in the centre of the dry ingredients and mix in wet ingredients until combined

Turn out on a board and knead gradually adding more plain flour if needed

This basic recipe will do for any filling that you wish to use

Terry's Tips: For a savoury tart omit the sugar and vanilla! You can make the pastry ahead of time, just cover with cling wrap and keep in a cool, dry place. Be sure to bring back to room temperature before using.

Unfortunately I do not have a gluten free option for this particular recipe but fortunately there are now recipes available for gluten free pastry, and you can buy gluten free shortcut pastry from the supermarket. As this recipe has been in my and so many others families for so long, I feel it deserves a mention.

Jennifer's Chocolate Nut Slice *GF

Ingredients - Pastry base

125 grams (4oz) butter
1 cup self-raising flour*
1/2 cup coconut
½ cup lightly packed brown sugar
½ cup salted peanuts (Macadamia nuts are nice too)

Ingredients - Chocolate Icing

60 grams (2 oz.) copha
125 grams (4oz) dark chocolate

Method

Pre-heat oven to 160°C
Melt butter, sift flour and combine with remaining ingredients
Press evenly into 18cm x 28cm square tin
Bake for 20 minutes or until dry to touch
Remove from oven
For the chocolate icing, stir chocolate and copha in saucepan over low heat
until melted and smooth
Pour over slice and cut into squares whilst still hot

Jennifer's Caramel Nut Slice *GF

A cooked tray of Jennifer's pastry base

Ingredients - Caramel Topping

200 grams butter
2 tablespoons brown sugar
1 can of reduced cream
½ cup macadamia nuts

Method

Melt butter and brown sugar in a pan over low heat, cook for five minutes
or until sugar has dissolved
Add cream and stir until completely mixed through
Pour over pastry base and sprinkle crushed macadamia nuts on top
Allow to cool and cut into squares

Terry's Tiramisu *GF

Preparation time: 1 hour (plus 2 hours refrigeration)
Serves 6-8

Ingredients

1 medium chocolate cake*
1 punnet sour cream or mascarpone
500 grams fresh cream
1 cup sugar syrup (Boil 1 cup water one cup sugar together for 5 minutes until sugar is dissolved)
4 eggs
¼ cup cocoa powder
¼ cup Marsala or Kahlua
½ cup strong coffee

Method

Mix ½ cup very strong coffee with the sugar syrup, ensure the syrup is cool before adding the coffee
Whisk fresh cream to a soft peak
In a separate bowl, whisk the eggs to a soft meringue then gently fold together, do not over mix
Using a rubber spatula gently fold through the mascarpone or sour cream
Slice choc cake into 3 x 1 cm slices

Layer all of the above into a glass bowl or individual parfait glass using the following steps

Place the first slice layer at the base of the glass bowl and brush with coffee syrup

Place ⅓ of the mascarpone cream mixture onto the cake then using a sieve dust the cocoa powder over the top of the cream mixture

Repeat this 3 times, finishing with a cream mixture layer on top and final dust with cocoa powder

Refrigerate to set for 2 hours before serving

Terry's Tip: Use a store bought Gluten free chocolate cake mix, Betty Crocker has quite a good one.

Elaine's Mango Dessert *GF

Preparation time: 30 minutes plus 4-8 hours refrigeration time
Serves 6-8

Ingredients

2 cups of boiling water

2 packets mango jellies
2 teaspoons gelatine
1 cup chilled carnation milk
2 eggs
400 grams or 2 mangoes, chopped

Method

Mix gelatine and jelly powder in a bowl
Pour the boiling water over the jelly mixture and stir until clear, leave to cool
Skin mangoes and chop into 1cm squares
In a separate bowl, blend eggs and carnation milk until it doubles in size
Fold mango and mango jelly mixture through the mixture and gently pour
into a serving bowl
Refrigerate until set

Terry's Chocolate, Raspberry, Pistachio Custard Cups *GF

Preparation time: 10 minutes
Cooking time: 5 minutes
Serves 6-8

Ingredients

400 grams chocolate sponge roll*
¼ cup orange liqueur
400 grams vanilla custard
1 teaspoon vanilla paste
¼ cup pistachio kernels, toasted and chopped
250 grams fresh berries

Berry Sauce Ingredients

½ cup water
½ cup caster sugar
300g frozen raspberries

Method

To make Raspberry Sauce, place sugar and water in a saucepan
Stir over low heat until sugar dissolves, approximately two minutes
Add raspberries and bring to the boil, reduce heat to simmer for 5 minutes
Remove from heat and leave to cool for 5 minutes
Transfer to blender and blend till smooth
Strain through a sieve to remove seeds and set aside
Cut sponge roll into 8 equal slices and brush both sides liberally with the orange liqueur
Cut each slice into 6 even wedges
Place one sponge wedge into the bottom of each cup and top each with 2 teaspoons custard, 2 teaspoons raspberry syrup, ½ teaspoon chopped pistachio and 2 raspberries
Repeat this layering 2 more times using 2 sponge wedges in each layer
Cover and refrigerate for 4 to 8 hours before serving

Terry's Tips: Substitute the chocolate sponge roll for any other gluten free sponge cake or GF Scotch finger biscuits, they're not as pliable but are just as tasty! A teaspoon or two of chocolate ganache in each layer makes the whole thing a little more decadent

Chocolate Ganache *GF

Ingredients

200 grams grated 70% dark chocolate
200 grams cream

Method

Place in a heatproof bowl over a saucepan of boiling water, stir constantly until the chocolate is melted and the cream is blended through, and then remove from heat

Meagan's Chocolate Truffles *GF

This mixture makes a very large batch of truffles, why make one when you can make many. My daughter Meagan knows just how quickly these truffles get gobbled up when family are around! They're also great to put into baskets as Christmas gifts.

Cooking time: 5-10 minutes
Preparation time: 1 hour
Makes lots of balls, depending on the size you roll!

Ingredients

625 grams cream
50 grams glucose
65 grams butter
625 dark chocolate (couverture)
625 milk chocolate (couverture)

Method

Bring cream, glucose and butter to the boil carefully
Over a pot of boiling water, melt chocolate and whisk until all lumps are clear
Pour the cream mixture into the chocolate and stir to combine
Place into a square container and refrigerate until set

Make small balls of mixture, roll the balls in chocolate and then in cocoa powder

Terry's Tips: You can also divide mixture into separate batches and add flavour or nuts to some of the mixtures. You can also coat in nuts, coconut or any other tasty sprinkle.

Triple Choc Muffins *GF

These muffins I adapted from a Nestles Recipe Card that came out of a box of baking cocoa in about 1970. Of course the Nestle products can be substituted for any others you can find.

Cooking time: 20-25 minutes
Preparation time: 15 minutes
Makes 12 Muffins

Ingredients

2 ½ cups self-raising flour*
½ cup Nestles baking cocoa
¼ cup sugar
1 cup Nestles milk chocolate bits
1 egg
1½ cups milk
100 grams butter, melted

Topping Ingredients

200g Nestles dark melts
¼ cup cream
1½ cups milk

Method

Preheat oven to 180°C
Line a 12 holed muffin tin with paper
In a large bowl, sift flour and baking cocoa and stir in sugar and milk chocolate bits
In a separate bowl, whisk egg and milk together then add to the dry ingredients
Add the melted butter mix well
Spoon into muffin cases
Bake for 20 to 25 minutes
Remove and cool on wire rack
In a bowl over boiling water, combine the dark melts and the cream until melted
Spoon the topping on to the muffins when cool

Chocolate Mousse *GF

Preparation time: 20 minutes plus 1-2 hours refrigeration
Serves 6-8

Ingredients

125 grams cream cheese
½ cup sugar
1 egg
250 grams Premium dark chocolate
600ml thickened cream

Method

Beat cheese, sugar and egg together until smooth
Break the chocolate up into small pieces and melt in a bowl over boiling water
Add the melted chocolate to the cream cheese mixture, stir through till well combined
Lightly whip the cream and fold into the mixture
Refrigerate for 1-2 hours
When ready to serve, pipe or spoon into glass bowls

Terry's Tips: You can also use chocolates cups or sweet shortbread casings. You can also use this mousse mixture as a filling for other desserts or cakes.

Terry's Coconut Ice *GF

Preparation time: 20 minutes plus refrigeration time
Makes 12 slices, depending on the size of your squares

Ingredients

1 tin coconut milk
¾ cup coconut oil
½ cup rice malt syrup
2 cups coconut desiccated

Method

Place coconut milk, coconut oil and rice malt syrup in a pot over low heat
and stir till melted
Remove from heat and add the desiccated coconut
Place half the mixture on a lined biscuit tray, making an even layer using
a spatula
Mix sugar free pink food colouring in to the other half and place on top of
the white layer, making another even layer
Cut into squares and refrigerate to set

Terry's White Nectarine And Vanilla Caramel Tarte Tatin *GF

Preparation time: 20 minutes
Cooking time: 20-25 minutes
Serves 6 to 8

Ingredients

250 grams castor sugar
50 grams unsalted butter
3 grams vanilla paste
8 white nectarines
1 sheet puff pastry*

Method

Preheat oven to 200°C
Place a pan on the heat and gradually stir in the sugar to make a caramel, once it's golden in colour, add the butter, stirring mixture until completely combined
Pour the mixture into an 8 inch shallow cake tin or medium size fry pan with metal handle
Place a medium pot of water on the stove and bring to the boil

With a sharp knife, mark an X on the top and bottom of each nectarine and place into the boiling water, slowly turning them over for 5 minutes, and then remove from heat

Place the nectarines into a bowl of cold water and gently peel off the skins

Slice the nectarines and lay them in a cake tin on top of the caramel making sure the inside is facing up

Cut pastry to the same size as the cake tin, using a fork mark the pastry lightly and then place it on top of nectarines

Bake in the oven for 20 minutes or until pastry is golden brown

Baklava *GF

This recipe comes from my neighbour Georgina Kolikias. It's a bit fiddly but definitely worth the time, so much nicer than anything you buy in a shop.

Preparation time: 40 minutes
Cooking time: 30-40 minutes
Makes 1 tray

Ingredients

2½ cups walnuts
1¼ cups blanched almonds
2/3 cup pistachios
1/4 cups caster sugar
1 teaspoon ground cinnamon
375 gram packet filo pastry
125g butter, melted

Syrup Ingredients

1 cup sugar
½ cup honey
¼ cup water
1 lemon, juice and zest
Whole cloves

Method

Pre-heat oven to 180°C

Line a 30x20cm tray with baking paper, lightly grease

Process nuts until finely chopped

In a bowl place the nuts, cinnamon and sugar, and mix well

Place filo pastry on a chopping board and place the tray on top and cut it to size using a sharp knife

Cover the pastry with a damp tea towel

Layer the six sheets of pastry on to the tray one by one, brushing each with melted butter

Spread half of the nut mixture over the pastry and repeat the filo and nut layers

Finish with filo, still brushing each sheet with butter

Press down firmly and refrigerate for 10 minutes

With a sharp knife cut through the filo in a diagonal pattern making diamond shapes

Bake for 30 to 40 minutes, until golden

Remove from the over and leave to stand until cool

For the syrup, combine all ingredients in a pot over medium heat, until sugar is dissolved

Simmer 1 minute without stirring, remove from heat and our over the Baklava

Set aside again until quite cool, slice into diamonds before serving

Chocolate Rum Mini Mousse *GF

Preparation time: 10 minutes
Cooking time: 5-10 minutes
Serves 4

Ingredients

6 egg yolks
1/3 cup caster sugar
125 grams dark rum
50 grams dark chocolate, grated

Method

In a heat proof blow over a pot of simmering water, heat the eggs and sugar together until light and fluffy
Whisk egg mixture continuously while gradually adding the rum, continue to whisk until the mixture is thick and creamy
Add the grated chocolate in batches, whisking gently until chocolate melts between each addition
Pour mousse into 4 cups or serving glasses
Serve with almond biscuits or almond wafers

Soft Centred Chocolate Cakes With Warm Sour Cherry Sauce *GF

Preparation time: 10 minutes
Cooking time: 5-10 minutes
Serves 6

Ingredients

185 grams dark chocolate, coarsely chopped
185 grams butter, chopped
3 egg yolks
1/3 cup plain flour (or corn flour plus ½ teaspoon baking powder*)
4 eggs
1/3 cup caster sugar
250 grams sour cherry jam
250 grams crème fraiche

Method

Pre-heat oven to 180°C
Grease a 6 holed muffin tin, sprinkle with flour
Place chocolate and butter in small pan, stir over low heat until mixture is smooth
Transfer into large bowl and stir in yolks and flour, whisk until light and fluffy

Fold chocolate mixture into the egg mixture

Spoon into prepared pan and bake for 10 minutes

Leave to stand for 5 minutes before removing carefully from pans, cakes should still be soft in the centre

Meanwhile, place jam into a pan and bring to the boil, add a little water to make a pouring consistency if needed

Skim surface and leave stand for 5 minutes

Serve the cakes with cherry jam and a dollop of cream fraiche poured over the top

Anne's White Chocolate Chip Brownies *GF

A good friend Anne Wilkinson passed on this delicious brownie recipe.

Preparation time: 15 minutes
Cooking time: 45 minutes
Makes 1 tray

Ingredients

200 grams butter, chopped
200 grams dark chocolate, chopped
1/3 cup cocoa powder
1 cup brown sugar
1 teaspoon vanilla essence
3 eggs, lightly beaten
3/4 cup plain flour, sifted (or corn flour with ½ teaspoon baking powder*)
1 cup white chocolate chips

Method

Preheat oven to 160°C
In a bowl over a pot of boiling water, melt the dark chocolate and the butter
Add cocoa powder, brown sugar, vanilla and whisk, then add the eggs and milk and mix well
Stir in the flour and white chocolate chips
Pour into a paper lined slice tray and bake for 40-45 minutes

Cherry Custard Cake *GF

This is a lovely moist cake to have with a cup of tea or coffee.

Preparation time: 25-30 minutes
Cooking time: 75 minutes
Serves 8

Ingredients

1 can pitted black cherries in syrup
250 grams butter, room temperature
1 cup castor sugar
1 tablespoon orange rind, finely grated
3 eggs
2½ cups self-raising flour*
2/3 cup milk
1 cup vanilla custard

Custard Ingredients

500 grams milk
125 grams sugar
5 egg yolks
60 grams corn flour
2 grams vanilla paste

Method

Preheat oven to 160°C

For the custard place milk and vanilla into a pot and bring to the boil

Add sugar and egg yolks together and whisk till light, and then add the corn flour

Once the milk has boiled pour it over the egg mixture, then place back into the pot and cook, stir until it's a thick consistency

Place custard into a tray, cover and refrigerator until required

Grease 24 cm round cake pan, line base and sides with baking paper

Drain cherries and pat dry with paper towel then set aside

Beat the butter, sugar and rind in a bowl until light and fluffy

Add the eggs one at a time, beating well between each addition

Stir in the milk and flour in two batches, add the orange rind

Spread half the batter over the pan evenly

Spread 1 cup of the custard over cake batter and then top with the remaining cake batter

Arrange the cherries on the top, pushing them in lightly

Bake for 75 minutes or until cooked when tested with a skewer

Turn onto a wire rack to cool slightly

Serve the cake warm with the remaining custard

Terry's Tip: A nice variation is to add orange rind and orange liquor in the pouring custard to taste.

Celia's Swiss Peach Dessert *GF

Celia Delaney gave me this lovely peach dessert recipe.

Preparation time: 5-10 minutes
Cooking time: 20 minutes
Serves 8

Ingredients

60 grams almonds, flaked
1 Swiss roll* or a GF biscuit*
¼ cup orange juice
¼ cup brandy
300 ml thickened cream, whipped
425 gram can peach slices

Method

Preheat oven to 160°C
Toast the almonds in the oven for 5-10 minutes until golden
Cut the Swiss roll into slices and place on a serving plate sandwiching each
slice with whipped cream so it's in the same shape as a Swiss roll
Mix the orange juice and brandy and gently pour over the roll
Cover the whole cake with cream and sprinkle the almonds over sides and top
Finish by arranging the drained peach slices on the top

Chocolate Pear Pudding *GF

Preparation time: 20 minutes
Cooking time: 25-30 minutes
Serves 8

Ingredients

2 x 800 gram canned pears
125 grams plain flour*
75 grams castor sugar
25 grams cocoa powder
1 teaspoon baking powder
1 teaspoon bi-carb soda
1 teaspoon vanilla
200 grams butter
2 eggs

Method

Preheat oven to 160°C
Drain the pears and layer onto the bottom of a square pie dish
Place flour, sugar, cocoa powder, baking powder, bi-carb soda, vanilla, butter
and eggs in to a bowl and mix for 10 minutes or until smooth
Place batter on top of pears and bake for 25 to 30 minutes

Eaton Mess Marcelle *GF

Preparation time: 20 minutes
Cooking time: 30-40 minutes
Serves 4

Ingredients

300 grams raspberries
50 ml caster sugar
50 ml framboise liqueur
80 grams meringue
22g clotted cream
430 grams mixed summer berries

Meringue Ingredients

100 grams egg whites
110 grams caster sugar
110 grams icing sugar
3 grams vanilla paste

Method

Preheat oven to 140°C

To make the meringue, whisk the egg whites and caster sugar together until firm

Fold through icing sugar until clear

Pipe onto baking trays and bake for 30-40 minutes or until firm to touch

To make the sauce, push the raspberries through a sieve over a bowl (discard the pips)

Stir in the caster sugar and framboise liquor

Once the meringue has cooled, break it into pieces and gently fold into clotted cream, then fold in mixed berries

Pile mixture into 4 pretty glasses and drizzle with the sauce

Decorate with mint leaves

Bon Vivant Flourless Chocolate Hazelnut Cake *GF

Preparation time: 40 minutes plus minimum 6 hours (or overnight) refrigeration
Cooking time: 15 minutes
Serves 8

Ingredients

4 egg whites at room temperature
100 grams caster sugar
150 grams ground hazelnuts
2 tablespoons dark cocoa powder
250 grams dark chocolate (60-70% cocoa) chopped into pieces

Method

Preheat oven to 180°C
Line a 23cm spring form cake tin with non-stick baking paper, base and sides
In a large bowl, whisk the egg whites until stiff, then gradually whisk in the sugar
Stir through the hazelnuts and cocoa using a large perforated spoon
Spoon the mixture into the prepared tin and smooth the top

Bake for 15 minutes or until a wooden skewer inserted in the middle comes out clean

Remove from oven and set aside until cool

Make Chocolate Mousse recipe

Spoon mousse mixture over the top of the hazelnut meringue

Smooth the top, cover and refrigerate for several hours or overnight before cutting

Remove spring form pan and paper before serving

Terry's Tip: Serve this recipe with a dust of icing sugar and a dollop of cream or ice cream

Terry's Rum Balls *GF

Preparation time: 10 minutes
Makes lots of balls!

Ingredients

250 grams icing sugar
1 level tablespoon cocoa powder
56 grams desiccated coconut
1 egg
1 tablespoon rum
½ teaspoon vanilla essence
125 grams copha

Method

Sift icing sugar, cocoa and desiccated coconut into a mixing bowl
In a separate bowl, beat the egg, rum and vanilla essence
Chop copha, place into a saucepan and melt on gentle heat (must only be lukewarm)
Pour all liquids into the mixing bowl and combine
Refrigerate until mixture is firm
Mould into 2½cm balls and roll into coconut, coloured decorates, chopped nuts or chocolate sprinkles

Melon In Champagne *GF

Preparation time: 20 minutes
Serves 8

Ingredients

1 rockmelon
1 honeydew melon
1 wedge watermelon
1 x 750ml bottle champagne
8 rose petals
1 egg white
50 grams caster sugar

Method

Remove flesh from melons with melon baller and arrange in champagne glasses, cocktail glasses or small bowls
Rose petals have been dipped in egg white then caster sugar
Prior to serving, pour champagne over melon

Terry's Tip: To really finish this off, you can decorate the glass or blow with grapes hanging over the side.

Terry's Butterscotch Tart

This is another old favourite dessert recipe and trying to make it gluten free would really spoil the flavour, I do miss it and felt that it would be a shame to not share it for those who aren't GF!

Preparation time: 40 minutes
Cooking time: 15 minutes
Serves 8

Biscuit Pastry Ingredients

1 egg
57 grams sugar
85 grams margarine
170 grams flour
½ level teaspoon baking powder
Pinch of salt

Filling Ingredients

½ cup brown sugar (firmly packed)
4 level tablespoons flour
Pinch of salt
2 cups milk
2 egg yolks
1 level tablespoon butter
1 tablespoon water

½ cup brown sugar
1 teaspoon vanilla essence

Meringue Ingredients

2 egg whites
4 level table spoons white sugar

Method

Preheat oven to 180-200°C
To make the biscuit pastry, beat egg and sugar until thick, add softened margarine and beat in thoroughly
Sift in the flour, baking powder and salt and combine
Turn out on a floured surface and knead lightly until firm
Roll out to fit 9" pie dish, prick base with fork and decorate the edge
Bake for approximately 15 minutes, set aside and allow to cool
For the filling, mix the brown sugar, flour and salt in a saucepan
In a bowl, beat egg yolks and milk and then gradually blend it into the flour mixture
Heat gently, stirring constantly until mixture boils and thickens, cook for two minutes then remove from heat
Place butter, water and sugar in a separate saucepan over heat, stir well until boiling then leave to boil gently for about 5 minutes to form the butterscotch toffee
Pour the toffee mixture into the thickened milk mixture, stirring until toffee is dissolved then add vanilla

Refrigerate mixture for approximately 30 minutes and then place in cooled tart shell

For the meringue, beat egg whites until stiff, add sugar gradually and beat until dissolved

Pile the meringue on top of the butterscotch tart, brown lightly with a blow torch (if you have one)

Golden Syrup Pudding *GF

Connie Maling and Camel Hinchcilff who are sisters and neighbours gave me this lovely recipe. Connie and Carmel said they have the fondest memory of their mother making this for them when we were children. Thank you for sharing it with me to share with everyone in my book.

Preparation time: 20 minutes
Cooking time: 90 minutes
Serves 8

Ingredients

1 dessert spoon margarine
2 tablespoons golden syrup
¼ teaspoon bi-carb soda
½ cup milk
1 cup sifted self-raising flour*

Method

Heat margarine and golden syrup in a saucepan
Dissolve bi-carb soda in milk and add to the saucepan
Stir in the sifted flour till combined
Place mixture into a greased steamer in a saucepan of boiling water and steam for 1¼ to 1½ hours
Serve with custard

Marshmallow Pavlova *GF

This recipe comes from one of my husband's sisters Helen Edwards. I have fond memories of Helen making Pavlova for many of our big family gatherings; it was a favourite amongst the kids and the adults!

Preparation time: 30 minutes
Cooking time: 1 hour, 30 minutes
Serves 8-10

Ingredients

4 egg whites
1 cup of caster sugar
1 teaspoon vanilla essence
1½ teaspoons white vinegar

Method

Preheat oven to 120°C
Beat egg whites and sugar for 20 minutes till it forms soft peaks
Fold through remaining ingredients until the mixture is clear
Spoon the mixture onto a foil lined tray making a circle and smoothing sides and top with a spatula

Bake on the middle shelf for 1¼ to 1½ hours or until the Pavlova is dry to the touch

Remove from the oven and when it's completely cold, transfer to serving plate or store in an airtight container until required

Terry's Tip: You can top this Pavlova with any fruit combinations you like and serve with whipped cream.

Hedgehog *GF

This is a very simple and very quick dessert that my mum Granny Smith used to make for the kids who always loved it.

Preparation time: 45 minutes
Cooking time: 5 minutes
Serves 8

Ingredients

500 grams morning coffee biscuits (or any similar gluten free biscuits)*
¾ cup desiccated coconut
250 grams butter or margarine
½ cup caster sugar
1 dessert spoon cocoa powder
1 egg, beaten

Chocolate Icing Ingredients

200 grams chocolate
200 grams cream
20 grams coconut

Method

Break biscuits into small pieces into a blow and add coconut

Melt butter, sugar and cocoa in a saucepan then add a beaten egg and bring to the boil

Pour over the dry ingredients and mix

Press lightly into a shallow tray and refrigerate to set for 30 minutes

For the chocolate icing, place the cholate and cream in a blow over a boiling saucepan and stir till combined

Remove from heat and stir in the coconut and leave to cool

When the log is set, remove from the tray onto serving dish

Use a spatula to spread the chocolate icing and sprinkle with coconut

Terry's Tip: You may need to sit the tray in hot water in the sink so the log is easy to remove from the pan. Or alternatively you can line the tray with cling wrap before pouring in the log mixture which makes it easy to remove.

French Chews *GF

This recipe comes from Margaret and Gus who are our neighbours when we relocate to Ellis Beach for the winter.

Preparation time: 30 minutes
Cooking time: 40 minutes
Serves 8

Ingredients

45 grams butter
½ cup sugar
2 egg yolks
½ teaspoon baking powder
50 grams plain flour or corn flour*
½ teaspoon vanilla

Topping Ingredients

½ cup demerara sugar
½ cup of walnuts or coconut (or mixture of both)
3 egg whites

Method

Preheat oven to 160°C

In a bowl, cream the butter, sugar, egg yolks, baking powder, flour and vanilla

Line a sandwich tin with baking paper and evenly spread the mixture over the base

For the topping, beat egg whites until stiff

Fold in the sugar, walnut and/or coconuts and spread evenly over the mixture

Bake for 35-40 minutes, making sure meringue is cooked (dry to touch)

Once completely cooled, slice using a serrated edged knife

Variation

Spread either stewed apricots or apricot jam over the biscuit base. Delete the walnuts (not the coconut) from the meringue. Personally I prefer this option.

Almond Macaroons *GF

These are great for after dinner or for afternoon tea. These are a must addition to any high tea occasion.

Preparation time: 20 minutes
Cooking time: 15-20 minutes
Make 1 tray (approximately 20 macaroons)

Ingredients

2 egg whites
½ cup caster sugar
110 grams slivered almonds
½ cup desiccated coconut
2 teaspoons rosewater essence

Method

Preheat oven to 150°C
Line a baking tray with baking paper
Beat egg whites and caster sugar together until the mixture has increased in volume and is thick and white
Add slivered almonds, coconut and rose water, stirring with a large metal spoon until just combined
Spoon teaspoonful's of the mixture 5cm apart onto the tray
Bake for 15-20 minutes or until pale golden and firm/dry to touch
Stand on a wire rack until the macaroons are cold

Cheesecake *GF

This is by far the easiest cheese cake ever!

Preparation time: 20 minutes
Cooking time: 25-30 minutes
Serves 8-10

Ingredients

1 packets scotch finger biscuits*
200 grams butter
150 grams cream cheese (room temperature)
2 lemon jellies* (or 2 cups of Bickfords Lemon cordial with gelatine)
1 can of evaporated milk (chilled)

Method

Make the jellies according to the instructions but using only half the water
Place the biscuits into a food processor to form a crumb and place in a blow
Melt the butter, add to the biscuit crumb and stir to combine
Press out into a spring form cake tin
Beat the evaporated milk until it doubled in size
Beat in the cream cheese
Beat in the cooled jellies

Pour over the biscuit base and refrigerate to set before serving
Serve with a dollop of cream or ice cream

Terry's Tips: There are plenty of garnishes that can be used for this cheesecake such as a sprinkle of nutmeg, grated chocolate, grated mint bar, any seasonal fruit or sliced preserved lemon. For variations you can add canned fruit such as chopped pineapple, peaches, apricots or cocoa to the cheesecake mixture.

Mocha Cheesecake Slice *GF

Preparation time: 45 minutes
Cooking time: 30 minutes
Serves 8-10

Ingredients

1 packet of scotch finger biscuits*
250 grams butter
*Or use Jennifer's slice base**
500 grams cream cheese
3 eggs
20 grams instant coffee
100 grams white chocolate, melted and cooled slightly
120 grams dark chocolate, melted and cooled
1 tablespoon boiling water

Method

Preheat oven to 150°C
Lightly grease and line a 20x30 slice tray with baking paper
Place the biscuits into a food processor to form crumbs, add the melted butter
Press firmly onto slice tray and refrigerate for 30 minutes
In a large bowl, using an electric beater, beat cream cheese and sugar until smooth
Add eggs one at a time, mixing each one in before adding the next

Divide mixture into two separate bowls

Dissolve coffee in the boiling water and add to one of the bowls, also add the melted white chocolate, mix well

Add the melted dark chocolate into the other bowl and stir to combine

Cover slice base with alternate spoonful's of white and dark chocolate mixtures

Drag a skewer through top to create swirls

Bake for 20-30 minutes until mixture is firm

Cool completely in the pan, before cutting into squares

Terry's Tips: Cut into small squares and give as gifts from your kitchen or longer bars for lunchbox snacks.

Easy Muesli Bars *GF

Preparation time: 20 minutes
Cooking time: 25-30 minutes
Serves 8

Ingredients

3 cups natural fruit muesli
3/4 cup self-raising flour or corn four*
2/3 cup dried apricots, chopped
2/3 cup desiccated coconut
185 grams butter, chopped
1/2 cup brown sugar
1/4 cup honey

Method

Preheat oven to 150°C
Lightly grease and line a slice tray with baking paper
In a large bowl combine flour, muesli, apricots and coconut
In a small saucepan combine butter, sugar and honey, stirring over medium heat until melted and smooth
Make a well in the dry ingredients and pour in butter mixture, mix well
Press evenly into the tray using a fork to prevent bar from crumbling
Bake for 15 minutes or until golden brown
Cool in pan before cutting into bars
Store in airtight container

Terry's Panna Cotta *GF

Preparation time: 20 minutes plus 3 hours refrigeration time
Serves 6-8

Ingredients

500 grams milk
75 grams caster sugar
3 leaves gelatine
375 grams crème fraiche
½ vanilla pod

Method

Heat the milk, vanilla bean and sugar together, bring to a simmer (be sure not to boil)
Place the gelatine leaves in ice water until soft, then drain and add to heated milk mixture and dissolve
Remove from heat and stir through the crème fraiche
Place into classes or moulds, cover and refrigerate for 3 hours or until set

Terry's Tips: This dessert can be served with fresh berries or sliced fruit, I like to serve it with poached plumbs.

Meagan's Date Tart *GF

Definitely saving the best till last, this recipe comes from my daughter Meagan who was taught this date tart recipe whilst she was working at Rock Pool under Head Pastry Chef Lorraine Godsmark. It is her favourite thing to make me for my Birthday. It's such a lovely dessert.

Preparation time: 40 minutes plus 3 hour refrigeration time
Cooking time: 75 minutes
Makes 1 tray

Tart Pastry Ingredients

250 grams cold butter, cut into cubes
38 grams caster sugar
1 large egg, beaten
30 grams milk
375 grams bakers flour or gluten free flour*, sifted
Pinch of salt

Filling Ingredients

8-10 fresh soft dates, halved, stones removed
180 grams egg yolks
78 grams sugar
600 ml single/pouring cream
½ vanilla pod

Extra

50 grams flour
1 egg yolk

Method

Place the flour, sugar and butter in a food pressor and blend until small butter lumps are formed

Add egg and blend until half the mixture is combined, then add the milk and mix until you have clear dough

If required place on the bench and rub the butter through the dough, wrap in cling wrap and refrigerate for 2 hours

Using a little bit of dusting flour on the bench, roll out the base and place into a 10 inch fluted cake tin, pastry should be about 3/4 cm thick

Refrigerate and rest pastry for 1 hour

Preheat oven to 200°C

Remove from refrigerator and blind bake pastry case for 20 to 35 minutes or until par-baked

Once baked brush the inside of the shell with egg yolk to seal any cracks that may have occurred during baking and place back in the oven for 2 minutes to seal then set aside on a cooling wrack

Preheat oven to 180°C

Cut dates in ½ and gently flatten the dates into the tart shell making sure that no air is trapped under the date, place the dates like a clock around the edge of the tart shell

Whisk egg yolks, vanilla seed and sugar together until extremely light and fluffy

Place cream and vanilla pod in a pot and bring to 79°C, ***do not boil***

Pour cream over egg mixture and gently stir until mixture is completely combined, give the bottom of the bowl a couple of taps on the bench to release any air bubbles

Place tart shell in the oven and pour the mixture on top

Bake for a total of 30-40 minutes, reducing the oven temperature by 10°C every 10 minutes until the tart is golden brown but still has a slight wobble in the centre, it will become firmer as it cools and it's important not to overcook the filling. If you feel that it needs more time it's safer to turn the oven off and leave it in the oven for a little extra time. Allow to come to room temperature before serving

Use a hot bread knife to cut slices

Terry's Tip: Meagan recommends not serving it with anything as the tart speaks for itself but I like a little dollop of cream on the side.

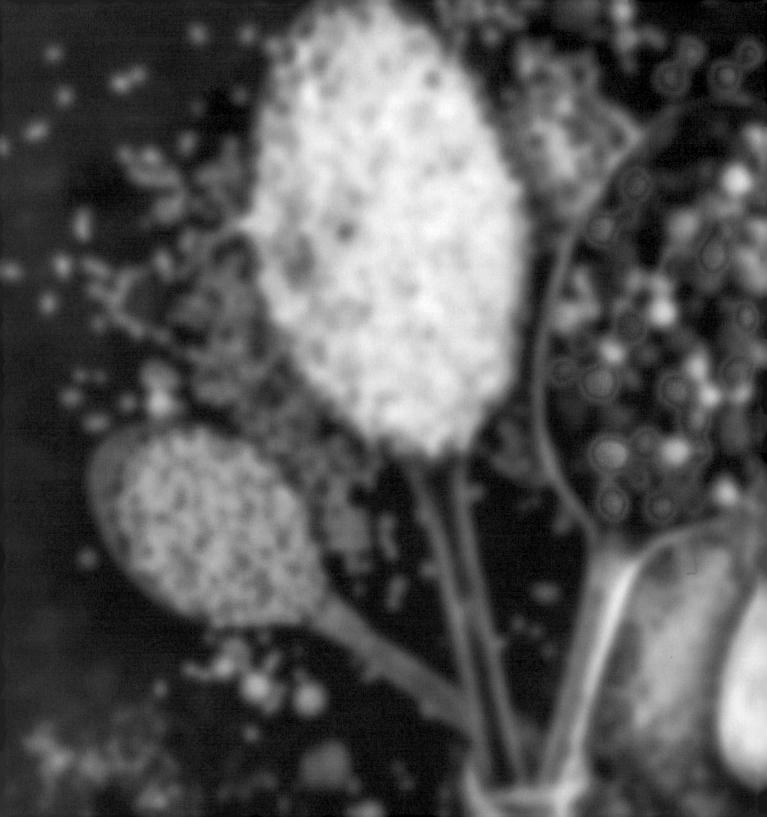

Pickles, Preserves, Sauces & Dressings

Pickles & Preserves

Mum's Green Pickles Recipe *GF

This pickles recipe can be used to pickle green tomato, cauliflower, cucumber and choko. I am sure this recipe came over with the first fleet. Growing up, everyone's home had homemade jars of pickles. I like to give these jars away as Christmas gifts or to the grand kid's school fetes.

Preparation time: 20 minutes (plus overnight)
Cooking time: 30 minutes
Makes 6 to 8 jars

Ingredients

1.2 kg cauliflower (or whatever you have chosen to be pickled)
250 grams sliced onions
2 tablespoons salt
500 ml white vinegar
2 tablespoons sugar
2 tablespoons all spice (in muslin bag)

Mustard Dressing Ingredients

1 level tablespoon mustard
2 level tablespoons curry powder
3 tablespoons cornflower
½ cup apple cider vinegar

Method

Prepare vegetables by breaking/slicing into small pieces
Place into a bowl with onions and salt, leave to stand overnight
Strain off all extracted liquid
Place vegetables into a pot with vinegar, sugar and a muslin spice bag containing allspice
Cook for 20 minutes then remove the spice bag
Stir in the mustard dressing and cook for a further 10 minutes
Spoon into sterilised jars and store

Granny Smith's Beetroot Relish *GF

Another Granny Smith family favourite, this beetroot relish is delicious, especially when served with lamb. The texture can be adjusted to your own liking, and I suggest it be somewhat chunky to give contrast to the smoothness of the lamb. A good side dish for tapas if the beetroot is cut into batons.

Preparation time: 30 minutes
Cooking time: 30 minutes
Makes 6 servings

Ingredients

6 medium beets, scrubbed and chopped
1 cup chopped onion
1 cup chopped red bell pepper
1 stalk celery, chopped
1 cup chopped cauliflower
½ cup white sugar
2 tablespoons salt
3 tablespoons mustard seed
1 tablespoon celery seed
1 cup white vinegar

Method

In a large pot, combine the beets, onion, red bell pepper, celery, cauliflower and sugar
Season with salt, mustard seed, celery seed and then stir in the white vinegar
Bring to a boil then reduce to low heat
Simmer stirring occasionally for 20 minutes or until vegetables are tender
Use immediately or store in sterilised jars

Terry's Tip: Omit peppers, celery and cauliflower for a pure Beet Pickle.

Tomato Relish *GF

This recipe was acquired by my mother (Granny Smith) from the ladies of the Seven Day Adventists, with the understanding that she would not make it and sell it. This was at least sixty years ago so I'm sure that her promise is well and truly outdated!

Preparation time: 20
Cooking time: 40
Makes 6 to 8 jars

Ingredients

1.4 litres vinegar
3 kg ripe tomatoes
1.5 kg onions
1 kg sugar
½ cup salt

Dry ingredients

1 level tablespoon mustard
2 level tablespoons curry powder
3 tablespoons cornflour*

Method

Peel and cut tomatoes, onions and place in a bowl
Sprinkle with salt and leave to stand overnight
Pour off liquid, place in a large pot and cover with vinegar
Bring to the boil, add sugar and boil for a further 10 minutes
Mix dry ingredients together, then add 1 tablespoon of vinegar to create a smooth paste
Add mixture to the pot and boil for a further 30 minutes, stirring regularly
Allow to cool slightly, add to warm sterilised jars
Seal jars immediately

Terry's Tip: Granny's recipe above says to pour off liquid, I don't because it's just too nice. I do however add a little more cornflour.

Choko Pickles *GF

I love choko pickles but unfortunately people do not grow chokos over their fences like they used too, they are now in short supply and reasonably expensive. This recipe was given to me by an elderly friend, Paul Benstead's mother, many years ago.

Preparation time: 15 minutes (plus overnight)
Cooking time: 20 minutes
Makes 10 jars

Ingredients

250 grams salt
1¼ litres water
2 kg chokos chopped
½ kg onions chopped
1½ litres vinegar
250 grams fresh ginger
½ kg white sugar
1 tablespoon curry
1 tablespoon mustard
1 tablespoon turmeric
1 teaspoon all spice
1 teaspoon pepper
1 cup plain flour or cornflour*

Method

Make a brine of salt and water

Pour over chokos and onions and leave to stand overnight

Drain off liquid and place into a large saucepan with 1 litre of vinegar, ginger, sugar and spices

Bring to the boil then reduce heat and simmer for 15 minutes

Mix flour with remaining vinegar and stir into choko mixture, cook for a further 5 minutes, stirring well

Allow to cool and pour into warm sterilized jars

Terry's Tip: Chop vegetables into smallish pieces if using for sandwich filling.

Bread And Butter Pickled Cucumber *GF

As with many of Granny Smith's recipes, this one too has been passed down from her Granny and is another family favourite.

Preparation time: 15 minutes (plus overnight)
Cooking time: 10 minutes
Makes 4 to 6 jars

Ingredients

4 large cucumbers
¼ cup cooking salt
1½ cups apple cider vinegar
1 cup water
¾ cup sugar
2 teaspoons mustard seeds
1 teaspoon all spice seeds
½ small red pepper

Method

Thinly slice the cucumbers and place in layers in a large shallow dish, sprinkling salt between each layer
Cover and stand overnight
Drain and rinse cucumbers under cold water
Combine vinegar, water, sugar, mustard seeds, all spice and 1 teaspoon of salt in a pan

Stir over low heat until sugar has dissolved, then bring to boil
Reduce heat and simmer uncovered for 5 minutes
Add the cucumbers, bring to the boil then remove from heat
Leave to cool
Transfer cucumbers into warm sterilised jars adding a few thin strips of red pepper to each
Fill the jars with vinegar mixture to within 1cm of the top and seal

Strawberry Jam *GF

This jam is quick and easy to make and any berry fruit will work just as well.
It is my own version of an age old classic and can be used as a dessert sauce
for cakes, on top of a pavlova or freshly made scones, etc ...

Preparation time: 5 minutes
Cooking time: 10 minutes
Makes 2 jars or 1 purpose

Ingredients

1 cup of sugar
2 cups of water
1 cup of strawberries washed and de-hulled (or berries of your choice)

Method

Place all ingredients into a heavy pot and bring to the boil
After 5 minutes, lower the heat and watch carefully until the mixture thickens
Remove from the heat and quickly test on a cold plate for jam consistency
Return to the heat for another few minutes if mixture is too runny

Terrys Tip: Be sure to watch carefully and do not leave the mixture unattended

Sauces

Rue Or White Sauce *GF

The base for many other flavours and the first sauce all of my children learnt to cook!

Preparation time: 5 minutes
Cooking time: 10 minutes
Makes 2 cups

Ingredients

3 tablespoons butter
4 heaped tablespoons self-raising or gluten free flour*
1 teaspoon salt (or according to taste)
2 cups milk

Method

Melt the butter in a saucepan
Add the flour and mix well to combine
Allow the combined flour and butter to cook for 2-3 minutes stirring constantly to ensure the mixture does not catch on the bottom of the pot
Add the salt
Remove the mixture from the heat and beat in the milk until smooth
Return to heat and bring to the boil, mixing constantly until mixture thickens

Parsley Sauce *GF

For the best sauce accompaniment to Corned Beef, add 3 sprigs of finely chopped parsley (or any herb to suit the occasion) to the white sauce.

Cheese Sauce *GF

For a cheesy sauce to add to pasta, lasagne or vegetable bakes (cauliflower or broccoli), add 1 cup of cheese (either cheddar or a mix of hard cheeses) to the white sauce, add extra milk if needed for pouring consistency.

Terry's Béarnaise Sauce *GF

Ingredients

Add to white sauce

2 tablespoons dry white wine
2 tablespoons apple cider vinegar
6 whole black peppercorns
2 shallots finely chopped
1 sprig fresh tarragon (dried tarragon does not have the flavour of fresh)
or fresh chervil
3 egg yolks
125 grams butter, chopped
1 garlic clove

Method

In a small saucepan bring vinegar, wine, peppercorns, shallots and tarragon
to high simmer and cook until reduced to approximately 2 tablespoons
Remove from heat and strain, reserving the liquid
Place egg yolks and strained vinegar mixture into a blender and process
to combine

Halve the garlic clove and rub on a warm pan, add the butter and melt until it starts to bubble then remove from heat

Very slowly pour butter through the tube of the blender while still hot to form a thick sauce

Stir through chopped fresh tarragon or chervil and season with salt and pepper

Terry's Tip: This sauce is the perfect accompaniment to a good steak!

Pear & Tarragon Cream *GF

A lovely summer time side dish or main for a luncheon.

Ingredients

2 tablespoons tarragon vinegar
2 teaspoons sugar
1 egg
1 pinch nutmeg
1 cup cream
1 tin sliced pear
1 baby cos lettuce

Method

Mix tarragon vinegar, sugar and egg together in a heat proof bowl over boiling water until mixture thickens
Remove from heat and allow to cool
Whip cream, and add to mixture and combine
Cool in fridge
To serve, pull apart the baby cos leaves and place individual leaves on a plate
Add pears to each lettuce leaf and spoon cream mixture on pears
Sprinkle with nutmeg

Blancmange Sauce Or Sweet Sauce *GF

Ingredients

Add to white sauce

1 tablespoon sugar
1 cup milk
1 teaspoon vanilla essence

Method

Beat the mixture and place in ramekins with stewed fruit either on the bottom or spooned over the top
Refrigerate until set

Custard *GF

Ingredients

Add to white sauce

2 beaten eggs
1 tablespoon sugar

Method

Beat the mixture to combine, be sure not to leave over the heat for too long as the eggs may curdle.

Terry's Tip: Add 1 teaspoon of vanilla essence for a Vanilla Custard.

Granny Smith's Lemon Sauce *GF

Ingredients

2 tablespoons cornflour*
2 teaspoons of custard powder*
1 cup cold water
2 tablespoons melted butter
2 tablespoons sugar
2 cups lemon juice
Zest of 1 lemon

Method

In a pot mix the cornflour, custard powder and cold water, stir until lumps are removed
Add the melted butter, sugar, lemon juice and lemon zest, stir and bring back to the boil, then remove from heat immediately

Terry's Tip: If the lemons are tart, taste the mixture to see if sweet enough, if not stir in another teaspoon sugar. This sweet sauce can be used to make a Lemon Pie or put in to jars and used as a Lemon Spread.

Dressings

Herb Dressing

Ingredients

1 anchovy fillet
¼ cup fresh herbs
2 tablespoons red wine vinegar
1/3 cup olive oil

Method

Combine all ingredients into a blender
Pulse until pureed
Season with salt and pepper

Simple French Dressing

Ingredients

1 cup olive oil
1 cup white vinegar
3 cloves crushed garlic
½ teaspoon sugar

Method

Add all ingredients to a jar
Replace lid onto jar and shake vigorously just before serving

Terry's Tip: Using the vinegar from a jar of pickled onions adds another dimension of flavour to the dressing. I pickle the garlic in the pickled onion vinegar and have it on hand for when necessary. This dressing stores in the refrigerator for weeks. My daughter Kristen likes to add ½ teaspoon mixed herbs (fresh or dry) to balance the garlic.

Independent Schools
Examinations Board

LATIN PRACTICE
EXERCISES

Level 2

R C Bass

www.galorepark.co.uk

GALORE PARK

Published by ISEB Publications, an imprint of Galore Park Publishing Ltd
19/21 Sayers Lane, Tenterden, Kent TN30 6BW
www.galorepark.co.uk

Design and typography Typetechnique

Printed by Replika Press Pvt. Ltd., India

ISBN: 978 0 903627 74 0

First published 2010, reprinted 2010

Details of other ISEB publications and examination papers, and Galore Park
publications are available at www.galorepark.co.uk

Cover image: Roman mosaic in the museum of Bardo in Tunis, Tunisia.
Image © Idealink Photography/Alamy

Contents

Introduction

This collection of practice exercises, previously published as *Ab Initio II*, is designed to provide material for pupils in their second year of learning Latin, particularly those preparing for the ISEB Common Entrance examination at Level 2. Companion volumes are available for Levels 1 and 3.

It may be used alongside courses such as *So you really want to learn Latin* and *Latin Prep*, both available from Galore Park, and provides extensive material for translation, both into and out of Latin, giving pupils the opportunity to revise or consolidate skills learnt in those courses. It may also be used as a free-standing course in conjunction with *Latin Practice Exercises Level 1*.

The vocabulary, grammar and syntax are deliberately geared to the Level 2 syllabus for Common Entrance. Five words from the Level 3 syllabus are included, however:

adeo = I go towards; alius = other; aut = either; relinquo = I leave; telum = spear.

It will not hurt to learn these words as and when they occur in the course.

An answer book, including mark schemes for the exercises, is available separately. For a full list of resources available visit www.galorepark.co.uk

A sequence of twelve test papers, *The Story of Perseus*, is included at the end of the book. It is suggested that these are not attempted before pupils have completed Chapter 3.

Nicholas Oulton
Series Editor
January 2010

Chapter 1

Revision

Exercise 1.1

Translate the following into English:

1. fuisti
2. amaverunt
3. currunt
4. videmus
5. scribebas

6. pugno
7. respondet
8. respondit
9. manebamus
10. clamant

1 mark for each question. Total: 10

Exercise 1.2

Translate the following into English:

1. ducis
2. dicis
3. luserunt
4. mittimus
5. movimus

6. discessistis
7. oppugnabas
8. ostenditis
9. paravit
10. posui

1 mark for each question. Total: 10

Exercise 1.3

Translate the following into English:

1. videmus
2. superaverunt
3. eratis
4. portabatis
5. audiunt

6. necavit
7. necant
8. movit
9. iussit
10. dat

1 mark for each question. Total: 10

Exercise 1.4

Translate the following into English:

1. constituerunt
2. cepit
3. cupiebam
4. ducebat
5. iecimus

6. laudatis
7. steterunt
8. portavisti
9. mittis
10. festinabamus

1 mark for each question. Total: 10

Exercise 1.5

Translate the following into English:

1. celeriter currebamus.
2. fortiter pugnabat.
3. diu navigaverunt.
4. numquam ludo.
5. bene scribis.
6. saepe flebant.
7. diu dormivi.
8. tandem discesserunt.
9. subito intravit.
10. semper bibit.

2 marks for each question. Total: 20

Exercise 1.6

Translate the following into English:

1. Romani magnum oppidum aedificaverunt. (4)
2. nauta pericula non timebat. (4)
3. turba feminarum in via stabat. (5)
4. multa verba dixisti. (3)
5. Romani multa templa deleverunt. (4)

Total: 20

Exercise 1.7

Translate the following into English:

1. oppidum novum muros altos habet. (5)
2. multi nautae celeriter appropinquant. (4)
3. hodie laboro. heri tamen nihil feci. (6)
4. Romani multa scuta portabant. (4)
5. multi viri boni in proelio pugnaverunt. (6)

Total: 25

Exercise 1.8

Translate the following into English:

1. nuntii in templum sacrum festinaverunt.
2. olim multi Romani clari erant.
3. dominus malus servum miserum necavit.
4. ancillae pulchrae cibum bonum parabant.
5. pueri mali magistros numquam audiunt.

5 marks for each question. Total: 25

Exercise 1.9

Translate the following into English:

1. magister puerum verbis iratis terruit.
2. gladiis et scutis semper pugnamus.
3. dominus multam pecuniam servo dedit.
4. parvum puerum hasta mea necavi.
5. poeta clarus librum bonum legebat.

5 marks for each question. Total: 25

Exercise 1.10

Translate the following into English:

1. verba nautarum mala erant. (4)
2. turbae servorum veniunt. (3)
3. muri templi alti et validi sunt. (6)
4. amicus pueri cantabat. (3)
5. verba magistri numquam audimus. (4)

Total: 20

Exercise 1.11

Translate the following into English:

1. ludere amant. (2)
2. servus pugnare cupiebat. (3)
3. dominus servum laborare iussit. (4)
4. laborare numquam cupio. (3)
5. nuntius currere constituit. (3)

Total: 15

Exercise 1.12

Translate the following into English:

1. lente ambulate, pueri!
2. librum scribe, poeta!
3. equos movete, agricolae!
4. vinum bibe, amice!
5. arma relinquite, nautae!

3 marks for each question. Total: 15

Exercise 1.13

Translate the following into English:

1. puer in via stabat.
2. servi contra dominum pugnaverunt.
3. in magno periculo sumus.
4. nuntius per viam cucurrit.
5. puella cum amicis ludit.

4 marks for each question. Total: 20

Exercise 1.14

Translate the following into English:

1. agricolane caelum diu spectabat? (4)
2. magisterne verba mala dixit? (4)
3. servine murum oppugnant? (3)
4. puerine scuta habent? (3)
5. dominusne multos servos et ancillas habebat? (6)

Total: 20

Exercise 1.15

Give the translation, person, number, tense and the first person singular of the present tense of the following verbs:

Example					
sunt	They are	3rd person	Plural	Present	sum

1. rident
2. oppugnabat
3. ponebamus
4. dedistis
5. steterunt

6. laboraverunt
7. constituunt
8. cucurristis
9. scripserunt
10. parabamus

5 marks for each question. Total: 50

4

Exercise 1.16

Give the translation, person, number, tense and the first person singular of the present tense of the following verbs:

1. veniunt
2. erat
3. portabas
4. necas
5. biberunt
6. dormiebas
7. iussit
8. monet
9. cepisti
10. dicebant

5 marks for each question. Total: 50

Exercise 1.17

Give and translate the following verb parts:

1. The 1st person singular, imperfect tense of **amo**.
2. The 2nd person plural, present tense of **sum**.
3. The 2nd person singular, perfect tense of **curro**.
4. The 3rd person plural, perfect tense of **pono**.
5. The 1st person plural, imperfect tense of **dormio**.

2 marks for each question. Total: 10

Exercise 1.18

Give and translate the following verb parts:

1. The 3rd person singular, present tense of **video**.
2. The 2nd person plural, imperfect tense of **bibo**.
3. The 1st person plural, perfect tense of **dico**.
4. The 3rd person plural, present tense of **festino**.
5. The 2nd person singular, perfect tense of **moneo**.

2 marks for each question. Total: 10

Exercise 1.19

Give and translate the following verb parts:

1. The 3rd person singular, perfect tense of **sum**.
2. The 1st person singular, imperfect tense of **teneo**.
3. The 2nd person singular, present tense of **rego**.
4. The 3rd person singular, present tense of **rideo**.
5. The 2nd person singular, imperfect tense of **facio**.

2 marks for each question. Total: 10

Exercise 1.20

Put into the plural and translate your answer:

1. oppidum oppugno.
2. equum habebas.
3. puellam spectavit.
4. periculum timet.
5. terram regebat.

2 + 2 marks for each question. Total: 20

Exercise 1.21

Put into the plural and translate your answer:

1. puella puerum amat.
2. magister librum iacit.
3. puer scutum habet.
4. ancilla cibum parat.
5. nauta murum aedificat.

3 + 3 marks for each question. Total: 30

Exercise 1.22

Put into the plural and translate your answer:

1. agricola hastam portabat.
2. vir periculum timebat.
3. dominus servum punivit.
4. puer magistrum audivit.
5. poeta librum scripsit.

3 + 3 marks for each question. Total: 30

Exercise 1.23

Put into the singular and translate your answer:

1. ancillas habebamus.
2. gladios portatis.
3. deas viderunt.
4. pericula timebatis.
5. viros laudavimus.

2 + 2 marks for each question. Total: 20

Exercise 1.24

Put into the singular and translate your answer:

1. servi templa aedificaverunt.
2. nautae scuta portabant.
3. pueri mali erant.
4. reginae terras regunt.
5. servi dominos necaverunt.

3 + 3 marks for each question. Total: 30

Exercise 1.25

Put into the singular and translate your answer:

1. nautae feminas non timebant.
2. agricolae agros amant.
3. oppida muros habebant.
4. magistri pueros puniebant.
5. puellae deos laudabant.

3 + 3 marks for each question. Total: 30

Chapter 2

Exercise 2.1

Translate the following passage. Line numbers are given on the left. New words are underlined in the text and their meanings given in the margin.

Discord gatecrashes the wedding party of Peleus and the goddess Thetis

1 olim in <u>monte Olympo</u> dei et deae <u>festum</u>
   <u>celebrabant</u>. cibum consumebant et vinum
   bibebant. <u>festum</u> <u>celebrabant</u> quod Peleus
   <u>Thetim</u> <u>in matrimonium ducebat</u>. Thetis dea

5 erat. Peleus vir <u>mortalis</u> erat. dei dea<u>eque</u> laeti
   erant. ridebant. subito tamen Discordia, dea
   mala, intravit. <u>ceteri</u> dei, ubi Discordiam
   viderunt, non laeti erant. non iam ridebant.
   non ridebant quod Discordiam non amabant.

10 clamaverunt: 'quid cupis, Discordia? cur hic
   stas? te non amamus. statim discede!'
   Discordia <u>nuntiavit</u>: 'me audite, dei! me audite,
   deae! <u>donum</u> habeo. <u>donum</u> pulchrum habeo.
   hic est.' deinde Discordia <u>pomum</u> <u>deposuit</u>.

15 risit discessit<u>que</u>. dei dea<u>eque</u> ad <u>pomum</u>
   <u>appropinquaverunt</u>. <u>pomum</u> spectaverunt.

monte Olympo = Mount Olympus
festum celebro, -are, -avi (1) =
  I hold a celebration

Thetim = accusative case of Thetis
  (a sea nymph, Greek form)
in matrimonium duco (3) =
  I marry
mortalis = mortal
-que = and (before the word it is
  attached to)
ceteri = the rest of

nuntio, -are, -avi (1) = I announce

donum, -i, n. = gift

pomum, -i, n. = apple
deposuit = put down

appropinquo, -are, -avi (1) =
  I approach

Total: 95

Exercise 2.2

1. From the passage give, in Latin, one example of each of the following:
   (a) a verb in the imperfect tense. (1)
   (b) a verb in the perfect tense. (1)
   (c) a part of the verb 'to be'. (1)
   (d) an imperative. (1)
   (e) a personal pronoun. (1)

2. **Discordia** (line 10). In which case is this noun? (1)

3. **risit** (line 15). Give the person, number and tense of this verb. Give the first person singular of the present tense of this verb. (4)

Total: 10

7

Translating 'and' into Latin

There are two ways of writing 'and' in Latin, as shown in the examples below:

Examples

1. the word **et** is used between two words

   Marcus **et** Sextus.
   Marcus and Sextus.

2. the ending **–que** is added to the end of the second word

   pueri puellae**que**.
   Boys and girls.

Exercise 2.3

Read these instructions carefully. For each question write out:
   (a) the same Latin sentence with the **et** replaced by a **-que** in the correct place;
   (b) an English translation of the Latin sentence.

Example

Marcus et Sextus sunt laeti.
(a) Marcus Sextusque sunt laeti.
(b) Marcus and Sextus are happy.

1. pueri semper currunt et clamant.   (1 + 5)
2. Iulia et Valeria sunt puellae.   (1 + 5)
3. agricolae et nautae veniunt.   (1 + 4)
4. currimus et ludimus.   (1 + 3)
5. amici rident et ludunt.   (1 + 4)
6. servus est fessus et laetus.   (1 + 5)
7. puer cibum et aquam habet.   (1 + 5)
8. contra Romanos et Graecos pugnamus.   (1 + 5)
9. agricolae hastas et sagittas habent.   (1 + 5)
10. pueri intrant et laborant.   (1 + 4)

Total: 55

Exercise 2.4

Translate the following into English:
1. Marcus Sextusque sunt pueri. (5)
2. rideo ludoque. (3)
3. puer puellaque currunt. (4)
4. servus timet fugitque. (4)
5. pueri currunt luduntque. (4)
6. servi dominique veniunt. (4)
7. magister pueros puellasque monet. (5)
8. dominus intrat servumque punit. (5)
9. puella intrat amicumque videt. (5)
10. pueri puellaeque rident luduntque. (6)

Total: 45

Exercise 2.5

Translate the following into English:
1. Romulus Remusque Romani erant. (5)
2. semper ridemus ludimusque. (4)
3. Valeria Aureliaque puellae Romanae sunt. (6)
4. magister Sextum Marcumque punit. (5)
5. Sextus Marcusque magistrum audiunt. (5)
6. magister puerum puellamque spectabat. (5)
7. puer agricolas nautasque timebat. (5)
8. servi cibum aquamque habebant. (5)
9. servi fessi miserique erant. (5)
10. templum sacrum pulchrumque erat. (5)

Total: 50

Exercise 2.6

Translate the following into English:

1. terruisti
2. rogaverunt
3. deleverunt
4. misimus
5. vidit
6. audivisti
7. constituerunt
8. clamavistis
9. reximus
10. venit

1 mark for each question. Total: 10

Exercise 2.7

Translate the following into English:

1. dixit
2. iussit
3. cucurrimus
4. nuntiavit
5. fecisti
6. mansimus
7. cepistis
8. appropinquaverunt
9. bibi
10. fuit

1 mark for each question. Total: 10

Exercise 2.8

Translate the following into Latin:

1. I have feared.
2. We loved.
3. They have been.
4. You (sing.) saw.
5. You (pl.) gave.

6. He heard.
7. We led.
8. She laughed.
9. I ruled.
10. They stood.

1 mark for each question. Total: 10

Exercise 2.9

Translate the following into Latin:

1. We moved.
2. I announced.
3. You (pl.) put.
4. We have been.
5. He decided.

6. I took.
7. You (sing.) wrote.
8. They threw.
9. We approached.
10. They departed.

1 mark for each question. Total: 10

Exercise 2.10

Put into the plural and translate your answer:

1. appropinquabam.   (1 + 1)
2. discipulus laborat.   (2 + 2)
3. servus pugnabat.   (2 + 2)
4. puer bonus est.   (3 + 3)
5. nauta navigavit.   (2 + 2)

Total: 20

Exercise 2.11

Put into the singular and translate your answer:

1. libri boni sunt.   (3 + 3)
2. gladios portabatis.   (2 + 2)
3. bella timemus.   (2 + 2)
4. nautae magnas hastas iecerunt.   (4 + 4)
5. servi muros altos aedificabant.   (4 + 4)

Total: 30

Exercise 2.12

Give and translate the following verb parts:

1. The 1st person singular, imperfect tense of **nuntio**.
2. The 2nd person plural, perfect tense of **navigo**.
3. The 3rd person singular, present tense of **aedifico**.
4. The 1st person singular, perfect tense of **sto**.
5. The 3rd person plural, perfect tense of **sum**.

2 marks for each question. Total: 10

Exercise 2.13

Put into the singular, and translate your answer:

1. puellae non cantant.   (2 + 3)
2. dona pulchra sunt.   (3 + 3)
3. servi muros aedificabant.   (3 + 3)
4. pueri scuta portaverunt.   (3 + 3)
5. discipuli magistros saepe timent.   (3 + 4)

Total: 30

Exercise 2.14

Give the translation, person, number, tense and the first person singular of the present tense of these verbs:

1. nuntiavit
2. appropinquabant
3. iecisti
4. oppugnamus
5. iussit

5 marks for each question. Total: 25

Exercise 2.15

Keeping the same person and number, put the following verbs into the imperfect tense and translate your answer:

1. appropinquaverunt
2. nuntiavit
3. navigavi
4. oppugnavisti
5. iussit

6. iusserunt
7. superavimus
8. stetit
9. deleverunt
10. dedimus

2 marks for each question. Total: 20

Chapter 3

Exercise 3.1

Translate the following passage. Line numbers are given on the left. New words are underlined in the text and their meanings given in the margin.

On Mount Olympus the three goddesses Juno, Athena and Venus argue over the golden apple

1	dei deaeque in <u>monte</u> Olympo erant. <u>pomum</u> spectabant. <u>pomum</u> pulchrum erat. <u>pomum</u> <u>aureum</u> erat. <u>haec</u> verba in <u>pomo</u> erant: '<u>hoc</u> <u>pomum</u> <u>aureum</u> feminae <u>pulcherrimae</u> est.'
5	<u>Iuno</u> regina deorum erat. <u>et</u> <u>soror</u> <u>et</u> <u>uxor</u> <u>Iovis</u> erat. dea Iuno <u>pomum</u> spectavit. verba legit. 'ego dea <u>pulcherrima</u> sum,' clamavit. '<u>pomum</u> igitur meum est.' dea Athena <u>pomum</u> spectavit. verba legit. '<u>erras</u>, Iuno,' clamavit,
10	'<u>pomum</u> meum est. <u>pomum</u> meum est quod ego <u>pulcherrima</u> sum.' dea Venus <u>pomum</u> spectavit. verba legit. '<u>erratis</u>, deae. ego <u>pulcherrima</u> sum. <u>pomum</u> igitur meum est. <u>pomum</u> <u>mihi</u> <u>tradite</u>!' sic tres deae de <u>pomo</u>
15	<u>aureo</u> <u>disputabant</u>. <u>omnes</u> <u>pomum</u> <u>aureum</u> habere cupiebant. ad <u>Iovem</u> appropinquare igitur constituerunt. <u>Iuppiter</u> <u>et</u> <u>pater</u> <u>et</u> <u>rex</u> deorum erat.

mons, montis, m. = mountain

pomum, -i, n. = apple

aureus, -a, -um = golden
haec = these
hoc = this
pulcherrimus, -a, -um = the most beautiful
et...et... = both... and...
soror = sister
uxor = wife
Iuppiter, Iovis, m. = Jupiter

erro, -are, -avi (1) = I am wrong

mihi tradite! = hand over to me!

disputo, -are, -avi (1) = I argue
omnes = (they) all

pater = father
rex = king

Total: 110

Exercise 3.2

1. From the passage give, in Latin, one example of each of the following:
   (a) an imperative. (1)
   (b) an infinitive. (1)

2. **pomo** (line 3). In which case is this noun? Why is this case used? (2)

3. **deorum** (line 5). Give the case and gender of this noun. (2)

4. **erat** (line 6). Give the person, number and tense of this verb. Give the first person singular of the present tense of this verb. (4)

Total: 10

12

Third declension nouns – masculine and feminine

	singular	plural
nominative	(given)	stem + **es**
vocative	(same as nominative)	stem + **es**
accusative	stem + **em**	stem + **es**
genitive	stem + **is**	stem + **um**
dative	stem + **i**	stem + **ibus**
ablative	stem + **e**	stem + **ibus**

Example

rex, regis, m. = king

	singular	plural
nominative	rex	reg**es**
vocative	rex	reg**es**
accusative	reg**em**	reg**es**
genitive	reg**is**	reg**um**
dative	reg**i**	reg**ibus**
ablative	reg**e**	reg**ibus**

Exercise 3.3

Give the correct form of the following nouns:

1. The nominative plural of **pater, patris, m.**
2. The genitive singular of **uxor, uxoris, f.**
3. The dative plural of **mons, montis, m.**
4. The ablative singular of **mater, matris, f.**
5. The genitive plural of **soror, sororis, f.**
6. The dative singular of **pater, patris, m.**
7. The ablative plural of **uxor, uxoris, f.**
8. The accusative singular of **soror, sororis, f.**
9. The accusative plural of **pater, patris, m.**
10. The vocative singular of **rex, regis, m.**

1 mark for each question. Total: 10

Exercise 3.4

Give the correct form of the following nouns:

1. The genitive singular of **rex, regis, m.**
2. The nominative singular of **uxor, uxoris, f.**
3. The dative singular of **mater, matris, f.**
4. The vocative singular of **pater, patris, m.**
5. The dative plural of **frater, fratris, m.**
6. The accusative singular of **mons, montis, m.**
7. The ablative singular of **soror, sororis, f.**
8. The accusative plural of **mater, matris, f.**
9. The ablative plural of **frater, fratris, m.**
10. The genitive plural of **pater, patris, m.**

1 mark for each question. Total: 10

Exercise 3.5

Translate the following into Latin:

1. Mountains (subject).
2. For the father.
3. King! (vocative).
4. Wives (object).
5. Brother (object).
6. Of the sister.
7. For the fathers.
8. Of the mountain.
9. For the king.
10. Of the kings.

1 mark for each question. Total: 10

Exercise 3.6

Translate the following into Latin:

1. By the mountains.
2. To the sister.
3. Brothers! (vocative).
4. Of the wives.
5. For the wife.

6. Sister (object).
7. Mothers (object).
8. To the fathers.
9. For the brothers.
10. Mothers (subject).

1 mark for each question. Total: 10

Exercise 3.7

Translate the following into English:

1. montem vidi. (2)
2. pater currit. (2)
3. uxorem meam amo. (3)
4. rex regit. (2)
5. matrem amamus. (2)
6. fratrem et sororem habeo. (4)
7. rex sororem pulchram habet. (4)
8. multos montes vidimus. (3)
9. ad montem altum appropinquabamus. (4)
10. uxor mea iam venit. (4)

Total: 30

Exercise 3.8

Translate the following into English:

1. Marcus frater Aureliae est. (4)
2. Aurelia soror Marci est. (4)
3. puella cibum patri parabat. (4)
4. puella sororem non amat. (4)
5. servi ad montem festinant. (4)
6. in montibus sunt multae viae. (5)
7. rex matrem patremque amabat. (4)
8. rex uxorem pulchram habebat. (4)
9. patrem bonum habeo. (3)
10. soror mea mala est. (4)

Total: 40

Exercise 3.9

Translate the following into English:

1. puer cum sorore semper pugnat. (5)
2. puella cum fratre semper pugnat. (5)
3. pater pueri iratus est. (4)
4. rex terram bene regit. (4)
5. rex pecuniam sorori dat. (4)
6. puella pecuniam regis capit. (4)
7. mater mea fratrem clarum habet. (5)
8. frater matris meae clarus erat. (5)
9. puer multa dona matri dedit. (5)
10. uxor regis pulchra est. (4)

Total: 45

Exercise 3.10

Translate the following into Latin:

1. I like high mountains. (3)
2. We saw the king. (2)
3. I have a sister. (2)
4. Mother is not coming. (3)
5. My father is good. (3)
6. My sister is sleeping. (2)
7. I love my mother. (2)
8. My mother is beautiful. (3)
9. My wife is frightened. (3)
10. We love our parents. (2)

Total: 25

Exercise 3.11

Translate the following into Latin:

1. I have a brother. (2)
2. My sister is beautiful. (3)
3. The wife was weeping. (2)
4. We saw the mountains. (2)
5. Parents like gifts. (3)
6. Mountains are tall. (3)
7. The king gave a present to his parents. (4)
8. Both brother and sister were running. (5)
9. I am handing over the money to father. (3)
10. The rest of the pupils were laughing. (3)

Total: 30

Exercise 3.12

Translate the following into Latin:

1. The king has a wife.
2. The girl praises the king.
3. Mother and father are approaching.
4. I love mother and father.
5. We are running towards the mountains.

3 marks for each question. Total: 15

Exercise 3.13

Translate the following into English:

1. et Marcus et Sextus pueri Romani sunt. (7)
2. et Valeria et Aurelia puellae Romanae sunt. (7)
3. et matrem et patrem habeo. (5)
4. soror mea et pulchra et clara est. (7)
5. magister et pueros et puellas saepe monet. (7)
6. vir magnam turbam et vidit et audivit. (7)
7. et rideo et ludo. (4)
8. Romani oppidum et hastis et sagittis oppugnaverunt. (7)
9. et mater et pater regis irati erant. (7)
10. frater meus et malus et saevus est. (7)

Total: 65

Exercise 3.14

Put into the singular and translate your answer:

1. reges festinabant. (2 + 2)
2. servi fratres habebant. (3 + 3)
3. puellae non appropinquabant. (2 + 3)
4. dona amavistis. (2 + 2)
5. viri feminas puniverunt. (3 + 3)

Total: 25

Exercise 3.15

Put into the plural and translate your answer:

1. mons altus est pulcher. (4 + 4)
2. puer patrem amat. (3 + 3)
3. rex sororem habebat. (3 + 3)
4. uxor bellum timet. (3 + 3)
5. mater discessit. (2 + 2)

Total: 30

Chapter 4

Exercise 4.1

Translate the following passage. Line numbers are given on the left. New words are underlined in the text and their meanings given in the margin.

Jupiter passes the buck to Paris, prince of Troy

1 tres deae, ubi ad <u>Iovem</u> venerunt, <u>haec</u> verba
   dixerunt: '<u>Iuppiter, pomum aureum</u> nos tres
   deae cupimus. quis est <u>pulcherrima</u>? lege!
   <u>nunc</u> lege!' <u>Iuppiter</u> perterritus erat. iram
5 dearum timebat. 'deae', inquit, 'vos <u>omnes</u>
   <u>pulcherrimae</u> estis. <u>omnes corpora</u> pulchra
   habetis. legere non <u>possum</u>. <u>iuvenem</u> tamen
   <u>scio</u>, Paridem <u>nomine</u>. in <u>urbe</u> Troia habitat.
   feminas pulchras amat. <u>ille pulcherrimam</u>
10 <u>leget</u>. Paridem rogate!'

   tres deae iratae erant. Paridem tamen rogare
   constituerunt. itaque ad Paridem <u>ierunt</u>. <u>iter</u>
   <u>longum</u> non erat. mox igitur ad Paridem
   <u>advenerunt</u>. Paris, ubi <u>lucem</u> claram in caelo
15 vidit, timebat. deae <u>omnia</u> de <u>pomo aureo</u>
   <u>narraverunt</u>. 'Iuppiter nos ad te misit, Paris. te
   deam <u>pulcherrimam</u> legere iubet. <u>nunc</u> lege!'

Iuppiter, Iovis, m. = Jupiter
haec = these
pomum, -i, n. = apple
aureus, -a, -um = golden
pulcherrimus, -a, -um = the most
   beautiful, very beautiful
nunc = now
omnes = all
corpora = bodies
possum = I am able, I can
iuvenis, -is, m. = young man
scio, -ire, -ivi (4) = I know
nomen, nominis, n. = name
urbs, urbis, f. = city
ille = he
leget = will choose

ierunt = they went
iter, itineris, n. = journey
longus, -a, -um = long
advenio, -ire, -veni (4) = I arrive
lux, lucis, f. = light
omnia = everything
narro, -are, narravi (1) = I tell

Total: 105

Exercise 4.2

1. From the passage give, in Latin, one example of each of the following:
   (a) a preposition. (1)
   (b) an imperative. (1)
   (c) an infinitive. (1)
   (d) an adjective. (1)

2. **dixerunt** (line 2). Give the tense of this verb. Give the first person singular of the present tense of this verb. (2)

3. **deae** (line 5). In what case is this noun? (1)

4. **habetis** (line 7). Give the person, number and tense of this verb. (3)

Total: 10

Vocabulary 4

iuvenis, iuvenis, m.	young man
urbs, urbis, f.	city
lux, lucis, f.	light
longus, -a, -um	long
nunc	now
narro, -are, -avi (1)	I tell
advenio, -ire, adveni (4)	I arrive
nomen, nominis, n.	name
iter, itineris, n.	journey
corpus, corporis, n.	body
flumen, fluminis, n.	river
mare, maris, n.	sea
opus, operis, n.	task

Third declension nouns – neuter endings

	singular	plural
nominative	(given)	stem + **a**
vocative	(same as nominative)	stem + **a**
accusative	(same as nominative)	stem + **a**
genitive	stem + **is**	stem + **um**
dative	stem + **i**	stem + **ibus**
ablative	stem + **e**	stem + **ibus**

Examples

opus, operis, n. = task

	singular	plural
nominative	opus	oper**a**
vocative	opus	oper**a**
accusative	opus	oper**a**
genitive	oper**is**	oper**um**
dative	oper**i**	oper**ibus**
ablative	oper**e**	oper**ibus**

Note (overleaf) the table of mare, which differs slightly from opus:

mare, maris, n. = sea

	singular	plural
nominative	mare	mar**ia**
vocative	mare	mar**ia**
accusative	mare	mar**ia**
genitive	mar**is**	mar**ium**
dative	mar**i**	mar**ibus**
ablative	mar**i**	mar**ibus**

Exercise 4.3

Give the correct form of the following nouns:

1. The nominative plural of **nomen, nominis, n.**
2. The accusative singular of **iter, itineris, n.**
3. The genitive singular of **corpus, corporis, n.**
4. The ablative plural of **flumen, fluminis, n.**
5. The dative plural of **mare, maris, n.**
6. The dative singular of **iter, itineris, n.**
7. The ablative singular of **nomen, nominis, n.**
8. The accusative plural of **corpus, corporis, n.**
9. The nominative singular of **mare, maris, n.**
10. The vocative singular of **flumen, fluminis, n.**

1 mark for each question. Total: 10

Exercise 4.4

Translate the following into Latin:

1. By name.
2. Names (object).
3. Bodies (subject).
4. To the river.
5. The sea (object).
6. By journeys.
7. Of the rivers.
8. Of the sea.
9. For the journey.
10. By rivers.

1 mark for each question. Total: 10

Exercise 4.5

Translate the following into English:

1. nauta mare non timet. (4)
2. iter longum et difficile erat. (5)
3. servi corpus portabant. (3)
4. multa itinera longa fecimus. (4)
5. aqua fluminis alta erat. (4)
6. sunt in urbe multa templa. (5)
7. oppida et urbes non amo. (5)
8. nomen regis Sextus erat. (4)
9. pater meus trans mare solus saepe navigat. (7)
10. amici itinere fessi erant. (4)

Total: 45

Exercise 4.6

Translate the following into English:

1. multa corpora in proelio vidi. (5)
2. iter iuvenum et longum et miserum erat. (7)
3. rex lucem claram in caelo vidit. (6)
4. nomen urbis Roma erat. (4)
5. puellae iuvenes pulchros saepe amant. (5)
6. pater multam pecuniam iuveni dedit. (5)
7. matrem patremque in urbe heri vidi. (6)
8. corpus nautae magnum erat. (4)
9. ad flumen mox venimus. (4)
10. itinere fessi, mox dormivimus. (4)

Total: 50

Exercise 4.7

Translate the following into Latin:

1. You (pl.) see the river. (2)
2. We are afraid of the sea. (2)
3. The sea is deep. (3)
4. My body is strong. (4)
5. The journey was long. (3)
6. I do not have a name. (3)
7. I saw many bodies. (3)
8. We do not often make journeys. (4)
9. The name of the boy is Sextus. (4)
10. I like rivers. (2)

Total: 30

Exercise 4.8

Translate the following into Latin:

1. The mother was afraid of the river. (3)
2. The king was making a long journey. (4)
3. On the journey we saw many young men. (5)
4. The sea does not frighten sailors. (4)
5. The woman had a beautiful body. (4)

Total: 20

Exercise 4.9

Translate the following into Latin:

1. The boy was standing in the river.
2. The name of the young man was Marcus.
3. We saw the rivers and the sea.
4. The water of the river was deep.
5. The waves of the sea were big.

4 marks for each question. Total: 20

Exercise 4.10

Put into the plural and translate your answer:

1. mater bona est. (3 + 3)
2. regem bonum laudo. (3 + 3)
3. fratrem habet. (2 + 2)
4. puella diu currebat. (2 + 3)
5. magister cucurrit. (2 + 2)

Total: 25

Exercise 4.11

Put into the singular and translate your answer:

1. iuvenes advenerunt.
2. urbes spectamus.
3. vina bibebamus.
4. corpora portatis.
5. luces vidimus.

2 + 2 marks for each question. Total: 20

22

Exercise 4.12

Give the translation, person, number, tense and first person singular of the present tense of the following verbs:

1. errabamus
2. fuerunt
3. tradiderunt
4. appropinquaverunt
5. nuntiavi

5 marks for each question. Total: 25

Exercise 4.13

Give and translate the following verb parts:

1. The 1st person plural, perfect tense of **rego**.
2. The 2nd person singular, present tense of **erro**.
3. The 3rd person plural, imperfect tense of **sum**.
4. The 1st person singular, imperfect tense of **trado**.
5. The 2nd person plural, perfect tense of **scribo**.

2 marks for each question. Total: 10

Exercise 4.14

Put into the singular and translate your answer:

1. flumina longa sunt.   (3 + 3)
2. urbes diu oppugnabatis.   (2 + 3)
3. dona amavimus.   (2 + 2)
4. pueri montes viderunt.   (3 + 3)
5. poetae narrabant.   (2 + 2)

Total: 25

Exercise 4.15

Put into the plural and translate your answer:

1. iuvenis currit.   (2 + 2)
2. iter longum est.   (3 + 3)
3. iam advenio.   (1 + 2)
4. rex urbem cepit.   (3 + 3)
5. urbs pulchra erat.   (3 + 3)

Total: 25

Exercise 4.16

Translate the following into Latin:

1. The journey was long. (3)
2. We have seen the light. (2)
3. He has a beautiful body. (3)
4. The slaves attacked the city. (3)
5. The young men threw missiles. (3)
6. The name of the king is Marcus. (4)
7. The man saw the girl in the city. (5)
8. We are playing in the river. (3)
9. Sailors are not afraid of the sea. (4)
10. Danger does not frighten the son of the king. (5)

Total: 35

Chapter 5

Exercise 5.1

Translate the following passage. Line numbers are given on the left. New words are underlined in the text and their meanings given in the margin.

The goddesses cheat

1 Paris perterritus erat. respondit tamen:
'omnes pulcherrimae estis, deae. nunc legere
non possum. cras redite! cras constituam!'

deae Paridi 'cras redibimus,' inquiunt. iratae
5 discesserunt. secreto tamen Iuno ad Paridem
appropinquavit. Paridi 'si pomum mihi trades,'
inquit, 'ego te virum potentissimum faciam.'
postquam haec verba dixit, discessit. Athena
quoque ad Paridem secreto appropinquavit.
10 Paridi 'si tu me leges,' inquit, 'ego te virum
sapientissimum faciam.' postquam haec verba
dixit, discessit. postea Venus ad Paridem
secreto appropinquavit. Paridi 'si tu me leges,'
inquit, 'ego tibi feminam pulcherrimam
15 coniugem dabo.' deinde discessit. Paris solus
nunc erat.

omnes = all
pulcherrimus, -a, -um = very
   beautiful
possum = I am able, I can
cras = tomorrow
redite! = return!
constituam = I will decide
redibimus = we will return
secreto = in secret
si = if
pomum, -i, n. = apple
mihi = to me
potentissimus, -a, -um = the most
   powerful
faciam = I will make
postquam = after
haec = these
sapientissimus, -a, -um = the
   wisest
postea = later

tibi = to you

coniugem = as your wife
dabo = I will give
solus, -a, -um = alone

Total: 85

Exercise 5.2

1. From the passage give, in Latin, one example of each of the following:
   (a) an infinitive. (1)
   (b) an imperative. (1)
   (c) a personal pronoun. (1)
   (d) a preposition. (1)

2. **dixit** (line 12). Give the tense, person, number and the first person singular of the present tense of this verb. (4)

3. **Paridem** (line 12). In which case is this noun? Why is this case used? (2)

Total: 10

Future tense: first and second conjugations

person	number	conjugation		English meaning
		1	2	
		love	warn	
1st person	singular	ama**bo**	mone**bo**	I shall love/warn
2nd person	singular	ama**bis**	mone**bis**	You (sing.) will love/warn
3rd person	singular	ama**bit**	mone**bit**	He/she/it will love/warn
1st person	plural	ama**bimus**	mone**bimus**	We shall love/warn
2nd person	plural	ama**bitis**	mone**bitis**	You (pl.) will love/warn
3rd person	plural	ama**bunt**	mone**bunt**	They will love/warn

Exercise 5.3

Translate the following into English:

1. portabimus
2. flebit
3. sedebitis
4. necabunt
5. appropinquabo
6. superabis
7. errabit
8. tenebunt
9. intrabis
10. nuntiabimus
11. flebo
12. dabimus
13. narrabitis
14. navigabis
15. pugnabunt
16. ridebitis
17. videbit
18. laborabimus
19. cantabitis
20. movebimus

1 mark for each question. Total: 20

Exercise 5.4

Translate the following into English:

1. aedificabunt
2. iubebo
3. respondebitis
4. stabunt
5. pugnabimus
6. oppugnabunt
7. clamabit
8. terrebitis
9. delebunt
10. dabitis
11. appropinquabimus
12. delebit
13. manebo
14. rogabo
15. ridebimus
16. videbo
17. sedebimus
18. stabit
19. monebitis
20. habitabunt

1 mark for each question. Total: 20

Exercise 5.5

Translate the following into Latin:

1. We shall stand.
2. They will carry.
3. I shall destroy.
4. He will have.
5. We shall approach.
6. You (sing.) will cry.
7. I shall overcome.
8. They will fear.
9. We shall call.
10. She will fight.
11. I shall answer.
12. You (sing.) will sit.
13. They will overcome.
14. She will laugh.
15. You (pl.) will sail.

1 mark for each question. Total: 15

Exercise 5.6

Translate the following into Latin:

1. She will stay.
2. You (pl.) will attack.
3. We shall stay.
4. You (sing.) will kill.
5. I shall hold.
6. We shall see.
7. They will watch.
8. They will weep.
9. He will frighten.
10. You (pl.) will hurry.
11. I shall move.
12. You (sing.) will approach.
13. We shall hold.
14. You (pl.) will enter.
15. They will ask.

1 mark for each question. Total: 15

Future tense: third, fourth and mixed conjugations and sum

person	number	conjugation 3	3½	4	English meaning
		rule	take	hear	
1st person	singular	reg**am**	capi**am**	audi**am**	I shall rule/take/hear
2nd person	singular	reg**es**	capi**es**	audi**es**	You (sing.) will rule/take/hear
3rd person	singular	reg**et**	capi**et**	audi**et**	He/she/it will rule/take/hear
1st person	plural	reg**emus**	capi**emus**	audi**emus**	We shall rule/take/hear
2nd person	plural	reg**etis**	capi**etis**	audi**etis**	You (pl.) will rule/take/hear
3rd person	plural	reg**ent**	capi**ent**	audi**ent**	They will rule/take/hear

person	number	sum	English meaning
		be	
1st person	singular	ero	I shall be
2nd person	singular	eris	You (sing.) will be
3rd person	singular	erit	He/she/it will be
1st person	plural	erimus	We shall be
2nd person	plural	eritis	You (pl.) will be
3rd person	plural	erunt	They will be

Exercise 5.7

Translate the following into English:

1. regemus
2. legam
3. advenietis
4. curram
5. trades
6. constituemus
7. eris
8. fugiam
9. mittent
10. cupietis
11. consumet
12. erunt
13. bibemus
14. curremus
15. mittet
16. ludemus
17. leges
18. constituetis
19. ludent
20. discedam

1 mark for each question. Total: 20

Exercise 5.8

Translate the following into English:

1. fugiet
2. eritis
3. scribemus
4. accipient
5. dormiet
6. discedemus
7. punient
8. ero
9. iaciam
10. pones

11. ostendemus
12. dormies
13. current
14. capiemus
15. erit
16. dormiam
17. veniam
18. capietis
19. accipies
20. dicet

1 mark for each question. Total: 20

Exercise 5.9

Translate the following into English:

1. currit
2. curret
3. regimus
4. regemus
5. festinabit
6. festinamus
7. est
8. erit
9. clamabit
10. bibet

11. bibit
12. ostendent
13. ostendunt
14. puniet
15. punit
16. videmus
17. videbimus
18. manebunt
19. manent
20. erunt

1 mark for each question. Total: 20

Exercise 5.10

Translate the following into English:

1. portabitis
2. parant
3. dabo
4. delemus
5. vocabimus
6. delebis
7. dormiemus
8. narrabit
9. habent
10. legis

11. dormimus
12. intramus
13. ridebitis
14. leges
15. habebo
16. advenient
17. fugiet
18. fugit
19. capiunt
20. habebis

1 mark for each question. Total: 20

29

Exercise 5.11

Translate the following into English:

1. heri servus laborabat. (3)
2. hodie servus laborat. (3)
3. cras servus fugiet. (3)
4. heri oppidum oppugnabamus. (3)
5. hodie oppidum oppugnamus. (3)
6. cras oppidum capiemus. (3)
7. heri pueri currebant. (3)
8. hodie pueri currunt. (3)
9. cras pueri current. (3)
10. heri multas puellas pulchras spectabam. (5)
11. hodie multas puellas pulchras specto. (5)
12. cras multas puellas pulchras spectabo. (5)
13. heri Romani scuta portabant. (4)
14. hodie Romani scuta portant. (4)
15. cras Romani scuta non portabunt. (5)

Total: 55

Exercise 5.12

Translate the following into Latin:

1. Many young men will arrive tomorrow. (4)
2. Help will come soon. (3)
3. My father will be making a long journey. (5)
4. The angry slaves will attack the walls. (4)
5. The boys will hurry to school. (4)

Total: 20

Exercise 5.13

Translate the following into Latin:

1. I shall drink wine tomorrow. (3)
2. Pupils will never listen to teachers. (4)
3. The young man will hurry to the town. (4)
4. The maidservant will never prepare dinner again. (5)
5. Good pupils will always work. (4)

Total: 20

Exercise 5.14

Translate the following into Latin:

1. I shall come to the city tomorrow. (4)
2. The king has a beautiful wife. (4)
3. The woman has a good husband. (4)
4. My wife was preparing a good dinner. (5)
5. We are making the journey now. (3)

Total: 20

Exercise 5.15

Translate the following into Latin:

1. The water of the river is deep. (4)
2. The wife of the king will not have money. (4)
3. We have come down from the mountain. (3)
4. You (pl.) saw the king on the journey. (4)
5. Who will be in the city tomorrow? (5)

Total: 20

Exercise 5.16

Put into the plural and translate your answer:

1. femina appropinquat. (2 + 2)
2. discipulus laborabat. (2 + 2)
3. prope flumen mansisti. (2 + 3)
4. puella donum amabat. (3 + 3)
5. iuvenis puellam vidit. (3 + 3)

Total: 25

Exercise 5.17

Put into the singular and translate your answer:

1. puellas non amamus. (2 + 3)
2. coniuges habemus. (2 + 2)
3. advenerunt. (1 + 1)
4. pueri hastas portabant. (3 + 3)
5. bene dormiverunt. (1 + 2)

Total: 20

Chapter 6

Exercise 6.1

Translate the following passage. Line numbers are given on the left. New words are underlined in the text and their meanings given in the margin.

Venus wins and promises Paris Helen, wife of Menelaus of Sparta

1 postero die tres deae redierunt. ante Paridem steterunt. 'Pari, nos te deam pulcherrimam nunc legere iubemus.'	postero die = on the next day redierunt = (they) returned ante + acc = before pulcherrimus, -a, -um = the most beautiful
Paris, quamquam iram dearum timebat, 5 clamavit: 'ego Venerem lego. Venus super omnes alias dea pulcherrima est.'	quamquam = although super omnes alias = above all others
Venus, ubi verba Paridis audivit, risit. laeta erat. Hera et Athena, ubi verba Paridis audiverunt, non riserunt. non laetae erant. iratae 10 discesserunt.	
Paris Venerem spectabat. 'ego te legi,' inquit. 'mulierem pulcherrimam uxorem meam cupio. ubi est?'	mulier, mulieris, f. = woman uxorem meam = as my wife
Venus Paridi respondit: 'mulier pulcherrima 15 Helena est. in Graecia in Sparta cum viro Menelao habitat. i ad Graeciam, cape Helenam, redi ad urbem Troiam! sic mulier pulcherrima tua erit.'	 i = go! redi = return!

Total: 95

Exercise 6.2

1. From the passage give, in Latin, one example of each of the following:
   (a) a verb in the perfect tense. (1)
   (b) a verb in the imperfect tense. (1)
   (c) a preposition. (1)

2. **risit** (line 7). Give the person, number and first person singular of the present tense of this verb. (3)

3. **verba** (line 8). Give the gender of this noun. (1)

4. **Paridi** (line 14). In which case is this noun? (1)

5. **Graeciam** (line 16). In which case is this noun? Why is this case used? (2)

Total: 10

Vocabulary 6

eo, ire, ii/ivi	I go
ineo, inire, inii	I go in
exeo, exire, exii	I go out
adeo, adire, adii	I go towards
redeo, redire, redii	I go back, return
pereo, perire, perii	I perish
transeo, transire, transii	I go across, I cross
ante + acc	before
super + acc	above
quamquam	although
alius, -a, -ud	other
mulier, mulieris, f.	woman

eo, ire, ii/ivi = I go

	present	future	imperfect	perfect
1st person singular	eo	ibo	ibam	ii/ivi
2nd person singular	is	ibis	ibas	iisti/ivisti
3rd person singular	it	ibit	ibat	iit/ivit
1st person plural	imus	ibimus	ibamus	iimus/ivimus
2nd person plural	itis	ibitis	ibatis	iistis/ivistis
3rd person plural	eunt	ibunt	ibant	ierunt/iverunt
Infinitive	ire			
Imperatives	**singular**	i	**plural**	ite

Exercise 6.3

Translate the following into English:

1. redibo
2. perierunt
3. ibas
4. ineunt
5. ii
6. ibis
7. eo
8. exit
9. ibant
10. transibunt
11. itis
12. rediit
13. exibo
14. ierunt
15. adierunt

1 mark for each question. Total: 15

Exercise 6.4

Translate the following into English:

1. pereo
2. ibitis
3. exibamus
4. transit
5. redii
6. exibunt
7. ibamus
8. periit
9. redibit
10. ibat
11. adit
12. rediimus
13. is
14. exii
15. iit

1 mark for each question. Total: 15

34

Exercise 6.5

Translate the following into English:

1. transierunt
2. ibit
3. imus
4. transibimus
5. eunt
6. peris
7. exibat
8. redierunt
9. adibunt
10. exibit
11. transeunt
12. redibunt
13. redibimus
14. pereunt
15. ibatis

1 mark for each question. Total: 15

Exercise 6.6

Translate the following into English:

1. periimus
2. ibimus
3. adeunt
4. ibam
5. eximus
6. exierunt
7. it
8. peribo
9. iimus
10. rediisti
11. transeo
12. peribamus
13. peribimus
14. ibunt
15. exibis

1 mark for each question. Total: 15

Exercise 6.7

Translate the following into Latin:

1. We are going.
2. They went.
3. They were perishing.
4. They are crossing.
5. We will return.
6. They went in.
7. I went out.
8. I will perish.
9. We were returning.
10. Go! (sing.)

1 mark for each question. Total: 10

Exercise 6.8

Translate the following into Latin:

1. I will go out.
2. I have returned.
3. They perished.
4. He has gone out.
5. You (pl.) were going.
6. He crossed.
7. To go in.
8. They were returning.
9. We will go towards.
10. He returned.

1 mark for each question. Total: 10

Exercise 6.9

Translate the following into English:

1. heri flumen transiimus. (3)
2. hodie mare transiimus. (3)
3. ad urbem eo. (3)
4. i, puer! (2)
5. ad urbem cras adibimus. (4)
6. per viam ibamus. (3)
7. multi iuvenes perierunt. (3)
8. pueri mox redierunt. (3)
9. crasne ad urbem redibis? (4)
10. celeriter exiit. (2)

Total: 30

Exercise 6.10

Translate the following into English:

1. quis ad urbem cras ibit? (5)
2. et ego et frater ad urbem cras ibimus. (8)
3. multi servi trans flumen transierunt. (5)
4. multi iuvenes in bello perierunt. (5)
5. mater paterque ad urbem mox redibunt. (6)
6. puer ex oppido statim exiit. (5)
7. vir, ubi in templum iniit, amicum vidit. (7)
8. nauta, itinere longo fessus, ad urbem tandem adiit. (8)
9. multi servi per viam ibant. (5)
10. rex iuvenes e templo exire iussit. (6)

Total: 60

Exercise 6.11

Translate the following into Latin:

1. The young man perished in the battle. (4)
2. Both mother and father were going to the city. (7)
3. The sailor has returned from the island. (4)
4. The boys will cross the river tomorrow. (5)
5. The slaves went out of the town yesterday. (5)

Total: 25

Translating ubi and quamquam into good English

Hint: move the 'when' or 'although' to the beginning of the English sentence.

Examples

servus, quamquam bene laborat, multam pecuniam non habet.

The slave, although he works well, does not have much money.
Although the slave works well, he does not have much money.
Although he works well, the slave does not have much money.

vir, ubi ad urbem venit, templa spectavit.

The man, when he came to the city, looked at the temples.
When the man came to the city, he looked at the temples.
When he came to the city, the man looked at the temples.

Exercise 6.12

Translate the following into English:

1. vir, quamquam multam pecuniam habebat, non laetus erat. (8)
2. nautae, quamquam undae magnae erant, non timebant. (7)
3. rex, quamquam clarus erat, uxorem non habebat. (7)
4. quamquam iter longum non erat, iuvenes fessi erant. (8)
5. liber, quamquam longus est, bonus est. (6)
6. mulier, quamquam pulchra est, virum non habet. (7)
7. puellae, quamquam perterritae erant, in aquam celeriter inierunt. (8)
8. servus, quamquam fessus erat, bene laborabat. (6)
9. Graeci, quamquam bene pugnaverunt, Romanos non superaverunt. (7)
10. rex, quamquam Romani appropinquabant, non timebat. (6)

Total: 70

Exercise 6.13

Translate the following into English:

1. Paris, ubi lucem claram vidit, magnopere timebat. (7)
2. servi, ubi dominum viderunt, timebant. (5)
3. pueri, ubi verba magistri audiverunt, laeti erant. (7)
4. iuvenis, ubi iter longum fecit, fessus erat. (7)
5. Romani, ubi Graecos superaverunt, urbem ceperunt. (6)
6. ubi ad urbem advenimus, ad templum festinavimus. (7)
7. ubi parentes meos vidi, laetus eram. (6)
8. servi, ubi diu laboraverunt, fessi erant. (6)
9. vir, ubi donum uxori dedit, discessit. (6)
10. nautae, ubi ad insulam advenerunt, urbem spectare cupiebant. (8)

Total: 65

Exercise 6.14

Translate the following into Latin:

1. I am already crossing the deep river. (5)
2. We are going to the city. (3)
3. Many men will perish tomorrow. (4)
4. Pupils never like teachers. (3)
5. The tall woman is approaching the temple. (5)

Total: 20

Exercise 6.15

Translate the following into Latin:

1. The mother of the king was beautiful. (4)
2. You (pl.) had many spears. (3)
3. I will give a present to the young man. (3)
4. The boys were running from the fields to the town. (6)
5. We were making a journey away from the city. (4)

Total: 20

Exercise 6.16

Give and translate the following:

1. The 1st person singular, future tense of **adeo**.
2. The 3rd person singular, imperfect tense of **sum**.
3. The 3rd person plural, perfect tense of **eo**.
4. The 2nd person plural, perfect tense of **rideo**.
5. The 2nd person singular, imperfect tense of **pugno**.

2 marks for each question. Total: 10

Exercise 6.17

Give the translation, person, number, tense and the first person singular of the present tense of the following verbs:

1. erit
2. dedisti
3. nuntiabunt
4. advenerunt
5. redibamus

5 marks for each question. Total: 25

Exercise 6.18

Translate the following into English:

1. multi iuvenes ad urbem cras ibunt. (6)
2. mulier, quamquam pulchra erat, coniugem non habebat. (7)
3. in itinere lucem claram vidimus. (5)
4. mater in villa sola manebat. (5)
5. et pater et mater in bello perierunt. (7)
6. ubi ad urbem advenimus, ibi diu mansimus. (7)
7. Marcus laborabat. ceteri discipuli prope flumen ludebant. (7)
8. iuvenem vidi. ad urbem ibat. (5)
9. dominus multa dona servis cras dabit. (6)
10. uxor regis multos servos habebat. (5)

Total: 60

Exercise 6.19

Put into the plural and translate your answer:

1. femina ibat. (2 + 2)
2. trans flumen transeo. (2 + 3)
3. puella cras veniet. (2 + 3)
4. ad urbem ibam. (2 + 3)
5. iuvenis librum scripsit. (3 + 3)

Total: 25

Exercise 6.20

Put into the singular and translate your answer:

1. ad oppida adibatis. (2 + 3)
2. mulieres pulchrae erant. (3 + 3)
3. mox adveniemus. (1 + 2)
4. iuvenes perierunt. (2 + 2)
5. etiam servi templa viderunt. (3 + 4)

Total: 25

Chapter 7

Exercise 7.1

Translate the following passage. Line numbers are given on the left. New words are underlined in the text and their meanings given in the margin.

Paris leaves Troy, goes to the Greek city of Sparta and kidnaps Menelaus's wife Helen

1 Helena mulier pulchra et clara erat. in urbe
Sparta cum viro, Menelao nomine, habitabat.
Paris vir clarus erat. in urbe Troia habitabat.
Troia erat urbs in Asia <u>sita</u>.

> sita = situated

5 Paris ex urbe Troia ad urbem Spartam
navigavit. ubi advenit, Paris e <u>nave</u> <u>descendit</u> et
ad <u>regiam</u> festinavit. ibi puellam Helenam vidit.
ubi Helenam vidit, <u>eam</u> statim amavit.

> navis, -is, f. = ship
> descendit = disembarked, got off
> regia, -ae, f. = palace
> eam = her

Paris Helenae 'te amo,' inquit, 'Helena. veni! ex
10 urbe Sparta navigabimus et ad urbem Troiam
ibimus! festina!'

Paris Helenam ad <u>navem</u> duxit. deinde
celeriter <u>fugerunt</u>. Paris et Helena ad urbem
Troiam navigaverunt. Paris laetus erat.
15 Menelaus <u>autem</u>, vir Helenae, non laetus sed
<u>iratissimus</u> erat.

> fugio, -ere, fugi (3½) = I flee

> autem = however

> iratissimus, -a, -um = very angry

Total: 100

Exercise 7.2

1. From the passage give, in Latin, one example of each of the following:
   (a) a conjunction. (1)
   (b) an adverb. (1)

2. **urbe** (line 1). In which case is this noun? Why is this case used? (2)

3. **nomine** (line 2). In which case is this noun? (1)

4. **ibimus** (line 11). Give the person, number and tense of this verb. Give the first person singular of the present tense of this verb. (4)

5. **fugerunt** (line 13). Explain the connection between this word and the English word *fugitive*. (1)

Total: 10

Vocabulary 7

navis, navis, f.	ship
autem	however
fugio, fugere, fugi (3½)	I flee

Exercise 7.3

Translate the following into English:

1. fugiunt
2. flebat
3. oppugnabis
4. cucurrerunt
5. constituerunt
6. discedemus
7. advenisti
8. aderat
9. iecit
10. misimus

11. superabimus
12. oppugnaverunt
13. currebas
14. superavit
15. erras
16. dormiemus
17. fuerunt
18. constituam
19. discessit
20. dabit

1 mark for each question. Total: 20

Exercise 7.4

Translate the following into English:

1. iussit
2. ponam
3. fugiemus
4. cupiebamus
5. timebat
6. nuntiavit
7. rexit
8. advenio
9. duxit
10. iubeo

11. adveniam
12. movemus
13. mittunt
14. tradidi
15. posuerunt
16. oppugnabatis
17. dicebat
18. iusserunt
19. erraverunt
20. damus

1 mark for each question. Total: 20

Exercise 7.5

Translate the following into English:

1. stas
2. dedimus
3. fugiebamus
4. movit
5. movet
6. fuit
7. aberant
8. scribemus
9. fugerunt
10. delebimus
11. discesserunt
12. appropinquabant
13. regebat
14. iaciebam
15. scripsit
16. tradidit
17. deleverunt
18. erunt
19. fles
20. stetit

1 mark for each question. Total: 20

Exercise 7.6

Translate the following into Latin:

1. We shall arrive.
2. They ran.
3. He ordered.
4. They decided.
5. They were watching.
6. They fled.
7. They will sail.
8. He announced.
9. She called.
10. They were.
11. They went.
12. He was walking.
13. We are sailing.
14. He is arriving.
15. I shall run.
16. They fought.
17. You (pl.) will send.
18. We shall flee.
19. You (sing.) are standing.
20. We were laughing.

1 mark for each question. Total: 20

Exercise 7.7

Translate the following into Latin:

1. They were building.
2. We were playing.
3. She went.
4. You (sing.) will stay.
5. I kill.
6. They were approaching.
7. We were drinking.
8. He was holding.
9. We were throwing.
10. He asked.
11. I shall announce.
12. They replied.
13. I shall order.
14. They were going.
15. He captured.
16. I am reading.
17. We were.
18. We sent.
19. You (sing.) have built.
20. He punished.

1 mark for each question. Total: 20

Exercise 7.8

Translate the following into Latin:

1. I shall return.
2. I heard.
3. We shall see.
4. You (pl.) have given.
5. They told.
6. We saw.
7. He destroyed.
8. I shall be.
9. They stayed.
10. We departed.
11. It is departing.
12. You (pl.) were perishing.
13. I have written.
14. We are.
15. We shall decide.
16. He was running.
17. They threw.
18. She was fighting.
19. I shall destroy.
20. He saw.

1 mark for each question. Total: 20

Exercise 7.9

Translate the following into Latin:

1. The ship was approaching.   (2)
2. We will attack the city tomorrow.   (3)
3. Sailors like ships.   (3)
4. Father did not have money.   (4)
5. The rest of the pupils were working.   (3)

Total: 15

Exercise 7.10

Translate the following into Latin:

1. Mother was on a ship.
2. We saw a ship near the island.
3. The slaves fled from the city.
4. The ships were returning to the island.
5. The ship was sailing on the river.

4 marks for each question. Total: 20

Exercise 7.11

Put into the plural and translate your answer:

1. iam fugio.   (1 + 2)
2. navis pulchra appropinquabat.   (3 + 3)
3. equus dormiet.   (2 + 2)
4. rex terram rexit.   (3 + 3)
5. puella periculum timebat.   (3 + 3)

Total: 25

Exercise 7.12

Put into the singular and translate your answer:

1. diu currebatis.   (1 + 2)
2. matres miserae flebant.   (3 + 3)
3. servi fugerunt.   (2 + 2)
4. agricolae agros habent.   (3 + 3)
5. discipuli libros legebant.   (3 + 3)

Total: 25

Exercise 7.13

Keeping the same person and number, put the following verbs into the imperfect tense, then translate your answer:

1. narravit
2. erraverunt
3. ambulavimus
4. risistis
5. timuerunt

6. pugnavit
7. mansi
8. cantavisti
9. vidit
10. clamavit

2 marks for each question. Total: 20

44

Chapter 8

Exercise 8.1

Translate the following passage. Line numbers are given on the left. New words are underlined in the text and their meanings given in the margin.

Menelaus appeals for help from other cities in Greece

1 Menelaus iratus erat. iratus erat quod Paris
uxorem, Helenam nomine, ad Troiam duxerat.
Menelaus hunc virum punire et hanc urbem
delere cupiebat.

> duxerat = had led
> hunc/hanc = this

5 nuntios igitur ad omnes urbes Graeciae misit.
hi nuntii haec verba dixerunt: 'audite, omnes!
Paris Helenam, uxorem caram Menelai, cepit.
ad Troiam fugit. propter hoc Menelaus iratus
est. hanc urbem delere cupit. arma parate!
10 naves et milites colligite! ad Troiam
navigabimus et Troianos puniemus!'

> omnes = all
> hi/haec = these
> omnes = everyone
> carus, -a, -um = dear
> propter = on account of
> hoc = this
> arma, armorum, n.pl. = arms,
>   weapons
> miles, militis, m. = soldier
> colligo, -ere, collegi (3) = I collect
> Troianus, -a, -um = Trojan

Graeci, ubi haec verba audiverunt, multas
copias paraverunt. copiae Graecorum ad
portum, Aulidem nomine, venerunt. Menelaus,
15 ubi has naves et hos milites vidit, laetus erat.
omnes salutavit. ad Troiam statim navigare et
bellum contra Troianos gerere et Helenam
liberare cupivit.

> copiae, copiarum, f.pl. = forces,
>   troops
> portum = port
> Aulidem = accusative case of Aulis
>   (a name, Greek form)
> has/hos = these
> saluto, -are, -avi (1) = I greet
> gero, -ere, gessi (3) = I wage
> libero, -are, -avi (1) = I set free

Total: 105

Exercise 8.2

1. From the passage give, in Latin, one example of each of the following:
   (a) an infinitive. (1)
   (b) a preposition. (1)
   (c) an imperative. (1)
   (d) a verb in the future tense. (1)

2. **nuntios** (line 5). In which case is this noun? Why is this case used? (2)

3. **misit** (line 5). Give the person, number and tense of this verb. Give the first person singular of the present tense of this verb. (4)

Total: 10

Vocabulary 8

colligo, -ere, collegi (3)	I collect
saluto, -are, -avi (1)	I greet
bellum gero, -ere, gessi (3)	I wage war
libero -are, -avi (1)	I set free
hic, haec, hoc	this
carus, -a, -um	dear
miles, militis, m.	soldier
copiae, copiarum, f.pl.	troops, forces
arma, armorum, n.pl.	arms, weapons
propter + acc.	on account of, because of

hic, haec, hoc = this

	masculine	feminine	neuter
singular			
nominative	hic	haec	hoc
accusative	hunc	hanc	hoc
genitive	huius	huius	huius
dative	huic	huic	huic
ablative	hoc	hac	hoc
plural			
nominative	hi	hae	haec
accusative	hos	has	haec
genitive	horum	harum	horum
dative	his	his	his
ablative	his	his	his

Exercise 8.3

Translate the following into English:

1. hic miles.
2. hic rex.
3. hoc scutum.
4. haec urbs.
5. hae urbes.
6. hic servus.
7. haec mater.
8. hi pueri.
9. hae naves.
10. hoc donum.
11. haec corpora.
12. hi reges.
13. hi milites.
14. hoc iter.
15. hic puer.
16. hi servi.
17. hi agricolae.
18. hoc flumen.
19. haec verba.
20. haec uxor.

2 marks for each question. Total: 40

Exercise 8.4

Translate the following into English:

1. huius puellae.
2. huius militis.
3. horum militum.
4. harum navium.
5. hoc dono.
6. hoc bello.
7. hac luce.
8. huius pueri.
9. horum servorum.
10. his verbis.
11. hoc gladio.
12. huic servo.
13. harum mulierum.
14. hoc vulnere.
15. hoc nomine.
16. his vulneribus.
17. his nominibus.
18. huic iuveni.
19. his fluminibus.
20. huius regis.

2 marks for each question. Total: 40

Exercise 8.5

Translate the following into English:

1. hic puer est Marcus. (4)
2. hoc bellum est malum. (4)
3. hi pueri sunt parvi. (4)
4. hae puellae sunt parvae. (4)
5. hanc puellam amo. (3)
6. haec verba audio. (3)
7. rex hunc militem punit. (4)
8. puella hunc cibum non amat. (5)
9. dominus pecuniam his servis dabit. (5)
10. haec flumina longa sunt. (4)

Total: 40

Exercise 8.6

Translate the following into English:

1. templum huius dei magnum est. (5)
2. libri horum puerorum boni sunt. (5)
3. multam pecuniam huic puero do. (5)
4. pecuniam his pueris non do. (5)
5. magister puerum hoc gladio necat. (5)
6. magister pueros his verbis terret. (5)
7. librum huius pueri lego. (4)
8. iuvenis, ubi haec verba audivit, discessit. (6)
9. Romani Graecos his militibus mox superabunt. (6)
10. hoc flumen sacrum est. (4)

Total: 50

47

Exercise 8.7

Translate the following into Latin:

1. This soldier.
2. These soldiers.
3. This city.
4. These cities.
5. This river.
6. These rivers.
7. These weapons.
8. These forces.
9. This light.
10. This journey.

2 marks for each question. Total: 20

Exercise 8.8

Translate the following into Latin:

1. These young men.
2. This mother.
3. These presents.
4. This shield.
5. These dangers.
6. This pupil.
7. These fields.
8. This teacher.
9. These walls.
10. This crowd.

2 marks for each question. Total: 20

Exercise 8.9

Translate the following into Latin:

1. For this girl.
2. Of these farmers.
3. To this queen
4. By this road.
5. Of these Romans.
6. With these arrows.
7. With this food.
8. For this horse.
9. Of these walls.
10. Of this book.

2 marks for each question. Total: 20

Exercise 8.10

Translate the following into Latin:

1. This ship was sailing to the island.
2. I saw this beautiful girl yesterday.
3. The messenger returned to this city.
4. I was carrying this body out of the town.
5. The soldiers have collected all these weapons.

5 marks for each question. Total: 25

Exercise 8.11

Translate the following into Latin:

1. The name of this girl is Flavia.
2. The walls of this city are tall.
3. The soldier has fought well with this sword.
4. The master will give a present to these slaves.
5. The girls liked the villa of this young man.

5 marks for each question. Total: 25

Exercise 8.12

Translate the following into Latin:

1. The forces were approaching. (2)
2. The master set free the slave. (3)
3. We greeted father. (2)
4. The soldier was fighting well. (3)
5. The young man will collect the weapons. (3)
6. The soldiers collected many weapons. (4)
7. The Romans had great forces. (4)
8. The king killed the soldier in battle. (5)
9. Many soldiers perished because of the war. (5)
10. The arms of the soldiers were new. (4)

Total: 35

Exercise 8.13

Put into the plural and translate your answer:

1. liberas. (1 + 1)
2. miles bonus est. (3 + 3)
3. navis cras adveniet. (2 + 3)
4. dominus servum liberabit. (3 + 3)
5. puer patrem salutavit. (3 + 3)

Total: 25

Exercise 8.14

Put into the singular and translate your answer:

1. scuta hastasque collegerunt. (3 + 3)
2. iuvenes fugiebant. (2 + 2)
3. milites pugnabant. (2 + 2)
4. mulieres cras redibunt. (2 + 3)
5. puellae equos amabunt. (3 + 3)

Total: 25

Exercise 8.15

Give and translate the following:

1. The 3rd person singular, perfect tense of **libero**.
2. The 1st person singular, imperfect tense of **saluto**.
3. The 2nd person plural, perfect tense of **gero**.
4. The 3rd person plural, perfect tense of **fugio**.
5. The 1st person plural, future tense of **eo**.

2 marks for each question. Total: 10

Exercise 8.16

Give the translation, person, number, tense and first person singular of the present tense of the following verbs:

1. exierunt
2. erat
3. gessit
4. bibemus
5. colligam

5 marks for each question. Total: 25

Chapter 9

Exercise 9.1

Translate the following passage. Line numbers are given on the left. New words are underlined in the text and their meanings given in the margin.

The Greeks assemble at Aulis, but their departure is delayed by contrary winds

1 Graeci multos milites et multas naves
Aulidem miserunt. Menelaus, ubi illos milites
et illas naves conspexit, laetus erat. Troiam
non amabat. illam urbem sine mora delere
5 cupiebat.

naves tamen navigare non poterant. naves
navigare non poterant quod venti adversi
erant. Graeci prope naves diu manserunt. nihil
faciebant. diu ventos secundos
10 exspectaverunt. nemo laetus erat. sed tandem
venti secundi erant

Menelaus militibus clamavit: 'comites, illi venti
nunc secundi sunt. parate naves! parate arma!
statim discedite!'

15 Graeci, ubi haec verba audiverunt, naves
celeriter paraverunt et Aulide navigaverunt.

Aulidem = to Aulis
illos = those
illas = those
conspicio, -ere, conspexi (3½) =
*   I catch sight of*
illam = that
sine + abl. = without
mora, -ae, f. = delay
poterant = (they) were able

adversus, -a, -um = contrary

secundus, -a, -um = favourable

exspecto, -are, -avi (1) = I wait for
nemo = no one

comes, comitis, m./f. = companion
illi = those

Aulide = from Aulis

Total: 85

Exercise 9.2

1. From the passage give, in Latin, one example of each of the following:
   (a) a conjunction. (1)
   (b) a preposition. (1)
   (c) a verb in the perfect tense. (1)
   (d) a verb in the imperfect tense. (1)

2. **manebant** (line 8). Give the person and number of this verb. Give the first person singular of the present tense of this verb. (3)

3. **naves** (line 13). Give the case of this noun. Why is this case used? (2)

4. **verba** (line 15). Give the gender of this noun. (1)

Total: 10

ille, illa, illud = that

	masculine	feminine	neuter
singular			
nominative	ille	illa	illud
accusative	illum	illam	illud
genitive	illius	illius	illius
dative	illi	illi	illi
ablative	illo	illa	illo
plural			
nominative	illi	illae	illa
accusative	illos	illas	illa
genitive	illorum	illarum	illorum
dative	illis	illis	illis
ablative	illis	illis	illis

Exercise 9.3

Translate the following into English:

1. ille servus.
2. illa navis.
3. illud bellum.
4. illi hostes.
5. illae urbes.
6. illa bella.
7. illa mulier.
8. illa arma.
9. illa corpora.
10. illud flumen.
11. illi equi.
12. ille comes.
13. illa puella.
14. illae copiae.
15. illa verba.
16. illud oppidum.
17. ille iuvenis.
18. illi comites.
19. ille amicus.
20. illi milites.

2 marks for each question. Total: 40

Exercise 9.4

Translate the following into English:

1. illius equi.
2. illis amicis.
3. illorum puerorum.
4. illi mulieri.
5. in illa urbe.
6. illarum puellarum.
7. illi deo.
8. illorum iuvenum.
9. illo itinere.
10. illis armis.
11. illis militibus.
12. illi servo.
13. illorum periculorum.
14. illa luce.
15. illis sagittis.
16. illorum magistrorum.
17. illius amici.
18. illarum feminarum.
19. illius urbis.
20. illi servo.

2 marks for each question. Total: 40

Exercise 9.5

Translate the following into English:

1. ille servus bonus est. (4)
2. illa puella pulchra est. (4)
3. illi milites fessi sunt. (4)
4. illa navis magna est. (4)
5. illud templum magnum et pulchrum est. (6)
6. illa verba mala sunt. (4)
7. illum puerum non amo. (4)
8. dominus illos servos saepe punit. (5)
9. magister illas puellas non amat. (5)
10. nomen illius pueri est Marcus. (5)

Total: 45

Exercise 9.6

Translate the following into English:

1. scuta illorum militum magna sunt. (5)
2. pecuniam illis servis cras dabo. (5)
3. dux arma illi militi dat. (5)
4. puer puellam pulchram illo gladio necabit. (6)
5. mater mea illa dona amabit. (5)
6. illa verba amo. (3)
7. multi iuvenes in illa urbe habitant. (6)
8. sunt multae naves in illo flumine. (6)
9. ubi sunt libri illorum puerorum? (5)
10. illud flumen sacrum est. (4)

Total: 50

53

Exercise 9.7

Translate the following into English:

1. hic servus bonus, ille malus est. (6)
2. haec insula magna, illa parva est. (6)
3. ille servus hunc dominum timebat. (5)
4. hic dominus illum servum terrebat. (5)
5. illi milites hanc urbem oppugnaverunt. (5)
6. illi iuvenes has puellas spectabant. (5)
7. haec navis ad illam insulam navigavit. (6)
8. illi servi ex hoc oppido fugerunt. (6)
9. hanc puellam in illa via vidi. (6)
10. ille dominus hos servos puniebat. (5)

Total: 55

Exercise 9.8

Translate the following into Latin:

1. That sword.
2. That woman.
3. That war.
4. Those horses.
5. Those girls.
6. Those temples.
7. That delay.
8. Those companions.
9. That soldier.
10. Those soldiers.

2 marks for each question. Total: 20

Exercise 9.9

Translate the following into Latin:

1. Those ships.
2. That light.
3. That name.
4. That city.
5. Those young men.
6. That journey.
7. Those rivers.
8. That danger.
9. That pupil.
10. Those books.

2 marks for each question. Total: 20

Exercise 9.10

Translate the following into Latin:

1. Of that boy.
2. Of that girl.
3. Of that war.
4. Of those boys.
5. Of those girls.

6. Of those wars.
7. For that slave.
8. To those slaves.
9. By those words.
10. By that present.

2 marks for each question. Total: 20

Exercise 9.11

Translate the following into Latin:

1. To those companions.
2. For that soldier.
3. Of that ship.
4. By that light.
5. Of those bodies.

6. To those young men.
7. To that king.
8. To that city.
9. By that name.
10. For those friends.

2 marks for each question. Total: 20

Exercise 9.12

Translate the following into Latin:

1. I like that girl.
2. I am watching those ships.
3. I am crossing that river.
4. I am setting free those slaves.
5. I am attacking that city.

3 marks for each question. Total: 15

Exercise 9.13

Translate the following into Latin:

1. The teacher does not like those pupils. (5)
2. That ship will arrive soon. (4)
3. The master never gives money to those slaves. (6)
4. The master of those slaves is wicked. (5)
5. The soldier wounded the friend with that sword. (5)

Total: 25

55

Exercise 9.14

Translate the following into Latin:

1. We attacked the city without delay. (4)
2. The companions have returned today. (3)
3. No one caught sight of the ship. (3)
4. Those soldiers were fighting. (3)
5. We are waiting for the queen. (2)

Total: 15

Exercise 9.15

Translate the following into Latin:

1. My companions will arrive soon. (4)
2. The king caught sight of the famous soldier in the crowd. (6)
3. The girl waited for the friend in the town for a long time. (6)
4. I saw this boy in the city. (5)
5. My companion perished in the war. (4)

Total: 25

Exercise 9.16

Put into the plural and translate your answer:

1. bellum diu gessit. (2 + 3)
2. mater exspectabat. (2 + 2)
3. comes currebat. (2 + 2)
4. puella pulchra erat. (3 + 3)
5. nauta navem conspexit. (3 + 3)

Total: 25

Exercise 9.17

Put into the singular and translate your answer:

1. frustra fugiebamus. (1 + 2)
2. milites discesserunt. (2 + 2)
3. illae naves magnae erant. (4 + 4)
4. dona mittemus. (2 + 2)
5. Graeci hastas collegerunt. (3 + 3)

Total: 25

Chapter 10

Exercise 10.1

Translate the following passage. Line numbers are given on the left. New words are underlined in the text and their meanings given in the margin.

Protesilaus: hero or half wit?

1   quod venti <u>secundi</u> erant, Graeci naves
    paraverunt. deinde in <u>eis</u> trans mare celeriter
    navigaverunt. ubi autem naves ad terram
    appropinquaverunt, nemo e Graecis e navibus
5   <u>descendere</u> cupiebat, <u>nam</u> dei haec verba
    Graecis <u>dixerant</u>: '<u>is qui</u> primus in terram
    <u>Troianam</u> <u>descendet, primus occidetur</u>.'

    diu Graeci nihil fecerunt. <u>inter</u> <u>eos</u> autem erat
    miles, Protesilaus nomine. hic miles <u>mortem</u> non
10 timebat. clamavit: 'spectate me, comites! ego
    <u>fortis</u> sum. ego <u>audax</u> sum. ego primus in terram
    Troianam <u>descendam</u>. <u>sic</u> ego clarus ero.'

    Protesilaus in terram statim <u>descendit</u>. ubi <u>is</u>
    descendit, ceteri Graeci <u>descenderunt</u>.
15 postquam Protesilaus <u>Troianos</u> vidit, contra
    eos <u>ruit</u>. multos ex <u>eis</u> <u>occidit</u>. tandem tamen,
    postquam multa <u>vulnera</u> <u>accepit</u>, periit. <u>sic</u>
    clarus <u>factus est</u>.

secundus, -a, -um = favourable	
eis = them	
descendo, -ere, descendi (3) = I climb down, disembark	
nam = for	
dixerant = had said	
is = he	
qui = who	
Troianus, -a, -um = Trojan	
primus occidetur = will be the first killed	
inter + acc. = among	
eos = them	
mors, mortis, f. = death	
fortis = brave	
audax = daring	
sic = in this way, thus	
ruo, -ere, rui (3) = I charge	
occido, -ere, occidi (3) = I kill	
vulnus, vulneris, n. = wound	
accipio, -ere, accepi (3½) = I receive	
factus est = he became	

Total: 105

Exercise 10.2

1. From the passage give, in Latin, one example of each of the following:
    (a) a demonstrative adjective. (1)
    (b) a third declension noun. (1)
    (c) an ordinal number. (1)

2. **venti** (line 1). Explain the connection between this word and the English word **ventilation**. (1)

3. **navibus** (line 4). In which case is this noun? Why is this case used? (2)

4. **fecerunt** (line 8). In which tense is this verb? Give the first person singular of the present tense of this verb. (2)

5. **vidit** (line 15). Give the Latin subject and Latin object of this verb. (2)

Total: 10

Vocabulary 10

is, ea, id*	that/he, she, it,
nam	for
ruo, -ere, rui (3)	I charge
occido, -ere, occidi (3)	I kill
mors, mortis, f.	death
vulnus, vulneris, n.	wound
inter + acc.	among, between
accipio, -ere, accepi (3½)	I receive

* Note the pronoun is, ea, id means 'that' (pl. 'those') but is also used to mean 'he', 'she' or 'it'.

is, ea, id = that / he, she, it

	masculine		feminine		neuter	
singular						
nominative	is	he	ea	she	id	it
accusative	eum	him	eam	her	id	it
genitive	eius	his	eius	her	eius	of it
dative	ei	to him	ei	to her	ei	to it
ablative	eo	by him	ea	by her	eo	by it
plural						
nominative	ei	they	eae	they	ea	they
accusative	eos	them	eas	them	ea	them
genitive	eorum	their	earum	their	eorum	their
dative	eis	to them	eis	to them	eis	to them
ablative	eis	by them	eis	by them	eis	by them

As a general rule, if is, ea, id is used in agreement with a noun, it means 'that', or 'those'. If not, it means 'he', 'she' or 'it'.

Exercise 10.3

Translate the following into English:

1. Menelaus miles Graecus erat. is vir bonus erat. (8)
2. Helena uxor Menelai erat. ea femina pulchra erat. (8)
3. in urbe est templum. id est templum magnum. (8)
4. Marcus filium habet. eum amat. (5)
5. Marcus filiam habet. eam amat. (5)
6. Marcus filium et filiam habet. eos amat. (7)
7. Marcus servum habet. pecuniam ei dat. (6)
8. insula magna est. multi incolae in ea habitant. (8)
9. Marcus multos libros accipit. eos semper legit. (7)
10. Marcus uxorem pulchram habet. nomen eius est Aurelia. (8)

Total: 70

Exercise 10.4

Translate the following into English:

1. Aurelia multos amicos habet. amici eius clari sunt. (8)
2. Marcus et Aurelia multos servos habent. servi eorum boni sunt. (10)
3. Marcus pecuniam eis saepe dat. (5)
4. Marcus librum legit. sunt in eo multa verba. (8)
5. Marcus vinum ad Aureliam misit. ea id nunc bibit. (9)
6. Marcus multa arma habet. arma eius nova sunt. (8)
7. Marcus multa arma habet. ea amat. (6)
8. rex servos amat. multam pecuniam eis saepe dat. (8)
9. servus aquam rogat. dominus eam ei dat. (7)
10. templum novum est. id nunc spectamus. (6)

Total: 75

Exercise 10.5

Translate the following into English:

1. magister hunc servum non amabat. eum igitur puniebat. (8)
2. Protesilaus fortiter pugnabat. Troiani tamen eum mox occiderunt. (8)
3. Graeci contra Troianos ruerunt. multos ex eis necaverunt. (8)
4. ille miles multa vulnera accepit. vulnera eius mala erant. (9)
5. dominus servum bonum, Sextum nomine, habebat. eum heri liberavit. (9)
6. navis magna erat. erant in ea multi nautae. (8)
7. magister multa verba dixit. nemo tamen ea audiebat. (8)
8. multae puellae appropinquabant. eas mox conspeximus. (6)
9. Romani milites boni erant. Graeci eos non superaverunt. (8)
10. agricolae multos agros habebant. agri eorum magni erant. (8)

Total: 80

Exercise 10.6

Translate the following into English:

1. ubi amicus venit, vir eum salutavit. (6)
2. magister meus uxorem pulchram habet. eam saepe video. (8)
3. illa femina pulchra erat. multi viri eam amabant. (8)
4. urbs magna erat. Romani eam capere constituerunt. (7)
5. hoc vinum bonum est. id saepe bibo. (7)
6. Graeci multa arma colligerunt. ea in navibus posuerunt. (8)
7. Menelaus et Helena Graeci erant. is clarus, ea pulchra erat. (10)
8. quod servi boni erant, dominus multam pecuniam eis dedit. (9)
9. puer, quod puellam amabat, multa dona ei dabat. (8)
10. auxilio eorum urbem cepimus. (4)

Total: 75

Exercise 10.7

Translate the following into Latin:

1. I have a brother. I like him. (4)
2. I have a sister. I like her. (4)
3. I have a name. I do not like it. (5)
4. I have horses. I love them. (4)
5. I have daughters. I love them. (4)
6. I have many presents. I like them. (5)
7. I do not like his brother. (4)
8. I like the girls; I do not like their mother. (6)
9. Their weapons are new. (4)
10. I have slaves. I give money to them. (5)

Total: 45

Exercise 10.8

Put into the plural and translate your answer:

1. scripsi. (1 + 1)
2. miles periit. (2 + 2)
3. vulnus accepit. (2 + 2)
4. mulier dormiebat. (2 + 2)
5. puer amicum habet. (3 + 3)

Total: 20

Exercise 10.9

Put into the plural and translate your answer:

1. comes currit.
2. puellam conspexi.
3. navem exspectabat.
4. vulnus accepi.
5. servus ruebat.

2 + 2 marks for each question. Total: 20

Exercise 10.10

Put into the singular and translate your answer:

1. amici fuerunt. (2 + 2)
2. reges currebant. (2 + 2)
3. milites occidimus. (2 + 2)
4. ancillae scuta non portabant. (3 + 4)
5. reges comites occiderunt. (3 + 3)

Total: 25

Exercise 10.11

Put into the singular and translate your answer:

1. Romani erant. (2 + 2)
2. vulnera mala sunt. (3 + 3)
3. comites pugnabant. (2 + 2)
4. servi fugerunt. (2 + 2)
5. ivistis. (1 + 1)

Total: 20

Exercise 10.12

Give and translate the following:

1. The 3rd person plural, imperfect tense of **exspecto**.
2. The 3rd person singular, perfect tense of **conspicio**.
3. The 1st person singular, future tense of **ruo**.
4. The 2nd person plural, imperfect tense of **occido**.
5. The 2nd person singular, present tense of **eo**.

2 marks for each question. Total: 10

Exercise 10.13

Give the translation, person, number, tense and first person singular of the present tense of the following:

1. conspexerunt
2. exspectabas
3. ruet
4. occidit
5. accepimus

5 marks for each question. Total: 25

Exercise 10.14

Translate the following into Latin:

1. I do not fear death.
2. The boy received a gift.
3. The Greeks will kill the Romans.
4. We received many wounds.
5. My companions have come.

3 marks for each question. Total: 15

Exercise 10.15

Translate the following into Latin:

1. We will charge against the Romans tomorrow.   (4)
2. We will attack the city with weapons.   (3)
3. Death will come to the old man soon.   (4)
4. The wounds of the king are bad.   (3)
5. The ship did not arrive today because of the delay.   (6)

Total: 20

Chapter 11

Exercise 11.1

Translate the following passage. Line numbers are given on the left. New words are underlined in the text and their meanings given in the margin.

The Greeks realise that capturing Troy will not be a five-minute job

1 Protesilaus <u>mortuus</u> erat. Graeci contra
muros Troiae ruerunt. fortiter et diu <u>sub</u>
muris pugnaverunt, sed <u>frustra</u>. urbem non
ceperunt. non multos Troianos <u>vulneraverunt</u>.
5 non multos Troianos occiderunt.

Agamemnon, frater Menelai, <u>dux</u> Graecorum
erat. non laetus erat. haec verba militibus dixit:
'Graeci, haec verba <u>vobis</u> dico: Troiam hodie
non capiemus. muri Troiae alti et validi sunt.
10 illi <u>cives</u> Troiani <u>fortes</u> sunt. muros bene
<u>defendunt</u>. ego vos <u>castra</u> ponere iubeo. bene
dormite! cras contra <u>hostes</u> iterum
pugnabimus.'

milites Graeci verbis Agamemnonis
15 <u>paruerunt</u>. castra posuerunt. fessi erant. mox
dormiebant.

mortuus, -a, -um = dead

sub + abl. = under

frustra = in vain

vulnero, -are, -avi (1) = I wound

dux, ducis, m. = leader, general

vobis = to you

civis, civis, m. = citizen
fortis, -is, -e = brave
defendo, -ere, defendi (3) = I defend
castra, -orum, n.pl. = camp
hostes, -ium, m.pl. = enemy

pareo, -ere, parui (2) + dat. = I obey

Total: 85

Exercise 11.2

1. From the passage give, in Latin, one example of each of the following:
   (a) an adverb. (1)
   (b) a noun in the genitive case. (1)
   (c) an infinitive. (1)

2. **mortuus** (line 1). Explain the connection between this word and the English word **mortuary**. (1)

3. **muros** (line 2). In which case is this noun? Why is this case used? (2)

4. **ceperunt** (line 4). Give the first person singular of the present tense of this verb. (1)

5. **pugnabimus** (line 13). Give the person, number and tense of this verb. (3)

Total: 10

Vocabulary 11

mortuus, -a, -um	dead
sub + abl.	under
frustra	in vain
defendo, -ere, defendi (3)	I defend
dux, ducis, m.	leader, general
civis, civis, m.	citizen
hostes, hostium, m.pl.	enemy
vulnero, -are, vulneravi (1)	I wound

ego and tu

	ego	English	tu	English
singular				
nominative	ego	I	tu	you
accusative	me	me	te	you
genitive	mei	of me/my	tui	of you/your
dative	mihi	to/for me	tibi	to/for you
ablative	me	(by) me	te	(by) you
note:	mecum	with me	tecum	with you
plural				
nominative	nos	we	vos	you
accusative	nos	us	vos	you
genitive	nostrum	of us/our	vestrum	of you/your
dative	nobis	to/for us	vobis	to/for you
ablative	nobis	(by) us	vobis	(by) you
note:	nobiscum	with us	vobiscum	with you

Exercise 11.3

Translate the following into English:

1. tu ludis; ego laboro. (4)
2. nos Romani sumus; vos Graeci estis. (6)
3. nos vos non amamus. (4)
4. vos nos non amatis. (4)
5. ego te non amo. (4)
6. tu me non amas. (4)
7. nemo me vidit. (3)
8. ego puellam amo. (3)
9. puella me non amat. (4)
10. te in urbe vidi. (4)

Total: 40

Exercise 11.4

Translate the following into English:

1. hostes nos oppugnant. (3)
2. Romani nos non amant. (4)
3. pater meus te amat. (4)
4. te puniam, serve! (3)
5. quis me vocat? (3)
6. magister te vocat. (3)
7. femina nos spectat. (3)
8. quis pecuniam mihi dabit? (4)
9. ego multam pecuniam tibi dabo. (5)
10. puellae nobiscum ludent. (3)

Total: 35

Exercise 11.5

Translate the following into English:

1. servus prope me stat. (4)
2. hostes contra nos pugnant. (4)
3. pater pecuniam tibi dat. (4)
4. dominus pecuniam vobis dabit, servi. (5)
5. servi ad me festinant. (4)
6. amici mecum ludunt. (3)
7. ego donum tibi dabo. (4)
8. magister dona nobis numquam dat. (5)
9. pater donum mihi, tibi pecuniam dedit. (6)
10. ille magister te, non me, amat. (6)

Total: 45

Exercise 11.6

Translate the following into Latin:

1. I am Roman; you are Greek. (6)
2. We are good; you are bad. (6)
3. I am giving money to you. (4)
4. He often gives money to us. (4)
5. Play with me, friends! (3)
6. We do not wish to play with you. (3)
7. That girl will never give me a present. (6)
8. The teacher will punish you, but not me. (6)
9. He is doing this for us. (4)
10. Come with us, mother! (3)

Total: 45

Exercise 11.7

Put into the plural and translate your answer:

1. te cras videbo. (2 + 3)
2. hasta servum vulneravit. (3 + 3)
3. rex mortuus erat. (3 + 3)
4. miles navem exspectabat. (3 + 3)
5. dux bellum non timet. (3 + 4)

Total: 30

Exercise 11.8

Put into the singular and translate your answer:

1. pueri mortui non currunt. (3 + 4)
2. cur nos monebitis? (2 + 3)
3. milites reges vulnerabant. (3 + 3)
4. cives oppida defenderunt. (3 + 3)
5. duces comites amabant. (3 + 3)

Total: 30

Exercise 11.9

Translate the following into English:

1. illi milites in proelio fortiter pugnaverunt. (6)
2. hunc civem in urbe heri conspexi. (6)
3. multae naves insulam contra hostes defendebant. (6)
4. quod milites bene pugnabant, dux eos laudavit. (7)
5. Romani bella contra Graecos saepe gerebant. (6)
6. arma militum Romanorum nova erant. (5)
7. comites ab insula in navibus sine mora discesserunt. (8)
8. hostes multos cives armis vulneraverunt. (5)
9. ille magister, quod ego numquam laborabam, me non amabat. (9)
10. copiae hostium multa vulnera a nobis acceperunt. (7)

Total: 65

Exercise 11.10

Translate the following into Latin:

1. The Roman citizen was dead. (4)
2. We were fighting against the enemy. (3)
3. The good citizens defended the city well. (5)
4. The spears wounded the soldiers. (3)
5. The enemy were fighting well for a long time. (4)
6. The citizens hurried to the city. (4)
7. The enemy wounded the king with arrows. (4)
8. Good leaders do not fear death. (5)
9. We saw the enemy in the city. (4)
10. The wounds of the citizen were bad. (4)

Total: 40

Chapter 12

Exercise 12.1

Translate the following passage. Line numbers are given on the left. New words are underlined in the text and their meanings given in the margin.

Achilles and Hector

1 Graeci Troiam <u>oppugnaverant</u>. urbem Troiam tamen non statim <u>occupaverant</u>. Troianos non <u>vicerant</u>. prope urbem Troiam igitur <u>castra</u> <u>posuerant</u>.	oppugnaverant = had attacked occupaverant = they had seized vicerant = they had conquered castra, -orum, n.pl. = camp posuerant = they had pitched
5 diu copiae Graecorum muros Troiae oppugnabant. eos tamen delere non <u>poterant</u>. <u>omnes</u> Graeci igitur <u>iratissimi</u>, Troiani <u>laetissimi</u> erant.	poterant = they were able omnes = all iratissimus, -a, -um = very angry laetissimus, -a, -um = very happy
<u>Priamus</u> rex Troiae erat. multos filios <u>fortes</u> 10 habebat. <u>nemo</u> autem <u>fortior</u> <u>aut</u> <u>clarior</u> <u>quam</u> Hector erat. vir magnae <u>virtutis</u> erat. <u>pro</u> Troianis fortiter pugnabat.	Priamus = Priam (a name) fortis, -is, -e = brave nemo = no one fortior = braver aut = or clarior = more famous quam = than virtus, virtutis, f. = courage pro + abl. = for
inter Graecos quoque erant multi milites <u>fortes</u>. Achilles autem <u>fortissimus</u> erat.	fortissimus, -a, -um = the bravest
15 Achilles amicum, <u>Patroclum</u> nomine, habebat.	Patroclum = Patroclus (a name)
quod Hector <u>Patroclum</u> in proelio <u>occiderat</u>, Achilles <u>iratissimus</u> erat.	occiderat = had killed

Total: 85

Exercise 12.2

1.   From the passage give, in Latin, one example of each of the following:
   (a) an adverb.   (1)
   (b) a preposition.   (1)
   (c) an infinitive.   (1)

2.   **oppugnaverant** (line 1). Give the Latin subject and the Latin object of this verb.   (2)

3.   **erant** (line 8). Give the first person singular of the present tense of this verb.   (1)

4.   **Troiae** (line 9). In which case is this noun?   (1)

5.   **habebat** (line 10). Give the person, number and tense of this verb.   (3)

Total: 10

The pluperfect tense

	1	2	3	3½	4
	had loved	had warned	had ruled	had taken	had heard
1st person singular	amav**eram**	monu**eram**	rex**eram**	cep**eram**	audiv**eram**
2nd person singular	amav**eras**	monu**eras**	rex**eras**	cep**eras**	audiv**eras**
3rd person singular	amav**erat**	monu**erat**	rex**erat**	cep**erat**	audiv**erat**
1st person plural	amav**eramus**	monu**eramus**	rex**eramus**	cep**eramus**	audiv**eramus**
2nd person plural	amav**eratis**	monu**eratis**	rex**eratis**	cep**eratis**	audiv**eratis**
3rd person plural	amav**erant**	monu**erant**	rex**erant**	cep**erant**	audiv**erant**

	sum, esse, fui	eo, ire, ii
	had been	had gone
1st person singular	fu**eram**	i**eram**
2nd person singular	fu**eras**	i**eras**
3rd person singular	fu**erat**	i**erat**
1st person plural	fu**eramus**	i**eramus**
2nd person plural	fu**eratis**	i**eratis**
3rd person plural	fu**erant**	i**erant**

Exercise 12.3

Translate the following into Latin:

1. He had loved.
2. They had carried.
3. We had stayed.
4. I had seen.
5. You (sing.) had sent.
6. They had put.
7. We had made.
8. You (pl.) had taken.
9. They had heard.
10. I had come.
11. She had slept.
12. He had punished.
13. You (sing.) had played.
14. He had given.
15. They had laughed.
16. We had fought.
17. They had departed.
18. I had read.
19. We had destroyed.
20. He had walked.

1 mark for each question. Total: 20

Exercise 12.4

Translate the following into Latin:

1. They had made.
2. He had seen.
3. You (sing.) had destroyed.
4. We had put.
5. I had laughed.

6. You (pl.) had punished.
7. He had made.
8. She had sent.
9. We had come.
10. They had taken.

1 mark for each question. Total: 10

Exercise 12.5

Translate the following into English:

1. amaveramus
2. ceperant
3. audiveras
4. rexerat
5. dederam

6. duxerat
7. moveramus
8. terruerat
9. responderant
10. miseram

1 mark for each question. Total: 10

Exercise 12.6

Translate the following into English:

1. posuerat
2. cucurrerant
3. discesseras
4. legeram
5. dormiveramus

6. ambulaveramus
7. fugerat
8. feceratis
9. riseramus
10. deleveras

1 mark for each question. Total: 10

Exercise 12.7

Translate the following into English:

1. manseramus
2. viderant
3. pugnaverat
4. intraverant
5. ceperat

6. monueras
7. biberat
8. dixerat
9. luseramus
10. occideratis

1 mark for each question. Total: 10

Exercise 12.8

Translate the following into English:

1. magister iratus erat quod riseramus. (5)
2. puer librum non legerat. (4)
3. pueri mali fuerant. (3)
4. puella puerum vulneraverat. (3)
5. verba non audiveramus. (3)
6. dominus laetus erat quod bene dormiverat. (6)
7. servi bene laboraverant. (3)
8. uxor discesserat. (5)
9. servus cibum paraverat. (3)
10 amicus multam pecuniam ei dederat. (5)

Total: 40

Exercise 12.9

Translate the following into English:

1. hostes laeti erant quod Romani discesserant. (6)
2. dei Romanos vicerant. (3)
3. numquam urbem deleverant. (3)
4. celeriter adveneramus. (2)
5. multa oppida ceperant. (3)
6. puer celeriter currebat quod magistrum iratum viderat. (7)
7. magister iratus eum conspexerat. (4)
8. miles validus eum terruerat. (4)
9. tandem is ducem occiderat. (4)
10. servus malus sororem vulneravit. (4)

Total: 40

Exercise 12.10

Translate the following into English:

1. puer diu laboraverat. (3)
2. dux iratus fuerat. (3)
3. milites bene pugnaverant. (3)
4. bene dormiveram. (2)
5. puer miser non riserat. (4)
6. proelium longum fuerat. (3)
7. hostes multas terras superaverant. (4)
8. dominus multos servos liberaverat. (4)
9. rex hostium ad flumen festinaverat. (5)
10. milites oppidum fortiter oppugnaverant. (4)

Total: 35

Exercise 12.11

Translate the following into English:

1. servi ex oppido cucurrerant. (4)
2. magister multos libros legerat. (4)
3. nuntius multa verba dixerat. (4)
4. servus multam aquam biberat. (4)
5. femina multa vulnera acceperat. (4)
6. puer donum ad patrem miserat. (5)
7. milites trans flumen transierant. (4)
8. puellam non conspexeramus. (3)
9. milites non bene pugnaverant. (4)
10. cives oppidum fortiter defenderant. (4)

Total: 40

Exercise 12.12

Translate the following into Latin:

1. We had conquered the enemy.
2. They had seized the city.
3. He had wounded the king.
4. We had defended the town.
5. I had seen the girl.

2 marks for each question. Total: 10

Exercise 12.13

Translate the following into Latin:

1. The leader had said many words.
2. The soldier had wounded the friend with a spear.
3. The enemy had charged against the town.
4. The sailors had waited for the ship for a long time.
5. The Greeks had collected many weapons.

4 marks for each question. Total: 20

Exercise 12.14

Give and translate the following:

1. The 3rd person plural, present tense of **occupo**.
2. The 1st person plural, imperfect tense of **defendo**.
3. The 2nd person plural, future tense of **vinco**.
4. The 2nd person singular, perfect tense of **vulnero**.
5. The 3rd person singular, perfect tense of **vinco**.

2 marks for each question. Total: 10

71

Exercise 12.15

Give the translation, person, number, tense and first person singular of the present tense of the following:

1. defendemus
2. ibat
3. vicerat
4. eritis
5. vulneravit

5 marks for each question. Total: 25

Exercise 12.16

Put into the plural and translate your answer:

1. dux clarus erat.   (3 + 3)
2. urbem defendis.   (2 + 2)
3. dominus servum vulneraverat.   (3 + 3)
4. regem numquam conspexi.   (2 + 3)
5. oppidum occupabo.   (2 + 2)

Total: 25

Exercise 12.17

Put into the singular and translate your answer:

1. vincemus.   (1 + 1)
2. hastae vulnerant.   (2 + 2)
3. duces pugnaverant.   (2 + 2)
4. Romanos vicimus.   (2 + 2)
5. cives mortui erant.   (3 + 3)

Total: 20

Exercise 12.18

Translate the following into Latin:

1. I do not have the courage.
2. The enemy were savage.
3. We will never beat the enemy.
4. They will seize the town tomorrow.
5. The Romans have conquered the Greeks.

3 marks for each question. Total: 15

Exercise 12.19

Translate the following into Latin:

1. That man has great courage. (5)
2. The courage of those soldiers was famous. (4)
3. These citizens were defending the town well. (5)
4. The soldiers were attacking the city with great courage. (5)
5. I saw my companion in the city yesterday. (6)

Total: 25

Exercise 12.20

Keeping the same person and number, put the following verbs into the imperfect tense and translate your answer:

1. occupaverunt
2. vulneravit
3. exspectavimus
4. mansimus
5. liberavistis
6. risit
7. salutaverunt
8. respondit
9. rogavit
10. dedi

2 marks for each question. Total: 20

Chapter 13

Exercise 13.1

Translate the following passage. Line numbers are given on the left. New words are underlined in the text and their meanings given in the margin.

Achilles, angry because of Patroclus's death, tells Hector that he will kill him. Hector is not impressed

1   Achilles iratus erat quod Hector Patroclum
occiderat. Hectorem igitur occidere cupiebat.

olim Troiani contra Graecos prope urbem
Troiam pugnabant. <u>omnes</u> fortiter pugnabant.   omnes = everyone

5   <u>tum</u> subito Achilles Hectorem <u>forte</u>   tum = then
conspexit. ubi eum vidit, ei clamavit: 'audi me,   forte = by chance
Hector! ego sum Achilles, <u>fortissimus</u>   fortissimus, -a, -um = the bravest
Graecorum. tu vir <u>crudelis</u> es. quod tu   crudelis = cruel
Patroclum, amicum meum, occidisti, ego te

10   occidam!'

Hector, ubi verba Achillis audivit, ei respondit:
'audi verba mea, Achilles! laetus sum quod
ego Patroclum, amicum tuum, occidi. ego te
non timeo. tu me non terres. tu <u>fortis</u> non es.   fortis, -e = brave

15   tu <u>audax</u> non es. veni! pugna! <u>victoria</u> mihi   audax = daring
<u>facilis</u> erit. ego te mox vincam!'   victoria, -ae, f. = victory
    facilis = easy

Total: 95

Exercise 13.2

1.   From the passage give, in Latin, one example of each of the following:
    (a) a verb in the pluperfect tense.   (1)
    (b) an imperative.   (1)
    (c) a personal pronoun.   (1)
    (d) a verb in the future tense.   (1)

2.   **urbem** (line 3). In which case is this noun? Why is this case used?   (2)

3.   **conspexit** (line 6). Give the tense and the first person singular of the present tense of this verb.   (2)

4.   **clamavit** (line 6). Explain the connection between this word and the English word ***exclamation***.   (1)

5.   **verba** (line 12). Give the gender of this noun.   (1)

Total: 10

omnis, -e = all, every

	masculine	feminine	neuter
singular			
nominative	omn**is**	omn**is**	omn**e**
vocative	omn**is**	omn**is**	omn**e**
accusative	omn**em**	omn**em**	omn**e**
genitive	omn**is**	omn**is**	omn**is**
dative	omn**i**	omn**i**	omn**i**
ablative	omn**i**	omn**i**	omn**i**
plural			
nominative	omn**es**	omn**es**	omn**ia**
vocative	omn**es**	omn**es**	omn**ia**
accusative	omn**es**	omn**es**	omn**ia**
genitive	omn**ium**	omn**ium**	omn**ium**
dative	omn**ibus**	omn**ibus**	omn**ibus**
ablative	omn**ibus**	omn**ibus**	omn**ibus**

Remember: omnes = everyone
omnia = everything

Example

omnes ridebant.	Everybody was laughing.
omnia paravimus.	We prepared everything.

75

Exercise 13.3

Translate the following into English:

1. rex nobilis.
2. reges nobiles.
3. opus difficile.
4. opera difficilia.
5. milites fortes.
6. omnia scuta.
7. omnes puellae.
8. viri tristes.
9. miles fortis.
10. vulnera crudelia.
11. filius difficilis.
12. iter difficile.
13. domini crudeles.
14. puella tristis.
15. dux nobilis.

2 marks for each question. Total: 30

Exercise 13.4

Translate the following into English:

1. omnia flumina.
2. omnes hastae.
3. dux fortis.
4. duces fortes.
5. feminae crudeles.
6. hostes fortes.
7. opus facile.
8. liber difficilis.
9. viri nobiles.
10. via difficilis.
11. verba crudelia.
12. verbum crudele.
13. servi tristes.
14. nomen nobile.
15. mater tristis.

2 marks for each question. Total: 30

Exercise 13.5

Translate the following into English:

1. dominum crudelem habeo.
2. opus facile facio.
3. omnia vina amo.
4. omnes libros lego.
5. omnes puellas specto.
6. omnia non porto.
7. librum difficilem lego.
8. ducem fortem laudo.
9. servum tristem video.
10. omnes pueros laudo.

3 marks for each question. Total: 30

Exercise 13.6

Translate the following into English:

1. servum fortem libero.
2. omnes puellas amo.
3. omnes non amo.
4. opera difficilia amo.
5. dominum crudelem occido.
6. milites crudeles timeo.
7. milites fortes laudo.
8. opus difficile facio.
9. omnia arma porto.
10. verba crudelia audio.

3 marks for each question. Total: 30

Exercise 13.7

Translate the following into English:

1. hic miles est fortis et validus. (6)
2. hi milites sunt fortes validique. (5)
3. illa puella nobilis est. (4)
4. hic liber difficilis est. (4)
5. dominus meus crudelis est. (4)
6. omnes pueri laborant. (3)
7. cur tristis es, puer? (4)
8. tristis sum quod magister crudelis est. (6)
9. non omnia opera difficilia sunt. (5)
10. hic rex nobilis est. (4)

Total: 45

Exercise 13.8

Translate the following into English:

1. magister crudelis omnes pueros punit. (5)
2. librum facilem legimus. (3)
3. hoc opus difficile non amo. (5)
4. omnes puellae ludunt. (3)
5. non omnes magistri crudeles sunt. (5)
6. servi tristes dominum crudelem timent. (5)
7. dominus nobilis servos laudat. (4)
8. frater meus omnia parat. (4)
9. itinera difficilia saepe facimus. (4)
10. servi tristes sunt quod dominus saepe crudelis est. (7)

Total: 45

Exercise 13.9

Translate the following into Latin:

1. An easy journey.
2. Difficult books.
3. A difficult war.
4. A sad girl.
5. Cruel masters.
6. All the soldiers.
7. Easy work.
8. A brave soldier.
9. Sad women.
10. All wines.

2 marks for each question. Total: 20

Exercise 13.10

Translate the following into Latin:

1. By an easy road.
2. To the cruel boy.
3. For the brave soldiers.
4. Of all the girls.
5. By a cruel wound.
6. For the noble master.
7. With all the spears.
8. Of a brave boy.
9. For the noble girl.
10. By a sad book.

2 marks for each question. Total: 20

Exercise 13.11

Translate the following into Latin:

1. The noble queen was sad. (4)
2. All boys like wine. (4)
3. The cruel king punished the brave soldier. (5)
4. All wars are cruel. (4)
5. The journey was not easy but difficult. (6)
6. The soldiers had fought well. (3)
7. We shall beat all the enemy. (3)
8. All the citizens were afraid. (4)
9. We do not like the cruel master. (4)
10. That king is noble. (4)
11. The wounds of all the citizens are bad. (5)
12. All the pupils have worked well. (4)
13. It is not easy to work well. (5)
14. The brave citizen fought against the enemy. (5)
15. We came to the city by an easy journey. (5)

Total: 65

Exercise 13.12

Put into the plural and translate your answer:

1. ridet. (1 + 1)
2. mater non timebat. (2 + 3)
3. puer patrem habet. (3 + 3)
4. miles urbem oppugnavit. (3 + 3)
5. discipulus magistrum audiebat. (3 + 3)

Total: 25

Exercise 13.13

Put into the singular and translate your answer:

1. sagittae vulnerant. (2 + 2)
2. servi oppida deleverunt. (3 + 3)
3. domini servos puniverunt. (3 + 3)
4. oppida diu defendebamus. (2 + 3)
5. viri currebant. (2 + 2)

Total: 25

Chapter 14

Exercise 14.1

Translate the following passage. Line numbers are given on the left. New words are underlined in the text and their meanings given in the margin.

Achilles fights Hector

1 Achilles Hectorem spectabat. Hector
Achillem spectabat. Hector vir fortis et <u>audax</u>
erat. Achilles tamen <u>fortior</u> et <u>audacior</u> <u>quam</u>
Hector erat.

audax = bold, daring

fortior = braver
audacior = more daring
quam = than

5 subito Hector <u>telum</u> suum iecit. <u>telum</u> ad
Achillem <u>volavit</u>. in scuto tamen Achillis
<u>haesit</u>. Achilles, ubi hoc vidit, risit. deinde
Hectori haec verba crudelia dixit: 'tu me non
occidisti, Hector. ego sum <u>fortior</u> <u>quam</u> tu.
10 ego sum <u>fortissimus</u> omnium Graecorum.
nunc ego te occidam.'

telum, -i, n. = spear
volo, -are, volavi (1) = I fly

haereo, -ere, haesi (2) = I stick

fortissimus, -a, -um = the bravest

ubi haec dixit, <u>telum</u> ad Hectorem iecit. <u>telum</u>
in corpore Hectoris <u>haesit</u>. Hector ad terram
<u>cecidit</u> mortuus. Achilles <u>laetissimus</u> erat. risit.

cado, -ere, cecidi (3) = I fall
laetissimus, -a, -um = very happy

Total: 80

Exercise 14.2

1. From the passage give, in Latin, one example of each of the following:
   (a) a personal pronoun. (1)
   (b) an adjective. (1)

2. **spectabat** (line 1). Give the Latin subject and the Latin object of this verb. (2)

3. **iecit** (line 5). Give the person, number and tense of this verb. Give the first person singular of the present tense of this verb. (4)

4. **Hectorem** (line 12). In which case is this noun? Why is this case used? (2)

Total: 10

79

felix, felicis = lucky

	masculine	feminine	neuter
singular			
nominative	felix	felix	felix
vocative	felix	felix	felix
accusative	felicem	felicem	felix
genitive	felicis	felicis	felicis
dative	felici	felici	felici
ablative	felici	felici	felici
plural			
nominative	felices	felices	felicia
vocative	felices	felices	felicia
accusative	felices	felices	felicia
genitive	felicium	felicium	felicium
dative	felicibus	felicibus	felicibus
ablative	felicibus	felicibus	felicibus

ingens, ingentis = huge

	masculine	feminine	neuter
singular			
nominative	ingens	ingens	ingens
vocative	ingens	ingens	ingens
accusative	ingentem	ingentem	ingens
genitive	ingentis	ingentis	ingentis
dative	ingenti	ingenti	ingenti
ablative	ingenti	ingenti	ingenti

	masculine	feminine	neuter
plural			
nominative	ingent**es**	ingent**es**	ingent**ia**
vocative	ingent**es**	ingent**es**	ingent**ia**
accusative	ingent**es**	ingent**es**	ingent**ia**
genitive	ingent**ium**	ingent**ium**	ingent**ium**
dative	ingent**ibus**	ingent**ibus**	ingent**ibus**
ablative	ingent**ibus**	ingent**ibus**	ingent**ibus**

Exercise 14.3

Translate the following into English:

1. miles fortis.
2. dominus crudelis.
3. templum ingens.
4. pueri felices.
5. magistri sapientes.
6. verba sapientia.
7. dux audax.
8. bellum triste.
9. proelia difficilia.
10. servus felix.

2 marks for each question. Total: 20

Exercise 14.4

Translate the following into English:

1. opus ingens.
2. domini difficiles.
3. fratres crudeles.
4. hostes audaces.
5. milites omnes.
6. verba omnia.
7. verbum sapiens.
8. templa ingentia.
9. servi fortes.
10. rex audax.

2 marks for each question. Total: 20

Exercise 14.5

Translate the following into English:

1. dominus crudelis servos omnes punit. (5)
2. omnes milites fortes sunt. (4)
3. non omnia bella sapientia sunt. (5)
4. libros difficiles numquam lego. (4)
5. templum ingens aedificamus. (3)
6. Roma erat urbs ingens. (4)
7. dux sapiens milites fortes semper laudat. (6)
8. non omnes reges crudeles sunt. (5)
9. iter longum et difficile facimus. (5)
10. magister puerum sapientem laudat. (4)

Total: 45

Exercise 14.6

Translate the following into English:

1. omnes milites Romani audaces erant. (5)
2. soror puellae felix est. (4)
3. omnes magistri sapientes sunt. (4)
4. illa puella fratrem sapientem habet. (5)
5. milites ducem felicem semper amant. (5)
6. servi opus difficile faciunt. (4)
7. omnes servi bene laborant. (4)
8. patrem sapientem puellae illius amamus. (5)
9. ad urbem itinere facili venimus. (5)
10. milites omnes mox capiemus. (4)

Total: 45

Exercise 14.7

Translate the following into Latin:

1. That tall soldier is daring. (5)
2. I have a wise father. (3)
3. Soldiers like lucky leaders. (4)
4. Not all men are wise. (5)
5. The enemy were brave. (3)

Total: 20

altior, altius = higher

	masculine	feminine	neuter
singular			
nominative	altior	altior	altius
vocative	altior	altior	altius
accusative	altiorem	altiorem	altius
genitive	altioris	altioris	altioris
dative	altiori	altiori	altiori
ablative	altiore	altiore	altiore
plural			
nominative	altiores	altiores	altiora
vocative	altiores	altiores	altiora
accusative	altiores	altiores	altiora
genitive	altiorum	altiorum	altiorum
dative	altioribus	altioribus	altioribus
ablative	altioribus	altioribus	altioribus

How to say 'than'

The Latin word for 'than' is **quam**. The nouns being compared are always in the same case.

Examples

puer est sapientior **quam** puella.   The boy is wiser than the girl.
puellae sunt sapientiores **quam** pueri.   Girls are wiser than boys.

Exercise 14.8

Translate the following into English:

1. hic miles fortis est; ille miles fortior est. (8)
2. ille miles fortior quam hic miles est. (7)
3. illud telum longum est; hoc telum longius est. (8)
4. hoc telum est longius quam illud. (6)
5. illa puella sapientior est quam hic puer. (7)
6. magistri sapientiores sunt quam pueri. (5)
7. magistri sapientissimi saepe sunt. (4)
8. hoc templum altius quam illud est. (6)
9. hoc opus non facile sed difficillimum est. (7)
10. milites Romani fortiores quam milites Graeci erant. (7)

Total: 65

Exercise 14.9

Translate the following into English:

1. milites audaciores quam cives sunt. (5)
2. illa puella pulcherrima est; puellam pulchriorem numquam vidi. (8)
3. ille magister iratissimus erat; magistrum iratiorem numquam vidi. (8)
4. ille miles audacissimus erat; militem audaciorem numquam vidi. (8)
5. illa mulier tristissima erat; mulierem tristiorem numquam vidi. (8)
6. Achilles miles fortissimus sed crudelissimus erat. (6)
7. Romani audaciores quam Graeci erant. (5)
8. urbes Graecae pulchriores quam urbes Romanae erant. (7)
9. omnes mulieres sapientiores quam viri sunt. (6)
10. Romani clari erant, sed Graeci clariores quam Romani erant. (9)

Total: 70

Exercise 14.10

Translate the following into Latin:

1. A very wise man.
2. A very high wall.
3. Very daring soldiers.
4. A very fortunate king.
5. A very cruel master.
6. Very long rivers.
7. A very difficult journey.
8. A very dear wife.
9. A very sacred temple.
10. Very easy tasks.

2 marks for each question. Total: 20

Exercise 14.11

Translate the following into Latin:

1. With very happy words.
2. On the higher wall.
3. To the very angry teacher.
4. For the very lucky boys.
5. Of a wiser man.
6. With a more beautiful girl.
7. For the very famous king.
8. Of very cruel masters.
9. For a very long war.
10. By an easier journey.

2 marks for each question. Total: 20

Exercise 14.12

Translate the following into Latin:

1. My son is very tall and very famous. (6)
2. Marcus is wiser than Flavia. (5)
3. Boys are wiser than girls. (5)
4. That temple is taller than this. (6)
5. I am looking at very beautiful girls. (3)

Total: 25

Exercise 14.13

Put into the plural and translate your answer:

1. dedit. (1 + 1)
2. magnum telum habeo. (3 + 3)
3. miles audax est. (3 + 3)
4. vir non festinabit. (2 + 3)
5. iuvenis gladium habebat. (3 + 3)

Total: 25

Exercise 14.14

Put into the singular and translate your answer:

1. non curremus. (1 + 2)
2. servi felices erant. (3 + 3)
3. hastae milites vulneraverunt. (3 + 3)
4. iuvenes tela timebant. (3 + 3)
5. itinera longa et difficilia sunt. (4 + 5)

Total: 30

Exercise 14.15

Give and translate the following verb parts:

1. The 2nd person singular, imperfect tense of **eo**.
2. The 1st person plural, present tense of **vinco**.
3. The 3rd person plural, perfect tense of **vulnero**.
4. The 3rd person singular, pluperfect tense of **maneo**.
5. The 1st person singular, perfect tense of **discedo**.

2 marks for each question. Total: 10

Exercise 14.16

Give the translation, person, number, tense and first person singular of the present tense of the following:

1. ruis
2. occupant
3. accipiebat
4. defendent
5. vicerat

5 marks for each question. Total: 25

Exercise 14.17

Translate the following into Latin:

1. That leader was daring. (4)
2. I have a lucky friend. (3)
3. The leader threw many missiles. (4)
4. Wise men often fear death. (5)
5. Many missiles wounded the leader. (4)

Total: 20

Exercise 14.18

Translate the following into Latin:

1. The missiles of the enemy were long.
2. The walls of the town were huge.
3. We attacked the city with many missiles.
4. The courage of the citizen frightened the king.
5. The soldiers' courage was great.

4 marks for each question. Total: 20

Chapter 15

Exercise 15.1

Translate the following passage. Line numbers are given on the left. New words are underlined in the text and their meanings given in the margin.

Achilles mistreats Hector's body

1 Achilles vir crudelissimus erat. corpus Hectoris
currui suo pedibus vinxit. deinde currum
circum muros Troiae egit, corpus Hectoris
trahens. omnes cives Troiani, ubi hoc viderunt,
5 tristissimi erant.

Paris filius Priami erat. frater igitur Hectoris
erat. quod Achilles Hectorem occiderat,
iratissimus erat. arma cepit, ex urbe cucurrit,
in proelium ruit. Achillem mox invenit. haec
10 verba ei dixit: 'Achilles, vir pessimus es. nemo
peior est quam tu. Hectorem, fratrem meum,
occidisti. ego tamen miles melior sum quam
tu. numquam effugies. nemo te servare
poterit. te nunc occidam.' Paris telum in
15 Achillem misit. telum in calce Achillis haesit.
Achilles ad terram mortuus cecidit.

currui = dative of currus = chariot
pes, pedis, m. = foot
vincio, -ire, vinxi (4) = I tie
circum + acc. = around
ago, -ere, egi (3) = I drive
trahens = dragging

Priamus, -i, m. = Priam (a name)

invenio, -ire, inveni (4) = I find
pessimus, -a, -um = very wicked
peior = more wicked
melior = better
effugio, -ere, effugi (3½) = I escape
servo, -are, servavi (1) = I save
poterit = will be able
calx, calcis, f. = heel
haereo, -ere, haesi (2) = I stick
cado, -ere, cecidi (3) = I fall

Total: 100

Exercise 15.2

1. From the passage give, in Latin, one example of each of the following:
   (a) a superlative adjective. (1)
   (b) a preposition. (1)
   (c) a verb in the pluperfect tense. (1)
   (d) an adverb. (1)

2. **occiderat** (line 7). Give the Latin subject and the Latin object of this verb. (2)

3. **urbe** (line 8). In which case is this noun? Why is this case used? (2)

4. **misit** (line 15). Give the tense and the first person singular of the present tense of this verb. (2)

Total: 10

Vocabulary 15

circum + acc.	around
invenio, -ire, inveni (4)	I find
servo, -are, -avi (1)	I save
effugio, -ere, effugi (3½)	I escape

Irregular comparison – a reminder

Positive	Comparative	Superlative
bonus = good	melior = better	optimus = very good/best
malus = bad	peior = worse	pessimus = very bad/worst
magnus = big	maior = bigger	maximus = very big/biggest
parvus = small	minor = smaller	minimus = very small/smallest
multus = much/many	plus = more	plurimus = very many/most

Exercise 15.3

Translate the following into English:

1. ego sum puer bonus, sed tu es melior. (8)
2. Sextus puer pessimus est. (4)
3. Iulius Caesar erat dux optimus. (5)
4. hoc templum est maius quam illud. (6)
5. Alexander Magnus miles melior quam Iulius Caesar erat. (8)
6. cibus matris tuae optimus erat. (5)
7. naves maximae appropinquabant. (3)
8. ego plus pecuniae quam tu habeo. (6)
9. Italia maior quam Britannia est. (5)
10. Britannia minor quam Italia est. (5)

Total: 55

Exercise 15.4

Translate the following into English:

1. illa puella minima est. (4)
2. hic puer maior quam illa puella est. (7)
3. plurimi milites oppidum oppugnaverunt. (4)
4. ille magister pessimus erat. (4)
5. puellae meliores quam pueri sunt, (5)
6. pueri peiores quam puellae sunt. (5)
7. milites Romani optimi erant. (4)
8. Romani milites meliores quam Graeci habebant. (6)
9. Graeci milites peiores quam Romani habebant. (6)
10. cives plurimi maximum oppidum defendebant. (5)

Total: 50

Exercise 15.5

Translate the following into English:

1. vulnus meum pessimum est. (4)
2. vulnus peius numquam accepi. (4)
3. montes Italiae maiores quam montes Britanniae sunt. (7)
4. muri Troiae olim maximi erant. (5)
5. milites in maximo periculo erant. (5)
6. hic agricola plurimos et maximos agros habet. (7)
7. sunt in agris plurimi equi. (5)
8. in maiore nave quam illa numquam fui. (7)
9. Graeci templa maiora et meliora quam Romani aedificabant. (8)
10. templa Romanorum minora et peiora quam Graecorum erant. (8)

Total: 60

Exercise 15.6

Translate the following into Latin:

1. A very bad boy.
2. Very good pupils.
3. Very many soldiers.
4. Very many ships.
5. Very good leaders.
6. A bigger temple.
7. A very small city.
8. Very big wars.
9. Smaller girls.
10. A very good teacher.

2 marks for each question: Total: 20

Exercise 15.7

Translate the following into Latin:

1. Not all teachers are very good. (5)
2. I have a few very bad pupils. (4)
3. We are carrying very big shields. (3)
4. That girl was very small. (4)
5. I have never seen a bigger ship. (4)

Total: 20

Exercise 15.8

Translate the following into English:

1. magister optimus.
2. flumen altissimum.
3. discipulus pessimus.
4. miles fortissimus.
5. milites fortissimi.
6. puella pulcherrima.
7. maximum oppidum.
8. plurimi pueri.
9. maxima turba.
10. flumen minimum.
11. hostes audacissimi.
12. servi pessimi.
13. liber difficillimus.
14. dominus crudelissimus.
15. vir nobillimus.
16. vinum optimum.
17. milites optimi.
18. liber longissimus.
19. liber optimus.
20. flumina longissima.

2 marks for each question. Total: 40

Exercise 15.9

Translate the following into English:

1. uxor pulcherrima.
2. verba sapientissima.
3. naves maximae.
4. hostes saevissimi.
5. mulieres pulcherrimae.
6. corpora maxima.
7. templa maxima.
8. templum maximum.
9. scutum maximum.
10. pueri laetissimi.
11. plurimae feminae.
12. aqua altissima.
13. puer felicissimus.
14. femina saevissima.
15. copiae maximae.
16. via longissima.
17. vir pulcherrimus.
18. caelum pulcherrimum.
19. ager maximus.
20. magister iratissimus.

2 marks for each question. Total: 40

Exercise 15.10

Put into the plural and translate your answer:

1. effugiebat. (1 + 1)
2. miles pugnabat. (2 + 2)
3. librum meum tandem inveni. (3 + 4)
4. civis tutus est. (3 + 3)
5. puella iuvenem timebat. (3 + 3)

Total: 25

Exercise 15.11

Put into the singular and translate your answer:

1. defenditis. (1 + 1)
2. naves veniebant. (2 + 2)
3. servi effugerunt. (2 + 2)
4. cives urbes servabant. (3 + 3)
5. corpora invenerunt. (2 + 2)

Total: 20

Exercise 15.12

Translate the following into English:

1. plurimi servi hostes timebant et ex urbe effugiebant. (8)
2. Romani opera difficiliora quam Graeci faciebant. (6)
3. quamquam dux multos hostes vicerat, nemo eum laudavit. (8)
4. omnes milites mortem in bello timent. (6)
5. cives Graeci sapientiores quam cives Romani erant. (7)
6. milites Romani multa oppida ceperant et multos hostes vicerant. (9)
7. plurimas puellas pulcherrimas in urbe heri conspexi. (7)
8. milites Romani pro civibus Romanis semper fortiter pugnabant. (8)
9. hi servi dominum crudelissimum habebant. eum non amabant. (8)
10. cives muros oppidi contra hostes maxima virtute defendebant. (8)

Total: 75

Exercise 15.13

Translate the following into Latin:

1. I am running around the wall. (3)
2. I found money in the street. (4)
3. The lucky slaves escaped. (3)
4. The king saved much money. (4)
5. The leader seized the town. (3)
6. The huge wall saved the city. (4)
7. The Romans conquered the Greeks with weapons. (4)
8. The farmer found a horse in the field. (5)
9. The weapons of the Romans frightened the enemy. (4)
10. The brave soldier saves his friend in the battle. (6)

Total: 40

Chapter 16

Exercise 16.1

Translate the following passage. Line numbers are given on the left. New words are underlined in the text and their meanings given in the margin.

The Greeks despair of taking Troy, but Ulysses comes up with a plan

1 diu Graeci urbem Troiam oppugnaverant. post
   multos annos fessi erant. quamquam fortiter
   pugnabant, urbem capere non poterant. 'quid
   faciemus?' inquiunt. 'num urbem capiemus?

5 muri Troiae altissimi et maximi sunt. eos
   delere numquam poterimus.'

   Ulixes, miles audacissimus Graecorum, ubi
   haec verba audivit, iratus erat. magna voce
   clamavit: 'audite me, Graeci! nolite stulti esse!

10 nos Graeci sapientiores quam illi Troiani
   sumus. Troiam mox capiemus. consilium
   habeo. consilium optimum habeo. consilio
   meo urbem delebimus. equum ligneum
   maximum aedificate!' Graeci igitur equum

15 ligneum maximum aedificaverunt.

post + acc. = after

annus, -i, m. = year

poterant = they were able

inquiunt = they said
num introduces a question which expects the answer 'no'; surely ... not?
poterimus = we will be able

vox, vocis f. = voice

nolite + infinitive = don't ...!
stultus, -a, -um = stupid

consilium, -i, n. = plan

ligneus, -a, -um = wooden

Total: 80

Exercise 16.2

1. From the passage give, in Latin, one example of each of the following:
   (a) a superlative adjective. (1)
   (b) a comparative adjective. (1)
   (c) an imperative. (1)
   (d) an adverb. (1)

2. **urbem** (line 1). In which case is this noun? Why is this case used? (2)

3. **muri** (line 5). Give the gender of this noun. (1)

4. **capiemus** (line 11). Give the person, number and tense of this verb. (3)

Total: 10

91

Vocabulary 16

post + acc.	after
possum, posse, potui (irreg.)	I am able, I can
vox, vocis, f.	voice

possum, posse, potui = I am able, I can

	Present	Future	Imperfect	Perfect	Pluperfect
1st person singular	possum	potero	poteram	potui	potueram
2nd person singular	potes	poteris	poteras	potuisti	potueras
3rd person singular	potest	poterit	poterat	potuit	potuerat
1st person plural	possumus	poterimus	poteramus	potuimus	potueramus
2nd person plural	potestis	poteritis	poteratis	potuistis	potueratis
3rd person plural	possunt	poterunt	poterant	potuerunt	potuerant

Infinitive	posse

Remember: The verb possum is preceded by an infinitive.

Examples

puella **currere** non potest.	= The girl is not able to run.
	= The girl cannot run.
ille miles bene **pugnare** poterat.	= That soldier was able to fight well.
	= That soldier could fight well.

Exercise 16.3

Translate the following into English:

1. potest
2. potestis
3. poterat
4. potuerat
5. poterit
6. potuimus
7. posse
8. potueras
9. poteras
10. potes

11. possum
12. poteramus
13. potuit
14. potuerunt
15. potueramus
16. possunt
17. poterunt
18. possumus
19. potuistis
20. potero

1 mark for each question. Total: 20

Exercise 16.4

Translate the following into English:

1. laborare possum. (2)
2. effugere potest. (2)
3. vincere possumus. (2)
4. exspectare non poteram. (3)
5. fugere poterant. (2)
6. redire non possum. (3)
7. currere non poteramus. (3)
8. oppugnare potuerunt. (2)
9. dormire non possum. (3)
10. pugnare non poteras. (3)

Total: 25

Exercise 16.5

Translate the following into English:

1. nautae ad insulam navigare poterant. (5)
2. hostes vincere numquam poterimus. (4)
3. milites urbem delere non poterant. (5)
4. servi ex oppido effugere non poterant. (6)
5. milites hoc oppidum capere poterunt. (5)
6. Romani tela iacere non poterant. (5)
7. ille rex bene regere non potest. (6)
8. cives urbem bene defendere non poterant. (6)
9. ille servus hoc vinum bibere non potest. (7)
10. ad urbem hodie venire non potuimus. (6)

Total: 55

Exercise 16.6

Translate the following into English:

1. quis ad templum cras venire poterit? (6)
2. hoc iter longum facere numquam poterimus. (6)
3. milites hoc flumen transire non possunt. (6)
4. dominus illum servum liberare non poterat. (6)
5. comites celeriter currere non poterant. (5)
6. magistri omnia facere non possunt. (5)
7. Graeci Romanos in hoc proelio vincere non poterant. (8)
8. hic vir librum longum scribere non poterit. (7)
9. multam pecuniam filio meo dare non poteram. (7)
10. milites fessi contra hos hostes bene pugnare non poterant. (9)

Total: 65

Exercise 16.7

Translate the following into Latin:

1. I can read. (2)
2. We could not escape. (3)
3. You (sing.) cannot laugh. (3)
4. I will not be able to work. (3)
5. They could not attack. (3)
6. I can sail. (2)
7. He could sing. (2)
8. They will be able to come. (2)
9. They could not see. (3)
10. You (pl.) can depart. (2)

Total: 25

Exercise 16.8

Translate the following into Latin:

1. This boy cannot drink wine.
2. The citizens will not be able to defend the town.
3. The pupils have not been able to do this.
4. The enemy could not find the citizens' money.
5. The leader could not prepare very big forces.

5 marks for each question. Total: 25

Exercise 16.9

Put into the plural and translate your answer:

1. mox ex urbe effugiam. (3 + 4)
2. rex nobilis est. (3 + 3)
3. urbem defendam. (2 + 2)
4. puellam videras. (2 + 2)
5. amicum exspectabat. (2 + 2)

Total: 25

Exercise 16.10

Put into the singular and translate your answer:

1. servi currunt.
2. amici effugiebant.
3. hostes invenistis.
4. milites servaveramus.
5. tela habebamus.

2 + 2 marks for each question. Total: 20

94

Exercise 16.11

Put into the plural and translate your answer:

1. it. (1 + 1)
2. oppidum numquam aedificavi. (2 + 3)
3. puer puellam amabat. (3 + 3)
4. dux militem fessum defendebat. (4 + 4)
5. fortiter pugnabo. (2 + 2)

Total: 25

Exercise 16.12

Put into the singular and translate your answer:

1. rediimus. (1 + 1)
2. illi cives effugiebant. (3 + 3)
3. muri ingentes erant. (3 + 3)
4. discipuli bene laboraverunt. (2 + 3)
5. mulieres templa spectabant. (3 + 3)

Total: 25

Exercise 16.13

Give and translate the following verb parts:

1. The 3rd person singular, present tense of **possum**.
2. The 2nd person plural, future tense of **servo**.
3. The 3rd person plural, perfect tense of **invenio**.
4. The 1st person plural, perfect tense of **eo**.
5. The 2nd person singular, imperfect tense of **vinco**.

2 marks for each question. Total: 10

Exercise 16.14

Give the translation, person, number and first person singular of the present tense of the following:

1. poterat
2. festinabamus
3. effugient
4. eramus
5. peribat

4 marks for each question. Total: 20

95

Exercise 16.15

Translate the following into Latin:

1. That wound was cruel. (4)
2. We fear the missiles of the enemy. (3)
3. They attacked our city with missiles. (4)
4. The enemy were noble. (3)
5. The journey is not long but difficult. (6)

Total: 20

Exercise 16.16

Translate the following into Latin:

1. The king escaped from the city.
2. The enemy attacked the smallest island.
3. The Romans were able to fight well.
4. The sailors sailed to the island.
5. By the courage of the soldiers we took the town.

4 marks for each question. Total: 20

Numerals – a reminder

cardinal numbers	
unus	one
duo	two
tres	three
quattuor	four
quinque	five
sex	six
septem	seven
octo	eight
novem	nine
decem	ten
undecim	eleven
duodecim	twelve
tredecim	thirteen
quattuordecim	fourteen
quindecim	fifteen
sedecim	sixteen
septendecim	seventeen
duodeviginti	eighteen
undeviginti	nineteen
viginti	twenty

ordinal numbers	
primus, -a, -um	first
secundus, -a, -um	second
tertius, -a, -um	third
quartus, -a, -um	fourth
quintus, -a, -um	fifth
sextus, -a, -um	sixth
septimus, -a, -um	seventh
octavus, -a, -um	eighth
nonus, -a, -um	ninth
decimus, -a, -um	tenth

Chapter 17

Exercise 17.1

Translate the following passage. Line numbers are given on the left. New words are underlined in the text and their meanings given in the margin.

The Trojans see the horse

1 Graeci equum ligneum maximum aedificaverant. antequam in navibus discesserunt, plurimos milites in equum posuerunt et equum in litore prope urbem
5 reliquerunt.

Troiani, ubi hunc equum viderunt, e portis urbis exierunt. attoniti erant. diu equum spectabant. unus e Troianis haec verba dixit: 'Graeci discesserunt. nonne eos vicimus? hic
10 equus donum nobis est. eum in mediam urbem trahite, cives!'

Troianus secundus autem magna voce clamavit: 'num hic equus donum est? Graeci dona numquam dant. Graeci homines fallaces
15 sunt. nolite equum in urbem trahere, cives! eum delete!'

tandem Troiani equum in urbem trahere constituerunt.

ligneus, -a, -um = wooden

antequam = before

litus, litoris, n. = shore

relinquo, -ere, reliqui (3) = I leave behind, I abandon

porta, -ae, f. = gate

attonitus, -a, -um = amazed

nonne introduces a question which expects the answer 'yes'; surely...?
medius, -a, -um = the middle of
traho, -ere, traxi (3) = I pull, I drag

num introduces a question which expects the answer 'no'; surely ... not?
homo, hominis, m./f. = person; plural: people
fallax, fallacis = deceitful
nolite + infinitive = don't ...!

Total: 90

Exercise 17.2

1. From the passage give, in Latin, one example of each of the following:
   (a) a verb in the pluperfect tense. (1)
   (b) a preposition. (1)
   (c) an ordinal number. (1)
   (d) an imperative. (1)

2. **equum** (line 1). Explain the connection between this word and the English word ***equestrian***. (1)

3. **navibus** (line 2). In which case is this noun? Why is this case used? (2)

4. **posuerunt** (line 4). Give the first person singular of the present tense of this verb. (1)

5. **viderunt** (line 6). Give the Latin subject and the Latin object of this verb. (2)

Total: 10

Vocabulary 17

noli/nolite + infinitive	do not ...!
nonne ...?	expects the answer 'yes'
num ...?	expects the answer 'no'
antequam	before
medius, -a, -um	middle of
homo, hominis, m./f.	man, person
relinquo, -ere, reliqui (3)	I abandon, I leave behind

Prohibitions – a reminder

Examples

noli currere, puer!	Do not run, boy! (sing. prohibition)
nolite currere, pueri!	Do not run, boys! (pl. prohibition)

Exercise 17.3

Translate the following into English:

1. noli ridere, puer!
2. nolite ridere, pueri!
3. nolite oppugnare, milites!
4. nolite effugere, servi!
5. noli exspectare, amice!
6. noli inire, iuvenis!
7. nolite navigare, nautae!
8. noli stare, pater!
9. nolite ludere, puellae!
10. noli discedere, mater!

3 marks for each question. Total: 30

Exercise 17.4

Translate the following into English:

1. noli flere, femina! (3)
2. nolite libros scribere, poetae! (4)
3. noli currere, miles! (3)
4. noli sedere, puella! (3)
5. nolite timere, comites! (3)
6. nolite hic manere, cives! (4)
7. nolite pugnare, pueri mali! (4)
8. noli festinare, serve! (3)
9. nolite cantare, filiae! (3)
10. noli me hic relinquere, amici! (5)

Total: 35

Exercise 17.5

Translate the following into English:

1. nolite oppidum oppugnare, milites! (4)
2. nolite verba magistri audire, pueri! (5)
3. noli iter longum facere, amice! (5)
4. nolite urbem contra hostes defendere, cives! (6)
5. noli hunc servum punire, domine! (5)
6. nolite illos servos liberare, domini! (5)
7. noli e templo exire, puer! (5)
8. noli pecuniam patri tradere, iuvenis! (5)
9. nolite in via stare, puellae! (5)
10. noli hoc vinum bibere, mater! (5)

Total: 50

Exercise 17.6

Translate the following into Latin:

1. Don't run, girls!
2. Don't approach, boy!
3. Don't charge, soldiers!
4. Don't return, friend!
5. Don't work, pupils!
6. Don't fight, comrades!
7. Don't attack, slaves!
8. Don't hurry, mother!
9. Don't reply, boys!
10. Don't fight, citizens!

3 marks for each question. Total: 30

Exercise 17.7

Translate the following into Latin:

1. Don't play in the road, boy! (5)
2. Don't wound the enemy, soldiers! (4)
3. Don't set free this slave, master! (5)
4. Don't cross the river, sailor! (4)
5. Don't listen to that teacher, pupils! (5)
6. Don't hand over the money, king! (4)
7. Don't attack the city, Romans! (4)
8. Don't throw your spears, slaves! (5)
9. Don't kill the king, slave! (4)
10. Don't drink all the wine, girl! (5)

Total: 45

nonne and num

Examples

nonne laborat?	He is working, isn't he?
	Surely he is working?
num laborat?	He isn't working, is he?
	Surely he is not working?

Exercise 17.8

Translate the following into English:

1. flet (1)
2. num flet? (2)
3. nonne flet? (2)
4. pugnant (1)
5. pugnantne? (1)
6. num pugnant? (2)
7. effugerunt (1)
8. effugeruntne? (1)
9. nonne effugerunt? (2)
10. num effugerunt? (2)

Total: 15

Exercise 17.9

Translate the following into English:

1. bene pugnabat. (2)
2. nonne bene pugnabat? (3)
3. num bene pugnabat? (3)
4. hic miles fortis est. (4)
5. nonne hic miles fortis est? (5)
6. num hic miles fortis est? (5)
7. Hector miles audax erat. (4)
8. nonne Hector audax erat? (4)
9. num Hector miles audax erat? (5)
10. num Hector fortissimus Troianorum erat? (5)

Total: 40

Exercise 17.10

Translate the following into English:

1. nonne cives urbem bene defendebant? (5)
2. num puer hoc fecit? (4)
3. num Graeci Romanos vicerunt? (4)
4. num omnes mortem timent? (4)
5. nonne illam puellam in urbe heri conspexisti? (7)
6. nonne matrem tuam amas? (4)
7. nonne Graeci multa arma collegerunt? (5)
8. num femina hoc facere poterit? (5)
9. nonne milites Romani in bello bene pugnaverunt? (7)
10. num hoc facere difficile est? (5)

Total: 50

Exercise 17.11

Translate the following into Latin:

1. We are Romans, aren't we? (3)
2. We are not Romans, are we? (3)
3. Are we Romans? (2)
4. You (sing.) are not running, are you? (2)
5. Are you (sing.) running? (1)
6. You (sing.) are running, aren't you? (2)
7. You (sing.) weren't laughing, were you? (2)
8. You (sing.) were laughing, weren't you? (2)
9. Were you (sing.) laughing? (1)
10. We won't escape, will we? (2)

Total: 20

Exercise 17.12

Translate the follwing into Latin:

1. This man is not very wise, is he?
2. These weapons are good, aren't they?
3. That journey isn't easy, is it?
4. You (sing.) saw that unhappy girl, didn't you?
5. We will attack this city tomorrow, won't we?

5 marks for each question. Total: 25

Exercise 17.13

Translate the following into Latin:

1. The man does not love his wife, does he?
2. The Romans will beat the enemy, won't they?
3. We won't be able to do this, will we?
4. That soldier received a wound, didn't he?
5. Death will come to everyone, won't it?

4 marks for each question. Total: 20

Exercise 17.14

Put into the plural and translate your answer:

1. clamo. (1 + 1)
2. regina adveniebat. (2 + 2)
3. puellam heri conspexi. (2 + 3)
4. mulier optimam cenam parabat. (4 + 4)
5. dux amicum reliquit. (3 + 3)

Total: 25

Exercise 17.15

Put into the singular and translate your answer:

1. colligebamus. (1 + 1)
2. voces semper audiunt. (2 + 3)
3. milites bene pugnaverunt. (2 + 3)
4. discipuli comites non habebant. (3 + 4)
5. cives duces audiebant. (3 + 3)

Total: 25

Exercise 17.16

Translate the following into Latin:

1. My daughter has a good voice. (5)
2. He is a wise man. (3)
3. Many men are not wise. (5)
4. The Romans will attack tomorrow. (3)
5. Do not leave the money there! (4)

Total: 20

Exercise 17.17

Translate the following into Latin:

1. We are listening to the voices of those girls. (4)
2. The boys are standing in the middle of the road. (5)
3. He left much money in the road. (5)
4. The citizens left their weapons in the city. (5)
5. All Roman soldiers had great courage. (6)

Total: 25

Exercise 17.18

Translate the following into English:

1. hostes vicimus. (2)
2. librum scripsit. (2)
3. multam pecuniam invenerunt. (3)
4. servi effugerunt. (2)
5. tela iecerunt. (2)
6. poeta cras veniet. (3)
7. vulnus accepit. (2)
8. pater meus discessit. (3)
9. ex urbe exierunt. (3)
10. illud verbum dixit. (3)

Total: 25

Chapter 18

Exercise 18.1

Translate the following passage. Line numbers are given on the left. New words are underlined in the text and their meanings given in the margin.

The Fall of Troy

1	Troiani equum in urbem <u>traxerunt</u>. laetissimi erant quod Graeci discesserant. laetissimi erant quod Graecos vicerant.	traho, -ere, traxi (3) = I drag
5	illa <u>nocte</u> igitur omnes cives <u>festum celebrabant</u>. multum cibi consumebant et multum vini bibebant. mox omnes Troiani dormiebant.	nox, noctis, f. = night festum celebro, -are, -avi (1) = I hold a celebration
10	media <u>nocte</u> milites Graeci, <u>qui</u> in equo erant, de equo <u>silentio descenderunt</u>. subito ad Troianos <u>dormientes</u> magnis <u>clamoribus</u> ruerunt. Troiani <u>se</u> defendere non poterant. multi Troiani gladiis Graecorum perierunt. inter hos erat Priamus <u>senex</u>, rex Troiae. Graeci <u>paucos</u> Troianos <u>vivos</u> reliquerunt.	qui = who silentio = in silence descendo, -ere, descendi (3) = I climb down dormientes = as they were sleeping clamor, clamoris, m. = shout se = themselves senex, -is, m. = old man pauci, -ae, -a = few vivus, -a, -um = alive
15	sic Graeci post decem <u>annos</u> urbem Troiam <u>dolo</u> ceperunt. maximam <u>partem</u> urbis deleverunt. Helenam ad <u>Graeciam reducere</u> nunc poterant.	annus, -i, m. = year dolus, -i, m. = trickery pars, partis, f. = part Graecia, -ae, f. = Greece reduco, -ere, reduxi (3) = I lead back

Total: 90

Exercise 18.2

1. From the passage give, in Latin, an example of:
   (a) a superlative adjective. (1)
   (b) a verb in the imperfect tense. (1)
   (c) a preposition followed by a noun in the accusative case. (1)
   (d) an infinitive. (1)

2. **vicerant** (line 3). Give the person, number and tense of this verb. Give the first person singular of the present tense of this verb. (4)

3. **urbem** (line 15). Give the case of this noun. Why is this case used? (2)

Total: 10

Reflexive pronouns – a reminder

singular		plural	
me	myself	nos	ourselves
te	yourself	vos	yourselves
se	himself/herself/itself	se	themselves

Examples

me necabo.	I will kill myself.
se amat.	He loves himself.
se defendunt.	They defend themselves.

se

	singular	English meaning	plural	English meaning
nominative				
accusative	se	himself/herself	se	themselves
genitive	sui	of himself/herself	sui	of themselves
dative	sibi	to/for himself/herself	sibi	to/for themselves
ablative	se	(by) himself/herself	se	(by) themselves

Note: secum with him/with her secum with them

Exercise 18.3

Translate the following into English:

1. ille puer se amat. (4)
2. Romani se necare constituerunt. (4)
3. Troiani se defendere paraverunt. (4)
4. illa puella se semper spectat. (5)
5. dux milites iter secum facere iussit. (6)
6. discipuli sapientes se numquam laudant. (5)
7. cives Troiani se fortiter defendebant. (5)
8. ille miles se gladio suo vulneravit. (6)
9. cives tristes hostibus se tradiderunt. (5)
10. multae feminae in flumine se spectabant. (6)

Total: 50

Exercise 18.4

Translate the following into English:

1. num hic senex mortuus est? (5)
2. multi perierunt, pauci effugerunt. (4)
3. nolite me relinquere, comites! (4)
4. clamores multorum senum audivimus. (5)
5. hi milites fortes se servare cupiunt. (6)
6. bene pugnate, cives! (3)
7. Graeci fortiores quam nos non sunt. (6)
8. nonne milites Graeci felicissimi erant? (5)
9. vos tuti estis, nos in magno periculo sumus. (8)
10. quis nos servare poterit? (4)

Total: 50

Exercise 18.5

Translate the following into English:

1. senex et fortis et audax erat. (6)
2. num ille puer in media via stat? (7)
3. non omnes cives fortes erant. (5)
4. ille dux hoc oppidum capere numquam poterit. (7)
5. hostes flumen transire non poterant. (5)
6. milites ducem felicem semper amant. (5)
7. pater meus vocem magnam habet. (5)
8. Graeci, ubi Troiam ceperunt, Helenam ad Graeciam reduxerunt. (8)
9. nonne Troiani urbem suam bene defendebant? (6)
10. clamores illarum feminarum perterritarum magni erant. (6)

Total: 60

Exercise 18.6

Translate the following into English:

1. dei deaeque, ubi deam Discordiam viderunt, iratissimi erant. (9)
2. Menelaus, ubi Paris Helenam cepit, nuntios ad omnes comites misit. (10)
3. Graeci, ubi de Helena audiverunt, copias ad Menelaum miserunt. (9)
4. copiae Graecorum, ubi trans mare navigaverunt, Troiam oppugnaverunt. (8)
5. Achilles, ubi Hectorem occidit, laetus erat. (6)
6. Graeci, ubi equum magnum aedificaverunt, eum prope urbem reliquerunt. (9)
7. Graeci, ubi equum prope urbem reliquerunt, discesserunt. (7)
8. Troiani, ubi equum viderunt, timebant. (5)
9. multi Troiani, ubi Graecos in media urbe viderunt, fugerunt. (9)
10. Graeci, ubi urbem Troiam deleverunt, ad Graeciam redierunt. (8)

Total: 80

Exercise 18.7

Translate the following into English:

1. hic vir, quamquam nauta est, aquam timet. (7)
2. Achilles, quamquam miles audax erat, pugnare non cupiebat. (8)
3. Graeci, quamquam Troiam diu oppugnaverunt, urbem armis capere non poterant. (10)
4. Graeci, quamquam milites meliores quam Troiani erant, non bene pugnaverunt. (10)
5. ego, quamquam sapientior quam multi homines sum, multam pecuniam non habeo. (10)
6. Troiani, quamquam urbem bene defenderunt, eam servare non poterant. (9)
7. miles, quamquam fessus erat, diu pugnavit. (6)
8. discipuli, quamquam magister sapientissimus erat, eum non amabant. (8)
9. quamquam vox senis magna erat, eam audire non poteramus. (9)
10. cives, quamquam hostes timebant, contra eos bene pugnaverunt. (8)

Total: 85

Exercise 18.8

Put into the plural and translate your answer:

1. audis. (1 + 1)
2. senex non timebat. (2 + 3)
3. telum longum erat. (3 + 3)
4. agricola equum habet. (3 + 3)
5. iuvenis hastam tenebat. (3 + 3)

Total: 25

Exercise 18.9

Put into the singular and translate your answer:

1. possumus. (1 + 1)
2. puellas reduxerunt. (2 + 2)
3. clamores hominum audivimus. (3 + 3)
4. discipuli non responderunt. (2 + 3)
5. milites proelia non saepe timebant. (3 + 5)

Total: 25

Exercise 18.10

Give and translate the following verb parts:

1. The 1st person plural, future tense of **reduco**.
2. The 3rd person plural, imperfect tense of **relinquo**.
3. The 3rd person singular, imperfect tense of **possum**.
4. The 1st person singular, perfect tense of **conspicio**.
5. The 2nd person plural, present tense of **bibo**.

2 marks for each question. Total: 10

Exercise 18.11

Translate, then give the person, number, tense and first person singular of the present tense of the following:

1. posuit
2. potuit
3. reduxerunt
4. effugisti
5. relinquemus

5 marks for each question. Total: 25

Exercise 18.12

Translate the following into Latin:

1. Many citizens were alive, weren't they? (4)
2. Few women were staying in the city. (5)
3. Don't be afraid, friends! I will be able to do this. (6)
4. Old men are wiser than young men. (5)
5. We slaves all have very cruel masters. (5)

Total: 25

Exercise 18.13

Translate the following into Latin:

1. Both men and women have loud voices. (7)
2. That soldier is more daring than this one. (6)
3. Surely Achilles was not the bravest soldier of the Greeks? (6)
4. The Trojans put the horse in the middle of the city. (6)
5. Wise men often like difficult tasks. (5)

Total: 30

Exercise 18.14

Keeping the same person and number, put the following verbs into the imperfect tense and translate your answer:

1. servavit
2. viderunt
3. superavi
4. aedificavimus
5. steterunt
6. timuerunt
7. delevistis
8. spectavit
9. responderunt
10. amavit

2 marks for each question. Total: 20

Test 1: The Story of Perseus (1)

1. Translate the following passage into good English:

Acrisius gets a warning

1 Acrisius rex clarus erat. <u>urbem</u> Argos regebat. filiam
<u>unam</u> habebat. <u>nomen</u> filiae Danae erat. olim dei
Acrisio nuntiaverunt: 'cave, Acrisi! filia tua filium
<u>habebit</u>. <u>hic</u> filius te <u>necabit</u>.' <u>haec</u> verba Acrisium
5 terruerunt.

urbs, urbis f. = city
unam = one
nomen = name
cave! = beware!
habebit = (she) will have
hic = this
necabit = (he) will kill
haec = these

(30)

2. (a) **erat** (line 1). Give the first person singular of the present tense of this verb. (1)
   (b) **regebat** (line 1). Give the person of this verb. (1)
   (c) **Acrisio** (line 3). Give the case of this noun. (1)
   (d) **terruerunt** (line 5). Give the number of this verb. (1)

3. Using the vocabulary given below, translate the following sentences into Latin:
   (a) I had a famous daughter. (3)
   (b) The words frighten the son. (3)

I have	habeo, -ere (2)
famous	clarus, -a, -um
daughter	filia, -ae f.
word	verbum, -i n.
I frighten	terreo, -ere (2)
son	filius, -i m.

Total: 40

Test 2: The Story of Perseus (2)

1. Translate the following passage into good English:

Acrisius tries to play safe

1   Acrisius verba deorum timebat. magnam igitur <u>turrim</u>
    aedificare constituit. ubi hoc fecit, filiam, <u>Danaen</u>
    <u>nomine</u>, in <u>turrim</u> posuit. deinde servos <u>Danaen</u>
    <u>custodire</u> iussit. 'sic tutus <u>ero</u>,' inquit Acrisius. tutus
5   tamen non erat.

turrim f. = tower
Danaen = the accusative case of Danae (Greek form)
nomine = by name
custodio, -ire, -ivi (4) = I guard
ero = I shall be

(30)

2. (a) **verba** (line 1). Give the gender of this noun. (1)
   (b) **deorum** (line 1). Give the case of this noun. (1)
   (c) **fecit** (line 2). Give the first person singular of the present tense of this verb. (1)
   (d) Give an example from the passage of an infinitive. (1)

3. Using the vocabulary given below, translate the following sentences into Latin:
   (a) The daughter was afraid of the god. (3)
   (b) The god frightens the slaves. (3)

daughter	filia, -ae f.
I am afraid of	timeo, -ere (2)
god	deus, -i m.
I frighten	terreo, -ere (2)
slave	servus, -i m.

Total: 40

Test 3: The Story of Perseus (3)

1. Translate the following passage into good English:

Jupiter pays Danae a visit

1 Iuppiter rex deorum erat. quamquam Iuno, regina deorum, uxor <u>eius</u> erat, multas alias feminas saepe amabat. postquam <u>Danaen</u> pulchram vidit, <u>eam</u> quoque amare constituit. in <u>turrim</u> igitur intravit et
5 <u>Danaen</u> amavit.

eius = his
Danaen = the accusative case of Danae (Greek form)
eam = her
turrim f. = tower

(30)

2. (a) **erat** (line 1). Give the first person singular of the present tense of this verb. (1)
    (b) **feminas** (line 2). Give the case of this noun. (1)
    (c) Give an example from the passage of a preposition. (1)
    (d) **vidit** (line 3). Give the person of this verb. (1)

3. Using the vocabulary given below, translate the following sentences into Latin:
    (a) The woman liked the queen. (3)
    (b) The queen sees the god. (3)

woman	femina, -ae f.
I like	amo, -are (1)
queen	regina, -ae f.
I see	video, -ere (2)
god	deus, -i m.

Total: 40

Test 4: The Story of Perseus (4)

1. Translate the following passage into good English:

Acrisius makes a worrying discovery

1   postea Danae filium parvum <u>peperit</u>. nomen pueri
    Perseus erat. Acrisius, ubi Perseum vidit, perterritus
    et iratus erat. clamavit: 'quis est pater pueri?' Danae
    respondit: 'pater pueri est Iuppiter, rex deorum.'
5   Acrisius et matrem et filium punire constituit.

peperit = gave birth to

(35)

2. (a) **pueri** (line 1). In which case is this noun?   (1)
    (b) **erat** (line 2). Give the first person singular of the present tense of this verb.   (1)
    (c) Give an example from the passage of an infinitive.   (1)
    (d) **matrem** (line 5). Give the gender of this noun.   (1)

3. Using the vocabulary given below, translate the following sentences into Latin:
    (a) The small boys are afraid.   (3)
    (b) The angry son was shouting.   (3)

small	parvus, -a, -um
boy	puer, pueri m.
I am afraid	timeo, -ere (2)
angry	iratus, -a, -um
son	filius, -i m.
I shout	clamo, -are (1)

Total: 45

Test 5: The Story of Perseus (5)

1. Translate the following passage into good English:

Acrisius thinks he has disposed of Danae and Perseus

1   Acrisius <u>Danaen</u> et Perseum in magna cista <u>clausit</u>.
deinde servos <u>cistam</u> ad <u>litus</u> portare et in <u>mare</u>
iacere iussit. Danae et Perseus perterriti erant. undas
timebant. tandem undae <u>cistam</u> ad insulam <u>pepulerunt</u>.
5   ibi senex, Dictys nomine, eos <u>invenit</u> et <u>servavit</u>.

Danaen = the accusative case of Danae (Greek form)
cista, -ae f. = chest
claudo, -ere, clausum (3) = I shut
litus, litoris n. = shore, beach
mare, maris n. = sea
pello, -ere, pepuli (3) = I drive
invenio, -ire, inveni (4) = I find
servo, -are, -avi (1) = I save

(40)

2. (a) Give an example from the passage of a conjunction. (1)
   (b) **iussit** (line 3). Give the first person singular of the present tense of this verb. (1)
   (c) **erant** (line 3). Give the number of this verb. (1)
   (d) **nomine** (line 5). In which case is this noun? (1)

3. Using the vocabulary given below, translate the following sentences into Latin:
   (a) The slave was afraid of the waves. (3)
   (b) I like the big island. (3)

slave	servus, -i m.
I am afraid	timeo, -ere (2)
wave	unda, -ae f.
I like	amo, -are (1)
big	magnus, -a, -um
island	insula, -ae f.

Total: 50

Test 6: The Story of Perseus (6)

1. Translate the following passage into good English:

King Polydectes takes a fancy to Danae

1 Danae et Perseus in insula laeti diu habitabant.
  Perseus iuvenis iam erat et mater eius femina <u>adhuc</u>
  pulchra erat. rex insulae, Polydectes nomine, ubi
  <u>Danaen</u> conspexit, eam statim amavit et <u>ducere</u>
5 cupiebat. Perseus tamen Polydectem non amabat. ei
  clamavit:'numquam matrem meam <u>duces</u>.'

> adhuc = still
> Danaen = the accusative
>   case of Danae (Greek
>   form)
> duco, -ere, duxi (3) =
>   I marry

(40)

2. (a) Give an example from the passage of an adverb. (1)
    (b) **habitabant** (line 1). Give the tense of this verb. (1)
    (c) **erat** (line 2). Give the number of this verb. (1)
    (d) **conspexit** (line 4). Give the first person singular of the present tense of this verb. (1)

3. Using the vocabulary below, translate the following sentences into Latin:
    (a) The woman liked the island. (3)
    (b) The good women were shouting. (3)

woman	femina, -ae f.
I like	amo, -are (1)
island	insula, -ae f.
good	bonus, -a, -um
I shout	clamo, -are (1)

Total: 50

115

Test 7: The Story of Perseus (7)

1. Translate the following passage into good English:

King Polydectes issues a challenge to Perseus

1 Perseus Polydectem non amabat. Polydectes Perseum
  non amabat. Perseus fortis erat sed iuvenis. regi
  igitur, 'Polydectes,' inquit, 'ego te non timeo. ego vir
  fortis sum.' 'si vir fortis es,' respondit Polydectes,

    si = if

5 'Medusam neca, deinde <u>caput</u> eius ad me <u>fer</u>!'

    caput, capitis n. = head
    fer! = bring!

(40)

2. (a) **erat** (line 2). Give the first person singular of the present tense of this verb. (1)
   (b) **regi** (line 2). In which case is this noun? (1)
   (c) **timeo** (line 3). Give the person of this verb. (1)
   (d) Give an example from the passage of a personal pronoun. (1)

3. Using the vocabulary given below, translate the following sentences into Latin:
   (a) Perseus kills Medusa. (3)
   (b) The boy was afraid of the girl. (3)

Perseus	Perseus, -i m.
I kill	neco, -are (1)
Medusa	Medusa, ae f.
boy	puer, pueri m.
I am afraid of	timeo, -ere (2)
girl	puella, -ae f.

Total: 50

Test 8: The Story of Perseus (8)

1. Translate the following passage into good English:

Perseus receives help from the gods

1   haec verba Polydectis Perseum terruerunt. hic,
     quamquam iuvenis fortis erat, Medusam timebat. dei
     tamen deaeque auxilium Perseo dederunt. gladium
     novum et scutum <u>politum</u> ei dederunt. Perseus, ubi
5   haec arma accepit, iam laetus erat. non iam Medusam
     timebat. ab insula navigavit et ad Medusam iter fecit.

politus, -a, -um = polished

(45)

2. (a) **ei** (line 4). Give the nominative masculine singular of this pronoun. (1)
    (b) **dederunt** (line 4). Give the first person singular of the present tense of this verb. (1)
    (c) **insula** (line 6). In which case is this noun? Why is this case used? (2)

3. Using the vocabulary given below, translate the following sentences into Latin:
    (a) The boys have new swords. (4)
    (b) We frighten the goddess. (2)

boy	puer, pueri m.
I have	habeo, -ere (2)
new	novus, -a, -um
sword	gladius, -i m.
I frighten	terreo, -ere (2)
goddess	dea, -ae f.

Total: 55

117

Test 9: The Story of Perseus (9)

1. Translate the following passage into good English:

Perseus kills Medusa

1 iter longum erat. Perseus tamen post multa pericula
  ad terram, ubi Medusa habitabat, tandem advenit.
  cum Medusa fortiter pugnavit et auxilio deorum
  eam occidit. ubi hoc fecit, <u>caput</u> eius <u>abscidit</u> et ad
5 insulam rediit.

caput, capitis n. = head
abscido, -ere, abscidi (3) =
  I cut off

(35)

2. (a) **iter** (line 1). Give the gender of this noun. (1)
   (b) **terram** (line 2). In which case is this noun? (1)
   (c) Give an example from the passage of an adverb. (1)
   (d) **fecit** (line 4). Give the first person singular of the present tense of this verb. (1)

3. Using the vocabulary given below, translate the following sentences into Latin:
   (a) They do not fear dangers. (3)
   (b) The god liked the island. (3)

not	non
I fear	timeo, -ere (2)
danger	periculum, -i n.
god	deus, -i m.
I like	amo, -are (1)
island	insula, -ae f.

Total: 45

Test 10: The Story of Perseus (10)

1. Translate the following passage into good English:

Perseus saves Andromeda

1   Perseus Medusam occiderat. ad <u>Graeciam</u> iam redibat
    et <u>caput</u> Medusae in <u>sacco</u> portabat. in itinere
    puellam pulchram conspexit. nomen huius puellae
    Andromeda erat. illa perterrita erat, quod <u>monstrum</u>
5   eam <u>petebat</u>. Perseus tamen eam servavit. <u>caput</u>
    Medusae <u>monstro</u> ostendit et in <u>saxum</u> id mutavit.

Graecia, -ae f. = Greece

caput, capitis n. = head
saccus, -i m. = bag

monstrum, -i n. = monster

peto, -ere, petivi (3) =
   I attack
saxum, -i n. = rock

(40)

2. (a) **occiderat** (line 1). Give the tense of this verb. (1)
    (b) Give an example from the passage of a preposition. (1)
    (c) **Medusae** (line 2). In which case is this noun? (1)
    (d) **conspexit** (line 3). Give the first person singular of the present tense of this verb. (1)

3. Using the vocabulary given below, translate the following sentences into Latin:
    (a) Perseus sees Medusa. (3)
    (b) We were carrying the frightened girl. (3)

Perseus	Perseus, -i m.
I see	video, -ere (2)
Medusa	Medusa, -ae f.
I carry	porto, -are (1)
frightened	perterritus, -a, -um
girl	puella, -ae f.

Total: 50

Test 11: The Story of Perseus (11)

1. Translate the following passage into good English:

Perseus surprises Polydectes

1	Perseus, ubi Andromedam servavit, ad <u>Graeciam</u> rediit. Polydectes, ubi Perseum vidit, iratus erat. 'quid hic facis?' Perseo clamavit. 'num <u>caput</u> Medusae habes?' Perseus respondit: 'Medusam occidi et <u>caput</u>	Graecia, -ae f. = Greece caput, capitis n. = head
5	eius hic habeo. specta!' <u>caput</u> Medusae Perseus ostendit. Polydectes <u>caput</u> spectavit et in <u>saxum</u> statim <u>mutatus</u> <u>est</u>.	saxum, -i n. = rock mutatus est = (he) was turned

(45)

2. (a) **Graeciam** (line 1). In which case is this noun? (1)
   (b) **rediit** (line 2). Give the first person singular of the present tense of this verb. (1)
   (c) **facis** (line 3). Give the person of this verb. (1)
   (d) Give an example from the passage of an adverb. (1)

3. Using the vocabulary given below, translate the following sentences into Latin:
   (a) Andromeda sees the islands. (3)
   (b) Perseus was looking at Medusa. (3)

Andromeda	Andromeda, -ae f.
I see	video, -ere (2)
island	insula, -ae f.
Perseus	Perseus, -i m.
I look at	specto, -are (1)
Medusa	Medusa, -ae f.

Total: 55

Test 12: The Story of Perseus (12)

1. Translate the following passage into good English:

The oracle is fulfilled at the city of Larissa

1 Perseus Polydectem occiderat. Danae, mater pulchra
Persei, tuta iam erat. diu Perseus et Danae laetissimi
habitabant. olim Perseus ad urbem Larissam iter fecit.
ibi <u>certamina athletica habebantur</u>. Perseus <u>discum</u>
5 iecit. <u>discus</u> forte <u>spectatorem</u> <u>icit</u> et necavit. hic
<u>spectator</u> Acrisius erat. dei <u>vera</u> dixerant: Perseus
<u>avum</u> suum occiderat.

certamina athletica
  habebantur = athletics
  contests were being held
discus, -i m. = discus
spectator, -oris m. =
  spectator
icit = (it) struck
vera = the truth
avus, -i m. = grandfather

(44)

2. (a) **urbem** (line 3). In which case is this noun? (1)
   (b) **iecit** (line 5). Give the first person singular of the present tense of this verb. (1)
   (c) **necavit** (line 5). Give the number of this verb. (1)
   (d) Give an example from the passage of a superlative adjective. (1)

3. Using the vocabulary given below, translate the following sentences into Latin:
   (a) Perseus kills the grandfather. (4)
   (b) The happy gods were watching. (3)

Perseus	Perseus, -i m.
I kill	neco, -are (1)
grandfather	avus, -i m.
happy	laetus, -a, -um
god	deus, -i m.
I watch	specto, -are (1)

Total: 55

Vocabulary: Latin–English

a/ab + ablative	*from, by*
absum, abesse, afui (irreg.)	*be away*
accipio, -ere, accepi, acceptum (3½)	*I receive*
ad + accusative	*to, towards*
adeo, adire, adii, aditum (irreg.)	*I go towards*
adfu-	*see adsum*
adsum, adesse, adfui (irreg.)	*be present*
advenio, -ire, adveni, adventum (4)	*I arrive*
aedifico, -are, -avi, -atum (1)	*I build*
afu-	*see absum*
ager, agri, m.	*field*
agricola, -ae, m.	*farmer*
alius, alia, aliud	*other*
altus, -a, -um	*high, deep*
ambulo, -are, -avi, -atum (1)	*I walk*
amicus, -i, m.	*friend*
amo, -are, -avi, -atum (1)	*I love, like*
ancilla, -ae, f.	*maidservant*
ante + accusative (preposition)	*before*
antequam (conjunction)	*before*
appropinquo, -are, -avi, -atum (1)	*I approach*
aqua, -ae, f.	*water*
arma, armorum, n. pl.	*arms, weapons*
audax, audacis	*bold, daring*
audio, -ire, -ivi, -itum (4)	*I hear, listen to*
aurum, -i, n.	*gold*
aut	*or*
autem	*however*
auxilium, -i, n.	*help*
bellum, -i, n.	*war*
bellum gero, -ere, gessi, gestum (3)	*I wage war*
bene	*well*
bibo, -ere, bibi (3)	*I drink*
bonus, -a, -um	*good*
caelum, -i, n.	*sky*
canto, -are, -avi, -atum (1)	*I sing*
capio, -ere, cepi, captum (3½)	*I take, capture*
carus, -a, -um	*dear*
celeriter	*quickly*
cena, -ae, f.	*dinner*
cep-	*see capio*
ceteri, -ae, -a, pl.	*the rest of*
cibus, -i, m.	*food*
circum + accusative	*around*
civis, civis, m.	*citizen*
clamo, -are, -avi, -atum (1)	*I shout* (verb)
clamor, clamoris, m.	*shout* (noun)

clarus, -a, -um	*clear, bright, famous*
colligo, -ere, college, collectum (3)	*I collect*
comes, comitis, m./f.	*companion*
coniunx, coniugis, m./f.	*husband, wife*
conspex-	*see conspicio*
conspicio, -ere, conspexi, conspectum (3½)	*I catch sight of*
constituo, -ere, constitui, constitutum (3)	*I decide*
consumo, -ere, consumpsi, consumpsum (3)	*I eat*
contra + accusative	*against*
copiae, copiarum, f. pl.	*troops, forces*
corpus, corporis, n.	*body*
cras	*tomorrow*
crudelis, -e	*cruel*
cucurr-	*see curro*
cum + ablative	*with*
cupio, -ere, cupivi, cupitum (3½)	*I want, desire*
cur?	*why?*
curro, -ere, cucurri, cursum (3)	*I run*
de + ablative	*down from, about*
dea, -ae, f.	*goddess*
decem	*ten*
decimus, -a, -um	*tenth*
ded-	*see do*
defendo, -ere, defendi, defensum (3)	*I defend*
deinde	*then, next*
deleo, -ere, delevi, deletum (2)	*I destroy*
deus, dei, m.	*god*
dico, -ere, dixi, dictum (3)	*I say*
difficilis, -e	*difficult*
discedo, -ere, discessi, discessum (3)	*I depart*
discipulus, -i, m.	*pupil*
diu	*for a long time*
dix-	*see dico*
do, dare, dedi, datum (1)	*I give*
dominus, -i, m.	*master*
donum, -i, n.	*gift*
dormio, -ire, dormivi, dormitum (4)	*I sleep*
duco, -ere, duxi, ductum (3)	*I lead*
duo	*two*
dux-	*see duco*
dux, ducis, m.	*leader, general*
e/ex + ablative	*out of*
effugio, -ere, effugi, effugitum (3½)	*I escape*

ego	*I*
eo, ire, ii/ivi, itum (irreg.)	*I go*
equus, -i, m.	*horse*
erro, -are, -avi, -atum (1)	*be wrong, I wander*
esse	*see sum*
et	*and*
et... et...	*both... and...*
etiam	*even, also*
exeo, exire, exii, exitum (irreg.)	*I go out*
exspecto, -are, -avi, -atum (1)	*I wait, wait for*
facilis, -e	*easy*
facio, -ere, feci, factum (3½)	*I do, make*
fec-	*see facio*
felix, felicis	*lucky, fortunate*
femina, -ae, f.	*woman*
fessus, -a, -um	*tired*
festino, -are, -avi, -atum (1)	*I hurry*
filia, -ae, f.	*daughter*
filius, -i, m.	*son*
fleo, -ere, flevi, fletum (2)	*I cry*
flev-	*see fleo*
flumen, fluminis, n.	*river*
forte	*by chance*
fortis, -e	*brave*
fortiter	*bravely*
frater, fratris, m.	*brother*
frustra	*in vain*
fu-	*see sum*
fugio, -ere, fugi, fugitum (3½)	*I flee*
gero, -ere, gessi, gestum (3)	*I carry on, do*
gladius, -i, m.	*sword*
Graecus, -a, -um	*Greek*
habeo, -ere, habui, habitum (2)	*I have*
habito, -are, -avi, -atum (1)	*I live*
hasta, -ae, f.	*spear*
heri	*yesterday*
hic	*here*
hic, haec, hoc	*this*
hodie	*today*
homo, hominis, m./f.	*man, person*
hostes, hostium, m. pl.	*enemy*
i-	*see eo*
iacio, -ere, ieci, iactum (3½)	*I throw*
iam	*now, already*
ibi	*there*
iec-	*see iacio*
igitur	*therefore*
ille, illa, illud	*that*
in + ablative	*in, on*

in + accusative	*into*
incola, -ae, m./f.	*inhabitant*
ineo, inire, inii, initum (irreg.)	*I go in*
ingens, ingentis	*huge*
inquit	*he said, she said*
insula, -ae, f.	*island*
inter + accusative	*among, between*
intro, -are, -avi, -atum (1)	*I enter*
invenio, -ire, inveni, inventum (4)	*I find*
ira, -ae, f.	*anger*
iratus, -a, -um	*angry*
is, ea, id	*he, she, it; that*
itaque	*and so*
iter, itineris, n.	*journey*
iterum	*again*
itiner-	*see iter*
iubeo, -ere, iussi, iussum (2)	*I order*
iuss-	*see iubeo*
iuvenis, iuvenis, m.	*young man*
iv-	*see eo*
laboro, -are, -avi, -atum (1)	*I work* (verb)
laetus, -a, -um	*happy*
laudo, -are, -avi, -atum (1)	*I praise*
lego, -ere, legi, lectum (3)	*I read, choose*
lente	*slowly*
liber, libri, m.	*book*
libero, -are, -avi, -atum (1)	*I set free*
locus, -i, m.	*place*
longus, -a, -um	*long*
luc-	*see lux*
ludo, -ere, lusi, lusum (3)	*I play*
lus-	*see ludo*
lux, lucis, f.	*light*
magister, -tri, m.	*teacher, master*
magnopere	*greatly*
magnus, -a, -um	*big, great*
malus, -a, -um	*bad, wicked*
maneo, -ere, mansi, mansum (2)	*I stay, remain*
mans-	*see maneo*
mare, maris, n.	*sea*
mater, matris, f.	*mother*
medius, -a, -um	*middle of*
meus, -a, -um	*my*
miles, militis, m.	*soldier*
milit-	*see miles*
mis-	*see mitto*
miser, -era, -erum	*wretched*
mitto, -ere, misi, missum (3)	*I send*
moneo, -ere, monui, monitum (2)	*I warn*
mons, montis, m.	*mountain*

mora, -ae, f.	delay
mors, mortis, f.	death
mortuus, -a, -um	dead
moveo, -ere, movi, motum (2)	I move
mox	soon
mulier, mulieris, f.	woman
multus, -a, -um	much, many
murus, -i, m.	wall
nam	for
narro, -are, -avi, -atum (1)	I tell
nauta, -ae, f.	sailor
navigo, -are, -avi, -atum (1)	I sail
navis, navis, f.	ship
-ne?	(open question)
neco, -are, -avi, -atum (1)	I kill
nemo	no one
nihil	nothing
nobilis, -e	noble
noli/nolite + infinitive	do not...!
nomen, nominis, n.	name
non	not
nonne ...?	(a question which expects the answer yes)
nonus, -a, -um	ninth
nos	we
noster, nostra, nostrum	our
notus, -a, -um	well known
novem	nine
novus, -a, -um	new
num ...?	(a question which expects the answer no)
numquam	never
nunc	now
nuntio, -are, -avi, -atum (1)	I announce
nuntius, -i, m.	messenger
occido, -ere, occidi, occisum (3)	I kill
occupo, -are, -avi, -atum (1)	I seize
octavus, -a, -um	eighth
octo	eight
olim	once (upon a time)
omnes	everyone
omnia	everything
omnis, -e	all, every
oper-	see opus
oppidum, -i, n.	town
oppugno, -are, -avi, -atum (1)	I attack
opus, operis, n.	task
ostendo, -ere, ostendi, ostentum (3)	I show
parens, parentis, m./f.	parent
paro, -are, -avi, -atum (1)	I prepare

pars, partis, f.	part
parvus, -a, -um	small, little
pater, patris, m.	father
patria, -ae, f.	country, homeland
pauci, -ae, -a	few
pecunia, -ae, f.	money
per + accusative	through, along
pereo, perire, perii, peritum (irreg.)	I perish
periculum, -i, n.	danger
perterritus, -a, -um	frightened
poeta, -ae, m.	poet
pono, -ere, posui, positum (3)	I put
porto, -are, -avi, -atum (1)	I carry
possum, posse, potui (irreg.)	be able, can
post + accusative	after
postea	later
postquam	after
posu-	see pono
potu-	see possum
primus, -a, -um	first
pro + ablative	for
proelium, -i, n.	battle
prope + accusative	near
propter + accusative	on account of, because of
puella, -ae, f.	girl
puer, pueri, m.	boy
pugno, -are, -avi, -atum (1)	I fight
pulcher, pulchra, pulchrum	beautiful, handsome
punio, -ire, -ivi, -itum (4)	I punish
quam	than
quamquam	although
quartus, -a, -um	fourth
quattuor	four
-que	and
quid?	what?
quinque	five
quintus, -a, -um	fifth
quis?	who?
quod	because
quoque	also
redeo, redire, redii, reditum (irreg.)	I go back, return
reduco, -ere, reduxi, reductum (3)	I lead back
regina, -ae, f.	queen
rego, -ere, rexi, rectum (3)	I rule
relinquo, -ere, reliqui, relictum (3)	I abandon, leave behind
respondeo, -ere, respondi,	

responsum (2)	*I answer*
rex-	*see rego*
rex, regis, m.	*king*
rideo, -ere, risi, risum (2)	*I laugh*
ris-	*see rideo*
rogo, -are, -avi, -atum (1)	*I ask, ask for*
Romanus, -a, -um	*Roman*
ruo, -ere, rui, rutum (3)	*I charge*
sacer, sacra, sacrum	*sacred*
saepe	*often*
saevus, -a, -um	*savage*
sagitta, -ae, f.	*arrow*
saluto, -are, -avi, -atum (1)	*I greet*
sapiens, sapientis	*wise*
scribo, -ere, scripsi, scriptum (3)	*I write*
scrips-	*see scribo*
scutum, -i, n.	*shield*
se	*himself, herself, themselves*
secundus, -a, -um	*second*
sed	*but*
sedeo, -ere, sedi, sessum (2)	*sit*
semper	*always*
senex, senis, m.	*old man*
septem	*seven*
septimus, -a, -um	*seventh*
servo, -are, -avi, -atum (1)	*I save*
servus, -i, m.	*slave*
sex	*six*
sextus, -a, -um	*sixth*
sic	*thus*
sine + ablative	*without*
socius, -i, m.	*ally*
solus, -a, -um	*alone*
soror, sororis, f.	*sister*
specto, -are, -avi, -atum (1)	*I watch, look at*
statim	*immediately*
stet-	*see sto*
sto, -are, steti, statum (1)	*I stand*
sub + ablative	*under*
subito	*suddenly*
sum, esse, fui (irreg.)	*be*
super + accusative	*above*
supero, -are, -avi, -atum (1)	*I overcome*
suus, -a, -um	*his own, her own, their own*
tamen	*however*
tandem	*at last*

telum, -i, n.	*spear, javelin*
templum, -i, n.	*temple*
teneo, -ere, tenui, tentum (2)	*I hold*
terra, -ae, f.	*land*
terreo, -ere, terrui, territum (2)	*I frighten*
tertius, -a, -um	*third*
timeo, -ere, timui (2)	*I fear, be afraid*
trado, -ere, tradidi, traditum (3)	*I hand over*
trans + accusative	*across*
transeo, transire, transii, transitum (irreg.)	*I go across, cross*
tres	*three*
tristis, -e	*sad*
tu	*you (sing.)*
tum	*then*
turba, -ae, f.	*crowd*
tutus, -a, -um	*safe*
tuus, -a, -um	*your (sing.)*
ubi	*when*
ubi?	*where?*
unda, -ae, f.	*wave*
unus	*one*
urbs, urbis, f.	*city*
uxor, uxoris, f.	*wife*
validus, -a, -um	*strong*
venio, -ire, veni, ventum (4)	*I come*
ventus, -i, m.	*wind*
verbum, -i, n.	*word*
vester, vestra, vestrum	*your (pl.)*
via, -ae, f.	*road, street*
vic-	*see vinco*
video, -ere, vidi, visum (2)	*I see*
villa, -ae, f.	*villa*
vinco, -ere, vici, victum (3)	*I conquer, beat, defeat*
vinum, -i, n.	*wine*
vir, viri, m.	*man*
virtus, virtutis, f.	*courage*
vivus, -a, -um	*alive*
voco, -are, -avi, -atum (1)	*I call*
vos	*you (pl.)*
vox, vocis, f.	*voice*
vulnero, -are, -avi, -atum (1)	*I wound (verb)*
vulnus, vulneris, n.	*wound (noun)*

Vocabulary: English–Latin

abandon, I	relinquo, -ere, reliqui, relictum (3)
about	de + ablative
above	super + accusative
across	trans + accusative
after (preposition)	post + accusative
after (conjunction)	postquam
again	iterum
against	contra + accusative
alive	vivus, -a, -um
all	omnis, -e
ally	socius, -i, m.
alone	solus, -a, -um
along	per + accusative
already	iam
also	quoque; etiam
although	quamquam
always	semper
among	inter + accusative
and	et; -que
and so	itaque
anger	ira, -ae, f.
angry	iratus, -a, -um
announce, I	nuntio, -are, -avi, -atum (1)
answer, I	respondeo, -ere, respondi, responsum (2)
approach, I	appropinquo, -are, -avi, -atum (1)
arms	arma, armorum, n. pl.
around	circum + accusative
arrive, I	advenio, -ire, adveni, adventum (4)
arrow	sagitta, -ae, f.
ask, ask for, I	rogo, -are, -avi, -atum (1)
at last	tandem
attack, I	oppugno, -are, -avi, -atum (1)
bad	malus, -a, -um
battle	proelium, -i, n.
be	sum, esse, fui (irreg.)
be able	possum, posse, potui (irreg.)
beach	litus, litoris, n.
be afraid of	timeo, -ere, timui, timitum (2)
beat, I	vinco, -ere, vici, victum (3)
be away, be absent	absum, abesse, afui (irreg.)
be present	adsum, adesse, adfui (irreg.)
be wrong	erro, -are, -avi, -atum (1)
beautiful	pulcher, pulchra, pulchrum
because	quod
because of	propter + accusative
before (preposition)	ante + accusative

before (conjunction)	antequam
between	inter + accusative
big	magnus, -a, -um
body	corpus, corporis, n.
bold	audax, audacis
book	liber, libri, m.
both ... and ...	et... et...
boy	puer, pueri, m.
brave	fortis, -e
bravely	fortiter
bright	clarus, -a, -um
brother	frater, fratris, m.
build, I	aedifico, -are, -avi, -atum (1)
but	sed
by	a/ab + ablative
by chance	forte
call, I	voco, -are, -avi, -atum (1)
can, I	possum, posse, potui (irreg.)
capture, I	capio, -ere, cepi, captum (3½)
carry, I	porto, -are, -avi, -atum (1)
carry on, I	gero, -ere, gessi, gestum (3)
catch sight of, I	conspicio, -ere, conspexi, conspectum (3½)
charge, I	ruo, -ere, rui, rutum (3)
choose, I	lego, -ere, legi, lectum (3)
citizen	civis, civis, m.
city	urbs, urbis, f.
clear	clarus, -a, -um
collect, I	colligo, -ere, college, collectum (3)
come, I	venio, -ire, veni, ventum (4)
companion	comes, comitis, m./f.
conquer, I	vinco, -ere, vici, victum (3)
country	patria, -ae, f.
courage	virtus, virtutis, f.
cross, I	transeo, transire, transii, transitum (irreg.)
crowd	turba, -ae, f.
cruel	crudelis, -e
cry, I	fleo, -ere, flevi, fletum (2)
danger	periculum, -i, n.
daring	audax, audacis
daughter	filia, -ae, f.
dead	mortuus, -a, -um
dear	carus, -a, -um
death	mors, mortis, f.
decide, I	constituo, -ere, constitui, constitutum (3)
deep	altus, -a, -um
defend, I	defendo, -ere, defendi,

	defensum (3)
delay	mora, -ae, f.
depart, I	discedo, -ere, discessi, discessum (3)
desire, I	cupio, -ere, cupivi, cupitum (3½)
destroy, I	deleo, -ere, delevi, deletum (2)
difficult	difficilis, -e
dinner	cena, -ae, f.
do, I	facio, -ere, feci, factum (3½); gero, -ere, gessi, gestum (3)
do not ... !	noli, nolite + infinitive
down from	de + ablative
drink, I	bibo, -ere, bibi (3)
easy	facilis, -e
eat, I	consumo, -ere, consumpsi, consumptum (3)
eight	octo
eighth	octavus, -a, -um
enemy	hostes, hostium, m. pl.
enter, I	intro, -are, -avi, -atum (1)
escape, I (verb)	effugio, -ere, effugi, effugitum (3½)
even	etiam
everyone	omnes
everything	omnia
famous	clarus, -a, -um
farmer	agricola, -ae, m.
father	pater, patris, m.
fear, I	timeo, -ere, timui (2)
few	pauci, -ae, -a
field	ager, agri, m.
fifth	quintus, -a, -um
fight, I	pugno, -are, -avi, -atum (1)
find, I	invenio, -ire, inveni, inventum (4)
first	primus, -a, -um
five	quinque
flee, I	fugio, -ere, fugi, fugitum (3½)
food	cibus, -i, m.
for	nam; pro + ablative
for a long time	diu
forces	copiae, copiarum, f. pl.
fortunate	felix, felicis
four	quattuor
fourth	quartus, -a, -um
friend	amicus, -i, m.
frighten, I	terreo, -ere, terrui, territum (2)
frightened	perterritus, -a, -um
from	a/ab + ablative
general	dux, ducis, m.
gift	donum, -i, n.
girl	puella, -ae, f.

give, I	do, -dare, dedi, datum (1)
go, I	eo, ire, ii/ivi, itum (irreg.)
go across, I	transeo, transire, transii, transitum (irreg.)
go back, I	redeo, redire, redii, reditum (irreg.)
go in, I	ineo, inire, inii, initum (irreg.)
go out, I	exeo, exire, exii, exitum (irreg.)
go towards, I	adeo, adire, adii, aditum (irreg.)
god	deus, dei, m.
goddess	dea, -ae, f.
gold	aurum, -i, n.
good	bonus, -a, -um
great	magnus, -a -um
greatly	magnopere
Greek	Graecus, -a, -um
greet, I	saluto, -are, -avi, -atum (1)
hand over, I	trado, -ere, tradidi, traditum (3)
handsome	pulcher, pulchra, pulchrum
happy	laetus, -a, -um
have, I	habeo, -ere, habui, habitum (2)
he said	inquit
he, she, it	is, ea, id
hear, I	audio, -ire, -ivi, -itum (4)
help (noun)	auxilium, -i, n.
her (own)	suus, -a, -um
here	hic
herself	se
high	altus, -a, -um
himself	se
his (own)	suus, -a, -um
hold, I	teneo, -ere, tenui, tentum (2)
homeland	patria, -ae, f.
horse	equus, -i, m.
however	autem; tamen
huge	ingens, ingentis
hurry, I	festino, -are, -avi, -atum (1)
husband	coniunx, coniugis, m.
I	ego
immediately	statim
in	in + ablative
in vain	frustra
inhabitant	incola, -ae, m./f.
into	in + accusative
island	insula, -ae, f.
javelin	telum, -i, n.
journey	iter, itineris, n.
kill, I	neco, -are, -avi, -atum (1); occido, -ere, occidi, occisum (3)

king	rex, regis, m.
land	terra, -ae, f.
later	postea
laugh, I	rideo, -ere, risi, risum (2)
lead, I	duco, -ere, duxi, ductum (3)
lead back, I	reduco, -ere, reduxi, reductum (3)
leader	dux, ducis, m.
leave behind, I	relinquo, -ere, reliqui, relictum (3)
light	lux, lucis, f.
like, I	amo, -are, -avi, -atum (1)
listen to, I	audio, -ire, -ivi, -itum (4)
little	parvus, -a, -um
live, I	habito, -are, -avi, -atum (1)
long	longus, -a, -um
look at, I	specto, -are, -avi, -atum (1)
love, I	amo, -are, -avi, -atum (1)
lucky	felix, felicis
maidservant	ancilla, -ae, f.
make, I	facio, -ere, feci, factum (3½)
man	vir, viri, m.; homo, hominis, m./f.
many	multi, multae, multa (plural)
master	dominus, -i, m.
master (teacher)	magister, -tri, m.
messenger	nuntius, -i, m.
middle of	medius, -a, -um
money	pecunia, -ae, f.
mother	mater, matris, f.
mountain	mons, montis, m.
move, I	moveo, -ere, movi, motum (2)
much	multus, -a, -um
my	meus, -a, -um
name	nomen, nominis, n.
near	prope + accusative
never	numquam
new	novus, -a, -um
nine	novem
ninth	nonus, -a, -um
noble	nobilis, -e
no one	nemo
not	non
nothing	nihil
now	iam; nunc
often	saepe
old man	senex, senis, m.
on	in + ablative
on account of	propter + accusative
once (upon a time)	olim
one	unus

or	aut
order, I	iubeo, -ere, iussi, iussum (2)
other	alius
our	noster, nostra, nostrum
out of	e/ex + ablative
overcome, I	supero, -are, -avi, -atum (1)
parent	parens, parentis, m./f.
part	pars, partis, f.
perish, I	pereo, perire, perii, peritum (irreg.)
person	homo, hominis, m./f.
place	locus, -i, m.
play, I	ludo, -ere, lusi, lusum (3)
poet	poeta, -ae, m.
praise, I	laudo, -are, -avi, -atum (1)
prepare, I	paro, -are, -avi, -atum (1)
punish, I	punio, -ire, -ivi, -itum (4)
pupil	discipulus, -i, m.
put, I	pono, -ere, posui, positum (3)
queen	regina, -ae, f.
question expecting the answer no	num ... ?
question expecting the answer yes	nonne ... ?
quickly	celeriter
read, I	lego, -ere, legi, lectum (3)
receive, I	accipio, -ere, accepi, acceptum (3½)
remain, I	maneo, -ere, mansi, mansum (2)
return, I	redeo, redire, redii, reditum (irreg.)
river	flumen, fluminis, n.
road	via, -ae, f.
Roman	Romanus, -a, -um
rule, I	rego, -ere, rexi, rectum (3)
run, I	curro, -ere, cucurri, cursum (3)
sacred	sacer, sacra, sacrum
sad	tristis, -is, -e
safe	tutus, -a, -um
sail, I	navigo, -are, -avi, -atum (1)
sailor	nauta, -ae, f.
savage	saevus, -a, -um
save, I	servo, -are, -avi, -atum (1)
say, I	dico, -ere, dixi, dictum (3)
sea	mare, maris, n.
second	secundus, -a, -um
see, I	video, -ere, vidi, visum (2)
seize, I	occupo, -are, -avi, -atum (1)
send, I	mitto, -ere, misi, missum (3)
set free, I	libero, -are, -avi, -atum (1)
seven	septem
seventh	septimus, -a, -um
she said	inquit

shield	scutum, -i, n.	troops	copiae, copiarum, f. pl.
ship	navis, navis, f.	two	duo
shout (noun)	clamor, clamoris, m.		
shout, I (verb)	clamo, -are, -avi, -atum (1)	under	sub + ablative
show, I	ostendo, -ere, ostendi, ostensum (3)		
sing, I	canto, -are, -avi, -atum (1)	villa	villa, -ae, f.
sister	soror, sororis, f.	voice	vox, vocis, f.
sit, I	sedeo, -ere, sedi, sessum (2)		
six	sex	wage war, I	bellum gero, -ere, gessi, gestum (3)
sixth	sextus, -a, -um		
sky	caelum, -i, n.	wait, wait for, I	exspecto, -are, -avi, -atum (1)
slave	servus, -i, m.		
sleep, I	dormio, -ire, dormivi, dormitum (4)	walk, I	ambulo, -are, -avi, -atum (1)
slowly	lente	wall	murus, -i, m.
small	parvus, -a, -um	wander, I	erro, -are, -avi, -atum (1)
soldier	miles, militis, m.	want, I	cupio, -ere, cupivi, cupitum (3½)
son	filius, -i, m.	war	bellum, -i, n.
soon	mox	warn, I	moneo, -ere, monui, monitum (2)
spear	hasta, -ae, f.; telum, -i, n.	watch, I	specto, -are, -avi, -atum (1)
stand, I	sto, -are, steti, statum (1)	water	aqua, -ae, f.
stay, I	maneo, -ere, mansi, mansum (2)	wave	unda, -ae, f.
street	via, -ae, f.	we	nos
strong	validus, -a, -um	weapons	arma, armorum, n. pl.
suddenly	subito	well	bene
sword	gladius, -i, m.	well known	notus, -a, -um
		what?	quid?
take, I	capio, -ere, cepi, captum (3½)	when	ubi
task	opus, operis, n.	where?	ubi?
teacher	magister, -tri, m.	who?	quis?
tell, I	narro, -are, -avi, -atum (1)	why?	cur?
temple	templum, -i, n.	wicked	malus, -a, -um
ten	decem	wife	uxor, uxoris, f.; coniunx, coniugis, f.
tenth	decimus, -a, -um		
than	quam	wind	ventus, -i, m.
that	ille, illa, illud	wine	vinum, -i, n.
the rest of	ceteri, -ae, -a	wise	sapiens, sapientis
their (own)	suus, -a, -um	with	cum + ablative
themselves	se	without	sine + ablative
then	tum	woman	femina, -ae, f.; mulier, mulieris, f.
then, next	deinde	word	verbum, -i, n.
there	ibi	work, I (verb)	laboro, -are, -avi, -atum (1)
therefore	igitur	wound (noun)	vulnus, vulneris, n.
third	tertius, -a, -um	wound, I (verb)	vulnero, -are, -avi, -atum (1)
this	hic, haec, hoc	wretched	miser, -era, -erum
three	tres	write, I	scribo, -ere, scripsi, scriptum (3)
through	per + accusative		
throw, I	iacio, -ere, ieci, iactum (3½)	yesterday	heri
thus	sic	you (pl.)	vos
tired	fessus, -a, -um	you (sing.)	tu
to	ad + accusative	young man	iuvenis, iuvenis, m.
today	hodie	your (pl.)	vester, vestra, vestrum
tomorrow	cras	your (sing.)	tuus, -a, -um
towards	ad + accusative		
town	oppidum, -i, n.		